The Elements of Private Investigation

An Introduction to the Law, Techniques, and Procedures

The Elements of Private Investigation

An Introduction to the Law, Techniques, and Procedures

ANTHONY D. MANLEY

CRC Press
Taylor & Francis Group
Boca Raton London New York

CRC Press is an imprint of the
Taylor & Francis Group, an **informa** business

CRC Press
Taylor & Francis Group
6000 Broken Sound Parkway NW, Suite 300
Boca Raton, FL 33487-2742

Printed on acid-free paper
Version Date: 20130211

International Standard Book Number-13: 978-1-4398-1542-7 (Hardback)

Library of Congress Cataloging-in-Publication Data

Manley, Anthony.
The elements of private investigation : an introduction to the law, techniques, and procedures / Anthony Manley.
p. cm.
Includes bibliographical references and index.
ISBN 978-1-4398-1542-7 (hardcover : alk. paper)
1. Private investigators--Legal status, laws, etc.--United States 2. Private investigators--Vocational guidance. I. Title.

KF2042.D48 M36
344.7305'289--dc22 2009022579

Visit the Taylor & Francis Web site at
http://www.taylorandfrancis.com

and the CRC Press Web site at
http://www.crcpress.com

Dedication

This book is dedicated to my wife, Emily.

Contents

Author's Note

Nothing should be construed as to how one should act or react based upon what is read or contained herein. The author accepts no liability of any type for damages, real, inferred, or imagined; or for any professional injury, personal injury, or property damage that might result from the use or misuse of any of the information, techniques, or applications presented or implied in this book. This book is intended as an educational and training publication and should not be considered as a substitute for advice and consultation with your own attorney; only an attorney can provide legal advice. New laws are enacted routinely, and court decisions affecting new and current laws are handed down daily. The author suggests that you use this book in conjunction with legal advice from your counselor, and the accepted procedures and current law in the state in which you are employed.

The commentary, citations, and case law described in this book have been summarized in most cases to illustrate a point under examination and are taken from previous holdings. For a full review of a particular case, the reader should refer to the published case citation.

Regarding state citations noted herein and elsewhere, precedent may be offered to a court when a holding has been handed down on a previous similar case from another state, and *only* when that state has no case for precedent, *may* the court defer to a decision from that other state. Federal holdings submitted or handed down to a state court will be binding in all states.

Note also, that throughout this book, the author has used *italics* for emphasis in order to highlight certain words and passages of importance to the reader.

Further, the designation of *Private Investigator* and *Private Detective* as used in this book should be considered synonymous in meaning, and may be abbreviated to the term *PI* or *agent* in an endeavor to be concise. In addition, because many states consider and regulate a private investigator as a security officer, whether so designated or not, the law, citations, and narration so described in this book are applied to private investigators, loss prevention officers, and security officers equally, because they, as "private citizens" are firmly incorporated into the laws and regulations that control this vocation and the inhabitants of our nation.

Preface

The duties, responsibilities, and obligations of private investigators are varied and complex. As may be found in many other state statutes, under New York State General Business Law, the description of a private investigator is specified as follows:

> A private investigator will be licensed to perform investigations as to the identity, habits, conduct, movements, whereabouts, affiliations, associations, transactions, efficiency, loyalty, reputation, character, credit, business or financial responsibility or any person, group of persons, association, organization, society, firm or corporation, or as to the origins or responsibility for crimes and offenses, the location and recovery of lost or stolen property, the cause or origin of, or responsibility for losses or accidental damage or injury to persons or to real or personal property, or to secure evidence to be used before any authorized investigating committee, board of award, board of arbitration, or in the trial of civil or criminal cases, including as to the credibility of any witness.
>
> *Rules and Regulations Title 19 NYCRR, Part 172, §172.1*

Today, technology is advancing at a rapid rate. Along with the ever-changing needs of our society and the possibility of loss or ruin due to numerous threats and risks, the

> The purpose of explaining in some depth the various liabilities that an individual or a business may face criminally or civilly is an effort to instill in the reader the fact that today we live in a litigious culture where excessive monetary awards have become all too common.

> Moreover, the private investigator must have a reasonable foundation of understanding regarding criminal and civil law so that such comprehension may be applied to his or her duties, accountableness, and investigative procedures.
>
> Consider therefore, that the most consequential and serious proceedings that a private investigator, loss prevention, or security officer becomes involved with will be as a defendant in a criminal or civil action, and that in finality, could result in incarceration, license forfeiture, loss of job, and financial disaster, whether the act committed was intentional or not.

private investigator must be familiar with a vast category of rules, requirements, and criminal and civil law that he or she never had to experience 50 years ago.

This book is intended for the novice just entering the field of private investigation. In essence, it is an attempt to introduce the newcomer to the various specialties within this vocation, the basic techniques and methods of the investigative process, and the criminal and civil laws that cover the actions of a private investigator. If nothing else, the author hopes to present the basic knowledge of what a private investigator can and cannot do in the performance of his or her duties.

Moreover, this book is offered not only as an introduction into the field of private investigation but is also for those who seek to broaden their raw ability or acquire further clarification. Consider this a fundamental presentation of the elementary investigative procedures, including some of the risks that an investigator may encounter, and how he or she can avoid repercussions by not acting in a litigious or criminal manner.

Finally, we must remember as a newcomer to the vocation, that we live in a litigious society where anyone who feels or perceives that he or she has been injured, defamed, falsely accused, or arrested; or suffered some type of loss or damage in any way can seek a large monetary award from the offender. In recent years, these awards have increased so dramatically that some jurists have reduced the juries' "judicious" reasoning to a more suitable settlement or resolution.

In any event, today's present rationale is that if a person or company commits some "wrong" against another person or group where "damages" can be proved, compensatory and punitive awards granted to the plaintiff should be substantial.

It is hoped that this book will provide guidance to the initiate in acquiring the proper performance and prudence within this field of employment.

The following is a partial description of the content of this book, which is divided into seven chapters, with each part being distinctive to the theme covered:

Chapter 1—Is a description of private investigation; the qualifications, licensing, and experience required; how the vocation began; and the code of ethics for the professional.

Chapter 2—Offers an overview of the law, American jurisprudence, the origins of criminal and civil law, the criminal justice system, criminal and civil liability and litigation, and how the law controls our responses and actions, which are securely established within the law regarding the restrictions placed upon the private citizen.

Chapter 3—Is a further discussion on the criminal and civil litigation processes; the court system, prelitigation, litigation, criminal and civil trials, hearings, testimony and behavior, and lawsuits.

Chapter 4—Describes the limitations placed upon the private investigator as a private citizen, criminal and civil liability concerns, unlawful actions, personal and privacy rights, and privilege and legitimate interests. This chapter also provides details on the rules of evidence, arrest procedures, privacy rights, search and seizure, eavesdropping, defamation, and the use of assorted electronic instruments.

The above chapters relate to the law and how it affects the consequences of any actions taken by a private investigator. Moreover, the text includes information on how private investigators should act and exemplify themselves in various circumstances and situations in an effort to present themselves as true professionals, and as a precautionary measure against criminal and civil litigation.

The following chapters attempt to illustrate the basic principles on the various and specific techniques, procedures, and management of diverse crimes, offenses, and investigations.

Chapter 5—Presents the fundamentals, including information on investigative techniques and processes; how to obtain information and intelligence; how to conduct an investigation, such as crime scene investigation and procedures, internal investigations, collection and preservation of evidence, case management; and the necessary steps to become a prolific and constructive investigator—communication and observation techniques, the art of the interview and interrogation, types of investigations and various areas of inquiry, and procedures for obtaining written and oral confessions, and statements.

Chapter 6—Is an examination of the vulnerability and threats against industry, institutions, and the public at large; espionage and sabotage; insurance fraud; accident investigation; fire investigation; and embezzlement.

Chapter 7—Highlights specific areas of investigation; the objectives, selection, behavior, and rules of undercover operations and stings; executive and celebrity protection; intellectual property protection; terrorism and bomb threats; and workplace violence and strikes.

About the Author

Anthony D. Manley retired from the Nassau County Police Department after 26 years as a patrol officer, plainclothes officer, detective investigator, and supervisor. Manley also served as a New York State certified police instructor at the police academy specifically in areas such as management, supervision, and operational standards. The last 10 years of service included an assignment to the Departmental Inspection Unit. This unit is a specialized squad of administrative officers that conduct detailed examinations and analyses of all commands, squads, and units within the department, concerning internal management and operational audits. This unit is under the command of and reports directly to the Commissioner of Police.

Since leaving the department, he served as a security consultant, including 11 years in contractual and proprietary management and administrative positions in the private retail sector. From 1992 to 2005, Manley was a certified New York State Security Guard Instructor, curriculum developer, and senior instructor for a large private school specializing in security officer training, disaster management, loss prevention, supervisory and management development, and assorted professional and management training programs and seminars.

Manley has earned an Associate Degree (AAS) in Criminal Justice, a Baccalaureate (BA) degree in Criminal Justice Management, and a Master's of Public Administration (MPA) degree.

Introduction: The Novice Private Investigator

To the general public, the terms *Private Investigator, Private Detective,* and *Private Eye* are synonymous in meaning, but in fact, the vocation covers a broad spectrum of duties and obligations. Gone are the days of the Hollywood PI who appeared to be surly, unkempt, and unshaven, with the ever-present turned-down fedora and trench coat. Along with an office that was dark, dim, and run-down, the PI was just one step away from being thrown out into the street by his landlord because the rent was constantly overdue. The romantic notion that all PIs deal only on behalf of sultry women rarely occurs except in the movies. Generally, today's PI is a retired police officer who has a background in investigation and knowledge of the law. Although most police departments frown upon it, past associations with police officers, police departments, and other law enforcement agencies can be of immense assistance to the PI in cutting corners or reducing effort and time in an investigation.

However, there has been an increase of candidates in this field, who have risen from the ranks of security and loss prevention officers because of their training, education, and a whole-hearted desire to enter into this vocation. Because security and loss prevention have become securely established in our present business world, businesses today make more use of private investigative agencies than ever before. And as a result, many young men and women have graduated from positions as security or loss prevention officers and entered into the private investigation field in hopes of better pay or a more adventurous and rewarding lifestyle. Moreover, colleges and universities that offer criminal justice and security administration degrees or instructional courses have been an active source of applicants for private investigation. There are also many private schools and business enterprises that offer training or courses in investigative techniques with successful students earning a recognized professional certification.

The type of activity carried out by private investigators can be diverse. The present-day PI can specialize in many specific fields or become a general "practitioner" covering all segments of investigation. In the instance of handling all forms of investigation, work will always be varied and sometimes demanding. Embezzlement, larceny, fraud, asset and background checks, and missing persons are just a few of the areas that can be anticipated by an investigator or investigative agency. There are many occurrences or incidents that are conducive to private investigation that a business enterprise may wish to employ. For example, many insurance carriers use PIs for investigations that cover life, auto, and property. In addition, crimes that detect espionage and intrigue require proficient intellect and expertise and, therefore, obligates the novice investigator to undergo extensive training.

Private investigators provide assistance in criminal and civil liability cases that include personal injury, insurance claims and fraud, child custody cases, preemployment or background verification, marital infidelity, and premarital screening. Fundamentally, investigators employ techniques in surveillance, conducting interviews and interrogations, performing background checks, gathering evidence, and verifying facts about individuals and corporations. Some private investigators may only work in the area of executive, corporate, or celebrity protection.

Today, because of his or her training and expertise, the PI is called upon many times as a professional witness, which involves the collection of evidence to support legal arguments or applications brought before the court, particularly in disputes among people and between businesses. A sound education and training, accrued expertise, knowledge of the laws that concern the PI, the attitude and demeanor that the PI exhibits, and a reputable professional work ethic will serve the PI and his or her employer well.

However, caution must be uppermost in the mind of a private investigator or security officer regarding any activity or procedure where liability can become an issue. The average American is much more knowledgeable with respect to their rights and in exacting compliance or atonement for a wrong or a perceived wrong committed against them, generally with some type of compensation awarded in their favor. It is not unusual to find frivolous lawsuits that are executed with the assistance of unethical attorneys. Consequently, it is for this reason that much of the narrative contained in this book focuses on nullifying the possibility of an action of criminal or civil liability based upon the deeds or misdeeds of a private investigator or a security officer.

There is no doubt that private investigation can be a risky business, since there is a much greater risk of a violent occurrence in this profession than in many others. There will be times where situations can escalate to physical contact and injury. The best defense in these events is dialogue and accord with the other party. Another suppressant is for the investigator to behave in a professional and assertive manner while acting as calmly as possible. Assertiveness is a characteristic that can be acquired, and the novice investigator should develop this important skill. Being able to talk oneself out of a troubling circumstance is an art, but it can be learned.

As long as private investigators act within the authority granted to them by their employer, and within the confines of the law, the courts will look favorably on their actions, their employer, and their client if a civil action is subsequently initiated. Therefore, private investigators must have some foundation in the interpretation of culpability and the basic laws that will concern them. If they do not understand the law and how to apply it to their mental state and physical actions, they most assuredly will become involved in false arrests and other wrongful acts.

We must remember that once a client (individual or corporation) employs a private investigator or a private investigative agency, that investigator or agency becomes an instrument (agent) of the client acting on his or her behalf. Subsequently, any behavior or activity contrary to law or common practice by that investigator is subject to criminal and civil liability. Additionally, any adverse action by the private investigator may reflect upon the client vicariously.

Presently, following any type of an incident where someone has been offended or harmed in some manner, or perceives that he or she has been adversely affected, that person most probably will seek legal counsel in an effort to gain some satisfaction or financial award. So it goes without saying that anytime there is an occurrence or an activity that can be attributed to some fault of that company or its personnel (gainfully employed or contractual), the person who has been aggrieved, harmed, or wronged in some manner will attempt to seek redress in the form of damages. And in most cases, damages mean money.

In this regard and when a wrong has been litigated or at least established to a degree, damages sought by the plaintiff in court can be *negated or reduced* when the investigator, agency, or client being sued can show that his or her actions, training, or precautions were conditioned on their professional behavior, legality, confidentiality, awareness, and concern toward any person, group, or enterprise that may be part of the investigation.

Chapter 1

A Short History of Private Investigation

It can be said that the first recorded use of spies (for the gathering of information) was during the early Egyptian and Sumerian eras. Spies have been around for thousands of years, and from that sinister beginning they can be considered the forerunners of present-day private investigators. The early investigators in our country were basically private police or bounty hunters employed by large businesses that had money or resources worth protecting. In essence, these individuals were hired to protect the enterprise and its property, and to investigate, arrest, or punish those who would commit a crime against the company. Railroads, express companies, and banks such as Wells Fargo were not above outright revenge and retribution in their attempt to discourage future thievery. Less known than Wells Fargo were Range and Stockmen Associations that banded together and hired men to act as their own personal rangers. Wielding considerable power over the ordinary cowboy, they crossed county and state lines to track cattle rustlers and thieves. They were greatly feared because of their ruthless and harsh treatment of captured outlaws.

One of the most distinguished private agencies was the Pinkerton National Detective Agency. Formed in 1850 by a Scottish immigrant, former deputy sheriff of Cook County, and chief of police of Chicago, Illinois, Allen Pinkerton initially specialized in railway theft and robbery cases. The Pinkertons were the professionals called upon when local police and other private detectives did not have the wherewithal or the power to track criminals across state lines. On one historical note, because of his reputation, Pinkerton and his agency were hired to protect Abraham Lincoln personally during his inauguration and appear to have suppressed an assassination attempt against Lincoln. Pinkerton also headed up the Union Army's

Counterintelligence Force, and his organization was a model for the federal agency, which later was to become the Federal Bureau of Investigation (FBI).

In fact, many law enforcement agencies began as private enterprises. Witness the U.S. Secret Service that was formed out of necessity after the assassination of Abraham Lincoln and which was initially protected by the private Pinkerton Detective Agency.

Pinkertons' activities were not without detractors and critics, however. Their harsh strikebreaking activity relating to coal miners known as the "Molly Maguires" (c. 1875 to 1876) and the iron and steel workers at Andrew Carnegie's steelworks in Homestead, Pennsylvania (c. 1892), damaged their reputation during those periods and furthered their distinction as "hired guns" for the wealthy.

Regretfully, at that time in our history between 1850 and 1900, most of these private agencies acquired an unfavorable reputation because of their unscrupulous and many times unrestrained activity against anyone that they knew or felt were a threat to the company they were employed to protect. It did not take long for individual states in the early part of the twentieth century to crack down on their illicit activity. Regulation of the private security industry began in California in 1915. As the years passed, the "private eye" held a seedy, sinister, unkempt, and disorderly appearance and usually dealt in circumstances more or less just within the law. However, in recent years, because of threats against our private and personal safety, our family, our employment and social welfare, and our society becoming more and more litigious, private investigation has become a well-accepted course of inquiry and discovery.

One interesting fact is that the Pinkerton logo, which was located on the letterhead and signage outside of their various offices, was "We Never Sleep," along with a symbol depicting an "open eye" and thereby originating the designation *private eye,* which was to become the popular term in our language relating to all private detectives.

Qualifications and Licensing

Police or Law Enforcement Officers versus Private Investigators

First, it is important to understand that basic police work and private investigation have little in common. Today, most police officers on patrol will respond to service calls (emergencies, disturbances, noisy neighbors, domestic commotion, to issue traffic citations, and so forth) or to crimes in progress or to reported crimes. Essentially, the police are *reactive* rather than *proactive.* A small percentage of police officers and designated detectives within a department are assigned to investigate crimes reported. And within these ranks, specialized squads, such as homicide, arson, robbery, burglary, and crimes against property, produce highly qualified investigators within their field of expertise. Many excellent police investigators in particular fields of endeavor enter the private sector, bringing their expertise. As an example, arson investigators, various types of fraud examiners, and auto theft investigators, to name a few, are of exceptional use and are highly sought after because of their training, credentials, and professional contacts.

There are no formal education requirements for most private investigative positions, although many investigators possess college degrees. A 2- or 4-year degree in Criminal Justice or a related program is helpful to the aspiring private investigator (PI). Moreover, many corporate investigators must possess a bachelor's degree, along with some type of certification, such as accounting, internal auditing, or business administration.

Today, most private investigative agencies and private investigators are made up of former police officers, ex-military, former investigators from other fields (various federal law enforcement, insurance, automotive), and former government secret or undercover agents. Their field of expertise enhances their professional talent and abilities. Recently, however, the ranks of private investigators have grown to include intelligent persons from colleges, private schools, and security agencies.

However, the classic bumbling literary figure of the "private eye" of the past, or the former police officer who decides to go into "private practice" as portrayed in books and other publications has little in common with actual private investigation as a full-time occupation. Unless the former detective investigator has a particular proficiency in an area that would be advantageous after he or she "retired" from the department, the failure to make the transition is all too common. Some may feel that their "contacts on the job" and former friends cultivated over time will help them. But sooner rather than later, they will find that the longer they are off the job, contacts and "friends" begin to "dry up."

As noted earlier, many have previous experience in other occupations. Certain professional designations such as Certified Public Accountant (CPA), Certified Fraud Examiner (CFE), and Certified Protection Professional (CPP) are highly regarded because of their exacting requirements for certification—examination and authentication of proficiency, codes of conduct, required preparation, and ongoing maintenance of their standing. These professional designations give status to one as an established and authenticated investigator, particularly in his or her specialty or a similar investigative accomplishment.

Upon leaving the public sector and entering the private sector, the newly licensed private investigator will find that running a private investigation service is a business, and as a business, there are certain business skills that must be possessed that were not required while a public officer. Many former officers become overwhelmed with business tasks that include accounting, tax and other sanctioned compliance, marketing, collections from delinquent clients, personnel problems, and the various overhead costs, such as rent, heat, electric, and telephone. More importantly, the position and authority of the private investigator are no more than that of a private citizen. It is not the same as a police officer who can flash his or her badge (and therefore the status of his or her office) and who has the control and authority to enter into areas of investigation that an ordinary citizen cannot.

Other than the specially trained police officers and military or federal agents noted above, applicants for private investigation should acquire and ultimately possess some knowledge and experience working for a well-rounded legitimate agency in all aspects of the business. Although many applicants may have criminal justice degrees, have loss prevention or security experience, or come from employment as former insurance fraud examiners or claims adjusters, the best training is gained by on-the-job experience under an accomplished professional.

Therefore, we can say that any investigative agency would consider those individuals who possess ingenuity, persistence, and assertiveness, along with good communication, writing, and analytical skills, and are competent in interviewing and interrogation as excellent candidates for the position of PI.

Licensing

Consider entry into private investigation as a vocation; it is not a profession. No degree is required, and in many areas of our country there are no apprenticeships and no ongoing training or instruction as a requisite. Other than a clean background and application for a license, very few states require some sort of experience. Licensing requirements vary considerably; a police officer with no investigative experience or one fired for incompetence after several years would be able to apply for a PI license. Some localities might require an applicant to possess a period of full-time work in a licensed private investigation agency. This period might be 1, 2, or 3 years. However, in many instances, an apprentice who spent the required period as an undercover agent operating a forklift vehicle would qualify.

A most important component in the professional life of a PI is the mandated licensing of anyone who wishes to practice or call oneself a private investigator. The majority of states and the District of Columbia require private detectives and investigators to be licensed. Licensing requirements vary widely; some states have few requirements, some have stringent regulations, and a few have mandatory training programs. At this time, six states have no statewide licensing requirements—Alabama, Alaska, Colorado, Idaho, Mississippi, and South Dakota.[1]

According to *PI Magazine,* a leading industry publication, with the industry's estimated annual sales at about $600 million, there are now about 60,000 licensed PIs in the United States, and approximately 29,930 of them are in the State of New York, a 14.5% increase since 2000. Moreover, the magazine estimates that 500 to 1000 licenses are handed out each month in the United States.[2] It is assumed that the rise of interest in this occupation has occurred because of the terrorism attack on September 11, 2001.

Most states and some cities require a certain number of years in the field of investigation, sometimes under the sponsorship or apprenticeship of a licensed PI, attending obligatory classes and passing a written exam. Some states consider a former police officer as having the requisite knowledge and experience in law and investigation to waive the aforementioned obligations. In either case, fingerprints will be taken, and a personal investigation will be conducted by the licensing authority. Finally, an application must be submitted along with the necessary fees. The right to carry a concealed weapon will also require a separate investigation and license in most states.

> To practice or pass oneself off as a private investigator (PI) without being licensed as such is a crime. Consider also that because rules and requirements may differ in each state, a PI cannot pursue leads or work in another state unless he or she is licensed in that other state *or* in the state in which he or she is licensed has reciprocity with that other state. Check with your own state regulations for the licensing requirements and the reciprocal agreements between each state.

Training

Although there are no academic requirements at this time for the licensing of a private investigator, the aspiring novice would do well if he or she would enter into a field of study that would lead to an associate's degree or a bachelor's degree in Criminal Justice, Police Administration, Police Science, Security Administration, or a similar program. Colleges across the country now offer curricula in these disciplines, including private schools that dedicate their course of study only in private investigation. A broad base of knowledge in various areas would include criminalistics; forensic sciences; legal principles; communication skills; computer investigation; case preparation and court presentation; evidence collection and procedures; intelligence and corporate espionage; the art of observation, investigation, interviewing, and interrogation among others. Realize also that some private investigator schools and various professional security and investigative organizations offer specialized training in certain areas. Examples could include in-service training or seminars on arson, criminal, insurance, or financial fraud investigations.

Investigators employed in the corporate sector generally may be required to have an associate's or bachelor's degree. Moreover, many times a Master of Business Administration degree may be required for the higher positions within the larger corporations.

However, we must not lose sight of the fact that on-the-job training is the best training for any novice investigator. Whether one is a retired detective or police officer who enters the field having a broad basis of law, investigation, evidence, and court presentation, for instance, he or she already gained some expertise during his or her years on the job. A new entrant into the field of investigation without any public-sector training must do the same, spending time learning from experienced investigators out in the field and in the office, initially doing menial chores and then graduating to more responsible duties. Many novices enter private investigation from positions in contractual or proprietary security businesses, having had a taste of investigation and wishing to better themselves. The investigative agency that looks to hire apprentices should consider those entrants who are intelligent, logical, and quick to learn and are go-getters and self-starters. The author has worked with many police detectives and private investigators who had no formal academic background but were spectacular investigators. Then there are those investigators who seem to have an inborn talent of solving cases based on one's initial or "gut" feeling, empathy, or perception, and conceptually delving into areas of investigation not ordinarily considered by others.

In-Service Training

Consider also that some PIs will be employed by an investigative agency, such as a novice just entering the field. Expertise will be gained, not only by experience and continuing attendance at seminars, conferences, and special curriculums, but also by in-service training within the group. In addition, acting as part of a team or group during an investigation should be regarded as training of a future leader or supervisor of such a team with the expertise necessary given time and the correct instruction. Other than the one- or two-investigator office, the leader of a team should include the following attributes:

- *Planning*—The preparation and planning of an operation to achieve the objective for a positive conclusion. Basically, this is the assignment of tasks as to who will do what, what they will do, and how they will do it. This segment can be reduced to a management technique known as *Organizing, Deputizing,* and *Supervising.*
- *Equipment*—The leader should have an overall knowledge of the technical details and operation of various equipment that will be used so as to achieve the tasks required of the team. All members of the team must be properly briefed concerning the type of equipment to be used in the operation.
- *Knowledge of the Law*—The leader must have a working knowledge of the law in general and be able and have access to relevant legislation that will or might be significant to the operation. Note that this should include a risk analysis regarding health and safety statutes and issues.
- *Instruction Techniques*—The leader should have the ability to impart information and knowledge that is particularly pertinent to the operation by quality instruction and presentation skills. Additionally, training programs must also be utilized for all investigators when work scheduling permits. Many leaders or supervisors have an aptitude toward teaching methods, but most will need some training. However, the leader who has the expertise, knowledge, and competence will most definitely convey his or her comprehension of the training at hand.

Employment Projections

Sources note that income for PIs has improved significantly. A PI could earn about $50.00 a day 30 years ago. Today, although very few in the business become really wealthy, industry insiders state that entry-level investigators can earn about $40,000 annually, and those with 10 or 15 years experience can make $80,000 to $120,000, with senior-level investigators earning $120,000 to $1,000,000 or more in a year.[3]

As described by the U.S. Department of Labor in their *Occupational Outlook,*[4] the more significant points pertaining to this vocation are as follows:

- Applicants typically have related experience in areas such as law enforcement, the military, private insurance investigation, or government investigative or intelligence positions. These individuals often apply their prior work experience in a related investigative specialty.
- Although not typical, a small number will enter the profession directly after graduation from college possessing a degree in criminal justice or police science.
- Because large numbers of qualified people are attracted to this occupation, there will be keen competition at the dominant elementary level. For those applicants without prior investigative experience, opportunities are best for entry-level jobs with investigative or detective agencies, the security or protection industry, or companies that offer in-house auditing or inspection functions.
- About one-third of all private investigators are self-employed.
- Work hours are irregular and sometimes boring, and the work can be dangerous.

The more glamorous positions for private investigators are those who specialize in a particular field of inquiry. These are described as follows[5]:

- *Legal investigators* specialize in cases that involve criminal and civil litigation and are employed by a lawyer or a law firm. They assist in the preparation of the case for court presentation, assist in preparing a criminal defense, locating witnesses, taking statements or depositions, serving legal documents, interviewing police and prospective witnesses, taking photographs, and gathering and assembling evidence and written reports for submission in court. They will testify in court as required and, once determined by the court, may be considered expert witnesses. This specialized area will include arson investigators, auto and insurance fraud investigators, missing persons, domestic and computer specialists, among others.

- *Corporate investigators* conduct internal and external investigations for corporations, which may include sabotage, espionage, fraudulent stock or billing procedures, embezzlement, various types of larcenies, drug use in the workplace, and civil and personal rights violations.

- *Financial investigators* develop confidential financial profiles and reports on individuals and companies that are or may be parties to large financial transactions. They may also search for assets in order to recover losses or damages awarded by the courts. They may be Certified Public Accountants (CPAs) or Certified Fraud Examiners (CFEs).

Future Growth

As previously noted, the Department of Labor sees keen competition in this occupation because many qualified people are drawn from the law enforcement and military fields as young retirees. However, the job outlook for the employment of private detectives and investigators is expected to grow faster than the average for all occupations through the year 2012. Moreover, in addition to growth, replacement of those who retire or leave the vocation for various reasons should create additional job openings. Therefore, there will be a need for those applicants who may gain entry from college and other related occupations.[6]

American companies have lost between $53 billion and $59 billion in proprietary information and intellectual property due to thefts in 2001 and more than $45 billion in such thefts in 1999 according to a recent survey by The American Society of Industrial Security.[7] Because many of today's significant crimes are segmental (one crime in particular) and international in nature, investigators have developed their interests, contacts, and inquiries all over the globe. Today's PIs are likely to be highly computer literate and able to speak more than one language.[8]

The increased demand for private investigators will be as a result of fear of crime, a perpetual increase in criminal and civil litigation, and the ever-increasing need to protect confidential information and property of all kinds. Additionally, the demand to protect the growing financial and commercial activity worldwide will require audit and control of internal and external financial losses.

Ethics, Liability, and the Law

The use of pretexts can be a valuable tool for a private investigator. Subterfuge may be regarded as unscrupulous to some, but, in fact, when used correctly and judiciously, can be considered legal and ethical. It can be a productive means of obtaining desired information easier and faster than may be had otherwise. A pretext can be defined as a person who pretends to be someone else in various modes in order to gain the information that is sought. This can be accomplished by the investigator acting as a utility repairman, a salesperson, a bank or credit card employee, a delivery person, someone conducting a telephone survey, or any other stereotype or deception in order to glean information. Posing as the subject in question to employees of newspapers, utilities, banks, or wherever and whoever else as a pretense in an effort to gain information is not uncommon, and if conducted with discretion would not be considered unethical.

However, if a private investigator is hired by an attorney for whatever reason, the use of pretexts cannot be condoned. Once hired, he or she is considered an agent of that attorney and is bound by the legal ethics and behavior that the attorney must practice. An attorney would do well to advise the investigator of any restrictions that might arise or areas that must be isolated from investigation. If the attorney wishes to be prudent with a newly hired investigator, in particular, he or she might put all restrictions enumerated in a written agreement. An example would be the interview of a witness for the other side without the knowledge of the opposing attorney. Also, a PI working in conjunction with the police or any law enforcement agency becomes an agent of that agency and must abide by the rules that subjugate officers in the public sector. This will also include situations such as entrapment in conjunction with the police or as an individual. To do otherwise places the investigator and possibly the attorney (if the PI is acting as an agent) in criminal and civil jeopardy. (See "Color of State Law," Appendix A.)

Private investigators must keep up with the changing rules and laws that pertain to their vocation. In particular, this should include the state in which one is licensed and employed. By joining or associating with local, state, and national professional organizations and associations dealing in private investigation and security agencies (see Appendix E), an investigator can be apprised of new laws, procedures, issues, and information that the investigator may have as a specialty. Moreover, association with these groups enhances camaraderie, networking, the promotion of business, and, more importantly, personal contacts with others in the various fields of inquiry and investigation.

Code of Ethics

The dedicated true professional adheres to a code of ethics in that it should be the intention of every private investigator to deal honestly and judiciously in all contractual obligations and endeavors with individuals and clients.

In addition, the private investigator:

- Will not knowingly violate any right or privilege guaranteed to any citizen protected by law.
- Will keep business records and reporting procedures lawful and truthful based on fact, and if opinionated, do so in an honest fashion.
- Will not allow his or her personal feelings, beliefs, or prejudices to interfere with any investigation regarding the truthful disclosure of facts and information.
- Will not betray, disclose, or violate any confidence placed in him or her by a client, employer, or associate unless given consent to do so.
- Will not engage in any entrapment of an individual for any purpose.
- Will not engage in or employ techniques, equipment, or devices that are forbidden by law or may threaten the life, limb, or safety of another.

- Will not accept an assignment or any employment where a personal conflict becomes an issue.
- Will not compete illegally or unprofessionally with other investigators in the advertisement or solicitation of work.
- Will not accept any commissions, benefaction, or allowances in any manner from other parties dealing with his or her client, employer, or associate in connection with the work or contract for which he or she is responsible.
- Will deal fairly, honestly, and equitably in all transactions with his or her client or employer. (This addresses excessive expenditures above true and authorized expenses, and the illegal "padding" of billing services.)
- Will explain the diversities and varied results of any investigation that may or may not be to the satisfaction of the client.
- Will not promise a definite satisfactory result to any client, which in so doing may corrupt the outcome of an investigation.

Personal and Corporate Insurance

Any private investigator who places himself or herself in a position of illicit, unauthorized, or unprofessional conduct in conflict with the licensing and professional standards of this vocation can be assured that a civil and possibly a criminal liability will likely result in financial uncertainty. Moreover, if the outcome or some part of an investigation is not to someone's liking for whatever reason, whether the client or the subject under investigation, without a doubt there may be some who will seek out any attorney willing to initiate a civil case if there is any chance of winning.

Although it may be expensive, the agency or the investigator or both should carry a comprehensive liability insurance policy with basic minimums of liability coverage carefully weighed. To not have any type of liability insurance for personal and business preservation is a poor business decision.

The Selection of a Private Investigation Agency

Most PIs are approached by individuals looking for a missing person or relative in various modes of disappearances, financial and asset searches, and insurance or matrimonial matters, to name a few. In addition, for various reasons and circumstances, a business establishment may wish to employ a private investigator. Whether because of an internal problem such as employee theft, sabotage, espionage, or collusion with venders, or an external problem such as an unlawful competitor's practice or a company takeover, the business may have a need to find and correct the problem.

It would do well for a prospective client to investigate his or her state Web site regarding the licensing of private investigators or detectives and investigative agencies prior to any exploration or contact with a private investigator. Initial inquiry would note if the state in which the client is located has some type of licensing requirements for an investigative business enterprise. Some states require that an "agency" must be hired rather than an individual investigator so that even if the agency is a one-man operation, the agency and the individual investigator must be licensed. Once the client has decided on a particular agency or investigator, a check with the licensing state department will show if the licenses are valid, and if there are any complaints or problems accrued against that agency or investigator.

It may be a benefit that the selection of an agency be compatible and knowledgeable with the business enterprise of the prospective client. In addition, he or she may wish to investigate the agency's Web site or make contact with the various professional security associations and organizations for compatible agencies that may be contacted. There should be at least three agencies where the principals or branch manager of each agency would personally appear for an interview. During this conference, the company can describe the problem and the agency could define their professional capabilities, how the problem can be corrected, what is needed, and the cost of the service. Of course, if a business confidant suggests an agency of fine quality and exceptional service, it may be considered by the company as one of the agencies to be interviewed. The following considerations must be taken into account in the selection of a private detective agency. For our purposes, the company individual who hires an investigator or agency will be noted as the "client."

1. *Experience*—A client may seek an agency that has been in business for a long period of time, believing that this is an indication of a competent firm. However, this does not hold true in some cases; rather, look for the experienced individual or individuals who have a proven track record. Some agencies may not require the experience and skills that are needed, reducing inexperienced personnel to a simple job such as surveillance, but in many cases invariably placing the agency and the client in civil jeopardy. Moreover, a smaller agency that may contain one or two investigators might be far more experienced than a larger agency with many unskilled investigators and a high turnover of personnel.

   In a best-case scenario, the principals or administrators of the agency should have at least 5 years of experience in conducting investigations or undercover operations in the client's particular business enterprise. Administrators, managers, and supervisors who are retired military or law enforcement officers with a background as detective investigators should be highly regarded because of their specific knowledge of the law and investigative procedure and experience.

2. *Ethics*—Agencies that advertise services or results that they are unable to provide because they do not have the expertise or equipment, or proclaim

superior accomplishments in an effort to compete with competitors do themselves and the industry a disservice. We must realize that at times, competent investigators will use deceptive procedures to gain information that can help them in the investigative process. Deception is considered a necessity in many instances, but it is also necessary that the investigator recognize when to draw the line and back off or become truthful when it is essential to do so.

Additionally, excessive expenditures, sometimes far above true or authorized expenses, padding the billing of services, and engaging in illegal or unethical behavior and procedures on behalf of the client are a few unscrupulous ways that could affect both the agency and the client. Most professional associations that cater to the fields of private investigation, security, and loss protection profess a code of ethics and integrity that they require their members to follow. Moreover, the PI should be cognizant that the client may possess or operate by a code of conduct that most assuredly could affect the operational procedures of the investigator.

3. *Law and Insurance Compliance*—Not all licensed PIs or agencies are bonded or insured. If local and state law require certain provisions and sanctions for an investigative agency to possess and operate within, copies of such licensing and certification should be provided to the client. This will include licensing, bonding, and insurance as obligatory within the state that the agency will do business. Adequate liability coverage should be one of the more important indications in selecting an agency and will indicate to a client the agency's financial responsibility. A copy of the *certificate of insurance* should also be provided representing at least a $1 million coverage in a comprehensive general liability, errors, and omissions policy at the time of contract signing. The insurance policy should be specific in design for the security and private investigation industry with the client named in the policy as "Additional Insured." Be mindful that one of the expenses that a struggling agency will drop is insurance coverage.
4. *Criminal and Civil Litigation History*—The client must be made aware of any criminal history of all personnel employed by the agency. Also, all civil litigation involving the agency and any of its personnel must also be made aware to the client. Failure to advise the client may render the contract null and void if found out at a later date.
5. *Education and Training*—The minimum education for all agents should be at least a high school or GED diploma. Administrators, managers, and supervisors would do well to have a college degree in public administration, business administration, or criminal justice, or some type of professional accreditation or certification in security, security administration, or loss prevention.
6. *Standards*—The following standards should apply to all investigators, agents, and undercover operatives (UCs):

- The applicant for entry into the agency must have a complete background check that will include a personality profile, criminal history, driver's history, financial and credit history, employment history, personal and professional references, education and military confirmation, and additional information.
- The agent must be fully trained prior to any individual assignment.
- The agent must be supervised in all aspects of his or her training and labor. Daily contact with undercover operatives must be a requirement.
- It is critical that the agent not have a history of alcohol or drug abuse. A drug-screening program is essential at the hiring phase and may be mandatory at times during the agent's employment.
- The client should have access to the agency's training manuals, review of the personnel records of the agent or agents to be assigned, and personal interview of the agent or agents who will be assigned.
- The client should be given an estimate of the fee expected by the agency for the work to be performed. Also, the client should authorize a "spending limit" for expenditures before the investigation commences, and so note in the contractual agreement.
- In this field of endeavor, there are too many variables that the investigator has little or no control over. No guarantees should be offered by the PI to a client other than the investigator's commitment to accomplish the best work possible for that client. *For a client to require a guarantee of success and the PI to acquiesce to such a demand only fosters unscrupulous behavior.*

7. *Professional Associations and Organizations*—Practically every state in the union has an association for private investigators and private detectives. In addition, there are many associations and organizations that cater to the specialized fields of endeavor within the province of private investigation. These might include the forensic sciences, financial auditing, arson investigation, specialized photography, and accident scene investigations. Membership may include networking, social activity, keeping abreast of changes in the industry, and legislative activity, among others. Active membership and professional certification in specific or applicable associations will show their standing and commitment to their vocation.

   A condensed listing of state and local private detective associations, along with national and international professional organizations, some of which may confer certifications in particular fields of endeavor, are located in Appendix E.

Other Professional Services

A client may wish to have his or her company seek the professional services of a private investigative consultant in an assortment of problems that could occur within or around the company's premises. In these situations, the primary agency contracted by a client should have the necessary expertise in assigning competent personnel in solving the issue in an *efficient, effective,* and *economical* manner.

In most instances, it may not require the services of an agent to go undercover, as the investigation may be overt rather than covert. Regarding internal money loss, most business embezzlements and white-collar crime leave a paper trail that in many cases cannot be concealed. If one digs deep enough, accurate determinations can be made with the necessary documentation. In any event, the use of outside consultants who have particular expertise in certain vocations should be considered, if necessary.

Consultation and inquiry could include the following:

- Examination by a certified public accountant.
- Internal auditors for the specific business, to include risk identification and analysis, safety and security surveys and threat potential, audits and inspections (building, fire, merchandise, etc.).
- Document examiners.
- Information security specialists (deterrents and encryption experts for the discovery of computer misuse and protection of proprietary data).
- Use of a qualified closed-circuit television (CCTV) installer, overt and covert.
- Security and safety consultants for the particular business.
- Burglar and fire alarm installers and systems providers.

In Conclusion

The private investigator, when meeting with a prospective client, should initially or soon thereafter present certain documents along with the final contract for scrutiny and the client's records. These documents should include the following:

- The licensing requirements and law relating to a private investigator and a private investigation agency in the state in which the agency is doing business.
- A copy of the licenses (including licenses of weapons, if required) of all investigators who will be assigned to the client's case.
- A copy of insurance liability coverage issued by the underwriting agency.
- An account of all academic and professional certifications and proficiencies acquired or possessed by the investigators employed by the investigative agency.
- A copy of all associations and fraternal and professional groups with which the agency and investigators have a membership in good standing.

- A list of satisfied clients, particularly those similar to the client in a comparable business interest. (However, references may be hard to come by because most former clients, including businesses or individuals, do not or may not wish to disclose any information concerning their association or hiring of a private investigator for whatever reason. References from law firms and similar businesses may be more easily obtained.)

Chapter 2

The Law

Introduction to American Jurisprudence

We must be mindful that a private investigator (PI) is not a law enforcement officer, does not possess police powers, and has no more legal authority than that of an ordinary citizen. A PI may be arrested and face criminal charges in a criminal court for any illegal action taken by him and not within the scope of his authority. Whether the investigator is exonerated in criminal court or not, he or she may still face civil litigation for any wrongs or perceived wrongs that a plaintiff believes were committed against him or her, and the burden of proof is far less than in a criminal court. Acquittal on a criminal charge does not exclude the initiation of a civil suit.

Today, most civil lawsuits against private investigators and security officers (and vicariously to their superiors) occur because of some overt act caused by a PI or security officer which was outside of his or her scope of employment. This could include such acts as an unwarranted assault or false arrest and detention, among other serious offenses.

The taking away of a person's liberty, placing that person in custody, and detaining him or her for a period of time is a serious matter that cannot be taken lightly under any circumstance. It does not matter whether the arrest was by a police officer, a private investigator, security officer, or an ordinary citizen—certain elements must be present for any overt action to consummate a legal arrest. Whatever justification exists, the actions of the person who makes the arrest will be carefully examined later at length in order to determine if such action was warranted and legal. Be assured that if unfounded, litigation will be forthcoming against the person who made the "arrest," and an award in the form of punitive damages can seriously affect the investigator or the security officer and the business enterprise, financially and in goodwill.

Regarding any business enterprise, we must bear in mind that along with injury, death, or the destruction of property, other serious consequences could significantly affect business and cause catastrophic financial loss. Along with a complete business disruption, the loss of goodwill, and the possibility of personnel without jobs, one of the more serious issues that could occur against a business entity is the awarding of monetary damages in a civil litigation lawsuit. And whether the award is compensatory or punitive, in many cases we will find that millions of dollars can be granted to the plaintiff. Moreover, the possibility of criminal charges filed against the corporation or individual officers of that corporation will entail the costly utilization of legal personnel and services, and regardless of whether there is an acquittal or not, civil litigation is sure to follow.

Whether it is private investigation or private security, anytime the actions or reactions of a PI or security officer entail the use of the law, he or she should be cognizant of his or her behavior. This will include how wrongful acts might affect the client, the employer, or the officer him- or herself. He or she should be cognizant of what the law is, why there are laws, how laws are enacted, and what the defenses or restrictions are that control his or her judgment and conduct. More importantly, the PI must know how a law protects the rights of the individual under investigation, and how to insulate oneself against any criminal or civil conduct. The novice PI would do well to review all the criminal codes and statutes in his or her state as well as those laws that will affect or control their vocation.

The Conception of Law

The following narrative will give a basic understanding of how laws, written or not, have protected and controlled the commonwealth from the beginning of recorded history. In addition, it is important that the private investigator becomes aware of the Criminal Justice System and how it operates; moreover, that there are two types of laws that control the private investigator's actions and make him or her subject to criminal charges or civil litigation if he or she commits a wrongful or harmful act.

With that sense of importance, a basic introduction to law and liability is presented below as an important component in the education and training of the novice investigator.

The Foundations of Our Law

The roots of our law can be traced as far back as 1900 BC, when the Code of Hammurabi was established by the Sumerians, whose civilization was located along the Tigris and Euphrates rivers in the Middle East. This code is the first known system of law where offenses and penalties were circumscribed. Consider also the Ten Commandments handed down by Moses to the Jewish people around

1200 BC. These commandments have been written into many of our present laws, which include offenses such as murder, larceny, and perjury.

Note also that ancient Greece initiated laws on property, contracts, and commerce, and began the system of jurors in legal cases. Moreover, they developed the philosophy that a society should be ruled by law and not by men. (This concept of law was the basis that our founding fathers adopted in setting up our Constitution, which includes The Bill of Rights.)

Subsequently overridden by Roman culture, these early roots gave way to a more categorized set of laws. Published in 450 BC, the Twelve Tables were a set of moral principles and practices that only Roman citizens were to follow. In time, all laws were brought together and codified. This code was called *Corpus Juris Civilus* (Body of Civil Laws) under Emperor Justinian I around AD 560. The *Corpus Juris* was considered the most complete set of laws up to that time and had a great influence on the countries controlled by the Holy Roman Empire During the fall of the Roman Empire, much of Roman law became part of the Canon Law of the Roman Catholic Church.

Canon Law came to England about AD 600 when the English inhabitants converted to Christianity. In reality, there was no law other than what the lords and kings of the various domains decided it to be. The feudal lords of the land had full authority to render whatever judgment they deemed necessary or warranted for control of the populace, obedience to the lord, and ultimately to the king. There was no clear-cut differentiation between customs, religion, morality, and criminal offenses. Punishment for the offender was haphazard and generally unfair. In one realm, the crime of poaching could bring torture or death in various forms. Another reign may not offer such a severe form of punishment, although it surely would be cruel. In other crimes, the offender could suffer the loss of a hand or mutilation or disfigurement by a branding iron. There was no established remedy for the common citizen regarding restitution of property loss or injury by another. Redress was practically nonexistent.

After the Norman Conquest of England by William the Conqueror around 1066, he and his successors attempted to unite England under a common rule. The Normans wanted a system of unity and control so that governing the populace was made easier and accountable, but they also wanted to curtail the power and unrestrained warfare among the various "manors," realms and principalities throughout the country.

Under the direction of William, the King's Court *(Curia Regis)* began to develop into a system of royal courts throughout England. Important decisions rendered in one county or shire by the justices of the King's Court were written in books. These books were called *reported cases* and included the key facts of the case, the issue of law, and the legal principles expressed by the justices, their decisions, and the reasons for their decisions. These reported cases became appropriate and applicable to the country as a whole and were known as *common law* because of their acceptance throughout England. However, this arrangement only covered actions where property, money, or injury was in question, and where money was sought as restitution. The king and his lords still had the power to mete out whatever punishment they wished upon the masses who may have committed some criminal act. It was not until the signing of the *Magna Carta* by King John in 1215 that the administration of justice and the relationship of the Crown (the exercise of royal power) were delineated somewhat to the people. Even then, the one source of justice was the King, who acted as judge, jury, and executioner. In the latter part of the seventeenth century, during the reign of King Charles II, Parliament was allowed to administer the laws of that time, taking absolute power away from the King. During that period, *Habeas Corpus* was introduced which was the introduction and establishment of a preliminary hearing or arraignment.

The American Form of Government

An Extraordinary System of Sovereignty and Administration Was Created by Our Founding Fathers

The government of the United States is considered a federal republic. The basic law that determines our American form of government is the *Constitution of the United States*. This document, adopted by the Constitutional Convention of 1787, in its written form notes a division of powers between the federal government and the state governments. It further describes the rights and freedoms of its citizens and the checks and balances of the three branches of power set up by our founding fathers which are specifically enumerated in this political document.

The Constitution is considered a "living document" in that the interpretation and amendments are ever changing depending on the times, sentiments, and prevailing beliefs of our citizens.

In 1789, the U.S. Constitution was formerly adopted by all 13 states and, in so doing, created a government framework for a new and unique legal system. The U.S. Government (federal) coexists with the governments of each state in the union. Each has authority in some areas but not in others. As an example, only the federal government can create treaties, handle foreign affairs, and issue a national currency, but it has no right to tax real property.

In addition, each state government has its own constitution that may be based on its particular history, philosophy, or other obligations. However, state law cannot contradict or be inconsistent with federal law because the U.S. Constitution is the supreme law of the land. Moreover, as in the federal constitution, state constitutions separate the power between the three branches of government also as a check and balance.

In addition to the national and state governments briefly described herein, there are other governments that Americans live under. Known as local government, this includes County, Town or Township, City or Municipality, Villages, and Special

Districts. Although these localities may pass and enforce their own laws and regulations, they are obligated to adhere to and not contradict federal and state law.

The Executive Branch

Fundamentally, the people elect senior officials of the *Executive Branch* of our form of government—the President and Vice President (federal), the Governor and Lieutenant Governor (state), and the Mayor or City and County Executives (local).

The Legislative Branch

In the *Legislative Branch,* we elect U.S. Senators (the Senate) and U.S. Congressmen (members of the House of Representatives) at the federal level; State Senators and State Legislators or Assemblymen at the state level; and Aldermen, Councilmen, ward leaders, and so forth at the local level (city, county, and township).

The Judicial Branch

Following that, the *Judicial Branch* has judges of the federal courts appointed for life by the President and confirmed by the U.S. Senate (Supreme Court, various Federal and District Courts throughout the country). The purpose of a life appointment is to neutralize any political pressure on a judge's reappointment to the bench or any forthcoming decisions. Depending on the individual state, we have elected or appointed judges at the distinct levels of state, county, and local administrations. (See "The Organization of Our Court System" below.)

The Three Branches of Government

Defined

The three branches or divisions of our government are further defined:

1. *Executive*—The executive branch of government conducts the administrative business of the nation or the state. In the federal government, the executive (the President of the United States) conducts the administrative business of the nation with the aid of his cabinet appointees. This would include the Secretary of State, Secretary of Defense, Director of Homeland Security, and the Attorney General, among others. It will also include various subdivisions, such as federal attorneys, federal police (Federal Bureau of Investigation [FBI], Secret Service, postal inspectors, Bureau of Alcohol, Tobacco, and Firearms [ATF], Drug Enforcement Administration [DEA], and so forth), and environmental protection officials, among many other subcategories of the executive branch.

At the state level, this branch consists of those officers in state government (the Governor, Mayor, County Executive, and their elected or appointees) and all the offices within those governments that enforce, regulate, or control the laws and regulations enacted by the legislature of each government entity. This includes various state and county attorneys, local and state police.

2. *Legislative*—Laws are enacted by the legislative branch of government and generally consist of two bodies. Whether it is the senators and legislators in a state government or senators and congressmen in the federal government, the members make, submit, and pass laws; impeach or remove officials; approve U.S. currency; and at the federal level also approve treaties and major appointments, among other obligations. Generally, laws must be passed by both houses of the federal or the state governments. The bill (proposed law) is then passed onto the appropriate executive, the President (federal) or the Governor (state), for his or her acceptance and enactment. If the bill is not acted upon or passed or is vetoed at this level, it may be returned to the legislature who may override the executive and pass the bill into law.
3. *Judicial*—The judicial branch includes courts and judges at all levels of government (local, state, federal) that will hear, try, and adjudicate crimes and offenses against the common good. Included in the trial process are the judge, the parties involved, the jury, the attorneys for each side, and the witnesses. In both criminal and civil trials, the *defendants* may be private individuals or corporations. In a civil trial, the *plaintiff is the complaining party seeking* redress against the *defendant* (the person or group being sued). In a criminal case, a *defendant* is the person or party *charged with the offense*, and the state (or the federal government) will prosecute the *defendant* on behalf of the *complainant or the people* (the state). In most criminal and civil cases, the party has a right to a jury trial if he or she wants one. However, if someone wishes to defend him- or herself and argue his or her own case, generally that person may do so. If after trial the criminal defendant is found guilty, or in a civil trial the plaintiff loses, both parties have the right to appeal the verdict to a higher court. These tribunals are called Appellant Courts or Courts of Appeals. The party losing the appeal at this stage may seek to have the case reviewed by the U.S. Supreme Court, which is the highest court in the land. The U.S. Supreme Court can accept the case and place it on the calendar or refuse to hear it and hand it back down to the lower court where the holding (the decision) will stand.

In actuality, the designation and assignment of powers peculiar to the three branches of our government were instituted to promote a system of checks and balances, in that it was an intended curtailment of dominance or control that one might attempt over the other.

The Criminal Justice System

The Criminal Justice System is a part of the U.S. form of government and consists of the following three jurisdictions:

1. *Law Enforcement*—The following have the authority to enforce the law, arrest or cite offenders, and bring the offender before the court to face the charge/s:
   a. Police officers, state troopers, fire marshals, district attorneys, state and local prosecutors.
   b. Federal agents within their scope of employment (FBI, ATF, DEA, Secret Service, Postal Inspectors, military investigators, and assorted regulating agencies and officials). If acting outside of their scope of employment, they act as private citizens.
   c. Peace officers (parole and probation officers, court officers, game wardens, park rangers, fire inspectors, etc.). Generally, depending on the state, the powers of peace officers are not as broad as those noted above. Only those officers in (a) and (b) are entrusted with full police powers.
2. *The Courts*—The judiciary at the various levels (police justice, district, county, state, and federal) will accept the charge, try the defendant, and if found guilty *beyond a reasonable doubt*, sentence the defendant to a fine or imprisonment. In a civil case, the court will make a decision on a *preponderance of the evidence*. The courts also have the ability to interpret the law and how it is to be executed. This area will include judges and magistrates, district attorneys or prosecutors and their assistants, court clerks, bailiffs, court officers, attorneys for the defense or plaintiff, and legal aid attorneys and staff for the indigent.
3. *Corrections*—This area includes local, state, and federal jails, prisons, penitentiaries, and correctional facilities. A person convicted of a crime can serve up to a year in jail (usually local) for a misdemeanor offense. A person convicted of a felony will serve at least 1 year in jail, and may be sentenced up to life imprisonment or death at a state or federal facility. Wardens, correction officers, or guards will control all defendants sentenced to incarceration. Parole or probation officers will control those defendants who have been released and paroled into their custody.

The Organization of Our Court System

As part of the Criminal Justice System, the courts in our country are structured as follows:

Federal Courts

The U.S. Supreme Court—The highest court in the land; tries lawsuits between the states; reviews decisions of federal appellate courts and specialized federal courts; in addition, may review decisions of the highest court in a state if a federal law or a constitutional question is in dispute.

U.S. Court of Appeals—Eleven courts, also known as circuit courts, sitting in 10 judicial circuits and the District of Columbia; rules on appeals from U.S. District Courts and decisions from U.S. Administrative Agencies.

U.S. District Courts—Numbering approximately 90 courts sitting throughout the United States, including Puerto Rico and the Virgin Islands; tries both criminal and civil cases, and sits as a Bankruptcy Court and Admiralty Court.

Other courts include: *U.S. Court of Customs and Patent Appeals, U.S. Court of Claims, Tax Court of the United States, U.S. Customs Court,* and the *U.S. Court of Military Appeals.*

State Courts (No two states have the exact same court systems, but all are similar in their general framework.)

State Supreme Court (may also be called *Superior Court, Appellate Court, Court of Appeals*)—Hears appeals from all inferior courts of record; serves as Court of last resort unless a constitutional question is in issue, which may be heard by the U.S. Supreme Court.

Intermediate Appellate or Appellate Courts (in some states only)—Hears appeals from lower courts of general and special jurisdictions and criminal courts.

Trial Courts

District, County, or Municipal Courts—General jurisdiction over civil suits and criminal cases.

Criminal Court—Hears criminal cases.

Family or Juvenile Courts—Has jurisdiction over domestic relations cases, juvenile delinquency, and youthful offender cases.

Probate Court—Probates wills and hears claims against estates.

Local Courts

Small Claims Court, Traffic Court, Police Court, Justice of the Peace—Generally no record of the proceedings are compiled or maintained and therefore frequently cannot be appealed to a higher court.

In addition, our court system is divided into two areas of concern and enforcement—*criminal* and *civil.*

See "The Division of Our Law" below and "The Court System" in Chapter 3 for further information.

Law Defined

In the United States, the source of every citizen's rights is delineated in two documents—the Constitution of the United States and the Constitution of the State of his or her residence. In addition, there are other certain basic rights that are not specifically documented but may be found in old *English Common Law* on which our legal system is based.

Our system of law is, in reality, two systems—national, and state and local. In addition, each system has three branches supposedly equal in power—the *executive,* the *legislative,* and the *judicial.* Although cumbersome to some, the U.S. system of law was set up by our forefathers to prevent an unrestrained all-powerful executive and an all-powerful national government from having unlimited authority over the populace, thereby setting up a system of checks and balances.

Laws are rules that govern society. They are guidelines—a set of rules and regulations established by society for the good of all the inhabitants within that society. And within these rules, a citizen can live in peace and comfort knowing that all inhabitants are protected and have equal personal and property rights under the law. Society, as the commonwealth, will determine what constitutes a crime or an offense, and once determined, laws will be enacted by the lawmakers (legislators) of that society. The norms and mores of society are ever changing. Moral principles and practices are capricious, and change may be slow over time or accelerated depending on the issue.

A crime is defined as such only when the populace circumscribe it to be. The legislature changes the law in response to social and political demands. What may be considered a crime today may not be a crime tomorrow, and is achieved by legislative actions or judicial rulings.

As an example, possession of marijuana may be a crime today, but next week marijuana may be legalized. However, it does not let the miscreant off the hook; if he was arrested for marijuana possession prior to the legalization, he still must answer to the charge because when the act was committed, it was still a crime.

In essence, our legal system sets down our obligations to each other; in substance, the system has enacted laws, rules, and regulations. It further prescribes the penalties for breaching these obligations and establishes procedures to enforce those obligations.

Our laws are based on the following:

Statutory Law (Written Law)—Are laws or regulations written down and promulgated by society through their legislators. These laws or regulations may be enacted by local, city, state, or federal government. For example, they may apply to the control of crime, someone's actions and behavior, a business or an agency, or a tax enactment, all for the common good. Statutes are constantly being enacted, amended, and repealed as society deems necessary.

Common Law—Carried over to our country from English Common Law prior to our present and ever-changing justice system, when most all inhabitants were illiterate and there was no written law, and where consistency of decisions was needed and resolved. Common law plays a strong role in our present legal system. Common law provides authority not set down in statute, affords defenses, and renders an interpretation of those statutes.

Case Law

The principle of case law is that a court must stand by its previous decisions (criminal or civil). It may be referred to as *precedent,* and lawyers will search for these precedents in previous decisions written and recorded to help in their present case. (See the definition of case law in the "Glossary.")

However, application of case law to the case at hand depends upon a few factors:

- Whether the present court has the same legal jurisdiction (state or federal).
- The level of the court in which the decision was made (lower or appeals court).
- The similarity of facts in both cases.

The Division of Our Law

There are two distinct divisions of law, *criminal* and *civil,* that cover most communal, personal, property, and business affairs, and which will be covered below in some detail.

Criminal Law

Criminal law is statutory law (written law), and the Criminal Justice System (police, prosecutors, judiciary, and corrections) will enforce the law and share a common goal to preserve the peace, prevent crime, and keep the community and its citizens safe.

Criminal law is concerned with the enforcement of *legal duties to act, not moral duties to act.* It includes an obligation to refrain from doing an illegal act or failing to act as may be required. In other words, when one commits a voluntary act or an omission to act that is illegal as legislated in the law, it is considered a criminal act. The basic elements of criminal liability include conduct by an individual who by his or her free will acts or fails to perform an act that the individual is physically capable of performing. Both corporations and individuals may be found guilty of criminal liability.

These laws are enacted to protect society—the inhabitants of the state (or in a federal case, the citizenry and residents of the United States)—where the act is considered a crime against the state, and the state will prosecute and punish the offender. A crime is an act against society, so that the prosecutor acts on behalf of the state, not the individual. Any fine or sentence laid against the defendant is paid to the state and not to that individual. The individual or the entity (an enterprise or corporation) charged in criminal court is the defendant, and the individual or entity making the charge is the complainant. In some cases, the state may be the complainant. The District Attorney, State Attorney, or federal U.S. Attorney will act as the prosecutor, and the defendant may be represented by a defense attorney, either hired by the defendant or appointed by the court.

> The person who commits an illegal act is arrested and brought before the criminal court to answer to the charge. Recognize the fact that because his offense or crime is a transgression against the people of the state, any sentence or fine imposed on the offender is paid to the state. Therefore, the state, not the complainant/victim, will receive any anticipated reparation other than to know that justice has been served. However, some judicial decisions may offer the victim some restitution, and if not, the victim has the opportunity to seek some type of compensation or repentance in a civil court.

Offenses Defined

An offense as defined in a law or regulation promulgated for the benefit of society. Offenses are divided into several categories:

- *Infraction*—Infractions are minor offenses such as traffic violations, where a fine can be imposed, and they are enacted by the state or local authority to control some type of conduct. It is not a crime, although there may be some sections of the traffic laws that are classified as crimes. As examples, these could include driving while intoxicated and leaving the scene of an accident. A citation or summons is issued to the offender because rarely is a summary arrest made by a police officer for an infraction. A private citizen cannot cite another person for a traffic violation, but in some states, the complainant (who witnessed the infraction) may appear in court to lay an information against the offender, and a letter or warrant to appear in court will be issued.
- *Violation*—A violation is an offense other than an infraction, where a minimal imprisonment can be proscribed but a fine is usually imposed. These are usually minor offenses prohibited in the state's criminal code or by local ordinances. It could include simple trespass, causing an environmental, health or physical hazard, public intoxication or disorderly conduct. A citation to the offender is usual, but an arrest may be made for a violation. It is not a crime and depending on a particular state's penal code, a private citizen cannot make an arrest for a violation and must appear in court as he would for an infraction.

> Infractions and violations are not crimes.

Most important for the purpose of this book are *misdemeanors* and *felonies* that are classified as crimes because they are considered much more serious offenses and, in effect, cause harm to the general public. These crimes include laws enacted by the state and federal governments to incorporate those egregious misdeeds that are contrary to the good order and safety of our society:

- *Misdemeanor*—A misdemeanor is an offense for which a term of imprisonment may exceed 15 days but cannot exceed 1 year if found guilty. The sentence is served in a county or local jail. In some states, minor crimes such as petit (or petty) larceny (e.g., any property valued at less than $1,000, depending on statutory law in your state), simple assault, harassment, and some sections of law concerning gambling, vice, and disorderly conduct are defined as misdemeanors.
- *Felony*—A felony is a more serious offense for which when found guilty, a term of imprisonment will exceed 1 year, up to a sentence of life imprisonment or death. Imprisonment will be served in a state prison or a state or federal correctional facility. Some crimes falling into this category are murder, rape, sodomy, arson, kidnapping, treason, grand larceny, or felonious assault (bodily harm causing serious physical injury or deformity).

> Only misdemeanors and felonies are crimes.

Concerning minor offenses and crimes and the authority granted by law to a private investigator and security officer (private citizens) to act or not to act when an offense occurs in his or her presence, see the section in Chapter 4, "Authority to Arrest by a Private Citizen."

Probable Cause

Generally, probable cause is more specific to the police than to the private person. But there has been case law where decisions have been rendered in which probable cause became an issue in favor of the security officer and his or her actions (and in actuality, can be extended to the private investigator). In essence, the courts have found that if a crime had been committed and that such an act was observed and committed in the officer's presence, it therefore constituted probable cause for the officer to act and make the arrest. Accordingly, at this time, probable cause required for the security officer to act has been broadened somewhat to include other factors that may lead up to probable cause.

The presence of probable cause to act in a given situation must be considered one of the most important determining factors that a private investigator or a security officer must rely upon before he or she initiates any overt action in an apprehension. It does not matter if the occurrence in question is a misdemeanor or a felony that the officer may become involved in; the facts must be present for probable cause before any response takes place. If the defendant in a criminal action is acquitted at a later time for whatever reason, the PI and security officer's actions concerning the arrest will be under scrutiny. If found that the apprehension was made with little or no probable cause, the former criminal *defendant* may now become a *plaintiff* in a civil suit against the PI or officer, the business owner or client, and whoever else was involved in the incident.

In any cause of lawful action against a person, there must be probable cause for a private investigator or a security officer to act.

A law enforcement officer is obligated to the same standard.

"Probable Cause" Defined

"Probable cause relates to reasonable cause; Having more evidence for than against... more than mere suspicion" (*Black's Law Dictionary*).

The terms *reasonable grounds, reasonably believes,* and *probable cause* may be considered synonymous in meaning:

- Probable cause may be defined as facts and circumstances that would lead a reasonably prudent person in like circumstances to believe the defendant (the perpetrator) is guilty;
- or, the existence of such facts and circumstances as would excite belief *in a reasonable mind acting on the facts* within the knowledge of the prosecutor, that the person charged was guilty of the offense for which he was or is being prosecuted;
- or, such *a state of facts and circumstances as would lead a man of ordinary questioning and prudence, acting consciously, impartially, reasonably, and without prejudice, upon the facts, within his knowledge,* to believe that the person accused is guilty;
- or, as a reasonable ground of suspicion, *supported by circumstance sufficiently strong in itself to warn a reasonable prudent man in his belief* that the person accused is guilty of the offense with which he is charged.

Probable Cause

To reiterate, probable cause is a conclusion reached by a *reasonable person* after examining all of the facts and circumstances relating to the question at issue, and once determining that an offense or crime did take place and was in fact committed by the perpetrator, an arrest of that perpetrator can take place.

Reasonable Person Defined

A reasonable person (in our case, a private investigator or security officer—a private person) may be defined as one of ordinary intelligence, experience, and judgment (the average citizen) who acts on what he or she reasonably believes to be true.

"Reasonable Grounds" Defined

The "Merchant's Privilege"—As we see in the meaning of the term *reasonable grounds,* as defined by some courts, the retail merchant (and his or her employees and agents) have been granted certain privileges (*merchant's privilege*) when it comes to the apprehension, arrest, and detention of a suspected thief.

Under these statutes, *reasonable grounds* may be defined as including, but not limited to, knowledge that a person has possession of unpurchased merchandise concealed on his or her person, which belongs to the retail establishment.

If *merchant's privilege*[1] or *defense to lawful detention* statutes have been enacted in your state, they most probably include the following:

- The merchant has a complete defense to any civil action if there are *reasonable grounds for the detention,* notwithstanding the outcome of any criminal action, the actual guilt or innocence of the accused, or whether or not a crime was in fact committed.
- The retail merchant has a defense in an action for false arrest and imprisonment for the detention of a suspected shoplifter *if the detention was reasonable,* even if the criminal action against the accused was dismissed.
- The retail merchant may act upon what appears to be true even though it may turn out to be false, provided he or she believes it to be true and the appearances are sufficient to justify such a belief.
- Additionally, in cases where merchandise has admittedly been taken with neither payment nor exculpatory explanation (a reasonable excuse for his or her actions), the merchant's *statutory defense is established whether or not the accused has the required intent to commit the crime.*
- Whether or not the accused is found guilty of the crime he or she was arrested for, the security officer must be conscious that his or her actions in the arrest and detention were based upon reasonable grounds and reasonable belief according to the law, so that in any event, the officer has the privilege of a defense.

But no matter whether there was complete justification to make an arrest, jury verdicts sometimes can cause bewilderment. Because facts and circumstances will define how the court or a jury will view a case and render a verdict, some previous decisions as described below will cause the security officer to use caution and question his or her own actions based on reasonable grounds.

Consider the following decisions:

> In a civil case, whether the defendant (the retailer) had reasonable grounds for detention or not *may* be considered a jury question.
>
> In a criminal case, the defendant's testimony (the arrested perpetrator) was that after he placed merchandise in a shopping bag without paying for it, he was leaving the store and headed for the street. While holding the inner vestibule door and facing inward, he was apprehended by a security officer. He immediately admitted he had not paid for the merchandise, but he further stated that he was about to pay and then proceeded to the counter, tendered a $20.00 bill, but was arrested. Evidence was insufficient to establish that the security officer had probable cause to make the arrest. The defendant was acquitted. This created a jury question of whether there were reasonable grounds for the arrest.
>
> If the *merchant's privilege* or similar law is applicable in your state, a merchant may use as an affirmative defense actions permitting a private individual to detain a subject in a reasonable manner, in which the merchant has probable cause to believe the subject was committing or attempting to commit larceny of merchandise on the premises of a retail mercantile establishment. But it will not be applicable as a defense in an action for false imprisonment where the subject who was detained was accused of stealing cash and not merchandise; therefore, the retailer could not invoke that part of the law.
>
> However, in another case, the storekeeper was entitled to invoke such a defense where it protects merchants in cases arising out of detention in a store, although *the plaintiff was not detained on suspicion of shoplifting but on suspicion of passing counterfeit money.*

"Reasonable Time and Manner" Defined

One of the more important points that a litigant's attorney will look for in order to substantiate and bolster his or her case is to find if his or her client, the plaintiff, was handled in a reasonable time and manner. The attorney will attempt to determine if the plaintiff was subjected to unlawful actions or delaying tactics, overly dragged-out procedures, embarrassing overexposure to the public, or any other exposure or procedure that "damaged" or harmed his or her client in some way.

Many laws affecting the businessman or client may define *reasonable time* to mean the time necessary to permit the person detained to make a statement or to refuse to make a statement, the time necessary to examine employees and records of the business establishment relative to the ownership and value of the merchandise or property stolen, the time required for the compilation of necessary reports, and ordinary arrest procedures prior to turning the defendant over to the police.

The manner in which a suspect is handled would be based on lawful and reasonable custodial and arrest tactics that may be found in several areas of the various criminal codes and criminal procedures, which include the necessary force that may be employed to effectuate an arrest, the protection of the accused and other persons, and detention procedures, among others.

Presumptions and the Burden of Proof

Regarding a civil litigation, except as otherwise provided by law, the burden of proof requires proof by *a preponderance of the evidence.* This is the opposite of a criminal action where all the evidence of the crime must be proved by the state *beyond a reasonable doubt.*

To sustain an action for *false arrest,* the *plaintiff* has the burden of proof in initially establishing specific elements that will constitute his or her claim for a false arrest. Notwithstanding, in any litigation regarding a false arrest case, the *defendant* has the burden of proving legal justification as an affirmative defense.

When the accused (the criminal defendant) becomes the plaintiff in a civil case and establishes what he or she believes to be the elements of a false arrest or an unlawful detention, the original complainant (now the civil defendant) has the burden of proving to the court that he or she had reasonable grounds or probable cause for the belief that the accused committed, was committing, or attempted to commit a crime.

The plaintiff need not prove the defendant lacked probable cause to make the arrest, but the *existence of probable cause is a defense by the defendant that will defeat the action.*

> *Reasonable grounds* or *probable cause* does not depend on the guilt or innocence of the accused or upon whether a crime has in fact been committed or attempted. The merchant or his or her agent (the security officer) may act upon what appears to be true even though it may turn out to be false, provided that the merchant or his or her agent believes it to be true and the appearances are sufficient to justify that such belief is reasonable.

Factors Leading to a "Probable Cause" Conclusion

Other than concealment and suspicious activity, which may or may not give rise to probable cause, some courts have noted that it would be almost impossible to list all situations that may indicate theft. However, these courts have listed some factors in their decisions for the security officer in leading to probable cause:

- It will be particularly relevant that the defendant (the accused) concealed the goods under clothing or in a container. Such conduct is not generally expected in a self-service store and may in a proper case be deemed an exercise of dominion and control inconsistent with the store's continued rights.
- Other furtive or unusual behavior on the part of the defendant should also be weighed. Thus, if the defendant surveys the area while secreting the merchandise or abandons his or her own property in exchange for the concealed goods, this may evince larcenous rather than innocent behavior.
- Relative, too, is the customer's proximity to or movement toward one of the store's exits. Certainly, it is highly probative of guilt that the customer, who was in possession of secretive goods, was just a few short steps from the door or moving in that direction, passing the last cash register in which he has the opportunity to pay for merchandise.
- Possession of a known shoplifting device actually used to conceal merchandise, such as a specially designed outer garment or carrying case with a false bottom, would be all but decisive of intent.

Of course, in a particular case, any one or any combination of these factors may take on special significance. And there may be other considerations that should be examined. So long as it bears upon the principal issue—whether the shopper exercised control wholly inconsistent with the owner's continued right—any attending circumstance is relevant and may be taken into account.

In conclusion, where a security officer has *reasonable grounds* to believe that a person is shoplifting merchandise from the store, these *Defense of Lawful Detention* or *Merchant's Privilege* laws give him or her privilege to stop and detain that person for a *reasonable time* and in a *reasonable manner* for the purpose of further investigation in order to determine if, in fact, a crime has been committed.

The PI or the security officer should research his or her state's civil and criminal laws that may make available to the retail merchant and his or her authorized employees any defense to an action for false arrest, false imprisonment, or unlawful detention.

Writ of Habeas Corpus

Defined

Habeas Corpus is Latin for "you have the body." A writ of *Habeas Corpus* is used when an attorney for a defendant or a person incarcerated wishes to challenge the legality of the imprisonment or the conditions in which that person is being held. A *Writ of Habeas Corpus* (literally meaning "produce the body") is an application to the court to order or direct the law enforcement officials (police, sheriffs, jail or prison administrators) who have custody of the prisoner to appear in court with the prisoner in order that the judge may determine that the incarcerated person is being held lawfully or not. Our federal and state constitutions provide for this type of relief, where in many other countries, police and military personnel may seize people and lock them up for months or years without charges being laid against them.

Habeas Corpus is a protection against illegal confinement, such as holding a person without charges, when due process obviously has been denied, bail set has been excessive, parole has been granted but release denied, the accused has been improperly surrendered by a bail bondsman or his or her enforcement agent, or probation has been summarily terminated without cause. The writ may also be used in child custody cases, deportation hearings, and federal district court challenging the constitutionality of a state court conviction.

Postconviction Strategy

A defendant convicted of a crime may have the ability through his or her attorney to challenge a guilty verdict or to correct a violation of a constitutional right.

The following motions or appeals may be made on behalf of the *convicted defendant:*

- *Habeas Corpus Petition to a State Court*—Requests that a State's Appeals Court order the jail or prison holding the defendant to release said defendant upon showing that the defendant is being held in violation of a state law or constitutional right.
- *Habeas Corpus Petition to a Federal Court*—Requests that a federal trial court order a jail or prison holding the defendant to release said defendant because such incarceration is in violation of the U.S. Constitution.
- *Motion for Acquittal*—Request by the defendant's attorney for the judge to decide that there is not enough evidence to have found the defendant guilty.
- *Motion for a New Trial*—Request to the trial judge to declare a mistrial and grant the defendant a new trial.
- *Appeal to the State Appellate Court*—Offering by the defendant's attorney that the trial judge made some legal error in the trial proceedings.
- *Petition for Rehearing to a State Appeals Court*—Request by the attorney for the defendant for the appeals court judges to change their own decision.
- *State Supreme Court Appeal*—Request to the highest court in the state to review and overturn the decision of the Appeals Court.
- *U.S. Supreme Court Appeal*—Request to the highest court in the nation to intervene and correct an error by a state court that violated a right as defined in the U.S. Constitution.

Civil Law

Civil law is a vast body of statutory and common law with private rights and remedies available to a citizen. Note that it includes the protection of *private rights,* not *public rights*. If the individual has been wronged, or perceives that he or she has been wronged in some manner, the individual can seek relief against another person or group in civil court for damages. The individual may hire his or her own attorney for representation in seeking damages. At this time in our litigious society, it is not uncommon for those persons employed in the private sector, such as security officers, private investigators, and others hired to protect people and property, to be placed in some type of litigious situation at some time in their career, where some remedy will be sought by a litigant for some wrong or perceived wrong committed against him or her. Usually the litigant seeks damages in the form of money, but not necessarily so. In those instances, the lawsuit may seek to change a procedure or a policy or just to correct a wrong.

> To reiterate, civil law refers to that law (a vast body of *statutory* and *common law*) relating to private rights and remedies sought by a party who has suffered a "wrong" or has been "damaged" in some manner. It may be further defined as a body of laws that deal with the relationship between individuals, whereas criminal law deals with offenses against the state (the people).
>
> Moreover, if a person suffers from some act, or a failure to act, when no privilege or right exists, and such act or failure injures the person, property, or reputation of another, directly or indirectly, it may be considered a civil wrong.

Civil Liability

Therefore, within civil law, civil liability includes the procedures for civil law actions based on a violation of a legal duty or standard of care which may result from an accident, an omission of an act or duty, or an intentional or a criminal act that the plaintiff may have suffered.

Whether the defendant in a criminal action is found guilty or acquitted, it has no bearing on the ability of that defendant, now a plaintiff, to initiate a subsequent civil action. Conversely, a private person (PI) who faces a criminal charge in a criminal court and is found guilty or not, may also face a civil lawsuit against him or her if the "wronged" party wishes to initiate such an action.

The Awarding of Damages

Civil damages may be received as *compensatory* or *punitive* If monetary damages are sought and won, the judge or the jury may award *compensatory remuneration* (for injurious pain, short- or long-lasting injury, medical bills, loss of employment, loss or damage to property) and *punitive reparation* (for the wrong committed; to establish that the wrong will not be tolerated).

Some wrongs may be identified as violations of contracts, warranties, and *torts*.

Tort Law

When a person commits an act or fails to act as he or she may be required, when there is no right or privilege to do so, and such act or failure to act injures the person, property, or reputation of another, either directly or indirectly, it is a *civil wrong*. This is also called a *tort,* and the commission of a tort is a civil act and not a criminal act. Although a tort and a crime may be the same or similar in many cases, the parties, burden of proof, and damages are different. The basic element of tort law is a lawful obligation that is owed to the *plaintiff* (the wronged party) by the *defendant* (the party that caused the wrong).

At times, and if appropriate, prior common law (court decisions, holdings) may be offered in defense by either party to the action. The individual or entity who initiates a civil action is the *plaintiff,* and the individual or entity being sued is the *defendant*. Both sides may be represented by an attorney—the attorney who represents the plaintiff and the attorney who represents the defendant.

Consequently, a tort is a private or civil wrong for which the court will provide a remedy in the form of an action for damages. A personal tort involves an injury to the person or to his or her reputation and psyche, as distinguished from an injury or damage to real or personal property.

To summarize, if a person suffers from some act, or a failure to act, when no privilege or right exists, and such act or failure injures or damages the person, property, or reputation of another, directly or indirectly, it may be considered a *civil wrong*.

Torts (civil wrongs) may be an *intentional wrong* (willful tort) or a *negligent wrong* (negligent tort) suffered by a person.

Intentional wrongs (false arrest, malicious prosecution, assault, libel, slander) and *negligent wrongs* (failure to offer a safe premises or environment, inadequate level of security, failure to act when required) may be experienced by a person who may then seek redress in court for that wrong. The plaintiff's complaint will note intentional or negligent wrongs, and it is possible that the PI or other employee committed an intentional wrong, while the company may have committed a negligent wrong, and there lies the position for a claim of *vicarious liability*.

Negligence Defined

It is important at this point to define the term *negligence* as it relates to civil law. As defined, negligence is the *omission* of doing something that a reasonable person, guided by those ordinary considerations that ordinarily regulate human affairs *would do,* or the doing of something that a reasonable and prudent person *would not do.*[2]

Negligence can be further defined in the sense that the business owner, facility manager, or the lessee of a premises failed to use *ordinary care* to reduce or eliminate an unreasonable risk of harm that was created by a condition on the premises which the owner, manager, or lessee knew or should have known about so as to exercise reasonable and ordinary care in removing or at least lessening the risk until it can be corrected in a timely manner.

Additionally, the failure to use such care as a reasonably prudent and careful person would use under similar circumstances can be characterized chiefly by a reckless, neglectful, or thoughtless act (an individual obligated or duty bound to commit a required act), or by inadvertence and inattention; an unintentional act by a person, which does not come within the standards established by law for the protection of the public at large (negligent wrong). This is contrary to "wantonness" and "recklessness" which are characterized by willfulness or full awareness—a voluntary or intentional act, either committed or omitted (intentional wrong).

Ordinary care is the action taken by the owner, manager, or lessee in a reasonable manner in light of what he or she knew or should have known about a condition, and the risks that may be or have been caused by that condition. Moreover, the failure of the owner or lessee to use such ordinary care is *proximate cause* for the injury or damage, in that in a natural and continuous sequence may produce an event, and without such cause, the event would not have occurred. Further, the plaintiff must show that for a proximate cause to be present, the act or omission that occurred and was complained of must be such that an ordinary person would or should have foreseen that injury or damage might reasonably result from that event, and failed to use ordinary prudence or care under the circumstances.

Criminal Culpability and Liability

A *crime* may be defined as a violation of law by the omission of a duty commanded *or the* commission of an act forbidden *by statute and conduct which unjustifiably and inexcusably causes or threatens substantial harm to an individual, a group of individuals, or the public interest. Criminal intent may not be required.*

Consequently, for any investigation that the private investigator may be concerned with, he or she must be cognizant that any *act* or *omission* required or mandated by law by an individual, employee, or a company places that person or company in jeopardy of criminal prosecution.

Culpability

Defined

A person is guilty of an offense when his or her conduct includes an act or omission and its accompanying mental state. Therefore, that person must have a culpable mental state where he or she intentionally, knowingly, recklessly, or with criminal negligence commits such an act or omission so dictated by statute. In essence, the subject must have intent to commit the crime, knows that it is a crime to do so, and has the ability and wherewithal to commit that crime. Culpability may also be considered when a person who was required to do or act as mandated by law or by his position, and in failing to act as required (an omission), death, injury, or damage occurred. Consider the following examples:

1. A person who enters a home without permission and with intent to commit a crime therein commits a burglary (acts knowingly and with intention).
2. A police officer fails to act as required by his sworn duties (which could be an omission) or is reckless or negligent in his actions, and because of these actions or inactions, a subject suffers a severe injury to his person causing him to become permanently paralyzed from the waist down. The officer is subject to civil liability and possible criminal action in failing to act as he was obligated, and the conduct was reckless and negligent by omission.
3. A railroad worker is assigned to a switching terminal and is required to monitor trains in all directions that may require switching from one track to another. The worker is drunk or falls asleep. Because of his action (or inaction), two trains collide head on, and many people are killed and injured. This worker failed to perform a duty and obligation required of his position; he was charged with many counts of manslaughter and assault.

Therefore, a person is *culpable* and subject to criminal and civil actions if he or she *has one or more* of the following *mental states:*

- *Intentionally*—By design, the presence of will in the act that consummates a crime; has a conscious objective to cause a result or to engage in such conduct.
- *Knowingly*—Intentionally, with knowledge and the ability to commit or complete the act.
- *Recklessly*—Commits an act that he or she is consciously aware of and disregards a substantial and unjustifiable risk that such a result will or could exist; a gross deviation from the standard of conduct that a reasonable person would render, or a person who creates such a risk by reason of voluntary intoxication.
- *Criminally Negligent*—Criminal negligence may be described as culpable carelessness; acting or omitting that which is required, and which a person of ordinary prudence would not have done or omitted to do.

Consequently, Culpable Conduct Means Criminal Capability; It Is a State of Mind

In general, a person cannot commit a criminal offense if he or she does not have at least one of the accompanying mental states described above in committing the act. Remember, if charged with a criminal act and whether found guilty or not, a person may also face civil liability.

The Defenses for Lack of Culpability

There are four reasons that a criminal defendant could apply for an affirmative defense when entering a plea of not guilty. The following are fundamental descriptions of each defense:

1. *Duress*—The defendant engaged in the offense or crime because he or she was coerced to do so or was threatened with imminent use of unlawful physical force upon his or her person or someone else, where he or she would be unable to resist.
2. *Entrapment*—The defendant was induced or encouraged to commit an offense or crime by a public servant in order to obtain evidence for prosecution against the defendant, where the defendant was otherwise not disposed to commit it. Inducement or encouragement means that the performance must be active in nature by the offender. Conduct merely affording a person the opportunity to commit an offense does not constitute entrapment.
3. *Renunciation*
   a. It is an affirmative defense where the defendant acted prior to the commission of a crime in which he or she facilitated, and made a substantial effort to prevent the commission of such crime.
   b. Where the defendant manifested a voluntary and complete renunciation of the criminal purpose, avoided the commission of the crime by abandoning his or her criminal effort, and if mere abandonment was insufficient to accomplish such avoidance, took further overt steps that prevented the commission of the crime.
   c. A renunciation is not voluntary or complete if it is motivated by the belief that circumstances exist which increase the probability of detection or apprehension of the defendant or another person in the criminal enterprise, or the defendant makes a decision to postpone the criminal conduct until another time or to transfer the criminal effort to another victim or another similar objective.
4. *Mental Disease or Defect*—The defendant engaged in a criminal act but lacked the criminal responsibility by reason of mental disease or defect, and at the time of the criminal act because of mental disease or defect, he lacked the

substantial capacity to know or appreciate the nature and consequences of such conduct, or that the conduct was wrong.

Liability

Be cognizant of one important fact:

Whether a defendant is arrested, found culpable, and convicted of a crime, or is acquitted of that crime, an individual (the complainant or victim—now the plaintiff) may sue in civil court for any damages suffered because of that criminal action. Litigation in one court does not negate an action in another court.

See also the section entitled "Civil Liability and Litigation" later in this chapter.

> Criminal law defines those offenses against the state (the people) and prescribes the punishment for their commission or omission. Crimes are circumscribed by legislation (statutory law). In addition to criminal prosecution for a crime committed, an individual may be liable in a civil litigation as a remedy to the person who may have been wronged by the actions of a private citizen or public official.
>
> The culpable actions by private investigators (private citizens) and the defensive remedies favorable to them can be readily defined in civil law and are easily applicable to criminal law. It is essential that private investigators understand civil liability and how such liability can affect them criminally, professionally, and financially.

Wrongful and Unwarranted Actions and Procedures

Scope of Employment

Defined

If a private investigator or a security officer commits an act that may be considered a wrong, the person who has been offended or injured may seek redress in civil court for damages as a plaintiff. If there is no breach of duty by the client or business establishment, but the PI or security officer committed an act within the scope of his or her employment by which there was an intentional or willful act where a wrong or some harm was suffered, the plaintiff may sue the PI or security officer. Moreover, if in violation of company policy or procedures, or a contractual agreement with a client, the manager, trainer, client, or employer could be added to the litigation (vicarious liability).

Further, the term *scope of employment* may be defined as any act or action that is intended to benefit or further the client's or employer's business, and not personal business, which becomes the test as to whether the client or employer is liable for damages due to such actions under the doctrine of *respondeat superior* (make the master answer).[3] But if the PI or security officer acts unlawfully, without reason, in violation of company policy and procedures, and without the authority and duty required of his or her employer or under the terms of an agency's contract with a client, that person acts outside of his or her scope of employment. Be aware also that acts forbidden by the client or employer or outside the confines of company policy may be found to be within the scope of employment. As an example, the question may arise, at what point does the threat or use of force by a PI or security officer in the performance of an arrest become excessive, and depart from the protection of a company's assets? Such an argument may have to be settled by the court.

Unauthorized Practice of Law

The unauthorized practice of law is defined as performing any service or rendering any advice that requires the provider to "possess legal knowledge greater than that which is possessed by the average citizen."[4] The practice of law also includes the giving of legal advice and counsel to others as to their rights and obligations under the law and the preparation of legal documents. These actions could apply to the preparation of civil demand letters, releases, and decisions to have each party mutually release the other from any alleged wrongful acts. Civil demand and releases are considered a tort act, and negotiation of tort settlements has been held to constitute the practice of law.[5] A defense claim that a third-party nonlawyer representative simply passed offers or other information back and forth between the parties has been disallowed.[6]

The private investigator must be cognizant that the Unauthorized Practice of Law differs or varies from one jurisdiction to another as to the definition of the "practice of law" but is generally considered a criminal offense and is therefore subject to penalties and forfeiture.

Criminal Impersonation

Licensed private investigators are not public servants (a public official). In essence, they are private persons engaged in a private occupation. If the private investigator (a private person) displays a badge, insignia, or a facsimile thereof so as to present himself as a public official, or acting, giving the impression or expressing themselves in words or actions as a public servant, pubic officer, police officer, or any law enforcement officer, that investigator is guilty of a crime and is subject to license forfeiture. See also, the section "The Color of State Law" later in this chapter, when acting on behalf of or on a request by a police officer when dealing with a defendant or a detained person.

Prints and Photos

Be aware that private investigators and loss prevention or security officers should not take fingerprint impressions of a subject in custody, whether that person is a defendant or not. Other than for a licensing process that may be authorized by the state, fingerprints should be taken only by police officers under sanctioned procedures. Some states restrict police officers to the taking of prints and photos from defendants under strictly controlled circumstances.

Many loss prevention departments take Polaroid® photos of persons arrested by their officers for future reference or for viewing by other officers within the department who may not be present at the time of arrest. If necessary to do so, and so as not to place themselves in a litigious situation, PIs and security officers should check their own state laws or legal counsel to determine if there are any restrictions pertaining to photographing an arrested subject in legal custody. If there are no impediments, photos should be taken prior to the arrival of the police, and not in their presence. In addition, photos taken for future reference should be contained in a secured photo album and not displayed in a security office where people other than security personnel can observe them.

Civil Liability and Litigation

There are several ways in which a company, an institution, or a person may be held liable in a civil action. In an effort to better understand the various liabilities that a PI may encounter or may have to investigate, the following examples are offered:

- Concerning the actions by a private investigator (or security officer):
  - A private investigator arrested or placed the plaintiff into custody without just cause—*an illegal act.*
  - The private investigator failed to have probable cause for the arrest and detention, but continued with the process and falsely requested of the police that the subject be charged with a crime, when in fact the investigator committed a malicious act—*false arrest and malicious prosecution.*
  - A private investigator detained the defendant for an excessive amount of time, over that which was required to process the subject, causing emotional trauma prior to requesting the presence of the police—*unlawful detention.*
  - A private investigator used derogatory or racial epithets against the plaintiff, causing emotional harm and embarrassment—*violation of civil rights and defamatory remarks.*
  - The private investigator, by his or her actions while consummating the arrest, embarrassed the plaintiff in front of his family, friends, or passerbys, thereby causing embarrassment, emotional trauma, and a loss to his reputation—*use of excessive force, derogatory remarks, excessive public exposure.*

- The private investigator unnecessarily used excessive physical force upon the subject causing an injury—*excessive force, assault, and battery.*

- A security officer, once proved to have knowledge of a security or safety violation, or any unsafe condition, failed to correct the condition or to act in a timely manner in safeguarding the plaintiff from injury—*failed to act within the scope of his employment.*

All of the above are intentional torts.

- During a report of a premises evacuation, which was a result of a fire in the building, the plaintiffs attempted to exit the building via a fire exit visibly marked as such but found it to be locked or blocked in some manner, thereby causing severe injuries or death to the plaintiffs because they were unable to exit safely.

The above is a premises liability—a negligent tort.

- An empty box was left in an aisle on the selling floor by a salesperson, and where a customer suffered an injury because she had tripped over the box and fell to the ground.

The above would constitute a negligent tort and a possible intentional tort by the salesperson.

- The company can be held liable if they hire an employee without a thorough background check or overlook certain prior behavior during the hiring process (or during the signing of or during the period of the contractual agreement), and the employee or the contractual employee thereafter commits a violent act while at work or in the process of his or her employment.

The above would constitute negligent hiring practices—a negligent tort.

- The company can be held liable if they have information regarding violent actions or possible violent acts, threats by an employee, sexual or other types of harassment, and no action or very little action is taken by management.

The above would constitute negligent retention practices—a negligent tort.

- The company or institution can be held liable for damages in a civil court for any security issue where any *foreseeable act* can be established. A *foreseeable act* in the sense that the owner or lessee of the premises failed to use *ordinary care* to reduce or eliminate an unreasonable risk of harm that was or may have been created by a condition on the premises which the owner or lessee knew or should have known about so as to exercise reasonable and ordinary care to correct or attempt to correct the risk.

The above would be a premises liability—a negligent tort.

Damages

Defined

Generally, damages are awarded to the plaintiff in the form of money, but not necessarily so. A plaintiff may seek a correction of some wrong such as in hiring practices, racial or gender discrimination, work-related circumstances, or other issues. Correction rather than money may be preferred in these cases. However, in cases such as these, the court may also award monetary damages.

Damages Can Be Awarded in Two Areas

Compensatory Damages—Awarded for injury; injurious pain; medical bills; loss of wages, work, or employment; damage to property; emotional distress; personal embarrassment; injury to reputation; defamation; and so forth.

Punitive (Exemplary) Damages—Awarded to the plaintiff and against the defendant/s above and in excess of compensatory damages for their malicious or willful actions as punishment for the wrong that was committed. Also as a message to the public and a signal to others who may face the same or similar conditions that the act was unjust, censurable, and should never have occurred.

Regarding willful torts (intentional wrongs), an insurance carrier for a company or agency has the right in New York State to refuse to become involved in a defense of this type of action. In a negligent tort (an auto accident, for example), the insurance carrier will cover the policyholder as defined in the policy. The policy will indicate that if the vehicle operator is committing a criminal act or is driving while under the influence of alcohol or drugs, liability coverage will or can be denied. Check with your own state to determine if the same procedure is applicable.

Foreseeability

The courts have found that a corporation and its employees can be held liable for conditions that arise on or within its premises, particularly where negligence can be established. *This could include actions off the business premises by company personnel and contracted employees.* If the corporation had prior knowledge or was aware of a particular condition, and if someone was injured or "wronged" in some manner by that condition, a plaintiff's attorney would most assuredly base his case on that prior knowledge.

For a business enterprise in particular, regarding those investigations that include negligence by an individual or the corporation, we must bear in mind that basically a person entering a premises open to the public has a reasonable expectation to believe that the premises is safe and secure. Moreover, it may be said that there is a duty for a corporation to hire employees judiciously, and to randomly and routinely conduct inspections and examinations in order to find and observe any and all dangers that may befall the inhabitants that come upon that premises. If and when these hazards or conditions are discovered, the corporation is obligated to correct, mitigate, or eliminate the danger in a timely manner.

Cautionary Note

Bear in mind that if a condition or a possible occurrence within a facility is observed or found to be a possible danger to employees, visitors, customers, patients, or students, for example, it must be addressed as soon as possible so that the condition is corrected. To do otherwise places the corporation and the security/loss prevention department at risk of criminal or civil liability.

Basis for the Lawsuit

In order to show a claim for negligence, the plaintiff must basically show the following:

- The company has a *legal duty* to take certain care and actions for the protection of employees, customers, visitors, and others coming onto its premises and for the actions of an employee.
- The company management knew or should have known that a crime or risk of injury or damage was *foreseeable* in the eyes of a reasonable person.
- The company failed to provide security and a safe environment, or a reasonable level of adequate security or safety to prevent such a crime, risk of danger, or injury suffered by the plaintiff.
- The company's failure was a *proximate cause* for the damage suffered in the claim by the plaintiff.
- The plaintiff suffered actual damages and seeks redress because of the company's breach of its *legal duty.**
- The plaintiff suffered damages because of the actions (acts or omissions) of a private investigator or a security officer acting within or outside of the *scope of his or her employment.**

- The plaintiff suffered damages because of the actions of a company employee or a contracted employee.*
- A claim of *vicarious liability* can be made if the actions of the individual employee can also be attributed to other persons, including the corporation.*

Elements of Liability for the Lawsuit

As far as the civil courts are concerned, the three elements regarding liability that will be examined by the court will be as follows:

1. Was there negligence?
2. Was there actual damage, loss, or injury?
3. Was the negligence the proximate cause of the damage?

In addition, the private investigator must be aware that if the awards (damages) granted to the plaintiffs are high (and many times excessive), the insurance rates will be affected by that rise. Ultimately, as with any loss, the cost of doing business will also rise, and in effect, the higher cost of products and services will be borne by the public. Many times, the costs over and above liability coverage will affect the bottom line of the business along with goodwill and public stature that a business has built up over time.

Defense by a Company in a Lawsuit

The best defense against liability for any business establishment (*regarding their employees*), particularly in-house and contractually hired PIs and security officers, is that *due diligence* be made in the following:

- The hiring process.
- The training process, or the accredited or certified training and licensing.
- The subsequent effective supervision of that employee.

In a defense against a premises liability claim, the corporation must show that it was or became aware of a dangerous or litigious condition on the premises and acted to correct the condition as soon as practical or in a timely manner.

See the next section, "Premises Liability."

* The company noted in the above instances could be the client who has employed the investigative agency, and the investigative agency along with its employees or contractual employees (*vicarious liability*).

To reiterate, an action in criminal court does not negate an action in civil court. A person charged (the defendant) may be acquitted in criminal court for an offense and subsequently sue the party who initiated that criminal action in civil court for damages. Conversely, one may charge a person for a crime and also sue in civil court for damages whether he or she wins in criminal court or not.

There are other areas of civil liability that the private investigator should be familiar with, including the following.

Premises Liability

The Question of Security Negligence

A businessman who maintains a premises upon which another can be expected to enter is under the affirmative duty to make every reasonable effort to remedy conditions that could *foreseeably* create or contribute to a dangerous hazard or crime-inducing risk. Essentially this has been interpreted as meaning that a *legal duty* is due those persons that enter upon a business owner's property by taking certain care in protecting those persons against harm and injury. If as a result of this legal breach of duty, actual damages may have been suffered, the plaintiff may seek redress in a civil court.

Courts have awarded damages against business and property owners for injuries sustained under dangerous and threatening conditions, in addition to harm received at the hands of criminal assailants on the common law theory of negligence. The relationship between the party who suffers an injury or some type of damage (the plaintiff) and the property or business owner (the defendant) will depend on the degree of care expected by the damaged party and the care required by the property or business owner.

The plaintiff, in order to initiate a civil action, must have had a legal right to enter and remain on or within the company's establishment. The establishment may be considered a public place open to the public in that the company may invite the general public at large to enter his premises for the purpose of selling his products or a myriad of other reasons for business activity. A theater, sports arena, or museum, for instance, gives license and privilege to the public once a fee for entry is paid. Once that fee is paid, unless notified of certain restrictions, the public will expect the same legal rights of security and safety. However, a person entering an establishment without paying the required fee commits a trespass.

Therefore, a plaintiff may fall into one of three categories—an *invitee,* a *licensee,* or a *trespasser.*

The Invitee

An invitee may be described a customer, browser, or visitor who enters a premises that is open to the general public. The public, whether a customer who is on the premises ready and willing to purchase merchandise, a person just "browsing," a person who pays an entrance fee to enter, or a visitor who is present legally for whatever reason is considered an invitee and has license and privilege to be on the premises. A museum, library, supermarket, office building with an open concourse or reception area, and, of course as noted, a retail establishment would fall into this category as a place of public access. Moreover, a business visitor is a person who enters a business establishment for the purpose of some type of business dealing or a business appointment with the business owner or his agent. An example might be a salesman who enters for the purpose of selling or offering a product or service. The business visitor also has license and privilege. Both the public and the business visitor are protected under the invitee concept.

The greatest degree of protection is given to the invitee in regard to negligence that may cause some harm or injury.

The Licensee

This would include contractors or workers who are hired, contractually or not, to come upon a premises for the purpose of repair, renovation, or other improvements. These workers enter the business establishment with an implied or express consent and are considered licensees but do not have the same protection as the invitee. A licensee has less protection because any knowledge of a dangerous condition will prevent any recovery for damages if such would occur. The licensee is expected to accept the property as he finds it and look out for his own welfare. In addition, the knowledge of any danger that may be known to that licensee, and then entering the premises expecting the property as he finds and knows of it, may preclude the licensee from any type of recovery.

However, the business owner and his agent have a legal duty to advise the licensee of any danger or dangerous condition they are aware of prior to that licensee coming aboard.

The Trespasser

The trespasser is a person who enters upon a property unlawfully. He does not have the implied or express consent of the business owner. In other words, he does not have license or privilege to enter thereon or therein. With just cause, a person may be given a trespass warning, orally or in writing, preventing that person from entering or remaining on or within a premises from that point on. Thereafter, if that same person is found on the premises at any time, he is considered present without license and privilege and could be charged with a trespass. Accordingly, persons who fall into this category as trespassers as defined in the law, and who enter the premises unlawfully for the purpose of committing a crime therein, escalate the trespass offense to the crime of burglary.

Anyone who enters on or within a premise without consent and without the right and privilege to do so has no legal recourse if some injury or damage befalls him. The owner or possessor of the property cannot be held liable for any harm or injury that may befall the trespasser. There have been some rare instances where a plaintiff with intent to or while committing a crime on a business premises suffered some injury, whether caused by his actions or not, and after a civil action subsequently received an award in court. There is no doubt that in many cases jury verdicts are incomprehensible.

Anytime there is the question of an injury or damage that a victim can attribute as being caused by negligence on the part of an individual or a business owner, we can be sure that there is the possibility that civil litigation will be initiated in the near future.

Vicarious Liability

Vicarious liability may be considered a form of *strict liability,* in that it is a liability without fault. This is somewhat different from a liability such as *negligence,* where such form of liability *requires a breach of duty,* and *intentional liability* which requires *intent or a willful act,* and where such intent gives rise to an injury or a wrong. Simply defined, vicarious liability places the accusation of that liability on one or more persons (or a corporation) for the actions of another.

If the plaintiff was harmed or wronged by an employee in the *scope of his employment,* redress may be sought against that employee *and* his superiors. Therefore, vicarious liability may be imposed on one person or company based on a civil wrong committed by another person. In any business enterprise, vicarious liability will most assuredly arise if the plaintiff can show that the business owner is or may be liable for the willful conduct of a security officer employed to protect the company's assets, and acts within the *scope of his employment.* In some states, criminal laws may also apply in addition to civil liability, where the actions by an employee are also held to be the responsibility of the business owner. An example in this case would be a bartender who serves an underage patron who may become inebriated, and after leaving the business premises then kills another or is killed in an auto accident. Similarly, a patron may consume enough liquor to become inebriated with the *knowledge or the assistance of the bartender,* and after leaving causes a serious accident. Some states hold the bartender criminally responsible in a situation such as this. However, if unable to prove a criminal act against the bartender, civil action most assuredly would be initiated against the bar owner and the bartender.

If a private investigator or security officer commits an act that may be considered a wrong, the person who has been offended may seek redress in civil court for damages as a plaintiff. Therefore, if the security officer commits an offense or wrong *outside the scope of his employment* (intentional wrong), the company may wish to disassociate from him by terminating that person's employment, and advising that person that he must seek his own counsel. Specifically, if a manager, employee, PI, or security officer commits a tortious act outside the scope of his employment, and if the plaintiff *cannot* establish liability on the part of management or the corporation, that person is individually liable for the damages caused by his actions. This usually occurs in criminal actions such as a false arrest or an assault without cause. In this case, the company may not be obligated to offer legal counsel, and the individual may have to suffer any damage award by himself.

If there is no *breach of duty* by the business establishment, but the private investigator or security officer did *act within the scope of his employment* by which there was an intentional or willful act where a wrong and some harm was suffered, the plaintiff may sue the individual investigator or security officer, his or her manager, trainer, employer, or agency. Further, the term *scope of employment* may be defined as any act or action intended to benefit or further the employer's business (see the section entitled "Scope of Employment" for further clarification). Be aware also that acts forbidden by the employer or *outside of the confines of company or agency policy* may be found to be within the scope of employment. As an example, the question may arise, at what point does the threat or use of force by an investigator or security officer in the performance of an arrest become excessive and depart from the protection of a company's assets. Such an argument may have to be determined by the court.

Essentially, the intent of a vicarious liability action is that monetary damages awarded to the plaintiff against a private investigator or a security officer may not be as great as they would be if the higher echelon or the corporation that is more financially secure were included in the lawsuit. In other words, the plaintiff will attempt to draw into the lawsuit as many people or businesses as can be attributable or connected to the action (zeroing in to where the "big money" is).

Products Liability

Other than the negligence noted under the section earlier in this chapter, "Premises Liability," the question of other vulnerabilities encountered by a manufacturer, distributor, or retailer obtainable as damages by a plaintiff is not uncommon. In other words, any company or person who makes, distributes, or sells a product may be responsible for that product causing harm to another person.

One of the more litigious areas of liability that a business owner may face is some loss or injury sustained by a customer after the purchase, which was caused by a product, article, or substance sold and carried by the merchant. This would include harm to a would-be customer while still on the retail premises caused by that product, article, or substance on display, offered for sale, or carried by the merchant.

Products Liability Defined

Products liability refers to all parties along the chain from manufacturer to retailer of any product that may have caused damage (injury) to another. This chain includes the manufacturer, assembler, wholesaler, and retailer, whether already sold or on display. Any product proven to contain inherent defects which causes harm to a consumer or user of the product, whether loaned, given, or sold, may be subject to a products liability lawsuit. The claim may be based on negligence, strict liability, or breach of warranty. The injured party must prove that the product was in fact defective based upon a design defect, a manufacturing defect, or a marketing defect.

If nothing else, it is not uncommon today for a business enterprise to be held strictly liable for product-related injuries, even when the product had been purchased years ago, was abused in some manner, was used other than designed, or was altered and made unsafe after the sale.

The plaintiff must prove that there is a causal connection between the product's defect and the injury or harm suffered by the plaintiff, and that such defect did in fact exist when the product left the hands of the defendant.

The manufacturer, distributor, or retailer will be held strictly liable for the unreasonably dangerous nature of the product. Unreasonably dangerous nature may include usefulness and desirability of the product, availability of other and safer products that meet the same need, likelihood of injury, and common knowledge and normal expectation of the danger among others.

The private investigator assigned to a case or the loss prevention officer of an establishment should be aware that any product or merchandise on display that may come in contact with a customer or visitor on premises, and where such contact could or may cause an injury to that person, that product is a potential hazard. Such hazards must be removed or safeguarded so as not to place the business in liability. The type of liability will depend on whether the hazard was unknown, known, or observed by company personnel, and if known or observed, whether action was taken to correct, remove, or make safe in a timely manner. Civil actions by a plaintiff regarding liability of a product once it is off the premises will initiate investigations by loss prevention management and insurance carriers.

Liability regarding the product will fall onto the manufacturer, distributor, or retailer under the following general areas:

- There was *negligent conduct* of the defendant in either the manufacture or sale of the product.
- There is an implied warranty of the product, in that the manufacturer or retailer warrants that the goods are of *good quality* and are fit for the *ordinary purpose* for which they are to be used.
- Liability of a product may be defined as the legal responsibility that a manufacturer, distributor, or retailer has to compensate persons who are injured as a result of using the product. This liability allows a person to sue for damages when he or she has been injured or his or her property has been damaged because the product was *defective.*

- The plaintiff must prove that there is a *causal connection* between the product's defect and the injury or harm suffered by the plaintiff, and such defect did in fact exist when the product left the hands of the defendant.

> But also consider that it is not uncommon today for the retailer to be held strictly liable for product-related injuries, even when the product had been purchased years ago, was abused in some manner, was used other than designed, or was altered and made unsafe after the sale.

Moreover, if the plaintiff suffers some misfortune based on a product, the plaintiff's attorney will attempt to affix liability regarding the product under the following general areas:

1. *Design Defect*—In that the product was defective or deficient in its manufacture or design, or was inappropriate for the purpose intended. Liability may also be based merely on the negligent conduct of the defendant in either the manufacture or sale of the product. In addition, the manufacturer, distributor, or retailer may be held strictly liable for the unreasonable dangerous nature of the product. Unreasonably dangerous nature may include usefulness and desirability of the product, availability of other and safer products that meet the same need, likelihood of injury, and common knowledge and normal expectation of the danger among others.
2. *Failure to Warn*—In that the manufacturer or retailer failed to warn the consumer of known faults or defects that could harm the user, and failed to reclaim, recover, or remove from sale the defective product in a timely manner. This may include the continued marketing of a product that is known or should have been known to be unsafe.
3. *Foreseeable Misuse*—In that the manufacturer or retailer should have known that the product may be used other than intended or may be used more severely than the purpose designed. This may include the probability of counteracting the implied warranty of the product, where the manufacturer or retailer warrants that the good or product is of good quality and is fit for the ordinary purpose that the product is to be used.

> A true example of a product liability case known to the author occurred when a retailer had sold a bed and mattress with the implicit warranty of "good quality" and fit for "ordinary use," but as stated in the civil suit subsequently filed, the bed was, in fact, "defective," causing pain and injury to the plaintiffs.

The civil case against the retailer and manufacturer (the defendants) was based on the plaintiffs (husband and wife) who had purchased a bed and mattress from the retailer just less than 2 years prior. On a particular night, the couple while in bed was engaged in sexual intercourse. During these marital relations, the bed became unstable, causing the wooden supports between the headboard and the footboard to crack and break, thereby causing pain and injury to both parties when they fell to the floor with the husband on top of the wife. The wife, in particular, claimed that she suffered a severe acute and chronic back injury, with ongoing medical and hospital expenses. The plaintiffs argued that they had threatening physical and mental injuries that would take years to correct, if ever. The insurance companies for the defendants refused to accept the couple's premise and decided to go to a civil trial.

The retailer and manufacturer argued that the "act" itself must have been so active and vigorous, far above normal relations, as to cause the bed to give way. Counsel for the plaintiffs pointed out that a bed is a bed and that such "activity" was common and expected by a married couple and that they expected with "ordinary use" the bed would be capable for the use intended.

The jury in this case found for the plaintiffs. The jury decided after trial that the couple did in fact suffer injuries and damages as proclaimed, and awarded the plaintiffs a large sum as compensatory money damages from both defendants, with the largest part of the award being paid in particular by the manufacturer's insurance company. No punitive damages were awarded.

In their decision, the jury stated that any bed should be made strong enough to sustain, support, and withstand the weight of any couple for sleeping and lounging and for under the conditions that the couple were engaged in, and accepted the plaintiffs' rationale that the bed was used in the normal and typical way it was expected to be used.

The decision was not appealed.

Contractual Liability

Rarely will the private investigator become directly involved with the insurance coverage that the business enterprise may require or the selection of the insurance carrier who will underwrite the policy contract. That is usually left to the company administration. However, we should become familiar with the terminology of *contract liability*.

In essence, your client, the agency that employs you, as well as yourself can be held liable for the negligent acts of another by means of a written or oral contract. In other words, liability for the negligent conduct of another person is incurred or implied through a contractual agreement. This will include all agency investigators or subordinates and any contractual security officers that may be hired from time to time.

Many times these insurance contracts may automatically cover premises and operations coverage, but depending on the insurance carrier, some contracts may be more or less specific in their coverage than others.

Private investigative agencies and contractual security guard companies will posses their own liability coverage, and the business to which they are contracted to should request an up-to-date copy of their insurance coverage. In addition, the client that contracts for the services of an agency or a security guard company should have insurance coverage for any liable actions caused by any company contracted by that client, particularly if liability can or could be vicariously proved.

Liability of Corporations

Any director, officer, or employee who is authorized to act on behalf of the corporation, or an officer of the corporation or any other agent in a position of comparable authority with respect to the formulation of corporate policy or the supervision in a managerial capacity of subordinate employees, is considered guilty of an offense when the following occurs:

- The conduct consists of an omission to discharge a specific duty imposed on corporations by law.
- The conduct constituting the offense is engaged in, authorized, solicited, requested, commanded, or recklessly tolerated by the board of directors, officers, or managers acting within the scope of their employment, or on behalf of the corporation.
- The conduct constituting the offense is a misdemeanor or violation, or a law defined by statute imposed as a criminal liability on a corporation.

Additionally, a person is criminally liable for any conduct that constitutes an offense which he performs or causes to be performed in the name of or on behalf of the corporation to the same extent as if the act or omission was performed on his own behalf. (In this regard, see "Public Company Accounting Reform and Investor Protection Act" in Appendix A. The Sarbanes-Oxley Act of 2002 (short title) was passed by Congress in January of that year.)

Civil Litigation Following Criminal Prosecution

Generally, a violation of criminal law does not exclude or otherwise affect any right or liability to damages, penalty, forfeiture, or other remedy authorized by law to be recovered or enforced in a civil action, regardless of whether the act or omission involved in such civil action constituted an offense in criminal law.

Civil Rights

Federal Civil Rights Act—42 USC §1983: Civil Rights Violations

Defined

Any act that can be construed as denying a citizen his or her civil rights as defined in the Articles of the U.S. Constitution is considered a federal offense. This would include, but is not limited to, cruel and unusual punishment, freedom of speech, assembly, and movement, freedom from harm, detention or imprisonment, free from unlawful search and seizure, right of privacy, and due process.

A violation under federal law as noted in the *Civil Rights Act, §1983 Action,* can be charged against a person even though he may be charged with a crime for that same act in state court; there is no double jeopardy. Whether a subject is found guilty or not guilty in a state court for a crime, that person may be charged with a civil rights violation in a federal court. Many times, federal action is determined by public or political pressure.

Basic Provisions of the Act

Section 1983 of Title 42 provides a broad spectrum of rights to every citizen as found in the U.S. Constitution. It denotes the above-described protections in addition to the right to sue state officials and *others* acting under the *Color of State Law* to deprive a plaintiff of "any rights, privileges or immunities secured by the Constitution and Laws."[7] Further, it provides that any person when *under the color of state law,* subjects another to a deprivation of rights secured by the U.S. Constitution will be liable to the injured party. The provisions as defined cover many facets of civil rights and are of particular importance to private investigators and security officers in the performance of their duties.[8]

> Note that the defendant (violator) may also be subject to this federal law over and above any state actions for unlawful conduct. *Double jeopardy does not apply.*
>
> Criminal and civil litigation in this area of law enforcement by the federal courts have become somewhat controversial, and these actions placing a defendant in "jeopardy" a second time are considered by many to be politically motivated.

To reiterate, double jeopardy does not apply concerning the enforcement of this law. In other words, whether the offender is charged in a state criminally or is sued in civil court, under this law, that same person can be charged in federal court for committing the same act.

The rationale established by these actions is that the victim was deprived of his or her civil rights under the U.S. Constitution and, therefore, the federal courts may act.

The Enforcement of the Civil Rights Act

The U.S. Attorney may act under Title 42 of the U.S. Code when a citizen's civil rights have been violated.

For example, if a private investigator or a security officer professed or identified him- or herself as a police officer in effecting an "arrest" or some custodial action, he or she could be charged in a state court as impersonating a police officer. A federal action could also be laid against the offender for acting under the "color of state law," whether found guilty or not on the charge in the state court.

As a further example, if a defendant is charged in a state court for murder and is found not guilty, the federal government may arrest and charge that same defendant in federal court for *civil rights violations* for the same act he or she had committed against the victim (in that the victim was deprived of life, liberty, and so forth, by the defendant in causing the death of the victim).

By the federal government seeking redress in a second court, the "public's concern of accountability" is satisfied, if not in one court, then the other; again note that double jeopardy does not apply in this case.

The "Color of State Law"

To be in violation of the part of the law contained in this Act, the violator must have *acted under the color of state law.* This federal statute prohibits those who act under the color of law from violating a person's rights and privileges. It is intended to protect a citizen from *illegal actions by a law enforcement officer or agency*—the misuse of lawful authority.

Therefore, the Federal Civil Rights Act can rarely be satisfied in the case of anyone except a state or government official. *However, if a private investigator or a security officer acts on behalf of, in cooperation with, or at the request of a law enforcement officer, his actions are subject to the same restrictions as the law assigns to that law enforcement officer.*

A §1983 action could also lie against the defendants *alleged to be police officers* who used excessive force, or a *citizen who collaborated with a police officer* in making an unlawful arrest.

Consequently, we can say that the following occurrences in which a private person (a private investigator or security officer) can be held accountable under this Act are circumstances that they must be aware and cautious of in their actions:

- Where a person's conduct (the private investigator or security officer) is the direct result of a state agent's encouragement or command. The "state agent" can be a police officer, sheriff, district attorney, or any law enforcement officer; the PI or security officer acts on that person's behalf.
- Where a private person (the private investigator or security officer) undertakes the performance and activities ordinarily exclusive to or only within the purview of a governmental entity. *This would include a citizen, a private investigator, or a security officer again who professes and acts as if he were a police officer.*
- Where the private person has been granted certain benefits by the state (or any municipal authority) of such a nature that the individual and the state are inseparably linked. Note that this may include private security officers contractually employed by a municipality or a school district.

The following court holdings refine the law:

- State statutes concerning the defenses accorded a retailer do not transform tortious conduct by a private merchant into an action undertaken by the state or under the color of state law in violation of 42 USC §1983.[9]
- A case is noted involving a citizen who collaborated with a police officer in making an unlawful arrest.[10] But in another case, a security officer employed by Alexander's Department Store was a SPO (Special Police Officer) appointed by the State pursuant to the New York Administrative Code (certain rights granted by a municipal authority).[11]
- Where the plaintiff was stopped in a store by store detectives for stealing a telephone answering machine and was handcuffed and taken to the security office. He was released a few hours later after issuance of an appearance ticket to appear at a later time to answer to the charge of petit larceny. A year later the plaintiff was acquitted of the charge. The plaintiff brought claim against the store under §1983 of the Civil Rights Act. The store argued that the store detectives were private citizens, and therefore, the store cannot be held vicariously liable.

  But the store detective who initially stopped the plaintiff was in fact an SPO appointed by the New York City Police Commissioner pursuant to the New York Administrative Code. Under the Code, a SPO possesses all the powers of a regular sworn police officer.[12] (This designation, rarely made, is a political appointment without civil service sanctions.)
- The court held that such a "police officer" with the power to arrest is a *government official and is subject to §1983 liability*. The store was held vicariously liable because the actions of the SPO were for Alexander's benefit and employees of the store "conspired" with the SPO in his actions.

Further, there was evidence presented that it was the store's unstated policy to arrest more readily minorities such as blacks and Hispanics, *so the store could be subject to an independent liability also,* along with the plaintiff's wife suing for emotional distress of seeing her husband taken into custody and placed in handcuffs.

- Where a private person and the State jointly act to deprive a person of his rights.[13]

It is not sufficient to make broad and conclusive allegations concerning the existence of an alleged conspiracy between private persons and state officials; the plaintiff must plead the facts with specificity.[14]

For example, a private investigator placed a suspect under arrest for burglary. The subject confessed to the crime he is to be charged with. Upon turning over the subject to the police, a police officer, knowing that he must advise the subject with a Miranda warning before any questioning by him, takes the investigator aside and asks him to question the subject on any other burglaries he may have committed. The private investigator thereafter continues his interrogation, and the subject does in fact admit to several other burglaries within earshot of the police officer. Soon thereafter, the police officer also charges the subject for the additional burglaries he admitted to.

Subsequently, the subject's attorney learns upon discovery that the private investigator acted on behalf of the police officer in violation of §1983, in that his client's civil rights were transgressed (failure to render the Miranda warning) and any admissions made cannot be used as evidence in court. Moreover, the attorney could place in peril any admissions made by the defendant when the investigator first questioned the suspect, if he can show that a police officer was in the vicinity or was observed by the defendant (a police-dominated atmosphere).

Remember and be aware that any private person (in our case a private investigator or a security officer) acting in any manner toward a suspect or anyone else at the behest of a law enforcement officer, or who portrays him- or herself in fact as a law enforcement officer, or gives the appearance that he or she is a law enforcement officer (which could lead to a charge of criminal impersonation of a police officer) and does not advise the subject of his or her legal rights as required, does so at the risk of criminal and civil litigation. (This is a §1983 civil rights violation.)

Chapter 3

The Criminal and Civil Litigation Process

Most people are not aware of the operation of the criminal justice system or the processes that take place within that system. The novice investigator should have some knowledge of the legal procedures that will or might take place in any interaction with another person, a client, or, in particular, one under investigation. In this segment, we will offer a basic view of the criminal justice system and how to act or react within that system.

We must remember that a private investigator (PI), or in fact any security officer, is not a law enforcement officer. He or she does not possess police powers and has no more legal authority than does an ordinary citizen. Private investigators may be arrested and face criminal charges in a criminal court for any illegal action taken by them and not within the scope of their authority. Whether the investigator is exonerated in criminal court or not, he or she may still face civil litigation for any wrongs or perceived wrongs that a plaintiff believes were committed against him or her. Remember that an acquittal on a criminal charge does not exclude the initiation of a civil suit.

Criminal law is statutory law (written law), and along with the Criminal Justice System (police, prosecutors, judiciary, and corrections) enforce the law and share a common goal to preserve the peace, prevent crime, and keep the community and its citizens safe. The person who commits an illegal act is arrested and brought before the criminal court to answer to the charge. Because his or her crime is an offense against the people of the state, any sentence or fine is paid to the state.

Complainant (The State) versus Defendant and Plaintiff versus Defendant

A point of clarification here is necessary. When a subject is arrested for a criminal offense, that person is the *defendant*, and is represented in a criminal court by counsel (*the defense attorney*). The person who arrested the subject is the police officer, security officer, or any person who wishes the subject be taken before the court to face the charges. Whoever makes the arrest or demands of a police officer that one be made is the *complainant*. The *complainant (or the police officer)* will swear to an "information" before the court requesting that the person named be brought into court to face the charge. An information is a "bill of particulars" in which the offense is detailed and the perpetrator is identified. The District Attorney or the Prosecutor will represent the complainant/state against the defendant. Also note that the crime committed is against the State (the people), and it is the State (on behalf of the complainant) that will prosecute the case against the defendant.

In a civil lawsuit, the subject who has been "damaged" in some way (unlawfully assaulted, false arrest, defamed, etc.) is the *plaintiff*. He or she is represented by an attorney (*plaintiff's attorney*). The person, group of people, or corporation that the plaintiff claims damages against is the *defendant*. The plaintiff may include in the action the investigator, his or her supervisor, his or her trainer, and the corporation he or she is employed by. This type of litigation is called *vicarious liability* and is essentially an attempt to bring as many persons into the lawsuit for the purpose of assigning responsibility or receiving as much compensation as possible. The belief is that just suing the investigator and winning the case will yield just so much money, but by including as many as can legally be added to the action, such implication would bring in much more remuneration.

The Court System

The Criminal Court

Before a criminal trial can take place, the subject must be charged in an indictment or a sworn information, which is a formal accusation or allegation that he or she has committed a crime, and that the subject must answer to the indictment or the complaint before a judge.

Minor offenses may be heard and disposed of in the lower courts. Depending on the state, these lower courts include Justices of the Peace, City Magistrates, and District Courts. Most arraignments take place in these lower courts. But when there is a Grand Jury indictment, the offense may be brought before a higher court for arraignment, preliminary hearings, and trial. These higher courts will include County Courts, Supreme or Superior Courts.

Prelitigation

Preserving Physical Evidence in a Criminal Prosecution

Depending on the police jurisdiction and local District Attorney procedures, stolen property recovered from the defendant may be photographed and returned to the owner or to stock so that the merchant will not suffer a loss of outdated merchandise when it is returned after adjudication at a later time. Two sets of photographs should be taken—one set for the police and one set to be attached to and made part of the private investigator's or security officer's report. Date, time, case number, description of items photographed, and signature or initials of the person taking the pictures should be noted on the rear of the processed photos. So as to give immediate access of photos to police, a Polaroid-type camera is adequate and acceptable in most jurisdictions. However, there are some police administrations that require all evidence be invoiced to the police property clerk for future court actions. The investigator will act accordingly. In the case of weapons or contraband recovered from the defendant subsequent to the arrest, and for which the defendant may also be charged for such possession, the investigator will act as directed by the police concerning the preservation of evidence and the identification of same for trial.

In any event, the private investigator will be guided by local police procedures in the handling of recovered property (proceeds of the crime) and any other evidence.

Obtaining Confessions and Witness Statements

If possible, a written and signed confession taken from the defendant is the most desirable in assigning an admission of guilt. If a written statement cannot be taken, any oral admissions or statements made by the defendant (or a witness for that matter), should be reduced to writing by the investigator as soon as practical. In any case, a witness should be present when the defendant reads and signs his or her written confession or when any oral admissions are made. As a matter of fact, two witnesses are preferred so as to rebut any subsequent contradiction made by the defendant.

> A confession or statement should not be taken or received under threat, duress, or promise. The court would prohibit a statement taken under these conditions from being offered as evidence and, in fact, may cast an unfavorable light on any testimony or other actions conducted by the investigator in the case.

Miranda warnings need not be made part of the statement or as a warning prior to any questioning because private investigators and security officers are not police officers. But if a police officer has knowledge of or asks the security officer to take a written statement or an oral admission, the security officer is then acting as an agent of the police officer and must issue the Miranda warnings. See Appendix A,

"Color of State Law" (Federal Civil Rights Act, Title 42 USC Section 1983) and pages 56–57 for the actions by an investigator when in the presence of or at the behest of a police officer.

It should be noteworthy that if the private investigator or security officer has the ability and is required to take a written confession from a defendant, or written statements from witnesses, the investigator and officer should have some training as to the format and what is required to be included in the confession or statement so that the writing will be able to stand up in court.

Concerning any confession taken from a suspected or possible defendant in particular, it should contain the pedigree of that person (that is, name, date of birth, social security number, if married, single, children if any, spouse's name, home address, telephone number, occupation and business addresses—as much identification as possible). A sentence should also be contained in the statement showing that it was freely given, and that all that is contained in the statement is the truth. Moreover, the written account must be dated along with witnesses to the defendant reading and signing the confession and so indicated by their signatures.

A written statement should be taken from a relevant witness or any person having direct knowledge of pertinent facts concerning the crime or the incident. This statement taken need not be so explicit as required in a confession; name, address, and telephone number may be sufficient. No further caveats are required. Hopefully, it will be signed by the witness and witnessed by the investigator. If not signed by the witness, notation should be made on the statement as to time, date, and location at which the statement was taken. If a written statement cannot be taken for whatever reason, the witness's identity should be noted, and any oral statements of importance should be reduced to writing, attributed to that person, dated, signed by the investigator, and attached to and made part of the incident or case report.

Generally, if the police are going to become involved because the incident is criminal in nature, it is best to let the police investigate in their capacity and not take confessions or witness statements. However, it should be noted that some police agencies look favorably on confessions taken by private investigators and security officers prior to their involvement, as long as they have the ability and expertise to do so. This is because Miranda warnings given to a suspect by the police might suppress any admissions that might be received during the interrogation process. But any statement, whoever takes it, becomes part of the case file and is subject to scrutiny by the defense attorney or the prosecutor at discovery or trial.

Some police agencies have procedures that vary with jurisdiction. Regarding criminal prosecution, it would be wise for the private investigator or security officer to determine what situations should be or will be handled only by the police and what incidents can and could be handled by private investigators and security officers.

In any case where the crime is of a serious nature, the police will interview or reinterview all witnesses, and the investigator or officer will be of great assistance in identifying to the police all witnesses involved.

Interviews by Unknown Parties and Damaging Remarks by Others

The private investigator must be aware that following any occurrence or incident where an investigation or litigation may be forthcoming, the investigator should be conscious of who approaches him or her, or attempts to glean information through an apparently normal conversation. In essence, do not answer any questions from anyone unless one is positively sure that the person requesting information is connected to your agency, your agency's client, or the company that you are contractually assigned to. Naturally, while in court and under oath, the security officer will be required to answer all questions truthfully, unless upheld on objection by the attorney representing you or your company.

Additionally, be mindful that any statements, however insignificant, made by you, the investigator, or anyone else at the scene of an incident, may be noted and held against you or another at a later time. Private investigators should not express any opinion, thought, action, or response that will place them or their employer in jeopardy of liability. Attempt to advise all associates present at any intercourse or assistance at a scene, if any, to remain as noncommittal as possible while doing what is required of them.

See also the box, "Cautionary Critique," at the end of this chapter.

Preparing Investigative or Case Reports

The objectives of a report are as follows:

- *Record*—Provide a permanent official record of relevant information and data obtained from the initial complaint, accusation, or request through the course of the investigation and its conclusion.
- *List Leads*—Provide information (active or that found to be nonproductive) to further advance the investigation for other investigators, to prevent duplication of effort, and to provide a rational basis for further inquiries or directions.
- *Prosecutorial Action*—Provide a statement of facts and evidence on which the case may form or be admitted in a criminal, corrective or disciplinary action.

Not everything can be committed to memory, and memory cannot remain unchallenged in a court of inquiry. Therefore, the private investigator must carry a notebook (which may be subject to discovery) that will later be used to transfer any pertinent information to a written formal report. Reports may come in different forms depending on the subject matter to be covered.

Some of these reports may fall into three categories:

1. *Administrative Memoranda*—This includes the agency's policies and procedures or specific business matters.

2. *Incident Report*—This may also be called an occurrence or case report. It provides a written record of an event, which may or may not require further investigation.
3. *Investigative Report*—This may be called a *case report* with various forms, reports, statements, and documents that will all be attached together or contained in a case jacket separate and apart from other cases under investigation. It will include a formal introduction to a client's initial contact with the agency, the problem or incident that the client wishes the agency to investigate, and any contractual agreements with the client. Depending on the case in question, it may also include witness statements, confessions, admissions, or other oral utterances reduced to writing, photographs, videotapes, recorded conversations, video and personal surveillance logs, property forms and logs, any supplemental reports or writings, and any activity performed by anyone who provided or contributed to the investigation or inquiry in question.

The most important report for an investigator is the *investigative report* noted above. A professionally compiled report requires expertise, guidance, and practice. It should note who, what, when, where, why, and how, and should be as complete as possible. The report must be accurate, concise, and legible. It must have clarity and brevity—a true representation of the facts as found by the investigator. Moreover, it must be objective in the findings.

However, it should not contain any opinions or inferences unless based on facts. Information that may be favorable or unfavorable to the case or the subject of the investigation should be included. Some reports may contain too much information not pertinent to the case, and may in fact diminish the data or information that the writer wishes to put forth. Moreover, the more information in a report not applicable to the case gives opposing counsel more of an excuse to challenge and question the truthfulness and accuracy of that report, or the proficiency and professionalism of the writer. The report should be developed logically and will be dictated by the nature of the case. Statements, confessions, or any admissions must be noted in the narration. The suspect and witnesses should be clearly identified, and any statements or confessions (including oral statements or admissions) should be reduced to writing and attached as enclosures and made part of the report.

All dates, times, locations, and notifications must be placed in chronological order and highlighted as a caption in bold type. All persons, suspects, and witnesses should also be noted in bold type so as to stand out and be easily located in the report. The report and each subsequent or supplemental report or page should be sequential, with the classification (larceny, forgery, and so forth) noted along with the case or file number, date, complaint or complainant (client), investigator assigned, and victim or business identified. Certain reports may also be maintained and filed chronologically or numerically within a category and contained in the case jacket. It also should be signed and dated by the investigator completing the form. All narratives contained in the report must be truthful, as they may be considered for admission as evidence at a trial or hearing. Consider also, that any notes, notations, or notebooks are also subject to discovery and admission as evidence and therefore should also be contained in the case jacket.

> It must be emphasized at this point that the private investigator must be cognizant of the fact that any report, statement, or writing compiled and submitted by him or her must be as truthful to the facts as possible. The private investigator must remember that he or she may have to swear under oath before a court or a hearing that all contained in the report or any narrative within that report is the truth.
>
> Consider also, that any formal written report compiled by a private investigator in the course of an investigation or as required by his or her employer (the agency) is a "business record," and to intentionally falsify a business record may constitute a crime in most, if not all, states.

Litigation

Grand Jury Action

Some states may differ as to the make-up or quorum for a Grand Jury. But generally, a grand jury is composed of 23 citizens but no less than 16 for a quorum. A quorum is required for the purpose of a finding. They will decide whether or not to indict the suspect after the district attorney (or an assistant district attorney) has presented the state's case (the evidence of the crime). If the grand jurors find a *prima facia* case to believe that the accused person committed the crime, they will return a "true bill"—an indictment. Only felonies and indictable misdemeanors will be presented to the Grand Jury (again, depending on the state). But upon investigation or inquiries of their own, grand juries may indict for any crime. If the defendant has not already been arrested and charged before the court, he will be arrested and appear for arraignment where the indictment will be presented against him.

Arrests Prior to Grand Jury Action

Prior to any Grand Jury action, if any, when a subject is summarily arrested and brought before the court, an *information* is drawn up and presented to that court where the subject is arraigned on the charge.

If an *indictment* (a *true bill* by the Grand Jurors) is sought prior to any court action, the next step after an indictment has been handed up would be the arraignment, where the suspect, now a defendant, appears at this formal hearing.

In addition, the *information* may also be sworn to and laid in the lower criminal courts for misdemeanors and felonies prior to any arraignment or Grand Jury action, and before an arrest takes place. The judge then issues a warrant for arrest of the defendant after accepting the sworn information.

An *information* that is sworn to before a judge or a police desk officer is in reality a *bill of particulars*, a *complaint, accusation,* or an *affirmation* that contains specific allegations in which the complainant swears that a crime has been committed, that it was committed by the defendant, and that the complainant wishes the defendant to face the charge or charges in court.

Arraignment

After a grand jury action where a true bill is handed down, the District Attorney may request that the person indicted surrender himself for arraignment, or an arrest warrant may be issued by a judge based on the indictment.

At any arraignment, the judge will ask how the defendant pleads to the crime as stated in the *indictment* or the *sworn information*. If the defendant pleads guilty, the case is set down for sentencing, but because defendant rights are such an issue today, rarely is a plea accepted other than a "not guilty" at arraignment. If a plea of not guilty is given, the judge may or may not set bail, may release the defendant on his or her own recognizance, or may remand him or her to jail. A date for trial is set in either case. If the defendant does not have an attorney, the court must make sure that he or she has one, usually before any plea is accepted. If the defendant is deemed poor and cannot afford an attorney, the court will provide one to serve him or her.

Discovery

At a hearing, the attorney representing either the defendant or the plaintiff attempts to obtain as much information from the other side as possible—*discovery*. This will include all facts, witness names, statements, evidence collected, and anything else of importance that the other attorney may need from his or her adversary in order to build a strong defense and to present a more informed case. In essence, it is a procedure where all parties of an action, criminal or civil, will commence the trial with as much knowledge as possible and withholding no secrets from the other.

Criminal Hearings—Actions before the Trial

At times a criminal defense attorney may request a hearing before the criminal court prior to a trial and many times before any Grand Jury action in order to determine if, in fact, a crime has been committed and the facts warrant the arrest of the defendant (*felony exam*). Or it may be in order to determine whether a witness' identification of the defendant is tainted, as in a lineup where unfairly suggestive procedures may be evident and therefore inadmissible as evidence (*Wade hearing*). Additional hearings of this type are conducted to discover and hopefully negate any evidence, statements, or confessions that are poorly or criminally obtained before the actual trial.

The Civil Court

A civil case begins when the plaintiff, the person who has been wronged or believes that he has been wronged, files a complaint in court containing a statement of his claim against the defendant. The wrongs that the plaintiff can seek as redress may include a false arrest, physical injury, loss of income, and harm to one's reputation, among others. The defendant in a civil case is the person or company being sued. The defendant, through his attorney, then files an answer with the court disputing all charges brought by the plaintiff. Once a case begins, the lawyers prepare for trial, which because of full trial calendars may take years. The lawyers look for witnesses favorable to their case, examine witnesses or evidence that may be used by the other side (discovery, evidence-based testimonies, examinations before trial [EBTs], depositions), collect evidence, do legal research, hire investigators and expert professionals, and file arguments and motions with the court relating to procedures in the case.

Civil courts are also generally divided by the types of cases they may handle, which usually concerns the amount of loss or the type of offense. Lower courts, such as District Courts, may at times also act as small claims courts, and may set a maximum amount of loss or recovery at no more than $5,000. Depending on the state, a lawsuit seeking damages above that amount would be heard in a higher court.

The Civil Lawsuit

Any business that wishes to stay in business has insurance to cover all perils from property damage, accidental and criminal liability, and other obligations. Unless a private investigator comes into this vocation with a law enforcement background, few novice investigators are familiar with the processes of a lawsuit. In that regard, it would do well to describe the process in some detail.

A civil lawsuit begins when an incident occurs and where someone has been injured, or wronged in some manner, and where that person will approach an attorney for counsel, and based on the facts and circumstances of the case will then initiate court actions.

There is nothing more disturbing for a corporation of any size than being served with or receiving a summons and complaint citing a civil action against all and everyone that may have been involved in an incident in question. Vicariously, that can include the initial actions or inactions by an employee who was or could have been involved in an incident, any assisting investigators and security officers, the employee's supervisor and manager, the store, the building or facility manager, and, of course, the corporation. Furthermore, in some instances, the police department and their officers are included for whatever part they may have played in the incident.

Along with noting the date, time, and place of occurrence, the lawsuit will list the wrongs committed by the individual or company personnel, the injuries or "wrongs" sustained by the plaintiff and others, and the damages demanded. Wrongs can include: false arrest, false imprisonment, assault, battery, pain and injuries suffered, medical expenses, slander, libel, civil rights violations, misfortune, emotional stress, and fear. Also included may be personal embarrassment; injury to reputation; loss of work, wages, or employment; and loss of services by a spouse; among others. Some of these "wrongs" do not have to occur only during an arrest or investigation, they could occur at any time during or after the incident, and in any confrontation with a dissatisfied or disgruntled individual or an injured person not properly protected or attended to.

Civil Hearings—Testifying at Depositions/ Examinations before Trial

A deposition is a more formal statement reduced to writing, signed and sworn to before a Notary Public. Basically, a confession does not differ from a deposition except that no Notary Public may be involved.

Examination Before Trial (EBT) is a formal hearing and may be considered a form of discovery. Basically, an EBT is testimony under oath, in response to questions asked by the opposing attorney with respect to the facts and circumstances surrounding the incident or occurrence.

Service of the Lawsuit or Intent to File Suit

Service of the lawsuit may be made by certified mail, a process server, or personally by the plaintiff or his or her attorney. In large business enterprises or companies that have the services of a loss prevention or security manager, that person will usually acknowledge or accept service regarding all lawsuits and will be the person in direct contact with the company's corporate risk manager, insurance broker, or insurance carrier. This low-level manager should be the person who should initially be the recipient of the lawsuit, because this manager and his or her department are the depository of all incidents and records of concern, are aware of all insurance coverage, have ongoing contact with insurance investigators and attorneys, and are most familiar with criminal and civil litigation. A senior manager or administrator on site may also be given the responsibility of handling some or all of these tasks along with or in the absence of the loss prevention manager.

Furthermore, in the larger business establishments, the importance of a Corporate Legal Affairs Department or a Risk Management Department cannot be overstated. Their counsel and guidance in the protection of all assets of the firm or organization against all risks can have a significant and reflective effect on the bottom line. All individual Loss Prevention or Security Managers within these large corporations must be attentive and responsive to these departments, particularly in the immediate advisement of all litigation matters.

In another type of service, a letter of representation with a possible additional notice of intent to sue will be sent (usually by certified mail) to the person or corporation of concern, requesting that the receiver advise their insurance carrier of such action and representation so that communication between the two may begin. This practice by a plaintiff's attorney is acted upon before any summons and complaint are laid in civil court, usually for the purpose of quick settlement.

In the case of an investigative agency or individual private investigator that may become involved in some type of litigation, service of the lawsuit will be received by the agency's owner or manager or the individual. Vicariously, the suit may include the investigator, the investigator's supervisors, the agency, and the client who contracted the investigator or agency.

The Trial Process

The Adversary System

Consider that a trial is a fair contest, in which lawyers contend to be an adversary system of justice, thereby creating it as the cornerstone of our legal system. It is basically a contest between two parties that have equal opportunity to triumph because each party has lawyers with equal foundation and familiarity with the law and know how to make the most of their talents. This may be particularly evident in criminal cases where the power of the state can overwhelm the individual to a great extent. In other countries, the court system is quite different than that in the United States. Many persons may face a judge who is in reality not impartial and who is both judge and prosecutor, holding that the defendant is guilty until proven innocent. Whereas in our system, the judge is supposed to be impartial and have an open mind. The public prosecutor (the District Attorney, State's Attorney or U.S. Attorney) has the burden to prove that the defendant did or could have committed the crime or offense that he or she is accused of. On the other hand, the lawyer for the accused need only raise a doubt in the minds of the judge or jury for an acquittal.

Whether it is a criminal or civil case that concerns an individual or a group, access to a lawyer is a right, in which he or she has a legal responsibility and obligation to the client who has been charged or wronged in some manner. A judge presides at a hearing or trial to determine that the public's interest is protected along with the rights of the parties involved. Knowing the law and the rules and procedures that can be applied, the judge will rule on the evidence to be submitted and the lawyers who may wish to bend or twist the law in their client's interest.

> Although not perfect, the legal system we have in the United States is the only one in the world where an individual may find evenhanded justice and protection from illegal prosecution by the government.
>
> Based on court judgements, mandates, and precedents, there is no other country so careful to protect the legal rights of a person accused of any type of crime or offense, or where a citizen has the right of redress in the appropriate court for a harm committed against them.

Testifying at Trial

The average citizen rarely enters a courtroom, and more rarely is called as a witness before the court. Most legal matters never reach the trial stage because they usually get settled for one reason or another. Because civil litigation is becoming more prevalent in our society, the PI has a greater chance of ending up in court than does the typical citizen.

When appearing at any hearing or when testifying in any court, the investigator should have a presentable appearance. The male investigator should wear a clean shirt, tie, and suit or sport jacket. The female investigator should wear a dress or a suit with a skirt or slacks. Jeans or dungarees should never be worn in court. Shoes should be appropriate and shined, and generally the investigator should be neatly groomed. The courtroom operates in a formal atmosphere. Out of respect, informal attire is considered inappropriate. The court and jury will consider the investigator as unprofessional and unsuitable if they appear in court wearing jewelry such as eyebrow, lip, tongue, or nose rings, or any other unsuitable adornment.

The investigator should also be on time, be attentive, and be responsive. As an investigator or security officer, you should review all reports and statements so as to refresh your memory prior to testifying. Generally, before any proceeding, you will be required to consult with the prosecutor or attorney representing you or your employer concerning the case in question, your testimony, and what to expect from both sides. Remember that the judge, jury, and opposing side are closely watching a witness's dress, appearance, demeanor, and presence of mind while on the stand.

While on the witness stand, you should speak clearly and loudly enough to be understood by the judge, the attorneys, and the jury, if any. Your head should be kept high with hands on one's lap, and try not to use hand gestures or become fidgety. You should answer all questions put to you by the prosecutor or any attorney truthfully and as briefly as possible. Do not attempt to clarify or add information not asked. The idea of the opposing attorney is to discredit or destroy your testimony. He or she will try to make you angry and try to confuse you in your testimony; he or she will become angry, rude, and annoying and will question your character, veracity, and integrity. Try to act and speak calmly, and do not become frustrated or angry with the attorney—realize that the attorney is just doing his or her job, whether you like it or not. Answer all questions honestly. If you do not know the answer, say so. If you do not understand the question, ask to have it repeated or clarified. Take your time in answering—the prosecutor or your attorney may wish to object to the question.

Behavior on the Witness Stand

When a private investigator, security officer, or any witness for that matter, is to testify in court, whether a criminal or civil case, he or she should be cognizant of the following:

- *Never Lie, Tell the Truth*—If you perjure yourself, you commit a crime. Never expound on an answer even though it is the truth. Provide *only the answer to the exact question that is asked.* It is all right to say, "I don't remember," or "I don't know."
- *Listen Carefully*—Pause before answering. Think and understand the question before you answer. Take your time. If you do not understand the question, ask that it be repeated or rephrased.
- *Never Guess*—If you do not know the answer, state simply that you do not know. Even if you "think" you know, you should only answer that which you *know* to be true. If you do not guess, then no one can make you appear to be lying or attempt to confuse you.
- *Never Answer Too Quickly*—A proficient attorney can fire questions at a very fast pace in an effort to confuse and rush a witness into making an incorrect or improbable statement or blurting out more than the witness may wish to. The witness should take his or her time, think every question through thoroughly, and answer truthfully but deliberately, factually, and concisely. Moreover, the attorney for the witness may wish to object to a question. If, at any time, your attorney makes an objection, stop talking immediately.
- *Keep Your Answers Simple*—Whenever possible, answer *yes* or *no.* Do not elaborate unless you are asked to clarify your answer. Use understandable language.
- *Do Not Exaggerate*—Give definitive answers. All answers should be well thought out and as short as possible. Do not give the impression of a braggart or a show-off.
- *Never Volunteer Information*—A question is asked for a purpose. If the answer is not explicit enough, another question will be asked. Do not try to second-guess or anticipate your attorney or the other attorney. Answer only the question asked and do not elaborate; stop when you have answered. Do not offer your opinion unless it is asked.
- *Be Alert to Trick Questions*—Do not let the opposing attorney put words into your mouth. Watch for the same question being asked with different words. Be aware of making comparisons or what you personally believe: "Wouldn't

you agree that…," "Are you telling me…," "Have you spoken with your lawyer before you entered the courtroom" (of course you did), "Have you ever lied?" (yes, but never under oath). One question that flusters most witnesses is "How much are you being paid for your testimony here today?" The witness should answer truthfully; "I'm just receiving my regular salary…it's my job, and I'm here because I was subpoenaed."

- *Never Argue or Lose Your Temper*—Proficient attorneys can easily goad or lead a witness into making rash statements, blurting out information helpful to their case, or making the witness look like an emotional idiot. Be patient and keep control of your temper regardless of the tone and content of the questions. Your complete testimony can be ruined if you fall into this trap. Do not become sarcastic or combative or behave in a "wise guy" manner. Answer questions from all attorneys in the same courteous manner.
- *Be Aware of Your Physical Actions*—Be attentive to the seriousness of your testimony. Try not to laugh or smirk, even though it might be a nervous reaction. Do not roll your eyes in a response to an action or a question, and do not permit a facial expression that may convey your thoughts or attitude to the judge or jury. If you are nervous on the stand, clasp and place your hands on your lap. In this manner, you will be less conscious of your nervousness by your hands being somewhat out of sight.

The Opposing Attorney

An attorney for the other side is not your friend in a court of law. His job is to free his client of any crime or civil retribution. The attorney for the other side will attempt to confuse, berate, and belittle you, call you a fabricator and a perjurer, condemn your testimony and your actions, and make other attempts to negate your testimony. Be aware that this stratagem is intentional and conducted to make you look like an untrained and unprofessional dimwit. Try to remember this and be mindful of these tactics. This attorney will jab and fling questions at you rapidly and relentlessly, hoping that you will slip with a wrongful or inaccurate answer and appear insecure. You can slow the attorney down and take control of the "conflict" by taking your time, mulling over each question, and asking that the question be repeated or rephrased. Nothing will rattle an attorney more than a witness who mulls over the question and takes his time to give a thoughtful and truthful answer.

In conclusion, private investigators must realize that their knowledge, demeanor, and presence in court will reflect upon any past actions they have taken or prior comments they have made, in or out of court. The more capable that an investigator appears to be, the more favorable weight that the judge and jury will give to his or her testimony and prior actions.

Cautionary Critique

All investigators should be aware that during a trial or any hearing, a person might approach them outside the courtroom in a friendly manner to pass the time of day and strike up a conversation. Consider that the inquisitor may be an agent for the other side. The novice private investigator must be conscious of an approach by anyone, particularly during recesses or breaks in court proceedings where court "observers" or "spectators" will begin "friendly" conversations with you in an attempt to glean any information or comments that can be passed on and used by the opposing attorney.

This is not an uncommon tactic, where after a court recess and the hearing resumes, the investigator or witness is called to the witness stand and is confronted with questions by the opposing attorney regarding comments made by the investigator or witness during that recess.

If approached, advise the "sociable" questioner that you cannot talk about or divulge any information regarding the case as directed by the prosecutor or your attorney. If the questioner persists, remove yourself from his or her presence and advise the prosecutor or your counsel of the incident as soon as practical.

Chapter 4

The Legal Powers and Limitations of a Private Investigator

Consider this chapter to be of utmost importance to a private investigator (PI) or any security officer. It will define his or her response and behavior in the apprehension and arrest of those persons who commit unlawful acts.

> The private investigator is not a sworn police officer or a peace officer. Therefore, the private investigator does not have the power and authority that a law enforcement officer possesses.

The legal authority of a private investigator (or a security officer) is *very* limited. The private investigator is considered a *private citizen* according to the law. As a private citizen, he or she has a legal right to make a *citizen's arrest under restrictive circumstances.*

Moreover, as a private citizen, the private investigator must be aware of the conditions required to make an arrest or to initiate a criminal complaint, and the authority to do so as dictated by the agency that employs that investigator.

Definition of Arrest

Arrest is defined as the restraining of a person and that person's freedom of movement, and the bringing of that person to legal custody to answer for the alleged offense or criminal act.

The restraint of a person's freedom (detention) can also be construed as *unlawful imprisonment* if the arrest is unlawful, and the private investigator or security officer may be held liable.

Criminal and civil law decree that *false arrest* and *false imprisonment* are synonymous in meaning.

If an arrest is to take place by a private investigator or a security officer (private persons), two controlling factors must be present:

1. The private investigator must detain or apprehend the person in question.
2. The person detained or apprehended is acted upon by and with the private investigator's intent of presenting the person under arrest to a police officer without unnecessary delay so as to answer to the alleged crime.

Types of Arrest

Actual Seizure, the Use of Force—The taking of a person into custody with the use of hands, restraints (e.g., handcuffs), or weapons. It is an actual seizure. It includes the touching of the person being arrested, or the use of threats for compliance.

Constructive Seizure—The taking of a person into custody without the use of force or weapons.

The Four Elements of Arrest by a Private Investigator or a Security Officer

1. The *intention of arrest* by a private investigator or security officer, in that he or she takes a person into custody, depriving that person of his or her movement or liberty (depriving a person of his or her constitutional right of freedom).

2. The *actual seizure of the person being arrested* by the one having the present power to control the person being arrested.

3. The *person being arrested must understand* that the private investigator or security officer is arresting and detaining the person then and there at the scene. Circumstances such as flight or physical resistance may not make this action possible.

4. If applicable, a *communication by an arresting officer* (a police officer) to the person in custody as to the private investigator's intent and purpose, then and there at the scene, to arrest the person.

Authority to Arrest by a Private Citizen

Generally, the descriptions and definitions described above and that follow in this chapter are commonly accepted in most if not all states. Newly hired private investigators (and security officers) should check with the criminal and civil laws in the state in which they are employed that would pertain to their activities and performance regarding arrest procedure and unlawful imprisonment.

Because the law regards the private investigator as a *citizen,* he or she has the basic right as any citizen to arrest a person who has committed a crime under the following circumstances:

- The *offense is committed in full view* of the private investigator.
    - The *offense must be a crime*—a *felony* or a *misdemeanor.*
    - The private investigator must be a witness to the crime then being committed.
    - The private investigator is aware that the crime that was committed must be classified as a *felony,* if not committed in his or her presence and is about to make an arrest, the private investigator must be positively sure a felony has been committed and that the person about to be arrested is in fact the perpetrator of that felony. In addition, a private person may make a felony arrest anywhere in the state in which the crime occurred.
- To prevent the consequence or continuation of a crime.
    - The private investigator *must witness the crime* committed.
    - The perpetrator is *in view at all times.*

To reiterate, in making an arrest, the private investigator must have the *offense within view,* and the offense is one of the following:

Felony—A crime that results in imprisonment of a person for *more than 1 year* in a state or federal penal institution. Examples include: murder, robbery, burglary, rape, grand larceny, and felonious assault.

Misdemeanor—A crime that results in imprisonment *not to exceed 1 year confinement* in a local or county jail. Examples include: petit larceny, harassment, loitering, disorderly conduct, public lewdness, and other minor offenses against the public order.

Check the laws of arrest in your state of employment as to certain restrictions for misdemeanor and felony arrests, during the day or night.

In addition, any person may arrest another person for a *felony* when the latter has in fact committed such a felony, and for any offense when the latter has in fact committed the offense in his or her presence. Such an arrest, if for a felony, may be made anywhere in the state. If the arrest is for an offense other than a felony, the arrest may be made only in the county in which such an offense was committed.

Moreover, if the crime is committed in his or her presence, the perpetrator may be arrested at any hour of the day or night (subject to the misdemeanor provision that this type of arrest must be sanctioned only in the county in which the act was committed).

Anyone making an arrest must inform the person whom he or she is arresting of the reason for such arrest unless he or she encounters physical resistance, flight, or other factors rendering such procedure impractical. In order to effect such an arrest, a person may use the necessary physical force that is justifiable.

Unless a particular state authorizes a private citizen to serve a warrant of arrest, the PI will not be empowered to execute any warrant. Only law enforcement officers have that authority. Check with local and state laws to resolve any questions regarding warrants or arrests made by a private citizen.

As required by state law, ordinarily the person making the arrest of another must without *unnecessary delay* deliver or attempt to deliver the person arrested to the custody of an appropriate police officer. Unnecessary delay may be equated to reasonable time and may be defined as the time required for the investigation of the incident, the interview of witnesses by the private investigator, and the processing of the defendant. The police officer upon receiving custody of the arrested person must then process that person as required by law.

The Use of Force in Effecting an Arrest

Justification of Physical Force by a Private Citizen

Once a private investigator or security officer has been granted the authority by his or her employer to effect arrests during the course of his or her duties, or to prevent an offense against persons or property he or she is employed to protect, the time will come when *justifiable force* may have to be used to consummate an arrest. Whatever physical force is used, private investigators must be prepared to justify their actions to the police if or when they become involved, or if and when a plaintiff seeks damages in court.

Therefore, under certain conditions, reasonable physical force may be used by a private person to consummate the arrest for any crime that takes place in his or her presence:

In Self-Defense—A person may use only that force which *reasonably* appears to be necessary to prevent the harm. That person may not use force likely to cause death or serious physical injury unless he or she *reasonably believes* that him- or herself is in danger of serious physical injury or death. If more force than necessary is used, the privilege of self-defense may be lost.

In the Defense of Another—When a person commits a forceful act in the defense of another person or persons (protecting person or persons from deadly force or serious physical injury), he or she must believe that such aid is necessary and that the victim has a right to defend him- or herself. This is a *privilege* authorized when the private investigator, security officer, or any citizen *reasonably believes such force is necessary* to prevent the threatened harm to another.

Cautionary Procedure

The private investigator must remember that he or she has the same powers of arrest that an ordinary citizen has, including the *necessary and reasonable physical force* that may be used to consummate that arrest, and *no more*.

Under *no* circumstances should the use of deadly physical force be used in effecting an apprehension or arrest of a suspect unless the private investigator or security officer can show at a later time that his or her life or the life of someone else was in *extreme danger of death or serious physical harm.*

A private investigator should not solicit assistance from anyone, whether passerby, spectator, or witness, other than a police officer or fellow investigator or security officer in the apprehension or pursuit of a suspect. The investigator, the agency, and the client become liable if the person assisting is injured or if that person acts wrongly against the suspect, and criminal or civil action is initiated because of that person's behavior.

The Use of Physical Force Defined

Remember that whatever type of physical force is used by the private investigator, he or she may have to justify his or her actions to the police, district attorney, or civil court.

Generally, the interpretations that follow may be considered those found in most, if not all, states in the union. The use of *physical force* upon another person, which would otherwise constitute an offense, is justifiable and not criminal under any of the following circumstances:

1. A person may use *physical force* upon another person in defense of themselves or a third person, or in defense of premises, or in order to prevent larceny of or criminal mischief to property, or in order to effect an arrest or prevent an escape from custody.
2. The use of *physical force* upon another person in believing it necessary to defend him- or herself or another person is applicable, *unless* the private investigator provokes or is the initial aggressor, *but* if he or she then withdraws and communicates such withdrawal, and if the other subject persists to continue and engage in the use or threatened imminent use of unlawful physical force, the private investigator or security officer is justifiable in the use of *physical force.*
3. A private investigator (private person) acting on his or her own account may use physical force, *other than deadly force,* upon any other person when and to the extent that he or she reasonably believes such to be necessary to effect an arrest or

to prevent the escape from custody of a person whom he or she reasonably believes to have committed an offense and who in fact has committed such offense.

A private person may use *deadly physical force* for such purpose when he or she reasonably believes such to be necessary to defend him- or herself or a third person from what he or she reasonably believes to be the use or imminent use of deadly physical force (deadly or serious physical injury).

A private person may use *deadly physical force* for such purpose when he or she reasonably believes such to be necessary to effect the arrest of a person *who has committed* murder, manslaughter in the first degree, robbery, forcible rape or forcible sodomy, *and who is in immediate flight therefrom.*

(Again, check your state's criminal code. The private investigator must be sure of his or her actions.)

4. At present, the majority of states hold that *deadly physical force may be used* when it is *reasonably necessary to deter the threat of death or serious physical injury.* A few states differ in that they hold that *deadly force may only be used when absolutely necessary to preserve one's own life.*

   But the private investigator may not use such force if he or she knows he or she can with complete safety to him- or herself or to another avoid the necessity to use deadly physical force by retreating. A private investigator, as a private person, cannot use deadly physical force if he or she has the ability to retreat or back off safely other than to immediately save his or her or someone else's life and the five serious felonies noted above. (Some states note that a person does not have to "retreat" if in his or her own dwelling.) A police officer does not have that privilege of withdrawal—he or she must stand fast and act.

   Also, in the case of deadly physical force, the private investigator may use it if he or she reasonably believes that such person is using or is about to use deadly physical force, or if the investigator reasonably believes that such person *is committing or attempting to commit* kidnapping, forcible rape, forcible sodomy, robbery, or arson (persons in extreme danger of serious physical harm or death).

5. The private investigator may use *physical force* upon another when he or she reasonably believes such is necessary to prevent or terminate the commission or attempted commission of damage to a premise. The investigator may use *deadly physical force* if he or she reasonably believes such to be necessary to prevent the commission or attempted commission of *arson.*

6. Further, a person in control of any premises, or licensed and privileged to be thereon or therein, may use *physical force, other than deadly physical force,* upon another if he or she reasonably believes such to be necessary to prevent or terminate a criminal trespass upon such premises.

7. A person may use *physical force, other than deadly physical force,* upon another to prevent or terminate the commission or attempted commission of larceny or criminal mischief with respect to property other than premises.

Regarding the private investigator's or security officer's ability while armed to use deadly physical force on a person in immediate flight from certain crimes previously described, he or she would be well advised to use caution and restraint in the pursuit of such behavior.

The probability of harm and liability concerning damage or injury to others is great, particularly during the heat of the chase when emotions and physical actions are intensified.

The following provides a summary of the use of physical force.

Physical Force

Physical force under the circumstances in which it is used, is readily capable of causing death or serious physical injury. Physical injury may be defined as protracted disfigurement, protracted impairment of health, or protracted loss or impairment of the functions of any bodily organ. It must be justifiable, *and* the private investigator must believe that the use of physical force is necessary to effect an arrest or to prevent escape from custody if the investigator reasonably believes such person committed an offense or such person did in fact commit such offense.

Deadly Physical Force

Deadly physical force is the necessary and justified force used to effect an arrest or control of a person not leading up to the more serious deadly physical force. The private investigator reasonably believes it necessary to:

- Defend him- or herself or a third person from what he or she believes to be the use or imminent use of deadly physical force or serious physical injury
- Effect the arrest of a person who has committed or attempted to commit murder, kidnapping, robbery, forcible rape or forcible sodomy, and the commission or attempted commission of arson.

Generally, the above narration on arrests and the use of force is applicable in most if not all states. However, there may be some distinction in content or application.

In order to have a more thorough understanding and overview of *arrests by a private person* and *the use of force,* the private investigator or security officer is urged to examine the criminal codes that cover arrest and justification of the use of force in the state in which he or she is employed. By such inquiry, a determination can be made as to the exact legal conduct he or she will be required to follow regarding arrest procedures, the use of force and unlawful imprisonment.

Aiding a Police Officer

In addition to the justification described above, there may be a section in the criminal code of your state that gives a police officer the authority to direct a private citizen to use the necessary force in assisting the officer in an arrest, in preventing the commission of an offense, or in an escape situation.

If during an incident a police officer requests the assistance of a private citizen, and that person refuses, or in any way does not assist that police officer, that person commits an offense that may be considered a crime.

Moreover, concerning police officers, the private investigator should be mindful that any action that may be considered as interfering with a police officer or a public servant in the performance of that person's duty *(obstructing governmental administration)* may constitute a crime in your state.

Police Officers as Private Investigators

Police officers may be restricted from certain private employment by the municipality that employs them. However, police officers if employed as private investigators theoretically are considered police officers 24 hours a day, and the courts can accept that theory as practice regarding the powers and restrictions allocated to a police officer's performance concerning arrests and other procedures.

Resisting Arrest

In most criminal codes, a person may not use physical force to resist an arrest, whether the arrest is authorized or unauthorized, which is being effected or attempted by a police officer when it would reasonably appear that the latter is a police officer.

Note that a defendant may be charged with resisting arrest only when such act—the resistance—is committed on a police officer. The private investigator (private person) does not have that endowment or authority. If the subject resists the arrest in any way, and other than a charge of assault against the subject, if applicable, his or her only recourse is justification in the use of necessary force as noted previously in this narrative.

Cautionary Note

A police officer is not required to take an arrested person into custody or to take any other action as described in this section on behalf of the arresting person (the private investigator or security officer) if he or she (the police officer) has reasonable cause to believe that the arrested person did not commit the alleged offense or that the arrest was unlawful or otherwise unauthorized. If such is the case, the police officer must release the subject. To do otherwise places the police officer in jeopardy of conducting a false arrest, of malicious prosecution, and so forth. Consequently, once released, we can anticipate that the person who had been placed into custody without reasonable cause will seek the advice of an attorney.

If the arrest is unlawful (without probable cause), then the private investigator or security officer, his or her supervisor, their employer, and possibly the client (via vicarious liability) are liable for damages to the person unlawfully arrested. Moreover, depending on the physical actions of the individual making the arrest, possible criminal liability may be considered.

Liability Concerns

Assault and Battery

Private investigators and security officers must be cognizant of the fact that in any type of a "stop" where the investigator lays his or her hands on the person of another, or comes in physical contact with another in any way, unless such occurrence happens during a lawful action, a plaintiff can lay claim to an assault and battery upon his person as part of his civil action. Because of the importance regarding confrontations and contacts with a subject suspected of a crime or not, it must be considered most important for the investigator to have some knowledge of what constitutes an "assault."

Definition of Assault

Assault is the threat or attempt to strike another, whether successful or not, provided the target is aware of the danger. The perpetrator must be reasonably capable of carrying through with the attack. Also, in some states, if the assault is with a weapon such as a sniping rifle, the intended victim need not be aware of the peril.[1]

Assault is any intentional, unlawful offer of corporal injury to another by force, or force unlawfully directed to the person of another, under such circumstances as to create a well-founded fear of imminent peril, coupled with the apparent present ability to effectuate the attempt if not prevented. As an example, assault can be further defined as an attempt or an offer to beat upon another without touching him, as if one would lift up his fist or point a loaded gun in a threatening manner at another. No actual touching is necessary if there is a threat of assault and the victim is aware of such a threat.

Definition of Battery

Battery is the actual intentional striking of someone with intent to do harm, no matter how slight. Negligent or careless unintentional contact is not battery no matter how great the harm,[2] but as it is not unlawful in this case, it may be challenged as a civil matter.

The least touching of another's person if done willfully in a violent or insolent manner or in anger constitutes battery, as does the unlawful beating or touching of the person without his consent by another.

There may be an assault without a battery. An assault may be committed without physical contact. Battery can only be committed by actually touching or striking the person of another.

Therefore, assault and battery can be defined as the unlawful touching of the person of another by the aggressor or by some substance put in motion by the aggressor (bullet, knife, baseball bat, etc.). If an unlawful attempt to do corporeal hurt to another is combined with an actual use of force, there is an assault and battery. The terminology "assault and battery" is not commonly used in criminal complaints today; it is usually referred to in civil actions.

There are several classifications or degrees in the crime of assault depending on the act—an actual hitting, if a weapon is used during the commission of the assault, the type and severity of the injury or injuries sustained, or just a threat.[3] Assault is both a criminal wrong, for which one may be charged and tried, and a civil wrong, for which the target may sue for damages due to the assault.

For further information on the various degrees or types of assault for which to charge a defendant in a criminal action, refer to your state's criminal laws.

The Elements of Assault and Battery

Overt Act—In an effort for the plaintiff to claim an assault, there must be an overt act, or an attempt, or the appearance of an attempt with force and violence to do physical harm or injury to the person of the plaintiff. Words not accompanied by a circumstance that would induce a reasonable apprehension of bodily harm are not sufficient. In the case of a battery, an unlawful touching of the person of another is sufficient.

Intent—A cause of action for assault requires that a person intends to inflict personal injury on the person assaulted, or to put him in apprehension of that intent to harm. In an action for battery, the person must have intended to make contact, and it is not required that the person who made the contact intended to do the injury. Malice is not a necessary element for assault and battery.

Lack of Consent

A plaintiff cannot recover damages for an assault or battery where he consented to the assault or the battery. However, the consent cannot be obtained by fraud or deceit, and the assailant cannot exceed the scope of the consent.

False Arrest and False Imprisonment

Defined

False arrest is merely another name for the tort of *false imprisonment*. It can be further described as the unlawful detention contrary to the will of the person detained *with or without the process of law*.[4] The private investigator must be aware that if he or she takes a person into custody, that person is arrested—freedom of movement has been taken away. If any arrest is proved unlawful, even if the PI believes that the arrest was lawful at the time, the person detained will surely seek legal counsel and thereby become the plaintiff in a lawsuit against the PI.

So then, regarding civil liability, any physical detention is an imprisonment,[5] and the detention can occur in a store, restaurant, hotel room, ballpark, bus, hospital, or any enclosure. As a matter of fact, throwing a subject up against a fence and holding him there can be construed as a false imprisonment if there is no probable cause to make an arrest.

The use of force is not a necessary element of false imprisonment, although it may aggravate the damages sought. Any act that restrains the subject, the person arrested, is sufficient.[6] Restraint of a person's freedom of locomotion does not have to be induced by force, but threat by conduct or words may be sufficient.[7]

In a *civil* case of false arrest, the *defendant* (person who made the arrest) has the burden of proving legal justification as an affirmative defense. The *plaintiff* need not prove the *defendant's* lack of probable cause, but existence of probable cause is a defense that will defeat the action.

The taking away of a person's freedom of movement is one of the significant elements considered when the *Bill of Rights* was drafted. There is enough case law that covers false arrest and false imprisonment for any private investigator to be aware of in any action he or she may take against another person. Caution must be a concerning factor when any thought of an arrest is to take place. Remember that one does not have to touch a person in order to consummate an arrest, though you may do so if necessary to control the subject. But placing one's hand on the shoulder of another can be considered an assault or at least a battery in a civil court.

Cautionary Procedure

One other thought should be taken into account. If a private investigator believes that the arrest he or she made was unlawful or in any way a wrongful arrest and wishes to release the subject, such release cannot be conditional upon the execution of any written statement, incriminating or otherwise. Moreover, once it is determined that the elements of the arrest are not present, it would be more advantageous to "unarrest" the subject and release him, rather than become involved in a serious action of false arrest and a subsequent malicious prosecution. Although "unarrest" is not a legal term and is not delineated in law, it is not uncommon for such an action to take place. If the released person decides to entertain a civil action and the court acts upon such litigation, the gravity of the case will be lessened and damages will not be as severe as they would be if the investigator continued to proceed. The reasoning here is not to aggravate or escalate the incident, but rather to stop it from becoming much more serious.

Malicious Prosecution

Misuse of the Legal Process

Malicious prosecution is a prosecution that is *begun with malice* and *without probable cause* to believe that the charge(s) and such action can be sustained, and which finally ends in failure.

The basics of malicious prosecution are as follows:

1. The defendant (originally the complainant—the person who made the arrest) commenced or continued a proceeding against the plaintiff, *knowing that there was little or no probable cause* to make an arrest *or* continue on to the prosecution.
2. There was an absence of probable cause for the proceeding, and the proceeding terminated in favor of the plaintiff.
3. The defendant was motivated by actual malice.

In these cases, the plaintiff can seek relief in civil court. (See a clarification of *Malicious Prosecution* in the "Glossary" at the end of the book.)

The Elements of Malicious Prosecution Defined

1. *The Commencement or Continuation of a Proceeding*

To satisfy this element, the proceeding must have commenced or was continued by the defendant against the plaintiff and must be judicial in nature.

Commencement of an action can include the serving of a summons, by mail or otherwise. A cause of action for malicious prosecution by the plaintiff does not arise out of a prior civil proceeding *unless* in that prior proceeding there was some interference with the person or property of the plaintiff, such as an arrest, attachment, injunction, receivership, or notice of pendency.

If the other necessary elements noted below are present, a prior criminal or extradition proceeding against the plaintiff will give rise to a cause of action *from* malicious prosecution.

2. *The Proceeding Terminated in Favor of the Plaintiff*

This element will be satisfied by any termination in favor of the plaintiff on the merits as the result of a judicial decision, regardless of the basis of that decision. A favorable termination can also be shown when there is an acquittal. Additionally, there are two other instances where a favorable termination can be found: first, any absent evidence of a fraud or compromise, the favorable termination of a prior criminal proceeding may be shown by the fact that the complaint was withdrawn, or that the complaint was dismissed for lack of either prosecution or evidence, or on a motion by the accused. Second, the voluntary discontinuance of a prior civil action by the plaintiff *not* as a result of a compromise, inducement, trick, or device of the defendant is a sufficient favorable termination to support an action for malicious prosecution against the defendant.

Conversely, a favorable termination is not shown where the ending of the prior action appears inconclusive or was effected by a settlement or some fraud, or where the plaintiff's case was dismissed because of the prosecutor's failure to procure a speedy prosecution or sentencing. Further, there is no favorable termination where there was an "adjournment in contemplation of dismissal," which is neither a conviction nor an acquittal, and therefore leaves open the question of guilt—or where the plaintiff's sentence was suspended, which is in fact a conviction. Also not a favorable termination is the prior action that the plaintiff complaints must be terminated *totally and not partially* in his favor, in that it is not enough that one cause of action against him was dismissed but that a second still awaits adjudication.

3. *There Was an Absence of Probable Cause for the Proceeding*

Generally, a defendant who had *probable cause* to subject the plaintiff to a reasonable detention has a complete defense to a cause of action for false arrest and imprisonment (see definition of *Probable Cause* noted earlier). Therefore, if probable cause exists for the initial action by the defendant, it will serve to bar any action by the plaintiff for malicious prosecution. However, the plaintiff can initiate an action for malicious prosecution *even though he has not been falsely arrested, imprisoned, or detained,* if the defendant between the time of arrest and detention and the time of prosecution knows some intervening fact *exonerating the plaintiff.*

4. *Defendant's Good Faith Belief*

The defendant's belief in the guilt of the person whom he charges with a crime is not enough to exonerate him in an action for malicious prosecution; *there must also be probable cause for the belief.*

5. *Reliance on Information from Others*

The defendant may show as justification of probable cause that he *had reasonable reliance on information received from others.* This rule has been applied where the defendant relied on a report of a private investigator and the word of an employee who had been in the defendant's employ for many years and had proved honest and reliable. Generally, to rely on this information only would not be enough without some type of corroboration.

6. *Mistaken Identification*

One can make a mistake as to the identity of another if the party acted reasonably under the circumstances in *good faith.* For example, the liability of a person who mistakenly identifies another as a criminal depends on the good faith and reasonableness of his identification, or the good faith of his reliance on a clearly sound identification by another person.

7. *Extent of Investigation by the Defendant*

The defendant has probable cause to file criminal charges against the accused *only* if he believes, and a reasonably prudent person in the same position would believe, that he has sufficient information to do so without further investigation.

8. *Plaintiff's Possession of Stolen Property*

Absent of some reasonable explanation by the accused, possession by the accused of recently stolen property belonging to the defendant is probable cause for his prosecution of an *appropriate charge* connected with the larceny thereof, and will avoid liability on the part of the prosecutor for malicious prosecution. (See *Criminal Possession of Stolen Property* for details on this crime in the "Glossary.")

9. *The Defendant Was Motivated by Actual Malice*

Malice is defined as conscious falsity, a wrongful act done intentionally without just cause or excuse. The plaintiff must prove the defendant commenced the criminal proceedings with *actual and not implied malice.*

Further, in the law of malicious prosecution, it means that "the prosecution was instituted primarily because of a purpose other than that of bringing an offender to justice" (*Black's Law Dictionary*).

Malice may also be defined as a condition of the mind that prompts a person to do a wrongful act willfully—that is, on purpose to the injury of another, or to do intentionally a wrongful act toward another without justification or excuse. Malice in law is not necessarily personal hate or ill will, but it is also that state of mind, which is reckless of law and of the legal rights of the citizen.

Malice may be inferred in several ways. It will be sufficient to show malice where the defendant commenced the prior proceeding because of a wrong or improper motive, or some intent other than to see that justice was served. Malice can be inferred from a lack of probable cause, the defendant's unnecessary zeal, eagerness, and activity, or from the total circumstances of the incident regarding the relationship of the parties and the objects of concern.

Malice may also be inferred by conduct inconsistent with proper motives. It may be presumed from gross or culpable negligence, such as the failure to make reasonable inquiries before beginning any proceeding, or from wanton and reckless disregard of rights of others, but not from ordinary negligence.

10. *Damage Was Suffered by the Plaintiff*

We must be cognizant of the fact that too often the actions by a PI or a security officer in any apprehension or confrontation will be subject to intensive review by the defendant and his attorney soon after the occurrence. This examination by the attorney is to determine if in fact the arrest and imprisonment were justified and legal. Basically the attorney will wish to determine that there was insufficient or no probable cause for the actions by the PI or the security officer against his client, or if any excessive force or abuses took place. In this way, the attorney is able to lay a defense in court for dismissal, and once dismissed, to initiate civil action against all parties concerned. If a civil action is considered, the defendant (*criminal*) now becomes the plaintiff (*civil*).

11. *Damages Recoverable by the Plaintiff*

The plaintiff can ask that *compensatory damages* (injury or harm to self or damage to property only) and *punitive damages* (awarded as punishment to the wrongdoer for the wrong he did) be found against the company or the employees. (See Chapter 2 for the definitions of compensatory and punitive damages.)

Damages for Malicious Prosecution

An action for damages concerning malicious prosecution may be brought by a person who has been *acquitted of a criminal action or for whom the termination of a civil suit was in his favor.* One who takes an unlawful active part in the initiation, continuation, or procurement of *civil or criminal* proceedings against another may be liable to that person.

Malicious prosecution actions usually involve "damage or injury" inflicted on the plaintiff's reputation, character, feelings, employment, business opportunities or employment, credit, health, and well-being. In addition, damages may be awarded for imprisonment, the cost of counsel to defend the prior action, mental suffering, and humiliation. A spouse has a cause of action for loss of consortium based upon the false imprisonment of the other spouse. Any other damages or injuries are restricted to the person who suffered the hurt, and not the spouse.

Note that although probable cause was present at the time of the arrest, some fact or facts could come to light at a later time that would eliminate that probable cause, and if probable cause no longer was present by the time of arraignment or indictment, and the complainant (the private investigator or security officer) continued the action, malicious prosecution may then be a fact. Where malicious prosecution was not established, and where a false arrest action was found for the plaintiff, such action would be limited to recovery as damages to legal fees incurred up to and including the arraignment.

Damages for Assault and Battery and False Imprisonment Regarding Malicious Prosecution

If established by the plaintiff, he may recover for the embarrassment, humiliation, pain, disability, discomfort, and inconvenience caused by the assault and battery. The plaintiff may also recover for emotional distress or mental anguish irrespective of whether or not a physical injury was sustained. Additionally, he may recover for loss of earnings and hospital and medical expenses that occurred as a necessary and direct result of the assault or battery. However, the plaintiff's family, whether present or not during the offense, may not recover for their own mental anguish and humiliation.

False imprisonment necessarily involves the element of an assault in a technical sense, but a battery is not an essential element of false imprisonment.

Under New York State law, civil damages against the person who made the false arrest or illegal confinement will be measured only *to the time of arraignment or indictment,* whichever comes first. If the *prosecution* of the criminal defendant *continues after arraignment* (without the prosecutor requesting a dismissal) *and up to the conclusion of that court action,* the tort of *malicious prosecution* can be sought against not only the person who made the arrest but also the prosecutor. If found that probable cause was not present for the arrest and the defendant is acquitted of the charge, the defendant, now a plaintiff, may sue for *false imprisonment* and *malicious prosecution.*

Check with your own state law regarding damages and the stipulations essential in this regard.

Malicious Prosecution and Vicarious Liability

Relevant to this offense, the security officer must be cognizant of *vicarious liability.* In tort law, vicarious liability refers to the liability assessed against one party due to the actions of another party. Simply put, the plaintiff may sue for damages against the investigator or security officer for his or her actions, and may include that person's supervisor, manager, trainer, the retailer or business owner, and whoever else can be made a party to the suit. The plaintiff's attorney will attempt to bring as many defendants into the lawsuit as possible in an attempt to increase the monetary award.

Unlawful Actions Concerning Personal Rights and Privacy

The Rules of Evidence

There are many different types of evidence that can be used in court against a criminal or civil defendant. Private investigators most probably will not become directly involved with the various types of evidence described herein, but knowledge of what is and what may not be considered evidence should be an important part of their training. Therefore, the private investigator should be aware of what constitutes evidence and what can be admitted in a court of law.

So then, in addition to that described below, evidence is found and collected in many forms and is to be considered a major element in the prosecution of any case, criminal or civil. Therefore, consider the gathering of evidence in statements and confessions (see Chapter 5, "Statements and Confessions") and search and seizure (see this chapter, "Search and Seizure"), among other areas, to be an important part of the investigative procedures of the private investigator.

Definition of Evidence

Evidence is a system of rules and standards by which the admission of proof at a trial or hearing is regulated. In a broad sense, it is the means or method by which any disputed or necessary matter of fact is proved or disproved.

Evidence may come in different forms; it can be *direct*—testimony by a witness who actually saw, heard, or touched the matter at issue—or *circumstantial*—facts or items that lead the mind to certain conclusions.

Physical evidence can be defined as *something tangible or material* of some nature, such as a written confession by the defendant, a bullet, weapon, blood, or an article of clothing. It can be further described as any element that helps prove that an offense was in fact committed, and that connects the perpetrator to that offense.

(For a complete list of the types of *evidence* and the significance of each, see the "Glossary.")

Evidence to be admissible in court must be *material* and *relevant:*

Materiality—If the fact that the evidence tends to prove is part of an issue of the case, the evidence is material. It must affect an issue of the case significantly. Evidence that proves something or tends to prove something that is not part of an issue of the case is immaterial. For example, Subject A is being charged with grand larceny, the theft of a pocketbook from a woman while she walked down the street. The defense attorney for Subject A puts forth the argument that the time of occurrence was 2 A.M., and the woman should not have been in that neighborhood at that time of night and therefore placed herself in jeopardy. This fact was unimportant to the case at hand and was therefore immaterial.

Relevancy—Evidence that tends to prove the truth of a fact at issue is relevant. For example, Subject A shoots Subject B intentionally with a loaded rifle from a distance of 1,000 feet. Evidence shows that Subject A is a hunter, is highly proficient with rifles, and is an instructor in target shooting and handling firearms. Such information can be admitted as being relevant.

Witnesses and Evidence Issues

Witness Competency

A competent witness is a person who is eligible to testify. Competency, which is both mental and moral, over the age of 13 is presumed. Mental competency relates to the ability to see, recall, and relate. Moral competency refers to the understanding of the truth and the consequences of false testimony. The court can accept the competency of a child if after examination the child has been found to have the mental aptitude that is acceptable and understands right from wrong. The credibility of a witness may be affected by his or her character and integrity or past transgressions.

Expert Witness

An expert witness is one skilled in some art, science, or trade to the extent that he possesses information not within the common knowledge. The testimony of an expert can be admitted on matters of a technical nature relevant to the case that may or will require interpretation that the judge and jury can understand. This can include physicians, ballistic and fingerprint technicians, and blood and DNA specialists. Once examined and satisfied by the court and accepted as an expert, he or she may testify to the issue in question.

Spontaneous Exclamations

Generally, it is accepted that if a person speaks or makes an utterance before he has time to reflect or fabricate a lie, he will speak the truth. It may defined as an utterance spoken at the time of a startling event or occurrence when during the excitement, shock, or surprise, such exclamations can be inferred as spontaneous and without deliberation, and can be introduced as evidence by anyone who heard such declaration. Note that the utterance in most cases, must *not* have been in response to a question.

The Exclusionary Rule

Evidence is *excluded* if it is not allowed by the court to be entered as evidence. This rule commands that where evidence has been obtained in violation of the privileges guaranteed by the U.S. Constitution, the evidence must be excluded at the trial.

Evidence obtained by an unreasonable search and seizure is excluded from evidence at trial under the Fourth Amendment of the U.S. Constitution, and this rule is applicable to all states.[8]

The "Plain-View Doctrine"

Consider also, that if a private investigator or security officer has the right to be in a certain place or area, and he or she happens to observe evidence or contraband in plain view, those items can be seized and will be admissible in court *(the plain-view doctrine)*. In other instances, as a private investigator or security officer, you are not an agent of the government, and thereby you have the right to search with *due notice*. For example, if a retailer or any business premises posts signs noting "All packages are subject to search" as company policy, entry into the business locale or site can be denied to a person who refuses to give access to a search of the package. Also, if certain company rules are noted to all newly hired employees as part of their hiring procedures that all packages, bags, and so forth are subject to inspection upon leaving the business premises or leaving at the end of the workday, the search is legal and they must submit or suffer termination.

"Fruit of the Poisoned Tree" Concept

In criminal law, this is the doctrine that states that evidence discovered due to information found through illegal search or other unconstitutional means (such as a forced confession) may not be introduced as evidence in court. The theory is that the "tree" (the original illegal evidence) is poisoned and thus taints that which "grows" or is gained from it. As an example, a confession, forced or not, was given by a defendant who was arrested for a larceny without being advised of his right to remain silent, and so forth (Miranda warnings). He subsequently told the police the location of the stolen property. Because the admission, oral or written, cannot be used against the defendant, the recovered stolen property cannot be introduced in court as evidence.[9]

Remember that the PI and security officer must have reasonable grounds or probable cause to act, and the action must be "fresh" in that it must relate to an event that is occurring at that time or occurred a short time prior, which is usually measured in minutes rather than hours.

Therefore, in any case with a private investigator or security officer, if and when the rights of a suspect are violated in any way, such as an improper arrest or false imprisonment, then any evidence arising from that arrest is inadmissible. Incriminating oral or written statements made by the suspect, recovery of stolen property, and any other evidence gathered as a result of that arrest will be inadmissible in court, and the case would be dismissed (*"fruit of the poisoned tree" concept*). The business owner, client, and the officers involved can be sure that civil litigation against them will follow.

Motion to Suppress Evidence

In a court of law, an attorney may attempt to suppress evidence on a motion based on the following:

1. Unlawful search
2. Illegal eavesdropping; evidence received without eavesdropping warrants
3. Offenses against the Right to Privacy
4. Unlawful confession
5. Poisoned tree concept
6. Illegal identification

Hearsay Evidence

During any investigation, investigators will come across a lot of "hearsay." This is information that the subject offers as secondhand knowledge or knowledge that was overheard by him or another person. It is not firsthand intelligence that a person heard which can be introduced as evidence. The courts will not accept a statement by a person who is a witness called at trial as evidence—utterances, remarks, or facts—stated by someone else. The reason for this is that attorneys on either side will not have the opportunity to challenge or question the actual person who spoke the original words.

Although "hearsay" cannot be introduced as evidence in a trial,[10] investigators can use information gathered in this manner to broaden their avenues of inquiry. However, depending on certain circumstances that may be described as a "dying declaration," such utterances may be introduced in court.

See Chapter 5, "The 'Hearsay' Rule" for additional information.

Judicial Notice

For certain facts that the court need not have proven by a formal presentation, the court is authorized to recognize and accept their existence without such proof. Whenever judicial notice is taken, there is no need to establish the merit of the evidence; there will be no dispute concerning it:

Of Fact (Discretionary)—Where a judge may accept the opinion or abstract offered by an attorney, for example, law of the land, law of the state, and law of other states.

Of Law (Mandatory)—Where a judge must accept as a fact evidence offered as commonly accepted knowledge, for example, standards of weights and measures, the seasons, and forensic evidence (once expert testimony is offered with the evidence), such as fingerprints, blood evidence, and DNA findings.

Privileged Communications

Privileged communication is not admissible unless the person holding the privilege consents to give it up. Communication between the following is considered *privileged*:

- Husband and wife
- Clergyman and confessor
- Psychologist and patient/client
- Attorney and client
- Doctor and patient
- Psychotherapist and patient/client

As a general rule, privileged information is determined by the nature of the information and the circumstances under which it was given. All conversation is not privileged.

Handling Evidence

The process of handling and identifying evidence may determine its use in a court of law or the conviction of a defendant. Generally, evidence should be handled by trained technicians, who are usually designated as crime scene or forensic investigators. Once an offense is reported to the police, they will control the gathering and processing of evidence.

However, there will be times when the private investigator will obtain some item other than a written statement or confession which could be designated as evidence. If a VCR tape taken from a closed-circuit television (CCTV) camera can be used to identify a crime or the perpetrator, it should be safeguarded by removing the plastic tab so erasure cannot be made at a later time. This would include safeguarding a compact disk (CD). Further, the cassette or CD, should be initialed and dated by the operator who made the tape or disk, and initialed by the investigator who received it. If the tape or disk is not turned over to the police as evidence, it should be secured in a safe place for future reference. Although not as critical as evidence controlled by police procedures, it is a good idea for the PI to identify a "chain of custody" to a tape or disk so the question of tampering can be fought. Photographs of evidence at a scene before being moved or handled, or photos of the scene itself are also important as evidence.

In any event, all evidence collected (including that noted above), weapons, tools, photos, and any object considered as evidence pertinent to the crime, should be inscribed at least with the investigators' initials, case number assigned, and date of collection, and so noted in detail in the case report. A very important detail includes when, where, and how the evidence or item was found and by whom. Items not easily marked should be placed in evidence envelopes, sealed, and imprinted with the necessary information. Other than indelible ink, a metal scribe may be used on metal or other hard objects.

Burden of Proof

Because under our law, no person is required to prove his or her innocence, the burden of proof for a conviction in court rests solely on the prosecution. In a criminal case, the prosecution has the burden of proving the accused guilty *beyond a reasonable doubt.*

This is in opposition to the defendant in a civil case, where the plaintiff need only *a preponderance of evidence* to prove his case.

Defenses

- *Ordinary Defense*—The burden is on the State.
- *Insanity*—The defendant was insane at the time of the crime.
- *Infancy*—The defendant was not old enough to understand the nature of the act or crime.

- *Justification*—The defendant was justified in his actions (i.e., self-defense).
- *Affirmative Defense*—The burden is on the defense.
- *Entrapment*—The defendant was entrapped into committing the act or crimes.
- *Renunciation*—The defendant renounced his or her intent before the commission of the crime.
- *Duress*—The defendant acted under duress because of some threat or act.

Search and Seizure

Search of the Person

Generally, concerning search and seizure, when it entails a personal search of a person, private security personnel are not regulated by the restrictions found in the Fourth Amendment as a law enforcement officer would be. The U.S. Supreme Court held in 1921[11] that search and seizures applied only to law enforcement and not to private persons. Subsequent decisions handed down in several state courts reaffirmed that position. For example, a security officer acting without any probable cause searches a young person's backpack and discovers a controlled substance illegally possessed. That officer could detain the youngster and turn him over to the police as a valid arrest, because a private person conducted the search. So it would seem that a private investigator acting in this manner would not be in violation in searching a person or his property.

Although it would appear that such an act is legal by a private person, a private investigator or a security officer should realize that caution must be used concerning the facts and circumstances surrounding a particular situation. A private person acting outside of the *scope of his or her employment*, attempting a search without any reason, or committing some outrageous conduct such as subjecting a person to a strip search, would be considered unreasonable force in the minds of many.

Moreover, the employment of a private investigator or a security officer by a governmental agency raises certain questions. To illustrate this, consider a private investigator or a security officer employed by a public school district. Such employment, depending on the municipality's control over the school district and its personnel, may place that officer under the *Color of State Law*. That private investigator or security officer may also be required to act according to the restrictions placed upon law enforcement officers when custody of a subject requires a search and seizure under Fourth Amendment guidelines. Extending this further, the service of a private investigator contracted to a public corporation or a municipality can place him or her under the purview of all civil and privacy rights.

However, after a legal arrest under probable cause, a search can be made *on the person* and anything *within his reach or distance* (the ability to reach overtly and grab something).

Therefore, the private investigator or security officer may conduct a search of the person for the following:

1. Weapons (for the protection of the private investigator, security officer, and others).
2. Access to items that could aid an escape.
3. Property taken by the perpetrator during the commission of the crime and so observed as being secreted.
4. Evidence used in the commission of the crime (e.g., an antisecurity device).
5. Evidence that could be destroyed.

In addition, if the defendant possesses any contraband legally seized from him and found to be illegally possessed (weapons, controlled substances), additional charges may be laid against him.

Consider the following case law:

- Searches must be *limited* to the arrestee's "person and the area from within which he might have obtained either a weapon" or "something that could have been used as evidence against him"[12] (". . . a search or seizure without a warrant as incidental to a lawful arrest has always been considered to be a strictly a *limited right*"[13]).
- *Unreasonable* search and seizures are protected by the Fourth Amendment, and in *Wolf v. Colorado,*[14] the Supreme Court held that evidence obtained in violation of the Fourth Amendment is inadmissible in a criminal prosecution.

The Search after the Arrest

Once the private investigator or a security officer has probable cause to make an arrest, a search of that person can be made under certain restrictions.

> A person who is subjected to an illegal search is protected by the Fourth Amendment.[15]

In general, you must meet the test of reasonableness by the following:

1. Probable cause.
2. Prevent a *general* search and undue harshness. (A search can be made on the person and anything within his or her reach or distance—his or her ability to reach overtly and grab something.)

To reiterate, the courts have held that if an arrest is *lawful*, a search by a police officer or a private citizen is *valid*, and that justification existed for a search incidental to the arrest. As an example, if an arrest was legal, and a search was made of the defendant in a legal manner, and a concealed unlicensed loaded weapon was found on the defendant, the defendant could additionally be charged with a weapons violation. This will include any contraband possessed in violation of the law.

Bear in mind, however, if the arrest was unlawful, then anything procured from that arrest is unlawful. See "fruit of the poisoned tree" concept above for details. This would include admissions, confessions, and any unlawful property or contraband taken or recovered from the subject.

There Are Two Types of Searches That a Private Investigator or a Loss Prevention/Security Officer as a Private Person May Conduct

1. A search of the person which is *incidental to a lawful arrest.*
   - A search to prevent harm to the private investigator, security officer, or others by the use of a weapon or instrument possessed by the person arrested.
   - Search for any weapon or implement that will facilitate escape.
   - Search for any item or instrument used in the commission of the crime.
   - To recover the proceeds of the crime (recovery of property).
   - To avoid the destruction of evidence.

2. A search with the *consent of the person* being searched, or the consent to search the property owned or under the control of the person who is the subject of the search.

Example

A security guard arrested the subject for shoplifting and was taken to the store's security office. A search was made of the subject, and the guard found a concealed loaded weapon on his person. Along with the larceny, the subject was also charged with the weapons violation. In court, the defendant's attorney contested that the search was illegal on the grounds that the security guard had no right to search the defendant fortuitous to the arrest. The court held that justification of searches incidental to an arrest applies whether made by a police officer or a private citizen and that the search was valid because the arrest was lawful.[16]

Consider also that if a private investigator or a security officer has the right to be in a certain place or area, and he or she happens to observe evidence or contraband in plain view, those items can be seized and will be admissible in court. This concept of law is considered *the Plain-View Doctrine*—the rule that a law enforcement officer may make a search and seizure without obtaining a search warrant *if* evidence of criminal activity or the product of a crime can be seen without entry or a search.

Example

A police officer stops a motorist for a minor traffic violation, and upon approaching, the officer observes a pistol or a marijuana plant on the back seat, giving the officer reasonable cause to enter the vehicle to seize the items.[17] This rule can also be applied to a private investigator or a security officer, who acting within the scope of his or her employment observes possible evidence under these conditions.

In other instances, private investigators are not agents of the government and they therefore have the right to search *with due notice.* For example, if a retailer or any business posts signs easily read upon entry and exit noting "All packages are subject to search" as a company rule, entry into the store can be denied to a person who refuses to give access to a search of the package. Also, if certain company rules are noted to all newly hired employees as part of their hiring procedures that all packages, bags, and so forth are subject to inspection upon leaving the building or facility, the search is legal, and they must submit. However, without *probable cause,* a search cannot be made if the search is denied by the subject, but the employee may be terminated for failing to adhere to company policy.

Employee Searches

A business enterprise may also have a policy concerning certain restrictions on employees, and as long as these policies are enforced equally, there is no loss of privacy. An example would be that all female employees must secure their pocketbooks in their lockers and, if they wish, make use of a clear plastic bag for the carrying of personal contents into the work area. This would include the restriction of all bags, valises, knapsacks, backpacks, and so forth, of all employees. Another example would be that all employees are subject to a bag check upon leaving the premises or work for the day. In this case, all employees leaving or leaving at a given time must be examined; the security officer may not act in a random manner or subject one employee and not another to the examination. This cannot be considered an unreasonable search and seizure under the Fourth Amendment of the U.S. Constitution, because it is not an action by a government employee, such as a law enforcement officer, but by a private person, a security officer, as per the employer's written policy and procedures.

Regarding searches conducted on employees, the employee has an expectation of privacy even if on the employer's premises. But if the employee has been advised of certain rules and regulations regarding employee conduct and what is expected of the employee, and such notification has been acknowledged by the employee, he or she must submit as may be required, although the situation could be delicate.

Company lockers can be considered one area of particular importance in this regard. If the lockers are provided to the employee, along with a lock or padlock under the condition that the locker can be searched at any time, and the employer or the employer's agent (security officer or manager, or a private investigator engaged by a client) has a master key for entry into that locker, a search without permission is legal. The employee must give access to that locker if he or she has read and acknowledged written company policy that his or her locker is subject to inspection at any time. The employee may refuse such access and no search of the locker can be legally conducted—probable cause exists and the contents of the locker are part of that cause if there is a serious public safety issue. There is a serious public safety issue. However, the employee can then be subject to termination of employment in this circumstance if such a refusal stands.

But if the employee provides his own lock and key and has not acknowledged the company's written policy or rules concerning examination of that employee's locker, the interior of the locker can be considered private property by the court and access can be denied.

Examination by a security officer or investigator of a private office or a private desk, or the opening of an employee's mail can be regarded as an invasion of privacy, since people have an expectation that these areas are private. Moreover, there is a greater risk of civil action if the security officer or investigator is working with or in cooperation with the police, as this will involve the issue of search and seizure and the color of state law and, therefore, criminal liability. A search of the contents of a desk may be made if the desk is communal or shared by more than one employee. If only one employee has use of a desk, that employee has an expectation of privacy, and no search can be made. The contents of an employee's desk will generally be viewed as private property if assigned to that one employee, but if the desk is communal, no protection exists.

The testing of new hires and present employees for drugs or drug use has raised issues of privacy and violations of the Fourth Amendment which many believe denies the right to search the person. For clarification on this matter, see the section on "Drug Testing" in this chapter.

Consent to Search

Consent searches, other than a search of a person incidental to an arrest, have been held to be more reasonable and binding by the courts.

> Whether the subject gives consent to search orally or in writing, the consent must have been given freely, intelligently, and without reluctance, fear, or provocation. To do otherwise, such evidence seized would come under "Fruit of the Poisoned Tree Concept" and could not be accepted in court.

If the consent was asked of the subject, and it was given orally, such conversation should be witnessed by at least one other person and so noted in detail on the written report following the occurrence. Written consent is considered more binding and, if used, should be compiled prior to any search. (See Appendix D for a sample "Consent to Search" form.)

As noted, permission to make a search of a person incidental to an arrest is not required. But if the subject under arrest owns or has possession of a vehicle in the retail or business establishment's parking lot which may contain stolen property from the officer's employer, consent should be obtained. Whether given orally or in writing, the search should be confined to the incident or investigation at hand. If the subject revokes the consent at any time, the security officer must cease the search.

If the PI or security officer is conducting an internal investigation, and any search of the employees' property on or off the business premises is required, a written consent form must be compiled. The security officer should be aware that some restrictions may apply in a case such as this, and counsel should be sought from the company's or agency's attorney. Additionally, if there is a crime involved or the employee may be subject to arrest, authority to conduct an off-premises investigation and search should be given to the police.

Criminal Possession of Stolen Property

A person may be charged with this crime when he or she knowingly possesses stolen property with intent to benefit themselves or a person other than the owner thereof, or to impede the recovery by an owner thereof. A charge of larceny (if applicable) may also be charged against the defendant.

A Search Other Than the Person

Generally, any search and seizure off the premises of a business establishment should be conducted by the police. Nevertheless, be mindful that if the subject has an auto parked in a parking field adjacent to the building or facility, or out of the immediate control of the subject, and gives consent for a search of the auto even orally with witnesses present, it will be more binding if the consent is in writing before a search is made.

However, if the arrested person denies permission to a private investigator or security officer to search an auto used and in possession by that person, and a search is made where stolen property is recovered, such a search and seizure may be considered illegal whether the auto is securely locked or not. The legality of such a seizure might be a question for the court to decide where property in full view is observed through a car window, and where the perpetrator cannot produce a sales slip for that property, and once recovered, an additional charge of *criminal possession of stolen property* was added to the original charge.

In such a circumstance where property is later considered illegally obtained and therefore may not be used against the defendant, the PI or security officer may have the satisfaction at least of making a recovery of the original owner's property to which the defendant cannot prove ownership and had no right to possess.

The private investigator or security officer would do better and be on safer ground if the police become involved in searching the contents of an auto. If a search is not made and the auto is impounded by the police for safekeeping because the perpetrator has been arrested and placed into the custody of the police, an inventory of the auto's contents will be routinely conducted by the police for security purposes. This is standard procedure for police departments so that the perpetrator or the owner of the auto cannot claim at a later time that property or an item was stolen or missing from that auto while in police custody. If property is found not belonging to the defendant, and where the defendant cannot prove ownership but that property can be identified as belonging to the client, retailer, or someone else, and is considered part of the proceeds of a crime, such seizure is legal, and the crime of *criminal possession* could be added to the initial charge.

In Conclusion—A Cautionary Note

To reiterate concerning search and seizure, we must be aware that the private investigator or any security officer must have reasonable grounds or probable cause to act. Further, the action must be "fresh," in that it must relate to an event that is occurring at that time or that occurred a short time prior, which is usually measured in minutes rather than hours.

If the rights of the suspect are violated in any way, any evidence, including oral or written statements made by the suspect and gathered as a result of that arrest, will be inadmissible in court, and the case will be dismissed ("fruit of the poisoned tree" concept). The private investigator, loss prevention/security officer, and possibly his or her employer and client can be sure that civil litigation against them will follow.

Closed-Circuit Television (CCTV)

The private investigator or security officer must also be cognizant that under the Fourth Amendment, *"The right of the people to be secure in their persons, . . . against unreasonable search and seizures . . ."* will include unlawful use of CCTV. A hidden camera placed in a restroom or other area where a person has an objective *expectation of privacy* would be considered a violation of law. Such action by a private investigator or loss prevention department would be considered a "search" and is subject to the Fourth Amendment's requirement of reasonableness and privacy. The individual who suffers this offense could initiate criminal and civil action.

The "Claim of Right"—A Defense by a Criminal Defendant

In any prosecution for larceny committed by trespassory taking or embezzlement, it is an affirmative defense that the property was appropriated *under a claim of right made in good faith.* The security officer assigned to retail or any business establishment should be acutely aware of this section regarding a person making a *claim of right* concerning merchandise or property, or in any instance where the possibility of a claim of right may become an issue.

A good example of an incident where a *claim of right* may occur could be described as follows:

> A person purchases or receives as a gift an expensive coat. He finds that the coat does not fit him or for whatever reason wishes to exchange the coat for another of the same value. He enters the store and rather than go through the store's procedure of returning the item and making an exchange, he goes directly to the coat department and selects a coat to his liking, takes that coat, and places the coat he is returning on the rack before leaving. In actuality, his motive was not to steal—there was *no intent* to steal—but he did, at least in a technical sense, exercise control of property belonging to another in which he had no right to do so. If all of the facts in this case are unknown (or not believed), and an arrest is pursued in this case, the subject could produce a defense under the *claim of right* made in good faith. If court action was taken and the reasoning accepted by the court, whatever charge was laid against this subject most assuredly would be dismissed. Consider also that if the subject found and produced a receipt for the original purchase, an arrest most probably would not have been made, or at least it would have provided a defense in court.

Moreover, a suspect can make a *claim of right* in a variety of situations, and a private investigator should be cognizant of this type of defense.

Warrants

Search Warrants

Search warrants are written orders (writs) by a judge issued on the written and sworn statement of a law enforcement officer or prosecutor. The warrant will specifically note and identify the location of the search (home, office, auto) and the articles or items intended to be seized (weapons, guns, drugs). Evidence unconstitutionally seized cannot be used as evidence in court, and no evidence can be admitted that was traced to this illegal evidence (*fruit of the poisoned tree*). The Fourteenth Amendment to the U.S. Constitution applies this rule to the states.

Bench Warrants

A bench (arrest) warrant is issued by a judge commanding the person named in the warrant to appear in court. It is customarily issued to a law enforcement officer to take custody of the person named in the warrant and bring that person into court before the judge. The officer may also receive a warrant of this type after swearing to information before a judge, being granted a bench warrant, and then seeking out the defendant for arrest. This type of warrant is issued for the arrest of a person who is charged with committing a crime, convicted of a crime but failed to appear for sentencing, owes a fine, or has been adjudicated in contempt of court.

Cautionary Note

A private person (private investigator, loss prevention/security officer) cannot solicit or request a writ of any type from a judge (unless via the police, prosecutor, or court officer, and *only they* will have the duty of executing the warrant), nor can he or she as an individual possess, enforce, or in any way act upon any type of warrant. This will include knowledge that a warrant has been issued and is in force.

Drug Testing

Questions may arise concerning drug testing, such as *if, when, and the right to do so* by a company. There are two conditions under which companies may test—at preemployment or randomly. Some companies have preemployment physicals as a standard procedure for employment in their company, but most do not.

A demand to test an employee would have to be based on the terminology "fitness for duty," where the opportunity to test a particular employee for specific reasons could be held. Such reasoning could include, if the workplace has been made unsafe for that employee or other employees, or that his work habits are contrary to the safety of his person or others, or that he is suspect in the use of a drug or other intoxicant. This reasoning may be based on the employee's appearance and behavior (actions and demeanor), in addition to physical evidence or information and belief from a trustworthy employee or employees. Ongoing written documentation of such activity or behavior would indicate the potential need for such testing and negate the possibility of mistreatment or illegality. But also consider that an incident of a serious nature that has come to the attention of management might require an employee's agreement to an immediate drug test before he or she may return to work.

As for random drug testing, whether individually or within the whole group of employees where everyone may be randomly subject to a drug test, there are many restrictions. Union contractual agreements, prior or present hiring agreements, personal civil rights, probable cause, the type and procedures for the test, whether such a test is applicable to a particular employment, and other considerations are open to close scrutiny by the legal profession. It is suggested that before a test of this type is seriously considered and contemplated, legal counsel be sought prior to any action.

Wiretaps and Bugs

Eavesdropping Defined

Generally, most states have defined the use of a "wiretap" or the recording under clandestine circumstances as *eavesdropping* when one unlawfully engages in wiretapping, mechanical overhearing of a conversation, or intercepting or accessing an electronic communication. Although anyone can be the target of covert eavesdropping, certain people have a greater risk than others because of their financial position, occupation, and status or distinctive expertise within that occupation, because they possess or have access to sensitive or secret information, and because of their legal or domestic situations. This could include industrial and scientific espionage, marriage difficulties, divorce litigation, union or labor problems, civil lawsuits and litigation, criminal litigation, insurance fraud, and nominated or elected officials who have been defamed or slandered or may have prior insidious backgrounds.

Because private conversations are expected to be private, many investigators believe that the preferred method of gaining information or obtaining intelligence is through the use of wiretap or bugging devices.

> Be cautious of entering into this field of inquiry; eavesdropping in any form is rarely legal or court sanctioned. Moreover, it is a crime when a person possesses any instrument, device, or equipment designed for, adapted to, or commonly used in wiretapping or mechanical overhearing of a conversation under circumstances evincing an intent to use or permit the same to be used in violation of law.

However, a private investigator must be cognizant of all forms of eavesdropping and the equipment that may be used. There are two types of eavesdropping techniques, *wiretap* and *bugging*, and they are subdivided into several categories.

Wiretaps

Wiretaps are the preferred method of obtaining information, as the quality of the transmission received will generally be of high quality. This technique involves tying into a wire or other conduit that is used for transmission. The type of transmission (communication) may be voice, fax, or electronic. Also, the transmission may be by telephone wire (hardwire), PBX cable, CCTV system, electronic, or any other communications instrument.

Wiretaps on company telephones can violate federal and state laws depending how the procedure is set up and conducted. Although it may be said that the employee's right to privacy may be balanced against the needs of the employer, consider this a no-win situation. If company management believes that a crime is or has been committed, and believes that one way to gain evidence would be through a wiretap, let the police do it. Once the crime is reported to the police department, the company can advise that a wiretap might be useful. The police will determine the benefits and legalities and obtain the necessary court order to set up the tap.

The more common wiretaps are as follows:

- *Hardwire Wiretap*—Where physical access is gained to a section of wire (a telephone hardwire line is tapped) and where the signal transmitted travels by the use of a second set of wires. This second set of wires is attached with a "slave" or similar isolation device, with the signal bridged back to a secret location. This type of apparatus is unlikely to be discovered by the untrained person, but once discovered, and with the proper equipment, the eavesdropper can easily be traced back to the listening location.
- *Soft Wiretap*—A modification to the software used by the telephone company phone system. This is generally done at the phone company but can be done at the place of business via PBX. This is considered the preferred method for tapping a phone where it is very tough to find it within the telephone

company's system (easy to locate but requires complete access to the inner operations of the phone company's computers—rarely given without court order). However, it may be easily caught on a PBX. This type of system is called remote observation (REMOBS), electronic switching system (ESS), or a translation tap. It is very popular with law enforcement, intelligence agencies, and large corporations. See *eavesdropping* terminology for definitions of these acronyms in the "Glossary."

Although not a wiretap in the covert sense, another type of "soft wiretap" is that many companies have a recording for incoming business calls that advises the caller that all conversations may be recorded for business or quality control purposes. This is considered legal as long as the announcement is made before a conversation takes place.

- *Record Wiretap*—Where a tape recorder is wired to a telephone tap. This is similar to a hardwire tap, but the tapes of the recording device must be changed on a routine basis. This is very popular with amateurs but is dangerous, because eavesdroppers can be easily detected and caught in the act of servicing the illicit recorder.

- *Transmit Wiretap*—By connecting a radio frequency (RF) transmitter to a wire (see below). This is a very popular tapping procedure for eavesdropping, but the RF energy produced can easily be detected by a competent "bug sweep" specialist, and its use increases the probability of being detected.

Bugging Devices

A "bug" is a listening device that is placed on, in, or within a specific area (auto, room, house, or on the person), and when placed or activated, intercepts and transmits communication (oral, optical, or geographic position) to a listener or monitor who may either be very close or somewhat distant from the "bug." There are several types of bugs used for specific purposes. Any of the following types of equipment can be combined in order to make a hybrid device:

- *Radio Frequency* (RF)—Radio frequency is the most used and common type of bugging system (consider the classic dry martini with an olive bug). A radio transmitter is placed in a device or the area to be "bugged." It is very easily detected but difficult to trace back to the person who planted it. The radio transmitter comes in various shapes and sizes and can be placed in or on an object. It can range from being in the olive in the subject's martini to on an overhead light fixture in a hotel room. These devices can be easily detected but are considered the most common because they are cheap and disposable.

- *Acoustic-Type Bug*—These "bugs" are simple in their use, without electronic implements, by simply and directly eavesdropping on a conversation with the naked ear. Access to any communication can be easily obtained by placing a stethoscope or a similar listening device, a rubber tube, or something as simple as a water glass against a wall. Basically, these objects may be placed anywhere sound may be transmitted or obtained, such as through power outlets, walls, vents, ventilation ducts, structural defects, and around windows, among other openings. This is considered the simplest of methods without the use of electronics.
- *Ultrasonic (or VLF) Bugs*—These convert sound into an audio signal that is above the range of the human ear. Audio pressure waves are used rather than radio waves or a radio signal. This technique is used to convert sound into an audio signal above the range of the human ear, and the ultrasonic signal is then intercepted at another location and converted back to audio.
- *Optical Bugs*—These are devices that convert sound or data into an optical pulse or a beam of light, such as active or passive laser devices. They are rarely used, as these bugs are easily detected and are generally expensive.

Any person who sets up, condones, or is part of an illegal or improper tap is subject to criminal arrest and civil litigation.

This is not to say that a private investigator cannot record a telephone conversation surreptitiously *as long as he or she is a party to that conversation.* Such a recording by an investigator where identification of the other person can be established and where certain admissions or comments are made by the other party may be considered of great use as evidence at a later time.

But, be aware that there may be some restrictions in some states concerning the legalities of a recorded conversation that you are part of. Check with your state law, your company attorney, and company policy on any situation where any recording of a telephonic conversation is to be conducted.

The aforementioned descriptions of eavesdropping devices are described here as a brief attempt to familiarize the private investigator with the equipment presently in use. Be apprised, however, that technology is upgraded daily, and what is in use today may be obsolete tomorrow.

Personal Recorder

Consider that the simplest of all covert devices used for eavesdropping is the audiocassette or voice-activated microrecorder. These units are cheap, easily operated, come in various sizes, and are well proven. Small digital models with a voice-activated mode will save tape time and can be easily hidden on the person or wherever desired. The only drawback in the voice-activated model is that loud ambient noise will cause the device to slip into a continual play. Many of these recorders can be used as a body-worn system with button microphones and the unit integrated into a briefcase or the pen in your pocket.

The pen bug is also widely used as a microphone and transmitter. Along with an ink reservoir, it can be used as a proper pen, and the receiver can be linked to a recording system allowing limitless playback. This can be a useful tool for the undercover agent attending meetings, discussions, and parties. In addition, the wearing of a "wire" along with a transmitter taped to one's body and the recording device located elsewhere, is an applicable method of taping a conversation.

The Art of Covert Eavesdropping

If properly installed by a skilled technician with premium appliances, wiretaps and bugs can be difficult to detect. However, it must be a consideration that no bug or wiretap is completely secure; given time to do the search, any bug or wiretap can be discovered by a trained technician with sophisticated instruments. Conversely, the PI must realize that unless he or she is a trained technician in the application and detection of these devices, such activity should be left to the expert.

The purchase of equipment and instruments required for detecting a carefully and scrupulously placed wiretap or bug is a major expense. For those private investigators who wish to become competent technicians in the use and detection of wiretap and bugging devices, the author suggests professional training and certification in this area.

Targets for Covert Eavesdropping

Anyone or any company can be the target for covert eavesdropping. However, some people, companies, or governmental agencies are more susceptible or are at greater risk than others because of several factors. In reality, anyone with money, power, or influence, or access to classified, sensitive, or personal information is at risk for being a target of eavesdropping, including those involved with the following:

- Law enforcement, intelligence, and counterintelligence
  - Drug Enforcement Administration (DEA), Federal Bureau of Investigation (FBI), National Security Agency (NSA), Central Intelligence Agency (CIA), Homeland Security, state and local police departments, and so forth
- Business information
  - Trade or scientific secrets, technology, intelligence
  - Computer information—software, data storage
  - Systems management and stock inquiries

- Labor problems, union activities, strike information
- New concepts, ideas, marketing
- Executives—corporate, private, or personal information

- Certain occupations
  - Public office, politicians, celebrities, or notable personage in society
- Financial
- Legal, litigation
- Political activism or demonstrations
- Insurance fraud
- Domestic, personal situations

Observable Warning Signs

Regarding an individual or a business enterprise, if anything that is said, written, or produced can increase someone else's condition, status, wealth, or influence, then consider that you or your company could be a potential target of eavesdropping.

The following indicators could be clues that the individual or the company is being infiltrated or spied upon:

1. Strange sounds, volume changes, static, popping, or scratching can be heard on your phone lines.
2. Sounds are coming from your phone's handset when it is hung up, the phone often rings when no one is there, a very faint tone is heard, or a high squeal or beep is heard for a fraction of a second.
3. Your AM/FM radio in your home or office, or your car radio suddenly develops strange interference. This applies to television in particular, because TV reception is sensitive to nearby transmitters.
4. You have been a victim of a burglary, or drawers or cabinets seem to have been rummaged through, but nothing appears to be taken in either case.
5. Door locks appear to be "sticky," harder to turn, or completely fail, indicating possible evidence of a lock being "picked" or manipulated in some way.
6. Certain items seem to appear in your home or office, but you are unable to determine how they got there.
7. Furniture seems to have been moved slightly.
8. Electric wall plates appear to have been moved or are slightly ajar. The smoke detector, clock, lamp, or exit sign in your office or home looks slightly crooked, has a small hole on its face, or has somewhat of a reflective surface.
9. A small bump or deformation has appeared on or in the baseboard near the floor, or a dime-sized discoloration has suddenly appeared on the wall or ceiling.
10. Drywall dust or debris is observed on the floor next to a wall, or small pieces of ceiling tiles or grit is observed on the floor or on the surface of your desk.

11. A vendor or business acquaintance presents you with an electronic device such as a desk radio, alarm clock, lamp, small TV, boom box, CD player, or calculator as a gift, which may contain an eavesdropping device.
12. Telephone, cable, plumbing, or air conditioning repair/service people show up to do work at your home or office when no one called them.
13. Telephone and utility workers are spending unusual periods of time doing "repair work" in the area of your home or business.
14. Telephone, utility, service, or delivery trucks are often parked nearby for long periods when nobody appears to be in them.

And more importantly, the target subject realizes the following:

15. Others know or become aware of your confidential business or professional trade secrets.
16. Secret meetings or bids seem to be less than secret.
17. People know more of your activities than they should.

> Consider that eavesdropping in any form is illegal unless it is sanctioned by a government entity by warrant or law. Wiretaps can be extremely difficult to detect if installed by a professional who has a high level of expertise. A wiretap or a bugging device is placed in an area in order to intercept communication and then transmit or conduct that communication to another area or listening location. The goal of eavesdropping is to gain intelligence or information that would be helpful to the recipient. Depending on the device used, the eavesdropper may be a few feet, hundreds of feet, or miles away from the subject (victim).

The Polygraph and Its Application

Most polygraph examinations are conducted by police departments and other law enforcement agencies. This also includes federal and state agencies in order to determine falsehoods in other public safety or national security matters.

Because of so many restrictions placed on the polygrapher and the rights granted to the examinee in the private sector, testing in this area is usually confined to certain investigations.

Process and Use Defined

Simply put, the polygraph, also known as a "lie detector," really does not detect lies, but in fact is based on the idea that a lie or lying leads to emotional conflict that can cause fear and anxiety. These emotions are then reflected as physical changes in the subject's body.

Once "hooked up to the machine," the polygraph will record four physical features—*the heart rate, blood pressure, respiration,* and *perspiration.*

The heart rate (pulse) is considered the most important response, with the galvanic response (perspiration) being the least important. The instrument will record these physical factors via four stylus-type pens on a wide sheet of graph paper extending from one side of the machine, and passing slowly under the pens as they record the responses.

The polygraph can be useful in the investigation of a crime or the probing for details of employee dishonesty after a crime has been discovered. In other instances, a business may need to replace a key employee almost immediately, but a detailed investigation into the applicant's background can be expensive and time consuming. Within certain restrictions, the utilization of a polygraph may be a more affordable solution with immediate analysis.

A polygraph examination cannot be forced upon anyone; it must be voluntary in that the subject must willingly submit to the exam. This restriction is applicable whether the examination is for an employment position or an inquiry as part of a criminal investigation. In any case, written consent must be obtained. If the examiner finds "deception" and in effect the subject fails the examination, it cannot be used against a defendant in a court of law, even if he voluntarily did submit. Conversely, if the subject passed the examination and was found to be truthful (no deception found), the defendant may attempt (with the judge's permission) to introduce the results on his behalf to show innocence. Controversial issues have arisen over polygraph test results and their admissibility in a court of law. Some states and jurisdictions have a complete ban on the admission of the results of a polygraph test, while some state and federal district courts allow such admission. Many appeals on the admissibility of polygraph tests are presently before the appellate courts throughout the country.

The Physics of the Polygraph

The use or attempted use of polygraph examinations can be the cause of controversy and civil litigation, so it is important to know what a "lie detector" test is and what it is not:

1. Polygraphs are used to narrow the list of suspects in a civil matter or a criminal investigation *and are restricted to certain controlling factors,* including a person's acceptance to submit to a polygraph exam and the following circumstances to be investigated—employee theft, sexual harassment, workplace disputes, civil disputes, marital and domestic problems (infidelity, drug use), and preemployment verification (of information received, qualifications, and criminal and drug histories). Note that an *employer* is further restricted in the use of a polygraph as illustrated in the next section, "General Restrictions for the Use of a Polygraph."

2. The lie is detected by the examinee's response to a question by the examiner, where physiological changes take place in the body when a lie is committed. In the case of deception, there is more than one type of physical change in the body, including an increase or decrease in blood pressure, heart rate, and blood volume. The components or devices connected to the examinee are rubber tubes placed across the chest and abdomen (to register respiration and movement), two metal fingerplates attached to the ring and index fingers of one hand (skin/sweat, galvanic response), and a blood pressure cuff on one upper arm (blood pressure, heart rate). These components are not harmful or uncomfortable.
3. Although considered to be very accurate, polygraph results can be affected by illness, pain, excessive coughing, mental or physical fatigue and heart conditions, breathing problems, tranquilizers, and depressants. Factors that might cause a "false response" to a question or questions because of nervousness or the emotional or physical state of the examinee might include a variety of procedures an examiner may use to determine the examinee's emotions and response capabilities, and factual analysis of the case in question.
4. It is possible to defeat or master the results of a polygraph exam in several ways. In an effort to inhibit or cloud emotional response, the subject could ingest sedatives just prior to the exam. Another way to hinder results would be to use biofeedback preparation in controlling pulse and respiration.

Essentially, if the examinee *knows* he is lying, the polygraph instrument will detect the lie. But it is possible to "beat" a polygraph test. Some examinees are sociopathic, and when telling a lie, they honestly believe in their mind the lie to be true. In these instances, the sociopath can beat the test or at least the question. In addition, if the subject is mentally unstable, results will be inconclusive, and a small percentage of participants cannot be tested, as they will neither pass nor fail. It is not unheard of within the profession that governmental undercover agents and spies receive intensive training in beating the polygraph with positive results. For further detail, see the section "Defeating the Polygraph Exam" later in this chapter.

5. Prior to the actual exam, the examiner will make certain that the subject is as comfortable as possible and will ask certain control questions in order to set a baseline. If the subject refuses to answer or evades the control questions, the examiner will cancel the test. Moreover, the professional examiner will be cognizant of the subject's mental and physical mannerisms, and if the examiner suspects that the subject has taken drugs or sedatives, which will or may affect

the test results, the examiner will terminate the test. Bear in mind that countermeasures by the examinee prior or during the test, such as drugs or body movements, can affect the test, but an experienced examiner will pick up on these deceptions and can either correct or reschedule the test for another time.

6. The law details the length of time for the test, which includes a pretest interview, the actual test, and the analysis of the charts resulting from the test. It also defines the examinee's rights, notification of the test, the review of questions to be asked, explanation of how the polygraph works and how the test will be conducted, the forms that must be acknowledged, and how many individual tests the examiner may conduct in a day.
7. According to the American Polygraph Association, the accuracy of polygraph testing over the last 25 years is estimated to be 85% to 95% for specific issue investigations. It has been found that the new computerized systems produce results closer to 100% accuracy. However, errors do occur and are usually caused by the lack of training and experience of the examiner, poor pretesting, and the wording of test questions, misinterpretation of chart results, equipment malfunction, and improper testing techniques. *Accuracy and verifiable results will depend on the expertise of the examiner.*

General Restrictions for the Use of a Polygraph[18]

The private investigator and loss prevention/security officer must bear in mind that an employee cannot be forced to take a polygraph test:

1. Generally, no employer is permitted to have a prospective or present employee submit to a polygraph test as a condition of employment or of continued employment. However, there are exceptions.

An Employer Can Legally Test or Question an Employee with the Use of a Polygraph Instrument under Two Circumstances

1. *Preemployment Verification*—Restricted to certain occupational duties including security officers or guards, or personnel who will be handling large sums of money or confidential information.
2. *Suspicion of Theft*—There must be an "economic loss" and is restricted as to how the employee will fall under the law as an examinee—for example, access alone is insufficient to provide "reasonable suspicion" for the required test.

2. The employee, once tested and believing that an error has been made in the testing procedure, has certain rights. He may request a second test, retain a second polygrapher for a second opinion (at his own expense), or file complaints with the state licensing board and the Department of Labor under the Employee Polygraph Protection Act (EPPA).
3. The results of the examination can be released to only authorized persons. This includes the examinee, anyone designated in writing by the examinee, the employer, firm, corporation, or government agency that requested the examination, and under due process of law.
4. Governmental agencies are basically exempt under the law concerning employees, present and prospective.

Polygraph Testing Restrictions in Criminal Investigation

Private Employers Are Entitled to Administer a Polygraph Test to Employees under the Following Circumstances[19]

1. The test is given in connection with an "ongoing investigation" involving economic loss (a monetary or property loss).
2. The employee had "access" to the property in question.
3. The employer has "reasonable suspicion" that the employee was involved in the incident under investigation.
4. The employer signs a statement containing the required information and provides it to the employee prior to the testing. (This statement will be supplied by the examiner.)
5. No action is to be taken against the employee unless there is additional supporting evidence of involvement or misconduct beside the results of the polygraph test.

The private investigation agency should use caution when hiring a polygrapher. The polygrapher should be a true professional—trained, educated, certified, and accepted as a member by the American Polygraph Association (APA). Moreover, he or she should be engaged in continuing education to improve his or her skills and remain current with new developments. The polygrapher should follow all the guidelines found in the law and provide all the required forms for the employer.

Polygraph examinations can be expensive, particularly if a large group of employees need to be examined regarding a crime. If used in the hiring process, some serious questions could arise, such as the legality, and the possibility of affecting the relationship adversely concerning the confidence and respect the new hire may have had for the employer. Many people feel that it is an invasion of privacy. Some states have banned polygraph exams as part of the hiring process, except for some specific governmental or sensitive positions.

The private investigator and the loss prevention/security department should consider the cost and the possible benefit in the use of this instrument. Depending on the seriousness and extent of the crime and the number of possible suspects involved, the expense may be the least of the problem. If the crime was committed within the jurisdiction of a police department and was reported to them, and that department has a reliable polygraph examiner on staff, the loss prevention/security administrator should let the police handle the case completely.

Considering that this type of inquiry is more specific in the investigative process, see Appendix A for a more detailed analysis of the Employee Polygraph Protection Act.

Defeating the Polygraph Exam

Although not readily admitted, polygraph examiners concede that professional criminals are the ones most likely to beat the polygraph. Moreover, anyone submitting to a polygraph exam who has a particular mental disease could also give erratic results. The private investigator should be aware that there are several books on the polygraph with chapters on how to beat the "lie detector." So then it can be said that anyone fearful of their results on a polygraph exam would consider some research into this field before agreeing to a test.

Some of the "tricks" offered by some sources include the following:

- Dampening emotional responses by the intake of sedatives.
- Practicing biofeedback movements in order to control one's pulse and respiration, including breathing techniques and muscle tightening.
- Producing erratic reactions to all questions by biting one's tongue, pressing one's toe into a tack located in a shoe, or contracting the anal sphincter at appropriate times.

Realize also that there are people who have been trained to beat the polygraph. Government spies and undercover agents having this type of training would benefit greatly in an interrogation of this type rather than someone who has never experienced or been trained in the characteristics of the polygraph machine.

Preexamination will include controls where the subject is instructed to say "no" to questions that the subject knows to be true or if true, is a lie. If the subject refuses to submit to the questions during a preexam that the examiner uses to set up the machine and procedure, it will be terminated. Generally, a good examiner can detect the subterfuge that a subject may wish to employ and construct corrections for a decent result, or if the results are exceptionally conspicuous, determine that the subject is deceitful in his or her attempt to control the test and that it must be terminated.

Privacy Rights and Civil Rights Violations

The Invasion of Privacy, Privilege, and Legitimate Interests

Defined

There is no doubt that an investigation can cause some emotional stress to both the guilty and the innocent. But for the plaintiff to engage in an emotional distress lawsuit, he must prove that the investigator engaged in some extreme or outrageous conduct that in fact caused severe emotional distress or personal embarrassment resulting in physical and emotional symptoms or bodily harm. The investigator should be cognizant of possible civil action alleging an invasion of privacy whether he or she is involved in an investigation of a person's personal life, preemployment, violation of company policy, the report of a crime, or any other investigation where an individual is involved.

Privacy

Publicity of private facts—*invasion of privacy*—can occur when an investigator makes a statement or reveals some type of information about an employee or an individual to another person not *protected by privilege.* The subject in question may also believe that some intrusion takes place when an investigator looks into the private matters of that person without having a *legitimate interest.* In other words, the investigator publicizes facts regarding another that are highly offensive to a reasonable person in which the investigator does not have a legitimate interest or passes on such information to one not protected by privilege.

Privilege

The term *privilege* relates to those persons who have an intrinsic interest in, are privy to, and have an interest in the investigation or its final results. This may be called *the closed circle* (those protected by privilege) and might include private investigative agency personnel, company security personnel, and select administrators or managers of concern as designated by the client or the employer.

Any person within this *closed circle* who violates the privilege obligation can be the cause of a legal action against the whole once this *privilege* is broken and any information about the investigation is *leaked* (public disclosure of private facts and information).

Legitimate Interest

The term *legitimate interest* can be defined as the total set of circumstances that would lead a reasonable, prudent, and professionally trained person to believe that an offense has occurred, is occurring, or will occur, and has the permission and authority to investigate such an offense. Basically, this could be less than probable cause but more than mere suspicion.

Procedures, expertise, and talent vary with different investigators and security officers, as well as to the type or seriousness of the investigation and how it is to be carried out. Therefore, the investigator should follow some simple rules in conducting a professional investigation:

- Although private investigators may initiate an inquiry or investigation into any process, procedure, possible or apparent loss, or suspicious activity or circumstances, they should have a *legitimate reason* to conduct an investigation on or into another person.
- They should respect the privacy and other rights of the people involved in the investigation.
- They should refrain from making any unnecessary comments or opinions to anyone, whether they are part of the investigation or not. This is not to say that private investigators, security officers, and their supervisors should not discuss among themselves feelings, thoughts, opinions, the direction or target of a suspect in the investigation, evidence gained or to be gathered, or the complete process of the investigation (keeping it within the *closed circle*).

An employee or any individual who is the subject of an investigation cannot initiate a slander or any form of a defamation action, when during an interrogation the investigator accuses the subject of a crime or some other offense, whether or not the subject is charged or punished in some way. No form of slander occurs when such accusations occur "privately" within the presence of only those people of concern—*the closed circle* (associate private investigators, security officers and their supervisors, police, or the subject's manager or employer), who are those *privileged* to hear and be present if and when an accusation may be made.

Additionally, the presence of a union representative at the request of the subject may be considered "privileged," and the union representative can be a party to the occurrence or accusation without any fault or wrong attributed to the investigator.

Disclosure of Confidential Information

For the private investigator, the area in which he or she may become involved would be in the case of an investigation of some criminal act, and where the employee or individual in question (the plaintiff) may be subject to public disclosures of private facts or information, or the publication by the private investigator (the defendant) of facts that place the plaintiff in a false light.

A publication may consist of any created article, composition, text, or written report in which the plaintiff is identified, *and such information becomes public knowledge.*

Truth Is No Defense Regarding an Action for Invasion of Privacy

Essentially, a nonpublic individual has the right to be free of public scrutiny, from public disclosure of embarrassing private information, from any intrusion of one's solitude or private affairs, or from any type of publicity that puts that individual in a false light to the public.

It is for this reason that all investigations, based upon fact or hearsay, should be confidential in all aspects. The case management supervisor and the private investigator should be cognizant that any written report or conversation regarding the subject in question must be held strictly confidential to only those personnel who may have business or a right to that information. This includes any activity or action prior to, during, or after the conclusion of the investigation. If information about the subject is exposed in some manner and becomes public knowledge, and the subject becomes aware of it and believes or perceives that a wrong has been committed, civil litigation may become a reality.

Preemployment Investigation

During the initial interview or screening process of new hires, some applicants may be subject to a more intensive background investigation than others. The private citizen is protected from having certain information revealed without his or her consent. To obtain that consent, all prospective employees must sign a release (see the example in Appendix D) giving the future employer permission to investigate all that may be required for the position that the subject is applying for. This task is usually relegated to the human resources/personnel department of the company.

Prospective employees who would expect to have an in-depth investigation into their background would include those who would handle any type of money or credit card transactions, some type of fiduciary administration or a position of trust, security officers, or any person in a sensitive or knowledgeable position where harm to the company could result because of that person's position and actions.

See also the possible liability regarding "Defamation" in the following section.

Defamation

The issue of defamation must also be of concern to the investigator because it may be the basis of a civil action or part of the litigation along with invasion of privacy. During any internal investigation or inquiry, investigators may open themselves to an accusation of having defamed a person's reputation or character. When accusations or comments are made that are later proved to be wrong, and those accusations or comments are made outside of the *closed circle*—those protected by privilege—then the person who has been accused has been defamed, *if in fact that person did not commit the act.*

Libel and Slander

A person may be defamed in two ways:

1. *Libel*—A malicious publication in printing, writing, signs, or pictures tending to blacken the reputation of one who is dead, or the reputation of one who is living.
2. *Slander*—Defamation by words spoken; malicious and defamatory words tending to the damage of another.

- Libel is the written word.
- Slander is the spoken word.

The Elements of Defamation

In a case where the plaintiff believes that he or she was defamed, the plaintiff must prove that the defendant used the following:

- Defamatory words or written material against the plaintiff which were untrue
- Such words or written material were said with malice
- Such act caused special damages

Regarding libel and slander concerning privileged communications, *malice* involves an evil intent or motive arising from *spite or ill will, personal hatred or ill will, culpable recklessness,* or a *willful and wanton disregard of the rights and interests of the person defamed.* Conversely, the person claiming the privilege must have acted in good faith under a sense of duty, with an honest belief that the statements that he or she made were true.

For the private investigator, the chances of an action that would include defamation is a possibility, and therefore, *the investigator should be aware of what he or she says, how and where it is said, and to whom.* No matter how minor an incident may be, comments elicited from you by the media, or made in the presence of witnesses or anyone who may become a witness, may surface at a later time and cause you to be placed in jeopardy. Private investigators must be aware at all times that their professional bearing, comments, and manner of speaking will all reflect upon them at, or subsequent to, the incident in question.

Defenses

In a defense of a defamation claim by the plaintiff, the following defenses may be used by the person accused of defamation:

1. *The statement was the truth*—A defamatory statement must be proven as a *false statement of fact.* It must be communicated to at least one disinterested third party; one who has no need to know of the information.
2. *The statement was not published*—If an investigator during interrogation accuses a suspect of committing a crime and the suspect later claims that the investigator made a slanderous allegation, a defense can be made on the grounds of nonpublication in that there was no third party present at this interrogation to hear the allegation. Moreover, if the suspect claims that he was defamed by reason that his superiors were advised of the investigation and his actions in the investigation, interrogation, and confession (if any), a defense may be made that the information was given to managers within the corporation who have the privilege to know and receive this information for various reasons, including training and safety and security matters.
3. *The statement was privileged communication*—The defense of privileged communication is one that is most frequently used. A privileged communication is one made to an *interested party*—one who needs to know. The most common defense in this area is a *qualified privilege communication.* If a suspect alleges that he was defamed by an investigator who made oral and written reports to his superiors (or an employer who has contracted the investigator), a defense can be made that the superiors enjoyed qualified privilege. The information was communicated in good faith to interested parties who needed to know the status and results of the investigation and the employee involved in order to properly oversee and manage the business of the company and the risks of this type of unlawful activity.

In a civil action for libel or slander based on a complaint against the defendant to the court, *the plaintiff may not recover in the absence of a showing that it was made maliciously and without probable cause.*

A person in the discharge of some public or private duty, legal or moral, or in the conduct of his or her own affairs and in a manner where his or her interest is concerned, and if expressed in a reasonable manner and for a proper purpose, enjoys *qualified immunity* against the imposition of liability in a defamation action. The communication must have been made in good faith to a person having a *corresponding interest of duty.*

The defamed plaintiff has the *burden of showing actual malice with convincing clarity.*

Sexual Harassment Conduct

The private investigator or security officer must be cognizant of the fact that different people may consider or perceive certain words, phrases, or actions (inappropriate or unprofessional behavior) as unacceptable, improper, or that which may constitute sexual harassment. Therefore, he or she must be constantly aware of how they interact in any manner with another person, whether privately or professionally. They may also have to investigate a charge of sexual harassment by one coworker against another. In these instances, they will be guided by company policy and procedures and may have to act in cooperation with the human resources or personnel departments of the company during the investigation and final outcome. In any event, they must be aware of the state and federal labor and criminal laws that define behavior such as this type of harassment.

Under federal law, sexual harassment is a type of discrimination defined by the U.S. Equal Employment Opportunity Commission (EEOC) as "unwelcome sexual advances, requests for sexual favors, and other verbal and physical conduct of a sexual nature." The complainant must prove that the behavior or conduct was pervasive and produced a hostile or intimidating work environment.

Gender is not an issue; the offender may be a woman against a man, a woman against a woman, a man against a woman, or a man against a man. Factors such as age, generation gap, and culture may determine how a person deals with an uncomfortable situation.

What constitutes improper or disrespectful behavior may be in the eye of the beholder—what may be an off-color joke or a suggestive remark may offend one person, but not another. Sexual harassment can include off-color remarks, pornography, sexually explicit literature, and pictures.

The complaint must be filed with the EEOC within 180 days of the incident. See "Civil Rights Act of 1964" under "Federal Civil Rights Law" in Appendix A.

Defined

Sexual Harassment—Any unwanted verbal or physical advance, sexually explicit derogatory statements or written material, or sexually discriminatory remarks made by someone, particularly in the workplace, toward any other person, male or female, which is offensive or objectionable to the recipient, which causes the recipient discomfort or humiliation, or which interferes with the recipient's job performance.

Violation of Civil Rights—Any act that can be construed as denying to a citizen his or her civil rights as defined in the Articles of the U.S. Constitution. A violation under federal law as noted in the Civil Rights Act, §1983 action, can be charged against a person even though he may be charged with a crime for that same act in state court; *there is no double jeopardy.*

The right of privacy is an additional consideration regarding civil rights.

Conduct That May Be Construed as Sexual Harassment

- *Touching*—The violation of personal space, caressing, unnecessary touching of any part of the other person's body, or brushing up against, patting, pinching, grabbing, or kissing.
- *Verbal*—Lewd comments, sexually explicit jokes, questions about personal life or behavior, whistling, and requests for dates.
- *Visual*—Posters, magazines, articles, or cartoons that may be considered as lewd to that person. Also staring, ogling, or offensive gestures toward that person.
- *Written*—The receipt of love letters or poems, particularly obscene letters or poems, and lewd or obscene written material.

- *Force*—Rape, sexual abuse, sexual misconduct, and physical assault.
- *Power or Threats*—The promise of a promotion in return for sexual favors or dates. The demand of sexual favors with the threat of loss of job, bad performance evaluations, or loss of promotion.

Sexual Harassment and Its Effects

Sexual harassment toward an employee can be the cause of several problems in the workplace. The private investigator or security officer should become aware by observation, investigation, or inquiry, particularly after being advised by the client or the human resources or personnel department of possible problems that are or may be affecting some personnel. This would also include any information received from actual or anonymous sources.

Some of the factors that may bring about this perception may be considered as follows:

Economic—Where there is overly noticeable turnover in personnel within one department or business area; where there is a noticeable rise in transfer requests or low productivity or interference with a person's job performance.

Psychological—Where a coworker is visually embarrassed, has loss of self-esteem, or has guilt or self-blame; also anger or emotional stress, the fear of the loss of job, bodily harm, and impressions of their peers.

Physical—Stress-related physical problems such as headaches, ulcers, and rashes; where it affects the recipient and his or her attendance or work performance.

Prevention of Sexual Harassment

Although it is almost impossible for the administration and management of a business enterprise to control one's behavior in regard to an act of sexual harassment, an investigator or security officer should be aware of the elements that constitute such sexually aberrant behavior. More importantly, he or she should be aware of the acceptable business practices that control behavior of this type and the possible instances that may initiate an internal investigation.

It has become common procedure in order to reduce liability that a company will have a policy of no nonsense/zero tolerance in regard to sexual harassment and its consequences. Remember that policy must be written and acknowledged by all employees.

This would include the following:

1. Knowledge and complete acceptance and enforcement of the company's policy and procedure concerning sexual harassment.
2. Compilation of a summary of any behavior reported or coming to his or her attention that may be construed as sexual harassment, whether there is a complaint or not. (A written incident report should be compiled in any event.)
3. Performance by employees of all duties in a professional and diligent manner.
4. Treatment of everyone with respect, including customers, visitors, and employees, without regard to gender, race, color, or religious or political affiliation.
5. Refrainment from making personal or derogatory comments about others, or making jokes to the detriment of someone else.

The private investigator and the security officer must remember that such offensive conduct may be considered illegal if the result of such behavior is perceived as harassment, or whether the act is committed on or against a male or female. In reality, it may be considered an act of a male on a male, male on a female, a female on a female, or a female on a male.

Closed-Circuit Television

At present, one of the most important tools that a PI or a loss prevention department may employ is the closed-circuit television (CCTV) camera. The means of surreptitious observation and detection in real time or time-lapse recordings can be a most effective tool in the reduction of loss in all sectors of concern. There have been studies that indicate that CCTV is an excellent deterrent to business crimes such as robbery, shoplifting, employee theft, and insurance liability claims. This has been determined by valid comparisons of similar businesses located in the same geographical area, with the only variable being whether the business in question used CCTV or not.

Overt CCTV

Some businesses feel that the presence of a TV camera may inhibit shopping or make the legitimate customer feel uneasy. One way to alleviate this potential problem is to house the camera in an opague plastic half sphere attached to the overhead. Legitimate customers are seldom aware of this type of contraption, with many not knowing what it is. But shoplifters and others with larcenous intent are fully aware of them, and they can serve as a great deterrent because the shoplifter cannot see if the camera is zooming or turning in their direction.

In contrast, the visible cameras located throughout a store or facility in both public and employee areas give notice that all behavior, suspicious or not, may or is being observed and recorded. These cameras would necessarily be used in those areas of recurrent loss or areas that are highly sensitive to loss particularly for those "spur-of-the-moment" thieves who will have second thoughts upon observing these cameras. Additionally, the use of systems connected to the point of sale for visual observation and recording reduces sloppy work habits, reinforces correct procedures, and identifies any collusive larcenous conduct between friends, relatives, and the cashier.

Covert CCTV

The technology of covert cameras and lenses has advanced so that the innocent looking motion detector or smoke detector attached to an overhead is in actuality a unit containing a camera, with the cost of this equipment the only limiting factor for its use. In a covert surveillance system, there is little doubt that ethical and legal issues will arise. The security officer must be aware that there are certain states where covert cameras are not allowed without proper notification, particularly in customer or employee dressing or locker rooms. As far as the use of visible or covert cameras in public and employee restrooms and locker rooms, it should be considered highly improper and illegal. Common sense would dictate that the privacy of a customer, visitor, or an employee should be held in the highest regard. Note also that if a covert camera is discovered by an employee under observation or a department under surveillance, it could provide ramifications such as union involvement, contractual violations, civil rights violations, and privacy issues.

Notwithstanding these problems, once discovered and the word gets out throughout the business premises, it could have a devastating effect on employee morale and the quality and quantity of work. However, under certain restrictions (privacy, privilege, and legitimate interest, noted earlier), the need to institute the use of a covert CCTV system may be necessary to investigate criminal behavior. The private investigator or the security department would do well to contact the company's attorney to review the need and potential risks involved in the use of covert systems concerning employees.

Covert Surveillance Issues

There will come a time when certain issues will arise concerning CCTV, two-way mirrors, coops, listening devices, or other types of surveillance or inspections that some people may consider an invasion of their privacy.

Basically, CCTV cameras in public areas, passageways, storage rooms, and so forth, can be used in the legal sense, in that employees and customers cannot expect the same right to privacy as they would have within their own homes. Certain rights of privacy are given up upon entering a public building or someone else's property. An employee or customer may be considered a guest in the place of business, and the merchant, retailer, or facility manager may make use and justify the use of cameras, two-way mirrors, or other types of surveillance based on the nature of work (for the employee), and the necessity for measures in combating and reducing theft of merchandise, property, and services committed by employees, customers, and visitors.

Because of the threat of terrorism and the interest of public safety, CCTV applications have increased and become more prevalent, particularly in certain facilities, venues, or public areas. Although the American psyche abhors constant surveillance in any manner for whatever reason, public opinion has generally accepted this intrusion because of this ongoing threat and the harm and serious consequences that a terrorist act could create.

However, there are certain restrictions that must be considered for the sake of propriety and decency when the use of cameras or one-way glass is contemplated. A valid case can be made by a person concerning his or her right to privacy when there has been an invasion of such privacy in certain areas of a public building. This would include the observation of people in lavatories, restrooms, locker rooms, or dressing areas, whether male or female, visitor, customer, or employee. A person using a public restroom has an *expectation of privacy,* and any installation of a hidden TV camera might well be considered a search or a privacy issue under the Fourth Amendment requirements of search and seizure.

No matter how serious a problem may be and the merchant's or facility manager's attempt to correct that problem, the possibility of some civil action or litigation, because of an invasion of privacy or the perceived notion of such an invasion, is not worth the risk. Moreover, some state statutes note that if a person enters a dressing or fitting room and is subject to being observed, the merchant or retailer *must post such written notice outside of the dressing room.* In this way, the person may then have the choice to enter or refuse the use of the room. Of course, the retailer who has this policy does harm to his business and goodwill, if nothing else. Therefore, it would be most prudent not to have any cameras or one-way mirrors in any dressing room for any purpose. There are other procedures that may be instituted to control theft when a dressing room is used to facilitate the crime. One procedure used in many retail establishments is an assigned employee making use of numbered tags for each garment taken into the dressing or fitting room by a customer, and the return of the same number of tags to garments upon leaving.

The Use of CCTV

On what occasion to record or not to record will depend on whether the TV monitors are constantly manned or not. Many loss prevention and security departments will record continuously in real time or in a time-lapse mode. Others may record only suspicious activity on tape when observed. In an effort to cut expenses and monitoring equipment, several cameras may be replaced by one *pan-tilt-zoom* camera. This camera has the ability to pan 360° and, when required, the capability to tilt and zoom in closely on a subject or occurrence.

The use of CCTV in loss prevention and the recording of criminal behavior is a proven factor, and the security manager would do well to make full use of this type of surveillance, as should the private investigator relevant to his or her investigation. If not already in use, inquiry into various types of equipment should be initiated, along with the allocated capital and a determination of where these cameras would be most useful.

Areas of Concern for the Placement of Overt or Covert CCTV Cameras

- Those areas conducive to loss, or of proven losses
- Those areas subject to surreptitious internal investigation
- Coverage of areas containing high-end merchandise
- Receiving and shipping docks
- Warehouse and storage areas
- Elevators, escalators, and rarely used passageways
- Garbage/trash disposal areas
- Entrances and exits (crowd control)
- High traffic areas
- Highly sensitive areas (cash offices or rooms, computer rooms, records storage, electric/telephone/utility rooms, etc.)
- Sensitive exterior areas, including spaces and areas hidden from public view
- Parking fields, garages, and multilevel stairways

Chapter 5

Investigative Techniques and Cautionary Procedures

The Investigative Process

Public- and Private-Sector Investigations

Bear in mind that a police detective or private investigator (PI) is accountable for a fair, ethical, and factual investigation that he or she may be committed to. Upon being assigned and arriving at a crime scene, the police investigator has several responsibilities. Most important is that he or she must determine if, in fact, a crime has taken place.

If so, certain procedures must be followed:

- Safeguard the crime scene; protect the scene from any or further contamination.
- Collect any and all physical evidence.
- Preserve this evidence for scientific analysis, and safeguard any and all evidence for future court presentation.
- Attempt to reconstruct the crime.
- Interview witnesses and evaluate or determine possible suspects.
- Interrogate possible suspects.
- Establish guilt once a suspect is identified.

Statements made by witnesses or suspects (oral or written) to an investigator are considered direct evidence. Remarks considered as hearsay cannot be admitted in court. *However, hearsay remarks may lead to further inquiry or investigation.*

Although a private investigator cannot be held to the same degree or standards as a police investigator, he or she can follow many of the same procedures in an investigation that are reviewed in this chapter.

The Collection and Presentation of Physical Evidence

Presenting physical evidence in court or at a hearing may mean nothing in many cases without an expert to present and explain it convincingly. Scientific evidence can be hard to understand or be accepted by the layman juror, unless the evidence can be explained in a credible manner. Once a witness convinces the court that he or she is an expert in the testimony about to be given and if admissible, such evidence may be introduced. However, attorneys for the other side have the ability to provide expert testimony that can destroy or contradict the original testimony. Some evidence can be irrefutable (fingerprints, DNA, blood work, etc.), but the gathering, collection, and custodial procedures of such evidence can be contested. Moreover, consider that a defendant's attorney can manipulate court procedure so that it benefits the defendant, particularly if the defendant has great amounts of money or social status to apply in his or her defense.

Objectives of the Investigator

A private investigator involved in a criminal investigation has the task of identifying and locating the guilty party and providing evidence in order to prove his guilt. *Investigation is an art—in fact, an applied art—not a science.* Therefore, it must be considered in terms of perception, precepts, and parameters rather than rigid theories.

As we will see, *a great investigator is a creative investigator*, and qualities such as intuition and inspiration can bring about a positive conclusion to an investigation. However, even with a methodic and exhausting process to any inquiry, we cannot deny that many times the outcome will be a matter of chance, where the investigator just happens "to be at the right place at the right time."

Intuition and Chance

Intuition—Because we can consider that the engagement of an investigation is an art, an example of one's intuition can be described as the sudden and unexpected insight that clarifies the problem where logic has run its course. Further, that right or wrong or fundamental principles about what is right or wrong can be intuited, without evident rational thought and inference. It can also be held to be similar to the "hunch," which is quite familiar to professional investigators. When acted upon, hunches can bring decisive results.

Chance—Consideration must also be given to fate or luck that often plays an important part of an investigation. Powers of observation, constant vigilance for the unexpected, along with enterprise, initiative, perseverance, and ingenuity can bring about the element of chance.

The investigator who solves the crime (that is, identifies and apprehends the perpetrator, and recovers or locates the stolen property) does not complete his or her objective of closing the case until the presentment of sufficient evidence to the court for a conviction.

However, we must consider that many crimes will not be responsive to a solution, mainly for lack of insufficient physical evidence, the absence of eyewitnesses, lack of a motive, and the indiscernible motives of the perpetrator.

Information and Intelligence

The fundamental reason that a private investigator or the private investigator's firm is hired is that the person doing the hiring needs some information that cannot be had in any other way. If it is a criminal or possible criminal investigation, the person hiring may not want the police involved at any time, or at least not initially. If the case is not criminal in nature, that person may wish to keep the investigation in-house. But in any case, the most probable reason a company solicits the services of a private investigator is because the company believes that its own security force is not up to the task, or the company has no security force on site. Moreover, they may arrive at a conclusion that with the services of an investigative firm, all legalities would be followed.

Therefore, the employment of a private investigator is to gather *information* and *intelligence,* and if the case is criminal in nature, to build a *prima facie* case for prosecution:

Information—Knowledge obtained with the use of your expertise and experience—inquiries, interviews, surveillance, and research into public and private records, newspapers, photographs, registers, and databases.

Intelligence—Information that has been gathered during the investigation and that is pertinent and relevant to the investigation. Once the information has been collected, it then becomes a plan of concentration of that knowledge for the assignment at hand.

Case Management

The Quest for Information—Research and Analysis

Circumstances Requiring Research

Depending on the investigation that the private investigator will be engaged in and the results that can be expected, research will be in-depth or superficial. An in-depth inquiry may be necessary if the matter concerns something serious in nature or that which comes to light once the investigation begins. This will include the following:

- A criminal case where the attorney for the defendant has hired you.
- A criminal case involving company personnel where such investigation could identify more than one perpetrator.
- Where the outcome or conclusion of an investigation could affect the corporation financially or criminally or cause public embarrassment.
- A civil case where the litigation will involve exceptional monetary compensation for the plaintiff or the defendant.
- A death or serious injury or injuries to more than one person, or where extensive property damage occurs.
- The initial investigation reveals information that:
  - A high potential exists for a similar event to occur.
  - More serious consequences could occur in the case of a similar event.
  - Several people are criminally or civilly involved or contributed to the event.
  - Risks of exposure, extortion, or coercion could be leveled or appear greater than previous estimates against the client/corporation that has hired you.
  - Additional technical examination and skills are required to analyze certain records, hazards, methods, systems, or processes (certified public accountants [CPAs], document examiner, safety engineer, etc.).
  - A person or persons have been identified as superior in some way to the client who has hired you, or have high public or celebrity stature, which may require an immediate personal consultation with the client before continuing the investigation.

Discovery Procedure

Regard *discovery* as the primary and the most important part of any investigation, inquiry, examination, research, study, or search. Although some of the terms noted herein are synonymous in meaning, they must all start with the initial processing of information, known facts, controlling factors, and intelligence particular to the case.

Once hired and obligated to the client and during the primary interview, the private investigator should begin with indicators or underlying factors and, given the information at hand, attempt to be as specific as possible. This interview and subsequent discovery will include the identification of potential sources of information that will or may be of assistance depending on the investigation. Research can reveal a large quantity of information during and after the interview with only a portion that will be relevant to the case. However, the more important would be informants (in-house personnel or outside of the company), supervisory or managerial personnel (involved or knowledgeable), company records, outside experts or consultants, service or technical departments of manufacturers, distributors, vendors, company accountants, and accounts payable/receivable clerks. Again, depending on the type of investigation, such inquiries may be evident and open or surreptitious in nature.

Company Records

Whether investigating an individual, a group of personnel, or some facet of the company, records maintained by any company can be an ideal source of information. Some records are saved because of government regulations, fiscal requirements, or good business practices, but in any event, they all leave what is known as a *paper trail.*

Generally, the following records are kept by most, if not all, business establishments:

- Company policies and procedures
- Training plans—types, instructions, materials, and schedules of personnel assigned
- Work rules and standards
- Safety and maintenance records
- Safety meeting records, safety directives, personnel accident records, and damage to property records
- Personnel and medical records—human resources may hamper or restrict your inspection of these records, but you do have the ability to inspect reports of injuries or sicknesses that occurred on the job (particularly worker's compensation cases)
- Employee reviews and performance evaluations
- Employee complaints and suggestions

Also consider the following:

- Building designs or plans
- People or vehicle traffic patterns in or around the business premises
- Location and type of safety fixtures, warning systems, emergency systems, ventilation, heating and cooling systems, and so forth

Analysis

Whether the case is an investigation into an incident such as an accident or injury, or a criminal affair involving a family, a friend, a colleague, or company personnel, a brief listing or checklist of as many facts as possible should be deemed as most important. Following that, a consideration should be given to each point of information received and analyzed.

Analysis is a systematic process in an effort to identify contributing factors, causes, reasons, effects, and possible correction or restitution, all in an attempt to close the case on a positive note:

- Identify the event or incident by the use of Who, What, When, Where, Why, and in many instances, the most important, How. These are the basic questions of any investigation or inquiry.

- List each incident or fact separately and in order of its occurrence. This step will identify a time sequence and will be helpful when organizing a large quantity of information.
- Examine each fact, and turn each into a question:
  - Who reported and who discovered the incident? Who had a motive? Who did it? If others are involved, who helped in the commission of the crime or incident? Who saw or heard anything?
  - What happened? What crime was committed? What were the actions of the suspect or perpetrator? What weapons or tools were used? What evidence exists to support or refute claims of suspect? What do the witnesses know or what do they not know? What was the motive? What was the cause and effect? What was the particular *modus operandi* or implementation used in this case?
  - When did the incident happen? When was it discovered and when was notification made and by whom? When was the victim last seen, by whom? When was the suspect located or perpetrator apprehended?
  - Where is the location of the incident? Where was the victim found? Where was the property of interest or the stolen property found? Where were the witnesses? Where was the evidence found? Where is the suspect now? Where was the suspect located or the perpetrator apprehended?
  - Why did this happen; why did this incident occur? Why or what was the reason it was done or committed?
  - How did the incident occur or come about? How was it completed (the *modus operandi*), and are there more than one person or factors involved? How did the suspect arrive at the scene and leave the scene? How did the suspect obtain the tools or weapons? How does the client wish to pursue a prosecution? Does the client only wish termination and restitution? How much restitution can be realized? How can the company (or the institution) correct or address the problem caused by this incident?

The Process of Case Management

Other than a criminal investigation lawfully empowered by law enforcement, the employ of a private investigator by a specific client would initiate an investigation.

In conjunction with the above factors described in the *Analysis* process above, a good investigation follows the following fundamental procedures:

1. *Direction*—The most important component in any investigation is the reason and purpose for the investigation. If an investigator is to have any part in an

investigation of any type, he or she must understand and be made clear as to the following:

a. What type of inquiry or exploration may be required?
b. Who or what is the focus of that inquiry?
c. What may be required to complete that inquiry?

2. *Collection*—The accumulation of information and evidence, in whatever form, is brought to a central location for examination.
3. *Collation*—At this stage, all information is scrutinized and compared to determine if it may or may not be relevant. At this point in the investigation, all vital data are compiled by *a person* who has complete knowledge of all the responsibilities and tasks of each investigator assigned to the team.
4. *Evaluation*—This is the stage at which all of the information and intelligence is fully examined and analyzed as to its relationship, value, and relevance to the investigation at hand.
5. *Dissemination*—Upon completion of the analysis stage, the investigation may be concluded and the intelligence may be shared with the client or interested parties. If not concluded, intelligence that has been gathered will direct the investigator to a new direction or level of investigation.

The private investigator must remember that any information gained will most probably be more than can be used in the current investigation. Rather than discard this information that was accumulated by inquiry, interviews, research, and so forth, it should be saved in some manner. The time and effort put into any exploration should not be wasted and may be useful when the present investigation moves in another direction, or may be useful in some future investigation. The PI will never know if and when it may become useful.

Realizing that all data collected from any investigation is confidential and must be protected as such, the PI would do well to place this information in an in-house computer database which will make collecting, storing, and retrieving that information much quicker and easier than if compiled as hard copy. Note that the private investigator should ensure that when obtaining and maintaining data, the data should conform to relevant laws. This will include photographs and documents that can be scanned or downloaded to the computer.

To summarize, records and data collected during any investigation must be legally obtained and retained and must be securely protected from misuse and any unauthorized disclosure.

In addition,

1. The information should be fairly and lawfully processed.
2. It must be accurate.
3. It should be adequate and relevant for its purpose and should not be excessive.

4. It must be processed for limited purposes and protected from disclosure regarding the civil and privacy rights of the investigation's target or anyone else contained in the data.
5. All data, statements, reports, photos, and evidence must be kept securely, with only particular personnel having access.
6. It should not be kept out of secured data files longer than necessary, other than for a particular investigation where a client would have access to this data, or when required or presented in a court of law.

The Significance of Observation

All humans receive information inherently and routinely through their five senses—*sight, smell, touch, taste,* and *hearing.* Our brain sifts and examines this information and lets our body know continuously to beware of hurt, harm, gratification, or comfort. The signals we receive could be called perception—what we perceive as insight and observation, and the assessment or processing of that information.

A good investigator must be constantly aware of his or her five senses, particularly during an investigation or when face to face with another person. The classic quote by Sherlock Holmes to Dr. Watson, "You have seen but not observed," recognized that observation was the primary investigative tool of that time period. Prior to computers and the forensic sciences, police relied upon documentation, physical evidence, witnesses, and observation to solve a case. Today, because we rely heavily upon modern technology, many of us have lost or have not developed our observation skills. Observation requires your complete attention and practice.

> Every rookie police officer or novice private investigator has overlooked a piece of evidence or discarded information that was relevant to a case under investigation, so that because of inattention, lack of experience, or failure to slow down and observe, has lost out on the clue that could have broken or led to the conclusion of a case.

In addition, and most importantly, do not rely on preconceived notions, because it will impede your perspective and your approach to the investigation. We all have a genius within us, and it is up to us, individually, to develop that genius and apply it to the problem at hand.

The ability to retain knowledge, particularly when scanned for a short period, takes training. Moreover, the description and recognition of people is a skill that should not be neglected. Sooner or later, you will be called as a witness in court where you will be expected to describe exactly what was observed or whom or what did you see. This type of "eyeball" evidence may be the only implication that links a subject to a crime or occurrence.

Observation of the Individual

As a training tool, the novice investigator should get into the habit of looking at people as a professional investigator. Acquire an overall impression of the subject—male or female; how tall; what age; tall or short; fat, chubby, or thin; color, length, and style of hair; color of eyes; glasses, shape and type; wearing a hat, type and color; wearing shoes or sneakers, color; beard or mustache, type and color; and tattoos or scars, if so, type and location on the body. Note also if the subject is wearing jewelry that may be obvious, such as ear, nose, or lip rings or excessive gold chains or bracelets.

Include a complete description of the subject's dress: Does the subject wear casual, formal, or work clothes? Are the subject's clothing out of the ordinary for the season? Do the subject's clothing fit in with what those around the subject are wearing? Describe apparel type and color that appear to be odd and obviously stand out.

When first observing a person, attempt to do a mental inventory. Does the person appear nervous, agitated, or under some sort of stress? Or does the subject appear relatively calm? Does the subject exhibit obsessive behavior, touching certain objects incessantly, or checking certain activities twice, such as closing or locking doors before leaving? Concerning the subject's personality, is he or she aggressive or passive with other people? Is he or she reclusive or gregarious?

Additionally, when observing a subject, we have to conclude that a person's physical appearance may be considered an illustration into one's behavior. A person's dress, tattoos, jewelry, hairstyle, and makeup will signify a great deal about that subject, particularly if the subject's appearance is outside of the norm. In that case, it would mean an unconventional lifestyle, especially noticeable when that person attends formal events. The location or abode of a subject can confirm much in the way of messy or chaotic living conditions. It could indicate that the subject is mentally ill, is indigent because of little or no income, has many people living within the same quarters, may be a squatter who has taken over an abandoned home or unit, or has strong traces of drug use or drug manipulation.

But most importantly, though people may change their dress and appearance, they rarely manage to alter their mannerisms. The way they walk, move, frequent certain locales or places, and particularly their personal habits are all important aspects of their character.

Observation of the Locale

One of the more important activities that a private investigator must be aware of at all times is the locale he or she is or will be working in. If assigned to a tail, does the subject fit in with the area he or she is frequenting or visiting? Is the subject's behavior and dress in accord with the locale? Must the agent fit the profile in dress and demeanor for the location or area that he or she will be working? Will the agent have to employ special measures for the safety of him- or herself or his or her associates?

If assigned to a stakeout, whether it is in a vehicle or a building, are special precautions required to negate or counteract the chance of discovery? What special requirements will be needed on a long-term employment of agents and to prevent possible discovery?

Depending on the nature of the investigation, the location and areas that the subject will be located in or passing through should be considered as important as the profile of the subject.

Becoming a Prolific Constructive Investigator

It can be said that observation is the imagination's servant, but effective observation requires hard work and practice. In an effort to enhance one's skills, the following components can be used as a guide in the observation process:

1. *Adaptation*—We need to adapt by perceiving the world, the scene, and the investigation through many eyes. For the investigator, *tunnel vision* must be considered a negative aptitude that will only frustrate the outcome. Put yourself in someone else's shoes—the office worker, the laborer, the lawyer or doctor, and the security guard. Placing yourself in situations or predicaments of that other person will broaden your capability to search, examine, and ultimately find (observe) things that were or could have been overlooked.
2. *Creativity—The best investigators are the creative ones.* Become a student of practical psychology, observation, common sense, and perseverance. Train yourself to look at things in a new perspective. For example, while at a scene of a crime, ask yourself obviously peculiar questions (to yourself, of course) that may direct you to other areas or new directions. Try to think as the subject or perpetrator would have thought in like circumstances. What would he have done? How would he have done it? How would he expect to get away with it? Would he need or have needed help in any way?
3. *Focusing*—Focus on the subject or the issue. The investigator must be constantly aware of what he or she is trying to accomplish. Careful and direct observation of the subject, location, document, or object will bring about further inquiry. Although uniformity can dull our senses, consider that everything is unique in some way. Examine the object or circumstance in detail, view it from different angles and different viewpoints. Ask questions. Observe the peculiarities that separate comparable or familiar objects found at the scene of an incident. Consider this attribute a refined skill that is worth development. Do not accept other people's observations as correct or infallible, whether a witness or a colleague. But do consider such observations as a reason for further inquiry. Double-check or corroborate all sources of information.

4. *Scanning*—Whether one is interviewing, interrogating, or has a subject under observation, that person's dress, demeanor, jewelry, hairstyle, and makeup will tell you an abundant amount of information about how that person fits in or places himself in society, and his reaction to that society. Physical appearance and dress often relate to one's behavior. A more relaxed lifestyle will lead a person to wear clothing and jewelry quite different from the norm or the general public. This will be particularly notable at more formal affairs such as court proceedings, weddings or funerals, business functions, or upper-scale restaurants. Moreover, a person's manner of speech and articulation could also characterize his or her education, ignorance, heritage, or origin. Other characteristics to certain lifestyles are tattoos, which may denote gang or club affiliation. Different types of tattoos usually denote a person's demeanor and dress, and certain tattoos may be commonly found on certain young adults. An example would be small flowers or butterflies located on many young ladies within the spectrum of our society. Prison tattoos are less professional and are therefore more obvious. When scanning a scene, observe any chaotic conditions, disturbance, items out of place, or anything not the norm. A person's living space and everything therein can usually give clues as to the occupant and his lifestyle.
5. *Document and Records Examination*—Other than a particular document that requires experienced analysis and expert certification and testimony of that analysis, the examination of stacks of records may be considered the most monotonous and many times tedious effort that a private investigator can be involved in. However, we must remember that in most cases any writing, document, or form leaves a paper trail. This is particularly true when a business or an agency requires forms to be compiled, ledgers, records, memos, directives, correspondence, or any other document, whether required to be maintained or not.

Of importance to any investigation, consider that a paper trail may provide evidence or affirmation to other indications and may be the most important lead to further inquiry.

When an investigation includes the examination of any writing or document, it must be approached with the mindset that the investigator will find what he or she is looking for. If a collection of similar records or documents is quickly scanned, important facts or information may be overlooked. A quick scan of a particular set of records may be practiced to get a general idea of what the writing is and how it will be of use to the investigation.

Regarding the investigation of a particular subject or department within a business, an initial start could be an examination of only those records compiled, maintained, sent, received, or handled by the subject. In many cases, that would include the subject's subordinates, superiors, or other departments or entities. Any connection, no matter how insignificant upon first analysis, may turn out to be the key to the successful conclusion of the investigation. Corporations in particular are required to maintain all written business documents, especially those regarding financial dealings. Partners and shareholders are entitled to access these records.[1]

Generally, if there is an irregularity, and if the investigator digs deep enough and long enough, he or she will uncover the sought-after information.

For further information concerning the significance of observation see the following sections entitled "Surveillance," "The Communication Process," and "The Observation Process" for helpful hints and strategies.

Types of Investigations and Covert Operations

Conducting the Investigation

The following procedures may be followed in the management of an investigation:

1. Information is gathered and acquired from the following sources:

- Conscientious citizens
- Records and files from corporate and public agencies
- Cultivated sources
- Informers
- Various occupations (bartenders, cab drivers, street walkers, employees of concern)
- Former criminals, associates or acquaintances, homeless persons, and addicts
- Anonymous tips or information from former or dissatisfied friends, associates, girlfriends, spouses, and so forth

2. A skilled interrogation of the suspect is conducted:

- A successful investigator must also be a successful interrogator. The suspect who is considered the perpetrator is expected to be in possession of most of the information necessary for a favorable prosecution, and if questioned intelligently and firmly, the suspect can usually be induced to disclose the information in question.

- Effectiveness will depend on the investigators' craft (expertise), logic, and psychological insight that he or she will use along with as much relevant information as can be accumulated. This will also include the vigorous questioning of one who is reluctant to divulge information.

As noted, a successful investigator must also be a successful interrogator. Interrogation is a skill—an art—an intellectual game that will be won by the person who is mentally faster and can immediately take advantage of an opening or a weakness.

3. Circumstantial evidence will be collected that will corroborate other evidence or can stand alone in convincing the court. This could include evidence such as the following:

- Blood, DNA, hair, fibers
- Ballistics, weapons
- Biology and pathology
- Fingerprints, footprints, palmprints
- Tools, tool marks, paint, glass, and so forth
- Document examination
- Surveillance photos, tapes, and recordings

Identifying the Perpetrator

- *Eyewitness Testimony*—The ideal identification.
- *Circumstantial Evidence*—Proof of facts or circumstances alone or in connection with other facts. (The identification of the perpetrator can be inferred.)
- *Motive*—Personal gain, desire for revenge, employment problems, arguments, quarrels, and angry statements.
- *Opportunity*—Physically possible to commit the crime, opportunity–means–access.

Larceny, Burglary, and Robbery—Motivated by economic gain.

Assault and Murder—For the professional, usually incidental to greed, disputes over division of spoils between coconspirators or operational or property rights; for the amateur, domestic situations, love, hate, desire for revenge; or when the offense is without motive, by reason of a deranged mind of the perpetrator.

- *Confession*—The major objective of any investigation; identifies the perpetrator and gives the motive, the opportunity, and the means, in the perpetrator's own words.

Procedures, expertise, and talent vary with different security personnel and investigators, as well as the type or seriousness of the investigation and how it is to be carried out. Therefore, the investigator should follow some simple rules in conducting a professional investigation:

- Although the loss prevention or security officer or private investigator may have the authority to initiate an inquiry or investigation into any process, procedure, possible or apparent loss, or suspicious activity or circumstances, he or she should have a *legitimate reason* to conduct an investigation on or into another person or incident.
- He or she should respect the *privacy* and other rights of the people involved in the investigation.
- He or she should refrain from making any unnecessary comments or opinions to anyone, whether they are part of the investigation or not. This is not to say that investigators, other members of the investigative team, and their supervisors should not discuss among themselves feelings, thoughts, opinions, the direction or target of the investigation, evidence gained or to be gathered, or the complete process of the investigation.

Conclusion

The final resolution in any investigation will be the following:

1. The facts necessary to prove the guilt of the accused in a court of law beyond a reasonable doubt must be gathered.
2. The existence of a crime must be established.
3. The defendant must be identified and associated with the crime and the crime scene.
4. Credible and competent witnesses must be available and willing to testify in court.
5. Physical evidence (along with expert witnesses) must be appropriately identified with the chain of custody established.
6. All of the above, presented in an orderly and logical fashion by the prosecutor.

Internal Investigations

Investigation of Loss—Theft and Shrinkage

For our purposes, loss (shrinkage) is described as the loss or possible loss of anything of value by known or unknown means. Initially and in actuality, there may have been no determination that the loss was due to some factor such as theft, damage, a paper loss, or just missing in some unknown manner.

Theft (larceny) may be described as property stolen from someone, in that the thief did take and carry away property belonging to another. The stolen property can belong to a business or retail establishment, an employee, a customer, a visitor, or any individual. If it is taken from the business facility or store, the theft can be internal (by an employee) or external (by a person who enters a business facility and shoplifts or commits a theft or fraud).

Shrinkage can be caused by several means. It includes internal and external theft, pilferage, intentional and unintentional damage, paper loss, and poor record keeping and stock control. The investigation will be directed toward a particular goal depending on the specific circumstances and conditions.

Other than an undercover operation, there are two types of methods for any investigation:

1. *Overt*—An overt investigation is sometimes unavoidable because the occurrence may be widely known by the workforce even before loss prevention has become aware of the problem. Some advantages or impediments to this are that the employees, once loss prevention is informed, will know that loss prevention officers are on top of the situation and are immediately involved in an investigation. There is also the possibility of outside auditors and investigators becoming involved in the investigation. Because of this close scrutiny, the thefts will cease. But, the perpetrator might become very cautious and lay low for a period, and then resume his or her activity at a later time.
2. *Covert*—A covert investigation of an incident or suspected incident of a theft, whatever type, consists of conducting the investigation as secretly and as discreetly as possible, with as few people as possible being aware of such an investigation. It may involve background investigations of the employees who could be involved, undercover operations, various surveillance methods in varying degrees, and prudent interviews in an attempt to gain information or evidence. The advantage of a covert operation is that the person or the perpetrators under investigation are unaware that they are under suspicion and will continue to commit their activities. In this way, if nothing else, the possibility exists that they will be caught in the act. Another advantage is that little reaction and attention will be perceived, and the investigation will not disrupt normal operations or the morale of the workforce.

Possible Beneficial Consequences

Although an investigation is performed for a particular purpose, there may be other unintended benefits that management may find useful. Collateral data may be forthcoming that may not be of any help in the investigation but could benefit the corporation by identifying conditions or procedures that could affect security, safety, and financial standing, some of which are as follows:

- Procedures are lacking and require instant rectification.
- Management supervision could be evaluated, identifying dislikes or problems with managers and supervisors and negative emotions and low morale among the personnel.
- Communication between management and subordinate personnel requires improvement.
- Safety committee (if operational) lacks direction or authority.
- Hazard control devices or procedures require immediate revision.
- Conditions of safety and security should be corrected.
- Company personnel consciously bypass or ignore certain safety procedures or security or access controls.
- Internal intelligence could include information about varied conditions in the workplace or with various job positions.
- Fiduciary and bookkeeping controls are lacking.

Ethics and Obligations

Obligation to Report a Crime to the Police

Because we have taken into account that a private investigator or security officer is a private person (a private citizen), it is every citizen's obligation to report a crime to the correct law enforcement authority.

In some states, a misdemeanor can be compromised (an agreement not to prosecute—a resolution with or without considerations). As an example, an employee is accused of and has admitted to a misdemeanor larceny of U.S. currency from his company and, subsequently, can have his employment terminated, restitution of any money stolen made to the employer (the victim), and not be prosecuted in any manner.

However, a felony cannot be compromised, and any crime of this magnitude should be reported to the police or a law enforcement authority for their determination and any action they might take.

As a private investigator, whether the investigation is conducted in-house or off the business premises, we must be considerate of the client or employer's position, and for whatever reason, his request to keep the results of the investigation in house and not report them to the police or in any public manner. Real-life management decisions such as this are not uncommon, mainly because of the negative publicity or harm to the company's goodwill that may ensue because of public disclosure.

The private investigator must be cognizant of the gravity of this type of behavior as to whether he or she is complicit in some manner in not reporting a serious crime, or in serving as an accessory to the crime (after the fact), in which the private investigator could become involved in a criminal action at a later time. The final decision by the private investigator will depend on the seriousness of the crime and the personal and professional ethics that govern his or her conduct.

Conversely, there will be some clients who have been so outraged as the victim of a crime that they will demand an arrest, no matter what. Investigators must not place themselves in a position of placating or complying with those demands. An arrest can be made only with probable cause—to do otherwise would place the investigator in criminal and civil jeopardy.

Deceptive Behavior

There is no doubt that a private investigator may have to use some type of deceptive or deceitful demeanor in order to elicit information when there may be no other way. The success of gleaning information personally or by telephone depends on one's ingenuity and self-assertiveness. Most information sought would include social security numbers, date of birth, home or apartment addresses, city, town, relatives, occupation, employment, credit and banking information, marriage, children, siblings, education, licensing and certifications, among others. The list of information that may be required and how it can be gathered during an investigation is only as extensive as the investigator's imaginativeness.

The use of some pretexts, whether in person or by phone, are described as follows:

- Pretending to be an employee of an electric, telephone, or water company, or a paging service.
- Pretending to be a delivery person (flowers, pizza, freight, etc.).
- Pretending by telephone to be a UPS or FedEx employee attempting to deliver a package but requiring address or other information in order to make the delivery.
- Passing oneself off as a credit or bank examiner or a bank employee checking account information, or acting in the pretense of a customer service representative or retail sales associate who "made a mistake" on a credit card purchase and wishes to confirm the subject's personal information.

The success an investigator can achieve will depend on the reasonable and believable comportment that he or she wishes to fabricate. Ordinarily the novice investigator will require some training and experience in this area before any adequate results are achieved.

Cautionary Note

The private investigator must be cautious not to pass oneself off as a public or law enforcement officer. To do so is a crime, which could incur arrest, loss of license, and possible civil liability.

> Moreover, the use of surreptitious behavior or deception to gain entry into or within a private premises or a building secured from the general public could place the investigator in criminal jeopardy (burglary, criminal trespass).

The use of deceptive behavior is a useful tool for the investigator and is generally considered a lawful use of this type of conduct. However, certain activity might cause concern, such as unscrupulous actions or a question of decency.

A General Classification of Employee Dishonesty

The Dishonest Employee

Ordinarily, the following types of dishonesty by employees can be found in all business enterprises. Dishonesty can be encountered in private and public enterprises and can encompass corporations from retail establishments, "blue chip" enterprises, large defense contractors, to bureaucratic entities.

The White-Collar Criminal

White-collar crime could include embezzlement of funds by executives and managers, accountants, and bookkeepers; kickbacks to buyers; the padding of expense accounts and vouchers; the making of payroll checks out to nonexisting employees; and theft from petty cash accounts. See also Chapter 6, "White-Collar Crime."

Dishonest Management Employees

These employees, because of their position or length of term within the company, have access to or security clearance concerning various assets. They include the security officer, who because of his or her status and position may have complete access to everything within the company.

The General Company Thief

This employee may be the office worker or anyone employed anywhere within the facility who routinely takes small items for his or her own personal use. Usually taken off premises, items may include pencils, pens, notebooks, paper, and other stationery supplies. Although this may appear to be minor to the employee taking these items, the expense of ongoing replacement to the company can be great.

Janitorial and Part-Time Staff

Many businesses employ a contractual janitorial service for housekeeping or general upkeep. Although most of these employees are honest and hard working, many are not because of poor wages, poor personal and work habits, and transitory work histories. Because they usually have access to all areas of the company, they have the ability to take and secrete items easily.

Consider also part-time employees, many who are teenagers (who at times seem to care less) or those in need of a second income and who work at night when there is little or no supervision. Under these conditions, they also have many opportunities to steal from their employer.

In addition, particularly in a retail business establishment, we have the following dishonest employees.

The Dishonest Cashier

The actions by this employee may include the following: the use of bogus void transactions to steal the same amount of cash relating to the transaction; the pocketing of cash from the customer rather than ringing up the sale (till tapping); the use of a company's refund policy to create bogus customer returns and pocket the money; the cashier "underringing" merchandise for friends, relatives, or other employees; a cash office employee or supervisor who may remove small amounts of cash from cash drawers prior to delivery to a cashier, and that will be considered minor errors by that cashier; also, the employee in charge of the cash office holding back cash from routine deposits or armored car pick-ups one or more days for various reasons (floating).

The Dishonest Customer Pick-Up or Service Department Employee

These employees include those who assist or load excessive, substituted, or unpaid merchandise into vehicles for a relative, friend, or employee, or a customer in return for a large "tip." Also included are those employees who work in the service department who commit to extra services or "undercover deals" for the customer and in return, are compensated for that service.

The Underwriting Salesman

This is the sales employee who intentionally miswrites or underwrites an item or merchandise regarding quantities or prices on a sales voucher or sales slip for friends, relatives, or personal financial gain.

The Receiving, Shipping, and Warehouse Employee

Working alone or in collusion with other employees, truckers, or deliverymen, this employee steals large items of merchandise by undercounting items received on the receiving dock, loading extra items into a truck off the shipping dock, issuing more expensive merchandise than purchased to a customer (warehouse worker), or stashing items outside of the facility for later clandestine pickup. This area would also include the mailroom employee whose responsibility is to ship via freightage or mail merchandise to customers, but will also include shipping stolen items to friends, relatives, and to oneself.

Why They Steal

Some common factors that can be attributed to or are characteristic of certain employees who may have an inclination to steal are as follows:

Substance Abuse—Alcohol or drugs; alcoholics and drug addicts are honesty risks. Their expense becomes greater as time goes by and therefore the need for cash to satisfy the habit. Their moral judgment becomes blurred, and any latent tendencies toward crime will arise. Count on problems that will occur on the job, including lateness, workdays lost, poor work habits, and of course, theft.

Gambling—Particularly the chronic gambler. Gambling is as much of a disease as alcohol and drugs, with the same abuses, problems, and tendencies. Caution must be used if gambling is discovered on the premises. It can cause morale problems, reduction of productivity, changes of attitudes, and the possibility of infusion of other illegal activity and unsavory characters.

Family Problems—A great tragedy such as illness or death in a family can cause unexpected or long-term hardship. People do many things that they would not do under normal circumstances. Divorce, alimony, childcare, maintaining a second marriage and family, bankruptcy, family budget issues, family health or legal problems, and addictions can lead a troubled employee to be vulnerable to the thought of stealing as expenses roll in and become overwhelming.

The Long-Term Employee—Whose honesty is taken for granted. These employees have more authority, freedom of movement, and ability to conduct business with little or no supervision. Sometimes hostile, the employee may tell people to "butt out." He may get annoyed, particularly when questioned or examined (a telltale sign for the auditor to inspect more closely). He may also appear to maintain a higher standard of living.

The Actor—Plays up to the boss or any superior. This employee becomes overly friendly with members of the security staff, does personal favors for anyone who he can curry favoritism with, and basically sets up smoke screens for himself.

The Rule Violator—This employee leaves early and comes to work late and takes long breaks; makes personal use of telephones, computers, and copy machines; smokes where not permitted; may use unauthorized exits when directed otherwise; fails to live by the rules; and shows a lack of responsibility in handling money and merchandise.

The "High-Roller"—This employee lives high or beyond his means, and while maintaining that status, may claim that he is the recipient of an inheritance or an estate. In order to meet his needs, this employee turns to ways in which he can satisfy his habits or lifestyle.

The Spendthrift—This employee cannot handle money and is always in debt. He is always borrowing from fellow coworkers and company plans or benefits (i.e., 401K, company credit union). He is an impulse buyer. Creditors keep calling or inquiring at his or her place of business.

The Disgruntled Employee—This employee is making up by stealing for what he believes should rightfully be his (such as failure to get a wage increase or benefits), or by committing thefts, damage, or disruption of business in order to "get even" with the boss or the company for some wrong or imagined wrong.

The "Joiner"—This employee succumbs to peer group pressure or goes along with the group so as to be accepted.

The Chronic Liar—This employee lies under pressure or to protect another, is afraid of punishment, is maladjusted, and lies frequently and without reason to do so.

The Mentally Unstable—These employees may be unstable or have guilt feelings and want to get caught, or are looking for attention.

How They Steal

Methodology

In order for a crime to be committed, one requires the intent, opportunity, and ability. Consequently, because intent and ability are indefinable components, only opportunity can be considered the controlling factor in crime deterrence by a loss prevention department. By setting up controls particular to an operation or function conducted by an employee, the opportunity to complete the act is diminished if not entirely eliminated. How well those controls are in place will depend on the reported and anticipated loss, the vulnerability of the operation or function, the appropriate resources and measures applied, and the management of those constraints.

Each criminal act committed by an employee will be specific to the function under his or her control or influence. Therefore, the private investigator, security officer, and, particularly, the undercover operator must become familiar with the procedures, tasks, and functions of all of the operations and departments noted here so that he or she are aware of the shortcomings, the potential for misdeed, and those controls that may be needed.

The following areas are considered vulnerable to some type of theft or misdeed and must have some type of restraint for the employee to adhere to and to make accountable for any job performance that might be subject to inquiry:

- Employees creating situations for easy theft by friends or relatives.
- Merchandise, property, or equipment taken out the "back door" by employees.
- Materials taken upon leaving for the day and counting on no bag inspection; expensive merchandise or proprietary information easily concealed on the person and removed from the premises.
- Collusion between employees from different departments.
- Check forgery or fraudulent issuance of checks.
- Embezzlement.
- Various types of thefts by night employees.
- Theft by day or night housekeeping crews.
- Manipulation of computers and systems for the benefit of others.
- Theft of computer time and proprietary information or programs.
- Theft of services such as use of telephone, fax machine, and copy machine, work time, sick time, and so forth.
- Worker's compensation fraud.
- Unauthorized access via keys or duplication of keys for larcenous purposes.

Some Indicators of Employee Theft

The following instances may indicate possible theft by an employee or the probability that theft has or may occur:

- Inventory shortages.
- During close observation of all employees during regular rounds or inspection by the security officer, he or she notices sudden movements, overfriendliness, or whispering by employees.
- Constant complaints by an employee about the company, compensation, the administration, or favoritism.
- Bragging to fellow coworkers about gambling winnings or losses.

- Visual signs of alcohol or drug abuse.
- Maladjusted employee who may be emotionally unstable, erratic in behavior, and unpredictable; or one who was well adjusted but who then becomes unstable, abusive, sarcastic, sullen, or withdrawn without any immediate apparent or known cause.
- Apparent signs of an employee living beyond his or her means, including expensive clothes, new cars, new home, infidelity, excessive alimony or child support, garnishment, bragging about his or her lifestyle.
- Accusing another coworker of suspicious behavior or theft.

The security officer or undercover operator who becomes aware of problems such as these or any leading indicator of wrongdoing among employees should consider close observation, the gathering of evidence, and ultimately management involvement. Any change in deportment or work habits could be a sign of potential vulnerability. Controls could include the routine testing by honesty shoppers, methodical checking of employees' packages upon leaving the business facility, but most of all, an active interest, conducted surreptitiously, should be directed to any employee who appears to fall into the above categories. We must consider that most employees are honest, and that only some will affect the company's shrinkage and losses and other security problems. Accordingly, each case or incident must be based on its own merits.

The Dishonest Security Officer

Bear in mind that one of the most important subjects in any business venture is that of the security or loss prevention officer who is dishonest. Here we have an employee who has been given particular confidence, responsibility, and trust over and above general company personnel, operating with less internal controls than management and their subordinates, and the ability to access all confines and spaces, including protected and secluded areas of the company.

This is an area in which any business enterprise must appreciate that personnel hired to protect the security and safety of the company, its employees, customers, and visitors, should be of the highest caliber and above reproach. Although infrequent, a security officer will succumb as a victim to his or her own weaknesses. In these cases, an investigative agency may be called upon.

Actions by a deceitful security officer might include monetary exchange for favorable actions and releases of persons arrested for a crime. This may include shoplifters, and minor thieves within the company. Moreover, other dishonest employees, who may or may not be in managerial or administrative positions once discovered by the officer, use blackmail against these employees to realize a financial gain.

Preemployment Inquiry and Job Satisfaction

How does one secure the services of an honest security officer? And once hired, how can we maintain that honesty and integrity at the highest level possible? The most generally accepted answer would be the application of intense preemployment investigation prior to hiring any security officer. This may include multiple interviews; criminal history; driving record; credit, financial, and personal reference checks; drug screening; and work and education verification. The ability or prerequisite of certification as a bonded employee would also involve an investigation by other individuals. Because of the nature of the position that the applicant is applying for and the responsibilities that will be expected of him or her, the hiring and application process should be considered more intense than that for any other job seeker. Consider also that a decent wage with promotional opportunities, appropriate salary raises, and suitable accolades should be additional indicators toward job satisfaction.

Integrity Testing

Following that, close supervision and the possible use of routine integrity testing of the individual officer may be considered. Although some businesses and police departments conduct ongoing testing of this type, it may be considered one of the most distinct factors in the development of low employee morale. No one wishes to be questioned or examined in any way as to his or her character, integrity, or veracity after they have been employed for a period of time. Procedural testing of this type can cause a debilitating consequence on a group of security officers where cohesiveness, camaraderie, and productivity can be affected. This will be particularly so for the long-time employee who is or has been considered an excellent officer in all ways. Once an employee has been surreptitiously tested and then finds out that he or she was the subject of such a test, the attitude and loyalty of that employee toward the company may be completely destroyed. No matter how the process is handled by management, the erosion of that loyalty may occur immediately, or for the group over a period of time if the process becomes a standard practice.

But make no mistake about it, morale will decline sooner or later. This may be considered the reason most loss prevention and security managers will not become involved in testing the honesty of their subordinates unless they have substantial reason to do so.

Nevertheless, it would be unwise to believe that a security officer or any employee would never commit a dishonest act. Depending on circumstances, the use of some type of testing may have to be considered in order to determine the guilt or innocence of the person under scrutiny.

Be mindful, however, if integrity testing is to be conducted within a business establishment, legal counsel should be obtained in order to determine that the reason and type of test might be considered judicious and legal.

There are some that question the use of integrity testing in that it may be considered a form of entrapment.

Entrapment

Simply put, entrapment may be defined as when the method used to obtain evidence was such to create a substantial risk that the offense would be committed by a person not otherwise disposed to commit it, *but that the subject was induced or encouraged to engage in such an act that would place him or her in jeopardy.* The inducement or encouragement must be active in nature. Conduct merely affording a person an opportunity to commit an offense does not constitute entrapment. In other words, setting a trap to catch a criminal in the act may be said to be proper. However, inducing or encouraging someone to commit the act is illegal.

Hiring and Supervising the Security Officer

In a study that included 69 law enforcement departments across the United States, it was shown that the use of personality tests commonly used in the hiring and application process has some validity in identifying those important relationships that may or are linked to corruption.[2]

In addition to the identification of personality traits, there are some factors or indicators that should be considered during the hiring process. These would include the following[3]:

- Tolerance of or toward others
- Willing and able to maintain long-term relationships
- Achievement oriented
- Willing to accept responsibility and blame
- More likely to be controlled by guilt or remorse

A business relies on its security force to be its eyes and ears in all aspects of security and safety, and expects officers employed by them to be above reproach. Therefore, there can be no doubt that such close inquiry of police candidates can be related to the same type of investigation for security officer applicants. Personality testing, along with close attention to an applicant's personal background and work history, would increase the probability of hiring an honest officer. How intense and essential the process may be would depend on the level of security expected and the requisite credentials of the applicant.

Once hired, there should be a probationary period that will include exposure to the company's policies and procedures, asset control policies, and necessary training for the position. Within this period, in particular, the officers' immediate supervisor must offer ongoing adequate and effective training and close supervision.

Whether during the probationary period of the security officer or subsequently thereafter, the supervisor must be cognizant of the following[4]:

- On-the-job misconduct (found to be the number one predictor of corruption). This would include violations of company policy, fraud, misappropriation of property, unlawful confiscation, pilferage, extortion, sexual misconduct, favoritism or preferential treatment, to name a few. No matter how trivial the transgression, a supervisor must be constantly observant and react immediately to any misbehavior by a subordinate.
- Difficulty getting along with others.
- Indications of immaturity, irresponsibility, and unreliability.

The question will arise that once the security officer has been hired and accepted as an honest and viable candidate in protecting the assets of the company, how do we maintain the same attributes we originally observed in the officer? *The answer is simply—effective supervision.*

A good supervisor must be constantly aware of the conduct and work habits of his subordinates. Their level of expertise, levelheadedness, honest reasoning, attitude, tenacity, leadership ability, and demeanor with others is important. But so, too, is the officer's complete acceptance of his department's mission, ability to work with little or no supervision when necessary, and aptitude for the required compilation and maintenance of records. Values such as these may be considered good characteristics of professionalism, competence, and confidence.

But the supervisor must also have the necessary attributes to receive a faithful and reliable reaction from his or her subordinate. He must have leadership qualities, be truthful, act with fairness in all dealings, promote excellence, praise good conduct and work, be able to admonish when necessary, seek innovation, and most importantly, possess high ethical standards.

However, there may come a time when a security officer commits an act of dishonesty. If so, and a determination of guilt is made, termination of employment must be the accepted norm. In other words, "zero tolerance" and, depending on the seriousness of the offense and company policy, arrest and prosecution may be mandatory. Other than that, if suspicion of unauthorized or illegal activity becomes known, the possibility of an integrity test or a sting operation may be required to resolve the question. If such an activity is warranted and authorized by upper management, the company may wish to hire an investigative agency that has some experience in this type of covert investigation.

Notwithstanding a valid suspicion or determination of a dishonest officer, the use of integrity testing as a routine policy within a loss prevention/security department should be avoided so as not to diminish or destroy the morale of the group.

Additional Types of Investigations

Firearms Investigation

Whenever a crime is committed with the use of a firearm, the police will become involved in the investigation. However, the private investigator should be informed and somewhat knowledgeable in what a firearms investigation entails.

America was the birthplace of the revolver, and has since become prolific and many times indiscriminate in their manufacture and distribution. As a consequence, most serious crimes committed in this country have entailed the use or possession of a firearm. Frequently, the crime that involves a firearm found at the scene will be solved simply by tracing the ownership of the gun. The evidence at a crime scene might only include the firearm, a bullet, a cartridge case, the wound, and the trajectory or distance of the bullet. Moreover, gunpowder residue may be found on the victim (estimating distance of discharge) or the perpetrator. An experienced technician should conduct testing in this area.

Tracing the Gun

A lethal weapon found at the scene of a crime must be traced as to ownership and history, or at least the last possessor. Who was the last owner? Was the weapon government property? Had it been? Official records may be consulted as to the history of the weapon, including information such as the manufacturer, distribution, sale, and owner. These records may be maintained by firearm manufacturers, dealers, and local, county, state, or federal sources. In cases such as this, the paper trail is most important in assigning ownership. In addition, if the weapon had been stolen from its rightful owner prior to the present crime under investigation, the preceding police report and investigation might direct the investigator to a suspect.

Be aware that many handguns may be of foreign manufacture brought into our country surreptitiously by service personnel during or after World War II, or the Korean or the Vietnam conflicts, and therefore have no record to track.

Nomenclature of the Firearm and Ammunition

Unless the novice investigator is familiar with firearms, he or she must have a rudimentary understanding of how to describe and identify a firearm and the ammunition used by that weapon.

A handgun (a pistol) may be classed into several types—*revolver, automatic, semiautomatic,* and *single shot.* A minimum description of a firearm would include the *type, make* (manufacturer), *model, caliber, serial number,* and *finish.* The serial number will be found on various surfaces of the weapon, and the most common examples of the finish may be *blue, nickel,* or *parkerized* (a dull gray appearance conducive to military weapons). Generally, the characteristics of a bullet and cartridge case and the markings found on each will usually identify the type of weapon used (revolver, semiautomatic pistol, rifle, shotgun, automatic rifle, or machine gun).

Expertise is needed to determine general characteristics of any firearm and the bullet used. Identifying characteristics will include the following:

- *Bullet*—Manufacturer, caliber, weight in grains, weight and type of powder, material (soft nose, dum-dum, lead, brass), cannelures (grooves on the curved surface), number of lands and grooves and direction of twist, contour or shape (although may be distorted), base (flat, hollow), and size and weight for shotgun pellets.
- *Cartridge Case*—If found at the scene, trademark, caliber, shape, markings, firing pin or breech face markings, extractor or ejector markings.

If a cartridge case was found at the scene, the initial indication would be that a semiautomatic or automatic weapon was used, and examination of extractor markings on the brass casing would confirm that fact. But if no cartridge case is found, it may not mean that a revolver was used in the crime, it may simply mean that the perpetrator picked up the brass before leaving.

Theft of Services

By an Employee

Concerning an employee who uses the services or equipment of the company that employs him or of another for personal use without permission commits a crime. This may include the personal use of a company computer, telephone or fax machine, or the copy machine, unless permission has been granted for such use. The "crimes" noted above may be considered petty in loss, and generally, the police will attempt to decline an investigation because of its trivial nature and the time and effort that may be required for a conviction. Other than the employer's policy for zero tolerance, and once caught, termination will be the norm, most companies overlook minor instances such as these with only a stern warning.

The theft of time can also be a serious offense, in that if the employee has the ability to misrepresent the actual hours worked, thereby increasing his or her weekly salary, an actual larceny has taken place. If the employee extends work and meal breaks in excess of the work rules or has another employee punch him in or out and thereby creating a false work record, an offense has been committed. Further, the misuse of sick time (worker's compensation) is not only an insurance fraud but also a theft of service. Instances such as these could and will affect the company in the long run, in addition to creating a low morale among those honest employees who become aware of these transactions. The company's reaction to these types of offenses depends on how the company's administration views it, and how far they wish to punish the offender.

By Other Means

Today the copy machine has become the favorite instrument for the professional and nonprofessional thief to copy and steal files and records without removing the originals from the premises. Unless caught in the act of copying, no one will ever know that sensitive and confidential information has been removed or compromised. In large businesses, many machines are located in various locations throughout the premises, usually separate and apart, out of general view or in discreet recesses. Controls in the use of a copy machine when large numbers of personnel have access, can include the use of closed-circuit television (CCTV); maintenance of logs at each machine noting time of use, number of copies, and name and department of the user; and keeping a close tab on the machine counter that numbers the copies produced. Theft of services is usually a misdemeanor in most states, and the offender making use of a copy machine under these circumstances commits not only a theft of services but also if applicable, the theft of business records and files.

Credit Card Fraud

Today, fraud with credit cards, and recently debit cards, has become so extensive that various types of business enterprises and banking institutions have suffered great losses.

Most states now include a *public benefit card* in their statutes along with credit and debit cards. It is considered unlawful for a person to use a credit, debit, or public benefit card when in the course of obtaining or attempting to obtain property or a *service* when that person knows such a card to be stolen, revoked, or canceled. In addition, a person is guilty of criminal possession of stolen property with intent to benefit self or a person other than the owner of the card, or to impede the recovery of the card by the owner, and when the property consists of a credit, debit, or public benefit card. Generally, a person who possesses two or more stolen credit, debit, or public benefit cards is presumed to know that such cards were stolen and is guilty of criminal possession, which may be considered a felony in most states. When used in the purchase of obtaining or attempting to obtain property or services, the perpetrator may be additionally charged with the larceny and unlawful use. Be aware that along with the local police agency, the U.S. Secret Service is now mandated to investigate these crimes.

Cheating Spouses

One of the more unpleasant (but lucrative) assignments for a private investigator is determining if, how, and when a person is cheating on his or her spouse or "loved one." One reason would be because of the insidious nature of the act upon a mate, which can bring on many insecurities, resentment, and an upheaval of the family unit. Add to that the probability of a confrontation between the offender and the offended, and the hostility between the investigator and the target which more often than not will surface sooner or later.

If this type of investigation is one of your fields of interest, the following is offered:

- Suspicions are discovered or accelerated with a sudden change in behavior by the disloyal partner.
- At the beginning of an affair, the cheater is more attentive to his or her spouse or loved one.
- Because of his guilty conscious, the subject will find unnecessary fault with the partner.
- The subject tends to lose interest in activities at home, with children, with relatives, and with friends.

Common indicators will include the following:

- Working excessive overtime without additional income realized.
- Returning home late or staying out late without reasonable excuses.
- Undergoing a change in sexual habits or a decrease in sexual interest with the partner.
- At the residence, receiving strange phone calls or calls coupled with whispered conversation, or the partner displaying sudden panic and hanging up when someone enters the room.
- Noticing smells of perfume or alcohol.
- Purchasing a personal pager.
- Often not being available at work.
- Excessively using the Internet, sending uncommon cryptic e-mail messages, and erasing the computer history.
- Logging additional mileage on the personal vehicle's odometer.
- Hiding or having phone or cell phone bills sent to another address or box office.
- Being unable to explain receipts or personal effects in wallet or car.
- Being unable to explain unusual gifts, travel, restaurant, motel/hotel, and other unknown charges on credit card billings.
- Having gas station credit card slips with uncommon or unknown locations.

Once determined that the spouse wishes to hire a private investigator and initiate an investigation, the investigator should consider the reason for the contract. It may be for a determination for a virtuous divorce hearing, a nullification of a prenuptial agreement, or strictly a vengeful action. Whatever the reason, the investigator should be aware of the circumstances surrounding the case in question before embarking on any investigation of this type.

Realize also that some cheaters are very shrewd and have an ability to cover their tracks, effectively leading another life. The cheater who is in control of his or her life can handle two sexual partners with ease and knows that much will be lost unless his personal affairs can be managed efficiently.

Counseling the Client (Complainant)

Prior to any initiation of an investigation into a cheating spouse, the investigator should advise the client that it would be in his or her interest to consider the following first:

- Contact an attorney if there is a possibility of any divorce proceedings, a separation, or a share of the family assets.
- However the outcome of the investigation, seek a therapist if the anguish and agony will be too great to bear, whether or not there is reconciliation.
- Prepare to remain calm and in control—do not resort to physical violence, and attempt to refrain from aggressive arguments. Remember that the offended spouse needs to come out ahead at the end of the relationship.

Tracing Missing Persons

Many times an investigator can often start and conclude an investigation without leaving the office. Thousands of people go missing every year for various reasons. Some may be missing because of some criminal act. However, many will be missing because they are running from some matrimonial or financial problems in their lives, which they may feel they cannot overcome or cope with. In addition, there are those "custodial interference" cases where one parent, estranged or not, takes or abducts a child in violation of a court order. Custodial interference and teenage runaways are among the most prevalent in missing person cases.

Generally, people who go missing leave a paper trail that can be followed. This trail can be followed by the use of a database or online data, which will be enumerated below. Other databases can also be of use in any inquiry of a missing person. This can include registers of birth, marriages, death, and social security, to name a few. Note also that persons who have a particular occupational expertise will usually follow that same path.

Many times a person wishing to "disappear" will change his or her name. If so, cross-reference a social security number, court records, or a secondary source, such as a credit reference or credit history. It has been said that 90% of information that an investigator needs to locate a "missing person" can be found through databases.

Realize, however, that a person who truly wishes to "disappear" for whatever reason, and has some knowledge of how to do it, need only keep away from relatives, old friends, haunts, neighborhoods, any numerical communication, or any trace of a reference to a name, in reality, completely erasing and distancing himself from his prior life.

Following are some of the areas of inquiry that an investigator might employ in the investigation of a missing person.

Skip Tracing and Missing Persons Searches

The term *skip tracing* originally meant tracking down and finding a person who was hiding from someone or something or just wished to disappear. Today, it can mean many things, including locating individuals or businesses for a variety of reasons.

Today, there is a growing industry of proprietary commercial databases that make an extensive assemblage of public records available online to the private investigator. Not too long ago, public records such as property deeds; death, marriage, and divorce records; and business name filings, fictitious and corporate, would involve a personal trip to the county clerks and county and state courthouses.

Finding a missing person or tracing anyone has been the essential element of the investigative profession. Much data come from credit headers, which is a portion of the credit record on each person that is available through several commercial services to licensed private investigators, insurance investigators, credit companies, and corporate personnel departments on new-hire checks. There are some governmental agencies (state and federal) that restrict access to certain data types or prohibit the sale of information to commercial databases for a profit. Full credit reports are more strictly controlled because of the Consumer Credit Reporting Reform Act (see Appendix A for details). There are times when information is not available or is hard to come by, and the investigator may resort to deceptive methods to gain that information. For the licensed private investigator, accessing information through illegal techniques can only harm the profession and the standard private investigators wish to achieve. We must realize that as misuse, misappropriation, and unscrupulous actions by investigators become the norm, government restrictions will become greater and more intrusive.

Consider that someone who wishes to "disappear" or actively attempts to hide his or her tracks for whatever reason should be deemed to be more difficult to locate than a person who simply lost contact with a family or friend. However, it is almost impossible not to completely leave some clue or indication as to one's whereabouts. Rarely does someone completely bury him- or herself with a new identity, as there will be some piece of information that can eventually uncover the subject's whereabouts.

Not too many years ago, any attempt to locate a missing person or to track down someone proved to be extremely difficult and somewhat arduous. It was time consuming, but if the investigator was persistent, results were usually positive. Today, we have computers to search central repositories of information and records that can easily be explored for the data requested. Ease of information did not exist as it does today. However, depending on the expertise and knowledge of the investigator, computer searches may not always be fruitful. Most times, computer use can be erratic and a bewilderment when some of the "hits" prove positive. Nevertheless, many files searched will give access to other paths of exploration for the investigator to follow. The key here is that persistence pays off with the explicit results.

During any trace search of a subject, the investigator must compile and maintain an activity log that will include dates, persons interviewed, records or databases examined, and any piece of information that might be helpful at a later date. Include also any information that was not helpful or was a dead end so that it may not have to be repeated.

If possible, the three elements of identification that an investigator should possess for a proficient search are the *subject's name, date of birth (or at least the approximate age), and the Social Security Number.* The necessity of obtaining at least two of these factors in any trace cannot be overstated.

A method should be set up, at least in the mind of the investigator, regarding a procedure of how and where to start the search. Primarily, the first step would be to determine where the subject was last seen or known to be; who was the last known contact; and names and addresses of relatives, friends, lovers, and business associates or partners. Also contact present and previous employers for personnel records that may show emergency contacts or employment references, determine present and former neighbors to be interviewed, and check out the last school attended (high school, college, or technical school, if any). Moreover, consider magazine subscriptions and book clubs that the subject may wish to continue in his or her new life without realizing a trace can be made after the publisher is notified of the new address.

If necessary, reinterview persons already questioned, particularly friends and relatives who may have been in contact with the subject since the investigators first interview. Leave a business card with everyone approached or interviewed so that they may contact you at a later time with possible updated information, not that all will do so, but someone may, and that someone may be all you need.

During a trace investigation, share your case file with an associate. A second opinion or another viewpoint may broaden the search or clarify information not previously perceived.

Make use of most or all of the areas of exploration noted below. For a more detailed list of places, bureaus, agencies, and organizations to search, see Appendix E.

Social Security

This is likely the most effective search tool for a missing person if the investigator possesses the Social Security Number (SSN) of the subject. And that may be the problem—gaining access to a SSN for a trace. A SSN verification can be made to validate the number along with the state and the year it was issued. Social security numbers are not randomly issued, and certain numbers will never be valid. If a subject states he or she originates from one state and was born or started their work history on particular dates, corroboration or contradiction can be comfortably assured as few people realize that these two facts are easily obtained. If the record is different than what information the subject furnishes, further inquiry should be made.

At this time in our society, the social security number has become the fundamental identifier in many of our records. This would include credit reports, driver licenses, employment records, worker's compensation files, tax records and forms, criminal history and arrest records, insurance applications, and insurance claims.

Practically everything the average citizen does today is cross-referenced by his or her SSN.

The *National Death Claims Index* is a database of claims requests for death benefits. The basic reason for the Social Security Administration to maintain this index is to ensure against fraud in that the SSN cannot be used again.

Credit Bureaus

The major credit bureaus offering SSN tracing are TRW, CBI, and TransUnion. These credit bureaus should be considered a major source of information because they maintain more than 200 million credit files that are updated daily. The SSN is highlighted at the top of a credit bureau file that will contain the name and address of the subject. Moreover, this file will note address updates as long as the subject's credit use is associated with the SSN, employment application, rental or home ownership application, or as a result of insurance and assorted utilities applications. At times, multiple SSNs will be uncovered, particularly if the subject is attempting to cover his trail. We must also consider that multiple numbers may have been entered in error by clerks initiating file information; however, these bureaus more often than not identify these inaccuracies and flag the number to the subject's other file.

A trace with the use of a SSN under the Consumer Credit Reporting Reform Act (CCRRA) does not require permission and therefore is not restricted in its use under federal law (see Appendix A). However, some states have laws that require the trace to be recorded at the bottom or end of the credit report noting the agency or company requesting the trace. Check with the state in which you are employed if this is mandatory.

Voter Registration

A search of voter registration files can be very helpful in locating a missing person or a person of interest. These records may be located in the offices of the County Commissioner of Elections or other similar title, and political office seekers who solicit and maintain voter files. Registration files will contain the full name, gender, date of birth, home address, county, town or city, and zip code. Depending on the state or county, they may also contain social security number, occupation, and telephone number. Online searches of voter registrations can be made in approximately 23 states at this time, with other states connecting and updating continually, usually on a yearly basis.

Uniform Commercial Codes (UCC)

This is a legal document required by a creditor offering public notice of a lien placed on certain property until the loan is satisfied. These certificates or notices of liens are usually filed with the county clerk in the county of concern and then maintained in a state depository. It can be said that if a UCC is filed, a loan or credit application preceded the UCC filing. The company that filed a UCC will have any updated information on the subject as a rule if the subject changes addresses. The data contained on this certificate will act as a source for other information.

National Provider Identifier

The federal government prepared well in advance of May 23, 2007 (date of full compliance), to assign new numbers unique to identifying all providers of health care services, supplies, and equipment in transactions conducted by public and private payers. This number is identified as the National Provider Identifier (NPI). The Health Insurance Portability and Accountability Act of 1966 (HIPAA) established procedures involving information related to health care and insurance matters. Overseen by the Department of Health and Human Services (HHS), this legislation focuses on exchanging information; standardizing electronic data exchange, claims codes, and transaction information; assigning unique identifiers (numbers) to providers and employers within the system; and improving security and privacy.

Essentially, the NPI was established to replace certain other identification numbers traditionally issued by health plans with a 10-position numeric identifier. Dentists, physicians, pharmacists, hospitals, health care facilities, health plans, and individuals and organizations providing health care services will be considered "covered entities." The intent of the NPI regulation is to adopt a standard unique identifier for health professionals and other providers and to eliminate multiple identification numbers now assigned by various health care providers.

The NPI will not replace identifiers that have been assigned by the Social Security Administration (SSA), the Internal Revenue Service Taxpayer Identifying Numbers such as the employer and individual identification number (EIN and ITIN), and those issued by the Drug Enforcement Administration. It will not replace a practitioner's license number because that number indicates that the licensee meets certain requirements for rendering health care. HHS Centers for Medicare and Medicaid Services is developing the National Provider System to capture all data necessary to uniquely identify a health care provider, and to maintain and manage that data.

It is unknown at this time how much access and availability to this data will be given to those outside of the health care sector. However, this is another step in assigning a uniquely permanent number to every inhabitant in the United States.

Forwarding Addresses

Initially, access to forwarding addresses was provided by the U.S. Postal Service (USPS) if the subject filed a change of address form prior to leaving that area. The investigator could request that information in person at the post office that serviced the last known address or could send a letter on business stationary. This information access was based on the Freedom of Information Act, and the post office charged $1 for the service.

This custom was done away with recently with the USPS empowering a few computer data companies to act as agents of a component known as the National Change of Address (NCOA) system. These agents purchased the change of address information on computer tapes. They would then resell these tapes to authorized online information providers. Moreover, the NCOA information base includes updated forwarding address data for magazine and newspaper subscriptions. Those subjects not compiling a change of address form at the post office usually change their address with subscriptions they may have and do not realize that this change may also be found on the NCOA system.

A search is completed online, and a service fee is charged by the information provider.

Driver's License and Vehicle Registration Information

This can be a good source of information, because almost all citizens drive and must renew their operators' license and auto registration with current address information. Also, many states require a recent photo when renewing a license. Knowing when a subject's license and registration last expired and when he or she is due to renew can lead to positive results. A search is made by name for a license or registration and by name or plate (tag) number for registration information. Inquiry is done state by state because there is no national database for this information. Most states offer this type of inquiry (license and registration) online for a fee, but there are some that do not offer this service to other than law enforcement personnel.

Traffic Citations/Appearance Tickets

This area of inquiry is often overlooked, but if the state in which the research is made maintains a record of traffic citations or summonses issued and gives access to the records, it can be productive. Basically, citations will note an abundant amount of information such as the type of violation, name, address, date of birth (DOB), license number, year and make of vehicle, auto registration number, and date of issuance. The citations are usually found at local traffic or district courts of the county or town where the citation is returnable.

Court Records/County Records/Criminal History

Bankruptcy, civil and small claims litigation, judgments, and notices of defaults and tax liens may provide a clue to other avenues of investigation.

A check of state and local police agencies for a criminal history may provide a full pedigree of the subject, along with names of associates who may also help in the investigation.

Online Crisscross Telephone Directories

Hard-copy crisscross telephone directories have been used by private investigators and law enforcement for years. With the contemporary use of computers today, online searches and acquired CD-ROMS have proved to be more useful than the telephone book. Because a search can be made in three ways (by name, address, or telephone number), the investigator has three chances to easily access the information sought. Basically, if the investigator has one of the above pieces of information, the other two can be had. Data can be had locally and nationally, so that the use of hard-copy crisscross telephone books is outdated.

An address search will note all subscribers on the street in question, thereby providing a chance to develop neighborhood sources, if necessary. Be alert when performing a search, and note that many single women and widows use only an initial in place of a first name, thereby enlarging the number of hits one may obtain.

CDs can be purchased for a nominal price. Information is updated routinely and appears to be more current than going online, but even these disks can be obsolete in a short period of time. If an investigative agency has considerable use for this service and wishes up-to-date information, it would be a good idea to subscribe to a company that provides this service.

Online Neighborhood Inquiry Searches

This type of search allows one to input a street and city and obtain a list of everyone who lives on that street for the purpose of conducting personal or telephone interviews. This is helpful in cases of tracing for last known address, and in developing neighborhood sources.

Marriage Records

Although these archives may not be current, a search of this type of record may offer information that will lead to other avenues of inquiry. Marriage records are usually recorded and maintained by the County Clerk in the county in which the marriage took place. Information contained in these records differs from state to state but may contain all or some of the following: names of the couple, maiden name, addresses, DOB of both parties, social security numbers, occupations, name of church or location of the marriage, and the name of the person who performed the marriage.

If the investigator has no knowledge of the county in which the subject was married (or if married), a search can be made of the state's vital records. Some states may charge a small fee for this service. One Web site for a search of vital records in any state is www.vitalrec.com/.

Credential Verification

The educational or professional license of a subject can be easily searched and verified, particularly for an applicant who requires verification of education, expertise, or competence for a position sought by that person. This investigation may include dates of attendance, degrees awarded, and dates of graduation or certification. Professional or practitioner licenses are usually accessed at the Department of State in the state in question or in state vital records.

Many businesses require background checks of new hires, especially those that will hold high-level or sensitive positions. This procedure serves two purposes: not only for the essential proficiency and professional certification, but also to negate or lessen any possibility of subsequent legal action by the new employee.

Conducting an Internal Investigation

An investigation begins when the loss prevention department becomes aware or a PI is hired and receives information that concerns a crime or other improper behavior, and is then required to determine what type of offense has been committed or what business practice or policy was violated, how it was violated, and by whom. The private investigator may also be hired to investigate an issue or subject surreptitiously which may not be crime related. The basis of eliciting this information can be from managers, employees, informants, business records and paper trails, violations of company policy and procedures, and observation and inquiry by security officers, to name a few.

The police will conduct an investigation only when a crime has been reported to them, and they will usually be assisted and guided by loss prevention or security personnel in their inquiry. The reason for this would be that loss prevention or security would be more familiar with the facility, the operations of various processes, and the employees. And, of course, the "crime" should be serious enough to warrant the attention of the prosecutor and the courts, otherwise the police may not become overly concerned. As an example, the police would look upon overtime abuse as minor and not worth the time and effort to process a person through the criminal justice system, even though the crime of "theft of services" had been committed. Because most investigations that occur within a business establishment involve employees and not hardened criminals, and those who have little or no criminal history, it is rare that businesses endeavor to prosecute an employee. However, if the police are requested to prosecute, the police and the prosecutor may look incredulously at the request finding that the offense is so minor as to not waste the courts' time on a trivial matter. Most often the business would rather get rid of the "rotten apple," attempt some type of restitution, or minimize losses by termination.

In large business establishments, the loss prevention manager or the chief security officer (CSO) will determine if a *prima facie* case exists, if an investigation is warranted, and how the investigation will be conducted. Agreement by the chief executive officer (CEO) or an administrative manager may be required, but the final decision must be left to the loss prevention manager or CSO. This is particularly so as the people in these positions are most familiar with the legalities and the fact that an employee has certain rights and specific cautionary criminal and civil factors must be considered.

If there is no senior loss prevention or security officer in one's employ, the client who has approached a private investigator will naturally leave the determination of the process to the investigator regarding the lawfulness of the occurrence or incident in question, the legalities involved, and whether to pursue an investigation with possible prosecution.

Once the decision is made to initiate an investigation, documentary or physical evidence is collected first. The second step would be the detailed observation by loss prevention personnel zeroing in on the problem and the people involved. Surveillance would be part of this process if required. Hopefully, this can be completed before any detailed interviews of employees take place.

Depending on the specific case, an overt investigation could include the following procedures within the interview process:

1. Determine the loss or damage to the business establishment—describe the type, amount and the total value.
2. Determine the place of occurrence or where the loss took place.
3. Determine the time period of the loss as close as can be discovered.
4. Determine if persons other than employees could be involved in the loss. This would include truckers/helpers, deliverymen, repairmen, salesmen, business associates, and industrial spies.
5. Evaluate all of the available information surrounding the loss and physical area of the loss.
6. If it has been established that the loss was a theft, then a crime has been committed, and loss prevention or the private investigator (with the permission of the client) may want to advise the police.

Interviews and Interrogations

The Interview Process

In any event, one of the most important skills an investigator could possess is the ability to gain as much information as possible during the *interview process*. Most investigators learn this ability through experience rather than by formal training. Following that, the most significant and meaningful skill that the investigator has assembled in the investigative and interview processes would be making use of the information he or she has gathered, and applying that knowledge in the *interrogation process*. By knowing all the pertinent facts and being in command of them, the investigator is able to confront the suspect in a more confident manner and, ultimately, has complete control of the interaction:

1. If the private investigator or security department wishes to conduct an investigation before any police involvement, there should be extensive interviews with all personnel who had or may have had access to the stolen property or the crime in general. Formal interview and interrogation procedures are to be followed at this point. Consider that word of the loss and investigation will spread rapidly.
2. Evaluate all notes and statements received from witnesses and persons of interest and through employee interviews and interrogations.
3. Follow up on inquiries, interviews, and interrogations as needed to clarify questionable facts and information.

4. Conduct follow-up inquiries and investigations of possible or apparent suspects based on interviews, interrogations, surveillance, and information received.
5. Investigate the possibility that the stolen items may still be on the premises or at some other private location. If a recovery of the stolen property is made, attempt to trace back the item to the perpetrator.
6. Be observant of an employee's increase in "wealth," spending habits, material goods, boasting, and flaunting.
7. Be observant for a motive, such as problems with drugs, gambling, or family finances.
8. Consider the use of a polygraph examination of all the suspects within the confines of the law.
9. The final evaluation in which the investigator concludes his report to management or the client regarding his or her findings and will include the following information:

- Whether the case is still active and the investigation continues.
- If the investigator is unable to continue further with the investigation because the facts and circumstances will not permit a continuance.
- If the investigation has concluded and the case is closed with an arrest, recovery, or prosecution of the persons involved.

10. Reports must be compiled and submitted by each investigator or agent involved in any part of the investigation. All written statements and confessions are to be attached to and made part of the report. All evidence must be marked, maintained in its original condition, properly safeguarded, and identified in the report. It is important for the investigator to remember that all evidence and any surveillance information or material must be legally obtained.

The Interrogation Process

Unless the suspect or suspects are caught in the act of committing the offense prior to or during the investigation and immediate action must be taken by the private investigator or the security officer, the interrogation process will take place as follows:

1. After completing the initial phases of the investigation and it has been decided that all *interviews and evidence* have been obtained that can reasonably be obtained, the investigator should begin the interrogation of the suspect or suspects. This will be the culmination of the investigative process in that it is calculated to elicit a statement of admission—a confession that will be legal and binding.

2. The definitive confession would be a written statement admitting to guilt, signed by the suspect, with such signature witnessed by at least two people.

3. If a written statement cannot be obtained or is unavailable, all oral statements made by the suspect should be taken down, reduced to writing, and made part of the report. Particularly note anyone who was present and witnessed an oral admission made by the subject. If possible, have that witness place in writing what he heard concerning an oral confession or statements. Oral statements include the suspect admitting guilt, describing his actions (how the suspect did it), and his past or present mental state concerning the incident (why he did it). In effect, it is any statement made by the suspect that places himself in jeopardy. In actuality, this writing is sort of a deposition in which a conversation took place between the investigator questioning the suspect and what was spoken by both. Within guidelines, oral admissions to a crime are acceptable as evidence in court.
4. The inference of guilt can take several forms. Even if the suspect does not actually admit to any wrongdoing, information can be obtained that can be incriminating, reduce his credibility, and destroy any defense he may raise in the future. If asked why he or she committed the crime (why he did it), the subject may just shrug his shoulders. The suspect may refuse to cooperate by directing attention elsewhere when questioned or may attempt to disrupt the interrogation by his actions. Consider also, that if the suspect refuses to answer or participate in the questioning, basically not saying a word, he "stands mute," and this can be considered in a court of law before a judge or jury as possible guilt, because an innocent person would deny guilt if he was in fact guiltless.

Threats or promises should never be made to a witness or suspect, otherwise any evidence or statements given may not be admissible in court. In any situation where voluntary consent is required (as in a search), the private investigator or security officer would be wise to obtain written authorization first. If the case is later presented at trial, the defendant's lawyer will certainly attempt to have any statement or evidence dismissed because of coercion, intimidation, promises, or illegal search and seizure. Do not place yourself in a position of losing a case in court because of sloppy or illegal procedures.

Q & A Sessions

Another type of interrogation is a Q & A (question and answer) session. A Q & A session is usually conducted by a District Attorney or an Assistant District Attorney before a defendant, customarily charged with a serious or egregious criminal act. Because it may be considered a highly publicized case, the purpose is to cover all legal points that may be discovered then or later and to produce a more tightly woven case for court presentation.

The Employee's Right to Representation

A private investigator employed by a business establishment to investigate a crime or other company infraction must be cognizant of certain restrictions regarding interviews and interrogations of employees who may have representation by right of membership in an authorized union, particularly so if the employee reasonably believes that he or she may be subject to some sanctions or disciplinary action. (See *U.S. Supreme Court–NLRB v. J. Weingarten, Inc.,* 1975, also known as the *Weingarten Rule.* See the "Glossary" for significance.)

Based upon the National Labor Relations Board, any employee protected by union representation through collective bargaining has certain rights regarding any criminal actions or wrongs that may have been committed. The most important right is that the employee has the privilege of a union representative to be present at any meeting, interview, or interrogation conducted by management or by an agent of the management. The right to representation exists even in cases where the employer concludes that there will be no discipline as a result of the interview or interrogation.

However, the employee must make the request to invoke this right to representation. If the employee wishes to forgo this guaranteed right or fails to make this request for representation, he or she cannot at a later time cry foul or unfair conduct by the employer in failing to provide adequate safeguards against self-incrimination.

If the request is made and a union representative is present to assist the employee, the employer has no duty to bargain or confer with the representative even if there is a suggestion or clarification of facts helpful to the employee. The employer is free to insist that the only interest at that time is in the employee's account of the matter under investigation.

The NLRB notes that the employer is not forced to interview or interrogate the employee once the request for representation has been made. On the other hand, the employer may refuse the request and has no obligation to justify his refusal for union representation to that employee if he wishes to do so. Under these circumstances, the employee may refrain from participating in the meeting with management in an effort to retain his or her right to representation. However, in any event, the employer is free to continue the investigation and may act on information obtained from other sources (*196 NLRB 1052*).

For further information on the interrogation process, see the section in Chapter 4, "Search and Seizure," and the section earlier this chapter, "Interviews and Interrogations."

The Investigation at a Scene of Occurrence

The Scene

Investigation is an important part of the job description of loss prevention and the duties assigned to that department. Whether the place of occurrence is an accident or crime scene, certain precautions must take place, depending on the situation or the seriousness of the occurrence. Once the emergency situation is under control, such as the fire being extinguished or the injured person attended to and removed from the scene, the security officer should then attempt to preserve the scene as much as it was when the occurrence took place. A scene of importance needs to be controlled as much as possible, and the security officer cannot do all that needs to be done without some help. If other security officers are not present to assist, a responsible employee or manager can be put to use in helping protect the scene.

The security officer should identify the complainant (if any) and all persons present during the occurrence, whether they witnessed anything of concern or not. If possible, attempt to separate witnesses so that any discussion between them will not be controlled or distorted by one over the other. If necessary and before taking any written statements that may be required, make sure the identification includes the name, address, age, date of birth, home and business telephone numbers, and a very brief recounting of what they observed and where they were when the incident took place. Such notations should be made in the officer's notebook that he carries, and will be maintained for future reference.

Anytime there is any remote possibility of subsequent civil litigation because of an accidental injury to a person, or because of the severity of the occurrence or injury, photos of the scene should be taken. In the case of an injured employee, photos may be helpful to that employee or to the company, depending on the occurrence. And in the case of a crime scene, photos taken before the arrival of the police or emergency personnel may be of some importance because a scene may inadvertently change or become contaminated because of people standing around and handling objects. If necessary, a diagram may be drawn of the scene with measurements noting windows, doors, and important objects. The security officer should note everything of importance upon arrival at the scene and while he or she is there. The officer should describe the conditions upon arrival and note if certain things or objects were out of place, or appeared to be placed in position to accommodate a prepared scenario. The area of the scene should be searched thoroughly for any evidence that would pertain to the incident, no matter how insignificant the officer may believe it to be.

Crime Scene Investigation

Once an investigator is assigned to a case, the search of the crime scene, if available and timely, may be the most important part of the investigation. Crimes of violence may involve a struggle, use of a weapon, or other physical activity, such as broken or disturbed articles or furniture. Moreover, the perpetrator may acquire and retain obvious physical signs of a fight or struggle or gunshot powder residue on his body or clothing. In crimes of personal gain, the proceeds of the crime may be found in the perpetrator's possession.

Physical evidence may serve to identify the perpetrator by means of clue materials, such as personal property, weapons, bullets and casings, tools, garments, bloodstains, fingerprints, and footprints. Traces of evidence can be found at any crime scene. Evidence may be found in the form of jimmy marks, pieces or threads of fabric, fibers, hair, glass, blood, paint, seeds, soil, filings, fragments, and semen stains, all depending on the character of the crime and the locale. Samples of these traces should be collected at the scene in anticipation that the suspect may carry from the scene trace evidence, and which if found on his person or clothing at a later time would thereby link him to the scene.

Crime Scene Search Procedures

Depending on the crime and the crime scene, and if the occurrence is not old, the investigator should follow the following procedures:

- Separate the witnesses (see the narrative in the previous section entitled "The Scene").
- Detain and question the person who reported the incident and all persons present at the crime scene.
- Safeguard the scene.
- Reduce or eliminate the number of persons entering the scene so as not to contaminate or destroy evidence.
- Do not touch or move any object.
- Watch where you step.
- Take photos and make drawings of the scene.
- Collect, preserve, and catalog all evidence found at the scene.

Generally, realizing that a private investigator will not have the expertise at a crime scene search as would a criminalist or a forensic expert, he or she should be aware of the requirements and procedures concerning the preservation of evidence at the scene of occurrence.

In reality, the *three major steps* in a crime scene search are

1. *Search*
2. *Collection*
3. *Preservation*

Outdoor Searches

If the crime scene encompasses an area such as a field or a large tract of land, the acceptable method of a complete search for any evidence linked to the crime or occurrence will depend on the size and extent of the search to be conducted. Method rather than intuition should guide the basic search, and the examination must be as thorough as possible. The following methods have proven their worth:

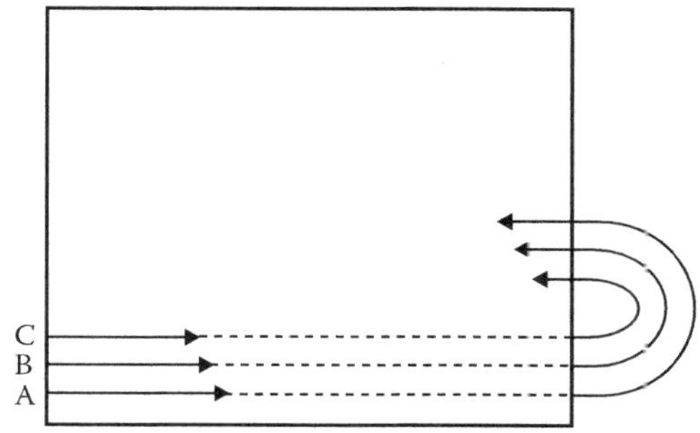

Figure 5.1 The strip method for an outdoor search.

1. *The Strip Method*—The area is blocked out in the form of a rectangle. Three searchers, parallel to each other, proceed slowly at the same pace to one side of the rectangle. At the end of the first stroll, the searchers turn and proceed back along new lanes, which will be adjacent to the first three lanes. (See Figure 5.1.)
2. *The Double Strip or Grid Methods*—A modification of the strip method described above, where the rectangle is transversed by the three searchers first parallel to the base of the rectangle, and when finished, then continued parallel to the side of the rectangle. (See Figure 5.2.)
3. *The Spiral Method*—Three searchers follow each other in the path of a spiral (circle) beginning on the outside and spiraling in toward the center. (See Figure 5.3.)

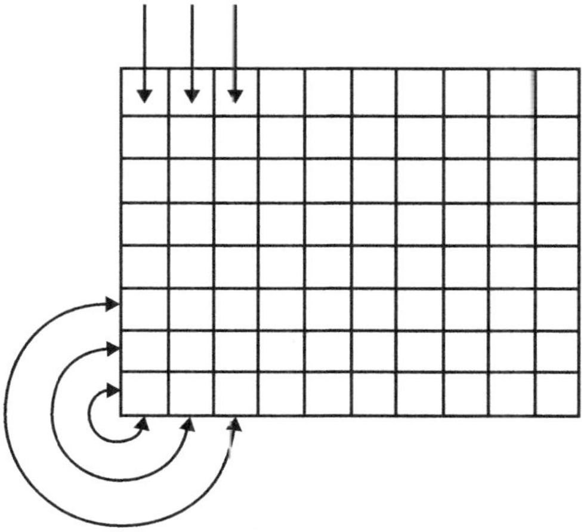

Figure 5.2 The double strip or grid methods for an outdoor search.

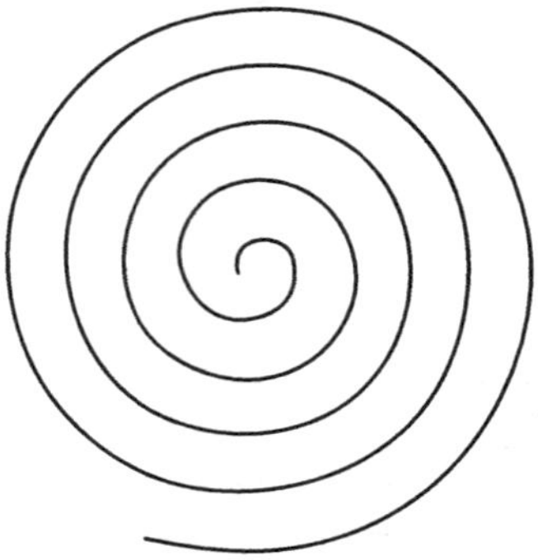

Figure 5.3 The spiral method for an outdoor search.

4. *The Wheel Method*—If the area to be searched is considered to be an approximate circle, the searchers gather at the center of the circle and proceed outward along the radii (spokes). Depending on the size of the search, the procedure may have to be repeated with additional radii. (See Figure 5.4.)
5. *The Zone Method*—A searcher is assigned to a portion or zone of a quadrant within a rectangle. Depending on the size of the area to be searched, each quadrant may be divided into another set of quadrants. (See Figure 5.5.)

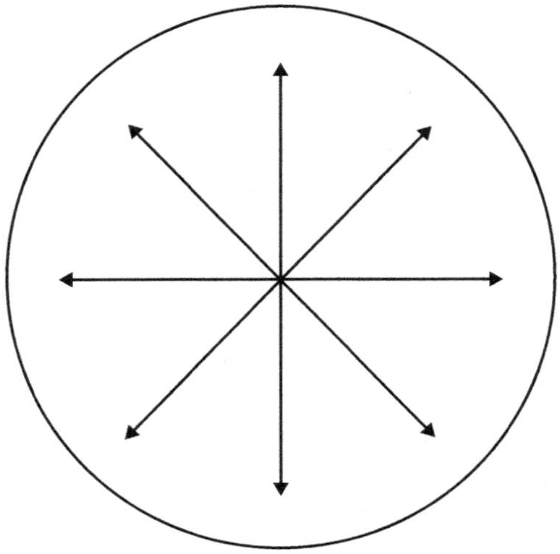

Figure 5.4 The wheel method for an outdoor search.

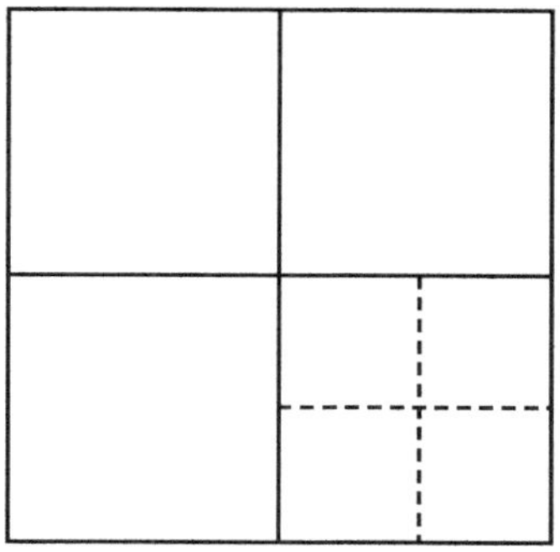

Figure 5.5 The zone method for an outdoor search.

Fingerprint Evidence

Defined

Fingerprints may be classified into three categories:

1. *Latent Fingerprints*—These are considered the majority of fingerprints that will be found at a crime scene. They are relatively unseen or invisible, and the impression must be developed by the use of powder, vapor, or liquid.
2. *Plastic Fingerprints*—These are fingerprint impressions that are depressed below the original surface. They may be found on such objects as butter, soap, putty, or melted wax.
3. *Visible Fingerprints*—These fingerprints may be left by fingers covered by a liquid or colored material such as blood, paint, grease, ink, or dirt.

The search for fingerprints should be made before any objects present are moved or removed from the scene of the crime. Outdoor scenes will present more of a problem than indoor scenes, simply because there will be fewer surfaces to examine for prints, and because of climate, the elements, and other environmental factors, deterioration of prints can occur rapidly.

An indoor scene search for fingerprints will depend on certain factors, which will include the *modus operandi* of the transgressor, and the existence of surfaces capable of retaining fingerprint impressions. Initially, though, observation and search should be made at points of entry and exit. This will include doorknobs, door panels, windows, windowsills, glass, and handrails. Thereafter, a circular or clockwise pattern around the scene will produce a more assured accounting of all articles to be searched.

Since DNA classification has become the ultimate method in identifying one person's body fluids from another, the lowly art of fingerprint identification has been placed somewhat on the back burner. In fact, however, fingerprint evidence is still considered highly reliable and is particularly acceptable by juries once properly introduced as evidence.

Once a jury has been introduced to evidence in the form of fingerprints, one does not need a Ph.D. degree to understand that fingerprints are specific and highly reliable based upon a contour map of ridges and whorls which is completely unique, and unlike the theories of DNA matching, rarely does one seriously doubt this assumption.

Basically, our fingers contain ridges and whorls that are unique from anyone else in that these ridge patterns (the swirled skin patterns on our fingertips) do not change throughout our lifetime; therefore, no two people have the same pattern of friction ridges, not even identical twins. These ridges contain rows of sweat pores, and mixed with body oils, they produce fingerprint impressions on a surface, particularly a smooth surface. Fingerprint and forensic experts use powders and chemicals to enhance the visibility of prints. We must remember that the quality of the print can be affected by the surface it was found and lifted from. However, with the use of computer enhancement techniques and other scientific methods, it is possible to pick up complete prints or fragments of prints that would otherwise be invisible to the naked eye.

If a print is already on file with the police or a federal agency, it can be matched to one found at a crime scene. Fingerprints may be on file in various jurisdictions and for various reasons because of the law, one's occupation, or employment requirements. Fingerprints also are a great tool in identifying crime victims and unknown persons.

Elimination Prints

Fingerprints are also taken for elimination purposes from all persons who were or could have been at a crime scene but are not at present considered suspects. These elimination prints will determine if the prints found at a crime scene are considered unknown or if there are no unknowns. If no unknown prints are identified, we can assume that one of the original group members who submitted to the elimination process could be the guilty party. If the print found at the crime scene does not match the group, we must assume that this print could belong to the suspect of the crime. However, we must also consider that if only identified prints are found, the suspect or perpetrator never left any. In other words, if no prints or unknown prints are found at a scene of a crime or incident, regard this as just one portion of the evidence—keep an open mind!

Fingerprints may last for a long period of time depending on the surface on which they are found or the surface effect of elements such as the sun, rain, water, or humidity. Be aware though that a suspect not familiar, authorized, or known to be at a location now considered a crime scene, may state that his or her fingerprint was left at some time previously and not at the time of the crime.

Techniques

There are some techniques used by crime scene searchers that may be employed by the average investigator as long as the surface is conducive to a fingerprint. These may include breathing on a surface causing a print to become visible, using a flashlight held at an angle to the surface revealing an impression not otherwise noticeable, or even examining a surface from different angles may produce the same results.

In regard to smooth, hard, and dry surfaces, using fingerprint powder is one of the best methods of making prints visible. Basically, the powder must not absorb water, it should adhere to all impressions of the print, and it should provide a contrast so that a photograph will take a good representation. White or gray powder will provide a sufficient contrast on dark surfaces. Black powder will serve as a contrast against light-colored surfaces. Cameras and chemical development of prints by fumes, immersion, or other scientific procedures should be left to the crime scene experts or criminalists. So, too, for fluorescent powders that are used for multicolored surfaces.

Under ordinary circumstances, it is considered advisable to leave the fingerprint impression on the surface where it was found, because its subsequent introduction in court in or on its original article or location will serve to enhance its value as evidence.

The lifting of fingerprints with the use of transparent tape or a rubber lifter (producing a reverse imprint) can cause several problems for those investigators with little experience. Unable to have complete adhesion, air bubbles or poor lifting methods would ruin the print for use as evidence. Air bubbles or creases in the tape will leave blank spots on the tape that may be unnoticed before being lifted. If the first attempt is unsuccessful, a second attempt is ordinarily useless.

The investigator should have some training and knowledge regarding the search for and the lifting of prints from various surfaces, in addition to the collection and preservation of prints.

Fingerprint Inconsistency

It appears that there is some recent controversy over the validity of fingerprint evidence. Scientists have found that there are similarities of print patterns among close relatives. This will occur because we inherit certain characteristics from our parents such as hair and eye color, face, body shape, and complexion. Although identical twins will have different fingerprint patterns, they may be closely related in classification. Scientists now believe that the notion that no two people can have the same fingerprints has little scientific basis according to a 2004 investigation by *New Scientist* magazine.[5] This can be considered in addition to with the human errors made in identifying and classifying fingerprints. Although more independent study is needed, fingerprints may not be a foolproof way of determining who did what. We can assume that defense attorneys will attempt to use this perspective to invalidate any fingerprint evidence that could add to a defendant's guilt.

The Collection and Preservation of Evidence

Photographs of the scene are considered evidence because they can show what and how the scene appeared at the time of the occurrence; therefore, they are of great importance if required at a later time. A scene can change, particularly in a retail environment where renovations are routinely commonplace, and will not appear as it was at the time of the occurrence. By the time the need to describe a scene takes place, many changes can occur, and hence the need for photos and, if necessary, hand-drawn diagrams noting measurements and distances. In addition, physical evidence collected at the scene may be defined as any material that will aid in identifying the problem, the people involved, the cause of the accident, or how the crime was committed. If the scene is of a serious criminal nature, the police will make use of a forensic team to search for clues and evidence. The security officer is not expected or prepared to lift fingerprints or collect hair samples or body fluids, for example. Some evidence may be so microscopic that only trained crime scene search investigators or fire marshals may be able to gather, preserve, identify, and present acceptable evidence in court.

See Chapter 4, "The Rules of Evidence," and *Evidence* in the "Glossary" for further definitions.

If the police are not involved in the investigation, the private investigator must then decide if the case is serious enough to warrant the search and collection of evidence for possible future inquiries or court action. Everything that may be considered evidence must be tagged, labeled, distinctively marked with the initials of the finder (a metal scribe is most useful in these cases), and identified with the case or incident report number assigned to the occurrence.

Marking

Solid objects collected as evidence should be marked for identification with the initials of the investigator receiving or finding the item. The identification mark should not be placed in an area where an evidentiary trace exists. A hard object may be initialed with the use of a sharp, pointed instrument such as a metal stylus. Indelible ink should be used for those objects that are softer or absorbent in nature. Use care for those objects that have great intrinsic value so as not to diminish their worth. These and smaller objects may be placed in containers or envelopes, and then sealed and labeled. If too large or cumbersome, a tag may be attached. Liquids or pastes should be retained in their original container and appropriately sealed and labeled.

Sealing and Labeling

If possible, each individual piece of evidence should be enclosed in separate containers and sealed with security tape so that the container cannot be opened without breaking the seal. The investigator's initials or name and the date of sealing should be noted on the seal in ink. Each time the seal is broken for whatever reason (court presentation, retesting), the name of the person who broke the seal, the date, and for what reason should be noted on the container, and it should then be resealed with a new security tape, again noting the investigator and date on the new seal.

If the object or item placed in a container or evidence envelope cannot be labeled with the appropriate information (as noted below), an evidence tag should be compiled and attached to the object.

The tag should contain the following information:

1. Case number
2. Date and time of finding the article
3. Name and description of the article
4. Location at time of the discovery
5. Name and signature of the investigator who made the discovery
6. Name of any witness or witnesses to the discovery

Documents, like any other evidence of concern, should also be marked. So as not to destroy or affect any type of examination, the acceptable method of marking would be on the back of the document, where the investigator places his or her initials and the date with a fine-tipped, indelible-ink pen. The document should then be placed in a clear plastic envelope and sealed with security tape, with the seal again initialed and dated. Appropriate identification information (such as the case number, investigator assigned, client or company name) should be placed on the back of this plastic envelope.

The Chain of Custody

Once collected and labeled, evidence should be placed in a secure area protected from any other employee. Only security/loss prevention personnel or the private investigator assigned to the case should enter into this secured area, because the continuity of evidence (the chain of custody) must be established to a certainty for a possible court hearing. To do otherwise would place the evidence in jeopardy of possible tampering or modification, and therefore possible suppression in court. The evidence must be identified as to where and when it was found, by whom, and how secured, with all this information carefully noted in the case or investigative report. Anytime the evidence is handled, removed, and returned to the secured evidence area for whatever purpose, it must be noted in subsequent entries to the report. This would include name of investigator, date taken and date returned, and for what purpose. As a safety measure, a positive approach of control is to repeat the information noted in the report on the rear of this evidence envelope (or an evidence tag, depending on the object secured) as to custody. Reasoning for this is to show that the chain of custody has not been broken, and the evidence has not been tampered with, altered, contaminated, or changed in any manner. Evidence protected in a secure area by security/loss prevention would usually be saved for those instances that might include subsequent civil litigation. Evidence collected and preserved for any future criminal prosecution must also be tagged, labeled, marked, removed, and secured by the police according to their procedures.

Although the chain of custody or evidence is not legally as applicable to the investigator or security officer as in the case of law enforcement, investigators and security officers would do well to follow the same guidelines as close as possible as an indication of a professional approach toward the preservation of evidence, chain of custody, and case management.

On some crimes such as sexual harassment, money loss, or embezzlement, the investigator may discover a document that will require professional examination in an effort to make a determination as to a suspect. Unless management wishes to keep the investigation in-house, security/loss prevention might consider reporting the incident to the police and letting their forensic detectives examine the document as part of their investigation. But if the incident is not going to be reported to the police and the investigation is kept in-house, it would be prudent for the private investigator and security or loss prevention department to have a qualified document examiner available for situations such as this.

If at a later time a PI is contracted and assigned for a follow-up investigation, or a similar investigation by the same client, the earliest reactions of the people involved, the investigation, statements, documents, notes, and any evidence collected and might be attributable to the initial incident are to be considered as significant support and benefit to the investigator, and will be passed on as part of his or her case preparation.

Documentary Evidence

This type of evidence must be considered of great importance in any criminal or civil investigation. Documents in one form or another may account for the greatest percentage of evidence that may be submitted and accepted in a court or hearing. Documents will include checks, claims, wills, codicils, certificates and records of all types, statements, letters, and memoranda.

Origination and authorship will be the initial steps in determining authenticity and admissibility. The following points will be open for questioning by a document examiner:

- The identity, make-up, and use of the record or book that may be considered evidence. Who compiled and maintained it and for what purpose? Is this the only record or is there a duplicate? Does the record show fiduciary information or data that will expose someone or the corporation criminally or civilly?
- The identity and the true signature of the writer or signer of the document, if found legitimate and applicable to the investigation.
- Comparison of handwriting and typewriting samples
- The determination whether there were any erasures, deletions, additions, or other alterations on the document.
- The age of the document.

- The source of the paper on which the document was printed or written on.
- The source and age of the typewriting, ink (liquid or ball point), or pencil markings.

Standards and Comparisons

In the determination of a questioned document, an important task for the investigator is providing suitable *exemplars* or standards from other sources with which the questioned writing or typewriting can be compared. An exemplar is a standard of writing from a known source or authorship that the technician may use for comparison. The exemplar (specimen) may be in the form of writing (script), printing, typing, or a stamp or seal impression. A requested standard is an exemplar prepared at the investigator's solicitation; nonrequest standards are those specimens made prior to the investigation. Depending on the investigation, the number of exemplars requested may be as high as 20 for comparison purposes. The exemplar should be of a similar type of paper, comparable pen nib or ballpoint, inks, or pencil used, and written in suitable and word form as the actual document text.

The major point to be made here is that the exemplar must be shown to be genuine for admittance as evidence. It must be shown that the exemplar is directly and unquestionably connected to the suspect. Because a suspect may not give any samples to the investigator for fear of incriminating himself and cannot be forced to do so, the exemplars must be given willingly. However, if at a later time this evidence is used against the defendant (former suspect), his counsel most assuredly will make the claim that the client was coerced into submission. This can be nullified by several means, such as a witness present at the time of the exemplar's production, CCTV, or a signed statement noting that the exemplars were given voluntarily.

The investigator should have some training in the taking of exemplars. What may be required depending on the investigation and particularly the suspect's attempts to disguise his writing by the speed, slant, irregularities, spelling, change of hand, and size.

Preserving the Document

The investigator can aid the document examiner by properly collecting, preserving, and transmitting the document. Remember that if the document is germane to the case and if it will be authentic and admissible, it should be considered important that a qualified and recognized expert become involved in the examination of that document.

- The document should be handled by the investigator or criminalist with wooden tongs or by wearing of surgical gloves.
- If possible, it should be placed and retained in a transparent plastic envelope when not under expert examination.

- Preserve the document from sunlight, humidity, dampness, or heat.
- Do not fold or make a tracing of the document. Mark each document on the back side in a neutral area with the case number, investigator's name or initials, date, and location where found. If unable to make markings in this manner, make the notations on the outside of the clear envelope.
- Advise the technician who will conduct the examination if you believe fingerprints are or may be present.
- And finally, make the appropriate notations in your notebook at the scene and ultimately in your investigative report as to the description of the document, where found, by whom, when, and its transportation to the examiner (the chain of custody).

Informants

Whether in the criminal, civil, or private sector, an informant is a valuable tool in any investigation. An informant may be cultivated surreptitiously or he may be voluntary. In either case, the reason for informing on another includes recognition, monetary reward, personal morality and ethics, or a desire to "get even." When used by law enforcement officers, the informant is known as a *confidential informant* (CI), and can be advantageous in gathering information on criminal activity or directing the officer toward the perpetrator. If the informant cannot direct the PI to a suspect or a perpetrator, many times information gathered can lead to new directions or further inquiries. An informant of this type, if shown to be reliable in the past, can be helpful in the basis of search warrants. The reasoning behind the designation "confidential" is that if his or her identity becomes known, retaliation may follow, or if nothing else, the informant as a source of information may "dry up." These are the major reasons that police officers and private investigators must keep the identity of their informants secret and known only to them.

Cautionary Note

We must consider, however, that opposing counsel may request of the court that the investigator reveal the name of the informant (the source of the information) so that this person may be examined on the witness stand.

The reasoning that the defense attorney will present is that the defendant has a right to face his accuser or the informant, and the information given should be subject to cross-examination.

The court may comply and demand that the informant be identified. Because there is no privileged communication that can be implied here, the private investigator will have to reveal his or her source. If not, he or she could suffer contempt of court and face jail time.

Before relying on any information used to support an arrest, the private investigator must be able to show that the informant in this case was reliable with information received based on past instances, and also how the informant gained this knowledge or the facts provided.

However, we must consider that in many instances, information may be received anonymously or by way of concerned citizens. A significant program for loss prevention is the "silent witness" or "hot line," where, if the informant wishes, information can be reported to the security office's telephone and recorded on voice mail anonymously or not. This type of program has been used effectively in the retail business where an anonymous person reveals pertinent information concerning a crime on premises. Substantial cash incentives for information given by a known or an anonymous employee leading to the termination or arrest of a dishonest employee should also be in effect and widely publicized as corporate policy. This policy should note the details of the monetary reward and the procedure that the employee is to follow. If the information is fruitful, the informant will be rewarded surreptitiously with his or her identity never known to anyone other than a select few within the security or loss prevention department.

Surveillance

Surveillance is the covert observation of persons, places, or vehicles for the purpose of obtaining information concerning the identities or activities of subjects. This activity can produce excellent results when conducted in a professional manner.

People are essentially creatures of habit, and they ordinarily elect to stay in their local area of residence and employment. The way that they walk, drive their cars, or habitually conduct their personal lives can pretty much be systematically noted. When and where a person shops, visits certain locales or specific places such as taverns, movies, or parks, or undertakes outdoor activities does not change a great deal and can be described as movement within his or her living and work environments. These routine tendencies can be very important to the investigator, as they will help to affirm the boundaries on the planning and surveillance arrangement of that individual.

Generally, most people are not very surveillance conscious and can be followed very easily by car or on foot. However, once they do become surveillance conscious, or become constantly aware of everything around them, they become very difficult to follow successfully.

The behavior or lifestyle of some people warrants close supervision or observation by authorities. Therefore, it can be said that such people are very conscious and cautious of everything they do, including their surroundings, as they will constantly be aware that they might be subjects of a surveillance operation. In these cases, surveillance must be very carefully prepared and organized, with the proper equipment and an experienced surveillance crew.

Some of the deterrents employed by subjects of investigation or surveillance can be as varied as CCTV and electronic detectors around their property to private security officers, guard dogs, and antibugging devices. Consequently, gaining useful information or acquiring helpful data on the subject's outside habits can be difficult. However, with time and patience, intelligence, no matter how minor, can be useful.

Surveillance may be divided into three types:

1. *Surveillance of Places*—Buildings, businesses, sites, locales, or homes that the subject or target will or may visit, work, or occupy.
2. *Surveillance of an Individual, Vehicle, or Group*—Tailing or shadowing a subject, associate, or target.
3. *Undercover Operations*—(See the section "Undercover Operations," in Chapter 7 for a detailed description.)

Within these types, surveillance may be considered to fall into three categories:

1. *Mobile or Moving*—Can be on foot or in vehicles.
2. *Static or Fixed*—Can be in various and diverse stationary locations or venues.
3. *Mixture*—A mixture of both.

Methods

The objective of the surveillance, location, and time of day will determine the method of the tail. Within the types and categories noted above, the following methods are described:

- *Loose Tail*—Employed when a general impression of the subject's associates and habits is required. Also employed where the target is not always in view, and can be left for periods of time without continual surveillance.
- *Rough Shadowing*—The tailing of a subject who is aware of the tail or is aware that he or she is under observation, and the agent must continue the tail for various reasons without any special precautions, or where the subject is a material witness and must be protected from harm or other influences.
- *Close Tail*—Where the surveillance is constant and may continue for a long period of time, and where extreme precautions are taken to ensure a constant surveillance of the subject, to prevent losing the subject, and to protect the agent from discovery or his presence.
- A *combination* of any of the above, where facts and circumstances will dictate an immediate change of deportment.

Surveillance of Sites, Places, and Locales

In criminal investigations conducted by the police, crimes that usually require this type of surveillance are crack or drug locations (use, sale, or manufacture), chop shops, gambling, and prostitution. PIs may conduct a surveillance of a location for several reasons, including the observation of an individual under suspicion for a theft or other offense in his employment, the uncovering of dishonesty among employees, or a case of infidelity in a divorce action.

Basically, the objectives of a site or locale surveillance are as follows:

- To detect criminal activities.
- To discover the identity of persons who frequent a particular establishment and to determine their relationship.
- To determine the habits of a particular person who lives in or frequents that location.
- To obtain evidence of a crime for a final conclusion or to prevent the commission of a crime.

Tailing or Shadowing an Individual

Tailing or shadowing may be defined as simply the act of following a person or vehicle, and the purpose for this action will depend on the nature of the investigation.

In police work, this would entail the detection of evidence of criminal activities in order to establish the associations of a subject, to locate a wanted person, and to protect a witness.

In the private sector, the investigator may wish to discover the associates and habits of an individual about to be hired for a position of responsibility, to determine the loyalty of employees in a company where thefts have occurred, to obtain evidence regarding a person under suspicion of theft or other offense, or to obtain evidence of infidelity.

The positive and categorical results in this type of surveillance will be determined by the requirements and appearance of the agent assigned:

- Be of average size, build, and general appearance.
- Have no noticeable peculiarities or mannerisms in appearance.
- Wear no conspicuous jewelry or clothing.
- Have nothing that will attract attention to his presence.
- Have the perseverance and ability to wait for hours at a time standing or sitting without showing any indication of impatience or irritation that would attract attention to your presence.
- Be resourceful and quick witted so that if confronted or observed by the subject under surveillance, you can conceive reasons or excuses for your presence in a given location.

Techniques

There are several techniques used by PIs in obtaining intelligence and information, or the applied observation of a targeted subject or location:

- Before the private investigator can decide the best procedure or action he or she is about to take in a surveillance, or in fact, in any investigation, the location and environment that the investigator is about to enter must be known. Preoperation intelligence should include such circumstances as if the subject will operate an auto or a motorcycle, travel in public conveyances, make use of a taxi, or be on foot. Moreover, knowledge of the subject's habits, social life, inclination for expensive tastes or expensive restaurants, associates, and places often visited will give an indication of how the agent will dress and conduct him- or herself in an effort to "fit in" to the lifestyle of the subject. The agent should be cognizant of the neighborhood where the subject lives, works, or frequents, so that he or she can act and dress to conform to that location. Additionally, the subject must be completely identified by description, such as physical appearance, type of clothing worn, and behavior and mannerisms.

  Questions such as the following will need to be answered: Will the location be in a rural, suburban, or city setting? Will the investigator have to enter certain buildings such as taverns, restaurants, factories, or shopping malls? Does the investigator have a working knowledge of map reading and the use of a compass and any other equipment he or she may be expected to use? The surroundings and conditions will dictate how the investigator will approach and conduct the assignment at hand. And as a cautionary procedure in any surveillance, the investigator must be cognizant of privacy laws that may be applicable to the circumstances he or she may find themselves in.

- Observing a location, residential or business, from another position or site (static) where the investigator has full view of all the comings and goings of the subject or occupants. This can be accomplished in an apartment or building that gives full view of the locale. If they can be utilized, the use of highly sensitive audio equipment and cameras could augment other evidence.

- The following of a subject, on foot or by auto, can be very tricky, especially if the target subject is cautious, insecure, and possibly vulnerable to observation. Particularly on foot, it is usual for novice operators to believe that they have been spotted. A good surveillance operative will get over this feeling as quickly as possible if he or she expects to become effective in surveillance methods. Experienced agents will attempt to monitor the subject properly, quantify any real behavioral concerns, and may note any changes in the subject's normal habits. The technique of following on foot will vary with the number of agents available, which can vary from one to six agents. A private investigator with a limited budget may be forced to conduct a tail by him- or herself. The reasoning for making use of more than one agent is to minimize the risk of detection by falling into the subject's line of sight too often or being forced to make an abrupt change of direction. If more than one agent is involved in the tail, prearranged signals should be considered mandatory. As an example, if agent A believes that he is about to be discovered, he may relay his intent to agent B to drop out by adjusting his hat, lighting a cigarette, or any other planned gesture that will convey his intent to the other agent.

- The following (tailing) of a subject in an auto by another vehicle can also be uncertain, as the target could constantly survey vehicle movement in the rearview mirrors. Erratic or jerky driving maneuvers will surely be seen in a rearview mirror, and any suspicious activity by a vehicle or vehicles will certainly neutralize the tail. A bug planted in or on the target vehicle would give the following vehicle enough information as to direction and location at a distance without close eye contact. In other instances, more than one vehicle is used to tail the subject, behind and parallel to the target, with those vehicles interchanging with each other so as not to arouse suspicion to one particular vehicle. Heavy traffic can cause problems. In these events, as close contact as possible without crowding him may be warranted rather than losing sight of the target vehicle. During night driving, headlights can sometimes be useful by using a toggle-like switch under the dash to control the headlights on, off, or each one individually.
- Involving two cars in tailing a suspect's auto can be much more effective than one, because the risk of detection can be reduced by interchanging vehicle positions. However, budget restrictions may force the investigator to rely on only one vehicle. Ideally, the surveillance vehicle should contain two operators—the driver and the passenger who will act as an observer and recorder. Unfortunately, a vehicle containing two people sitting at a stationery location for a period of time will cause some suspicion, even from the average citizen. If there are two operators, one could leave the vehicle and tail on foot if the target parks and leaves his vehicle. Anyone in a vehicle or on foot should wear dark clothing, because bright or colorful clothing stands out. The idea is to blend into the scene around the target. This includes the auto as well as all team operators.
- There is a tendency for inexperienced investigators to become easily convinced that they have been uncovered or "made" by the subject under surveillance. Professional investigators find that this is rarely a basis for the belief and can be attributed to the self-consciousness of the investigator because

of inexperience. As the novice investigator becomes more accomplished in surveillance techniques, the more value he or she will add to the agency that employs them, and the easier this activity will be to perform.

Logs

In any event, and whatever type of surveillance takes place, a log compiled and maintained of the subject or location under surveillance will or may form the basis of the report. Because activities observed during a surveillance may become part of evidence introduced at a trial or hearing, may be used in the cross-examination of a witness, or may become the basis of interrogation within that process, it is important that all information collected be recorded chronologically in log format.

The log may be brief as to the entries but relevant to the issue:

- The date and time, agents assigned.
- The period of the surveillance.
- The location under observation.
- The time of arrival and departure of agents assigned.
- Vehicles and agents involved in a tail.
- Description of the subject's vehicle and the route of the vehicle.
- Description of the location under surveillance.
- Telephone calls made by the subject or agent.
- Conversations overheard.
- Persons in contact with the subject.
- Photographs taken and identified by date, time, location, subject, and agent involved.
- As complete a description as possible of places visited by the subject.

Team Surveillance Operations

During a surveillance operation where the target is being followed on foot and the investigator is assisted by an associate or as a member of a team, each should have a good understanding of the roles each member will play, as well as the knowledge of the communications that will be used in the surveillance process. As well as radio communications, there should be an understanding to communicate nonverbally. Using a pattern of physical signs will enable everyone involved to move and operate as one. When radio communication is not appropriate, a series of signs specific and known to one's partner or the team can be used effectively without detection by the target. Examples of this include: exaggerating the movement somewhat in the use of hands and arms to indicate direction, scratching the head, looking at one's watch, removing a hat or some other motion that all agree on. On static surveillance situations, hand signals can be useful between team members located at a distance from each other. Moreover, during lengthy surveillance periods at a particular location, team members should change with each other at regular intervals. Of course, moving in and out of a static location must be conducted with stealth.

If an operative inadvertently happens to come too close to the target and there is some contact or communication between them where the surveillance could be compromised, resourcefulness and ingenuity may be all that the operative can rely on. In a case such as this, a good cover story can usually be all that is needed.

The use of accents (not one's own) by an investigator while attempting or in a deceptive mode, undercover or conducting a surveillance, can be dangerous and a dead giveaway.

Dress, Equipment, and Supplies

Whenever a private investigator is involved in any investigation or surveillance, he or she must be properly equipped for any circumstance. The choice of clothing worn by an investigator during surveillance or while on a tail should be as discreet and nondescriptive as possible. There will be times where there is no chance to change clothes, but one can still alter his or her appearance to a great degree. Carrying a newspaper or a shopping bag that can be folded and placed in a back pocket, taking off one's tie or jacket and placing them in the shopping bag, or even folding one's coat over the arm can alter a person's depiction to a great degree. Even the use of a baseball cap or fedora that can also be folded out of sight or if viable even a change in footwear carried in the trunk of your vehicle can alter one's appearance.

The choice of clothing is an important aspect of any surveillance. In a static surveillance, the investigator should wear dark clothing, and when undertaking a moving surveillance, the dress of the investigator should not be outstanding so as to fit in with the surroundings at that time. The idea here is to become a "gray person"—the kind of individual who fits in with his surroundings and to whom no one takes notice.

The following items are to be considered of importance in the PIs profession:

- *The investigator's automobile:*
  - Should be in good running condition, check all lights, warning systems, oil, full gas tank, windshield washer fluid, and all other fluids.
  - The color of the vehicle should be dark rather than light in color, with no decals or other identifying marks or markings.
  - The vehicle should not contain any whips, aerials, extra lights, decals, bumper stickers, or special registration plates.
  - The vehicle should contain the vehicle registration certificate, local, area and state maps, first aid kit, camcorder, camera (including VCR tapes, recordable CDs, and film as required), and a fully charged handheld radio.

- Because the investigators may find themselves in unfamiliar territory and therefore become confused or lost, the vehicle should contain the necessary maps of the area in which the subject of the surveillance will be mobile in, and an auto-mounted compass.
- All equipment, paperwork, and statement paper should be kept out of sight, properly contained in the trunk of the vehicle. The interior of the car should be clean and neat, with nothing that would indicate the driver's occupation or purpose.
- Various articles and a change of clothing should also be carried in the trunk so that a change in appearance can be made on short notice.

- *The investigator's personal equipment*:
  - Proper license and identification.
  - A fully charged cell phone that is programmed for easy dial-up with the telephone numbers of police emergency or associates and team members.
  - Covert radio equipment with throat mike and earpiece.
  - Pen, pencil, notepad.
  - A good wristwatch that can be easily read day or night.
  - A lightweight compass.
  - Change for tolls, meters, and telephones.
- A large, heavy cell metal flashlight that can be used also as a protective weapon when needed since blackjacks, saps, or billy clubs are unlawful.
- *Also, as may be required*:
  - A handgun (if necessary as part of the assignment, properly trained and licensed to carry).
  - Protective clothing, including stab/bulletproof vests, again depending on the type of environment or the investigation at hand.
  - Pepper spray or a mace-like substance for personal protection (legally possessed).
  - Handcuffs (see the "Restraining Devices" section later in this chapter).

Cautionary Activity

The agent should be conscious that if the subject who is under surveillance and who is shrewd and constantly aware and guarding against a "tail," he may have one of his own associates follow him at a reasonable distance in order to determine or observe that the same person is constantly in the rear of his confederate. Therefore, if the agent believes this to be the case, he or she must keep a lookout to the rear in order to be satisfied that no one is "following" him or her.

Regarding personal equipment, it is not inconceivable that at some time in an investigation, the agent may be placed in a compromising position where he or she is discovered, is a victim of an assault, or faces a dog attack. An encounter with a dog, whether just barking or outwardly aggressive, is not uncommon. A barking dog can awaken the whole neighborhood if it occurs during the evening hours, thereby placing the agent in a possible compromising position. Consider that when the police are called to a particular neighborhood during a dark quiet night for a possible prowler, they can usually track the prowler from property to property or location to location by barking dogs as the prowler attempts to leave furtively and proceeds through each location. Therefore, consider neighborhood dogs as a problem when committed to a surveillance site, particularly on a dark, quiet night.

But there may be times when dogs may present a more serious problem. A confrontation by a vicious dog may require the use of some animal spray or deterrent if one is quickly available. If not, it is now down to you and the dog. Animal experts state that whatever you do, *don't run* (the dog will win). Stand your ground facing the dog, and attempt to remain as calm as possible. Dogs can sense fear. Do not make any sudden movements or wave your arms around or kick out. Keep facing the dog but *do not make eye contact* with the animal—keep your eyes on the dogs' back, not on its head. Looking directly into the eyes of a dog may incite an attack. As the situation appears to calm, back away slowly. If an attack does occur, use whatever means that you can bring to hand, such as the dog spray, a stick, a brick, or anything else that can be used as a weapon to fend off the dog. Striking the dog in the throat, between the chest and throat, or between the base of the skull and the back will usually stop the attack.

Further, regarding personal protection, when in a room, the investigator should make sure to be between the subject and the door so that an exit from the area can be made quickly. Keep your vehicle as close as possible and parked in a position that will enable you to leave the area quickly and easily or, if necessary, to facilitate a fast getaway. Parking in this manner should not include parking facing into a dead-end street or parking near the property under surveillance where you have to drive past it and may be observed. While in the vehicle, keep all doors locked. In traffic, keep well back from other vehicles, with enough room to maneuver your vehicle in any situation.

Consider also that it is important that all investigators be qualified at the minimum in basic first aid and be inoculated or protected as may be required and obligated against blood-borne pathogens such as HIV, and hepatitis A, B, and C. Also, seek immediate medical help after a serious confrontation with a dog attack and plan on an immunization for rabies. Unfortunately, one cannot guarantee that you will never become a victim of violence of some type. Plan for the basis that you will likely become a victim and you will most probably keep out of trouble and away from serious harm.

Weapons used by an attacker might include a pistol, rifle, shotgun, baseball bat, club, broken bottle, or anything that can cause a severe injury. The investigator should consider attending a self-defense or personal protection school that offers fast, easy, and effective defenses against the more common attacks.

Possession of a handgun by licensed private investigators will surely require a pistol permit issued by most if not all local or state authorities. Possession of billy clubs or blackjacks (considered concealable weapons), handcuffs, and noxious substances such as pepper spray and mace are or may be illegal to possess depending on local or state law. Check with your local and state statutes concerning the licensure and possession and use of these implements.

If found to be legal, use caution and discretion in their use. Unlawful, improper, and aberrant behavior in handling these devices will certainly initiate criminal and civil action against the offender.

Restraining Devices

Generally, the only restraining device that a security officer or a PI may possess or use in the scope of his or her employment would be handcuffs. However, there are many localities and jurisdictions that forbid the use of handcuffs other than use by law enforcement officers. The rationale given is that handcuffs can and have been used as a weapon to pummel or punish another person, or that they may be tightened around the wrists to be used as "pain compliance" in order to control a defendant.

Handcuffs are used only to restrict the movement or prevent the escape of a defendant, or to protect the defendant or others from harm. If permission to possess and use a set of handcuffs is granted to the officer or investigator by his or her employer or agency, and the governing or licensing agency grants legal possession and use, the officer or investigator should have some training in application and procedures. This should include how to restrain the subject with handcuffs, how tight they should be, and to possess only those cuffs that can be double locked in order to prevent covert unlocking by the subject. If the subject complains of illegal or unauthorized use of handcuffs in that the handcuffs were used unlawfully or in a brutal or angry manner, and subsequently initiates a claim in a criminal or civil action, the mandatory and recorded training can be used as a defense.

Chemical sprays, noxious substances, electronic devices, or any implement used to control or disable a subject should never be used, because most if not all would be illegal in the state of your employment. The public generally disapproves of any use of these devices except by law enforcement. The possibilities of liability claims are too great to be considered.

Investigative Photography

Fundamental Equipment

The primary objective of a private investigator is the gathering of information that can be used as evidence or further inquiry. Other than personal evidence given by a witness of what was seen, heard, or touched, photography in two forms may stand-alone as evidence or can be essential to corroborate other evidence. Though many investigators possess and use film cameras and VCR video camcorders (reliable equipment presently on hand), the more up-to-date investigator or agency will have progressed to new technology with digital cameras and camcorders.

Photos or video confirm what you, the investigator observed. Nothing remains the same—scenes change, buildings and the rooms contained therein may be destroyed or renovated, furniture may be moved about, and evidence that was fundamental to the case may be removed. The taking of photos is a permanent, accurate, and impartial record of something that was observed by the investigator or someone else, and this documentation may be used as a reference or evidence in court.

Moreover, a photo records a specific appearance of something and details or reveals that which may not have been observed at the time the photo was taken. Most important for the PI is that certain elements be met. To ensure admissibility in court of photographs taken by the investigator, the following are to be considered minimal requirements:

1. The scene or object that is to be represented and photographed must be material or relevant to the investigation or the issue at hand.
2. Photographs or video must not appeal to the emotions or sensitivity of others, or tend to unduly incite prejudice or the sympathy of the court or jury.
3. The investigator must photograph or video the scene or object as is; it must be free from distortion (perspective, point of view, or exposure) and any misrepresentation of the scene or object it purports to depict.
4. Each photo should be marked as to case number, person who took the photo, date, time, description, and location where the photo was taken.

Private investigators must have some fundamental training and experience in the use of cameras and camcorders. Their camera equipment must be professional and fit to the task at hand. Many film cameras in use today by investigators are 35-mm single-lens reflex (SLR). However, the use of the film camera has become outdated.

The problem of maintaining negatives and prints, particularly if excessive in nature, has been lessened to a great degree by new camera technology introduced in the past few years. The compact SLR digital camera has all the features that were found in the more expensive outdated SLR film cameras with several added features. The more features that a camera has, including the capacity to zoom in on a subject from a great distance, creates more opportunities of picture-taking in all types of conditions.

No film is required and compact memory cards inserted into the camera have the ability to take and hold 300 or more pictures depending on the amount of storage on the card. The picture or images, which are in color, can be reviewed on the camera's LCD monitor, and retaken immediately, if necessary. The memory card can be removed and inserted into a printer for hard-copy prints or a computer for storage to a CD for easy access at a later time. These digital cameras have become highly sophisticated and easy to use, so much so that regular film cameras are becoming obsolete.

Camcorders on the other hand have been around for some time. These instruments may be used to record ongoing action or incidents in real time. They have been very successful in matrimonial cases, accident fraud (particularly worker's compensation), employee larceny, and other work-related offenses. Again, recent technology has accounted for current camcorders in digital modes, and they have been highly useful because they can be used for both DVD camcorder and digital still camera formats.

Accident Investigation

The type of accident or crime will dictate the photographs that need to be taken. Auto accident investigation requires detailed picture taking in that there are eight major photos that must be taken. The vehicle must be identified—front and back shots should include the registration plates, including a shot of each of the VIN plates located on the dash and door post. The pictures should include the following angles of the vehicle: 12, 3, 6, and 9 o'clock. Subsequent to that, photos should be taken at angles of 2, 5, 7, and 10 o'clock. Thereafter, photos should be taken distant and at close range of all vehicle damage, and any trace evidence such as paint or blood. Attempt to use some measuring device in these shots which should be at a 90-degree angle. Some of the photos may have to be taken at a distance and at close range so as to get a proper perspective of the vehicle and what needs to be represented.

The Art of the Interview and Interrogation

There are two distinct differences in performance concerning the use of interviews and interrogations during an investigation.

> *The interview is the first step in the investigative process in that it is not accusatory in nature.*

When an investigator makes inquiries or asks questions of someone, he or she is attempting to verify or gain information that will assist him or her in the investigation being conducted. Because the conversation is an attempt to gain information, it is directed toward witnesses, passersby, or anyone who may have seen, heard, has knowledge of, or was present at a scene in which the investigator wishes to inquire; the endeavor is meant to be friendly and not aggressive or confrontational. It is a way of ascertaining facts, witnesses, and evidence, and whether the incident is criminal or not in nature.

An interrogation is another matter, as it is considered accusatory.

The subject is now the focus of the investigation, and the interview now becomes more aggressive as the interrogator zeros in on the subject based on information or evidence gathered. The most important point that the novice investigator must remember is that during an interrogation, the subject who is questioned cannot successfully present a false scenario consistently. In other words, a good interrogator will remember and zero in on the inconsistencies during the questioning. Interrogation may be considered "an art whereby through the use of questioning and observation the truth is elicited from a suspect by sound reasoning and understanding without the use of threats or promises."[6]

Consider also that an interrogation is the art or process of asking questions in order to gain information from a subject who is unwilling to give up or provide that information. Accordingly, the investigator must realize that no two human beings are alike, and that how they think and react to different circumstances in different environments will color their demeanor and answers. People who have had negative experiences with the police or other higher authorities will be less susceptible to answering questions that might place them or someone else in jeopardy. Law-abiding citizens are more likely to answer all questions and readily assist the investigator, unless they have something to hide. Moreover, intelligent and sophisticated people may be somewhat cautious in answering questions, whereas a simple or naïve person is more likely to be controlled or intimidated by the investigator.

However, the fabrication, insinuation, or trickery by the interrogator that he or she has more or certain "knowledge or facts" in the case in order to deceive or make a subject more vulnerable *cannot be understated.*

Consequently, in an interrogation, the investigator must find or discover the "key" to each subject. As noted above regarding fabrications or trickery, this might include discovering or appealing to one's conscience, religious beliefs, and emotional state, or listening to reason. Constantly getting back to and rephrasing certain questions in various ways will, in time, confuse the subject. The interrogator must present him- or herself as having more knowledge of the incident or the subject under questioning. If the investigator is organized and consistent, emphasizing certain points that the subject avoids or presents as unclear or deceptive, the subject will realize that the investigator is competent and hard to deceive. Whereas an incompetent interrogator who assails the subject with aimless questions and has no organization to his or her strategy will lose all respect from that subject, who will easily give the investigator little if any information.

Routine Investigations (Not Criminal in Nature)
Interviews

1. Anytime a private investigator or a security officer asks questions of another concerning an incident, it is an interview.
2. An important interview will be for the purpose of gathering information for insurance purposes and possible future civil litigation.
3. In cases of personal injury, damage to personal or company property, criminal activity, product liability, and apprehensions and arrests, to name a few, certain inquiries, questions, and actions by the investigator must take place with witnesses and persons involved.
4. Information gathered for forms and reports that should have been compiled along with any photographs applicable to the case in question must be reviewed, put in writing, and copies made part of and attached to the case file.
5. Witness statements must be obtained in writing or at least the interview reduced to writing along with the identification of the subject interviewed, and attached to and made part of the final case file.

Criminal Investigations

Interviews

1. The interviews are not accusatory but are basically a conversation between the interviewer and the interviewee in order to determine the facts.
2. The investigator has little or no evidence at this point.
3. There are no formal charges against any subject or any suspect, and there are no overt indications that any suspicions are being formulated.
4. The investigator takes notes for future reference and begins to form a strategy.

Interrogations

1. The guilt of the suspect is reasonably certain in the mind of the investigator.
2. The investigator now dominates the conversation, and the tone of the interaction becomes accusatory.

3. Evidence against the suspect is known or is insinuated so as to mislead the suspect into a false comfort.
4. The interrogation of the suspect must be private with no interruptions or distractions of any kind.
5. The investigator takes no notes during the interrogation so as not to give the suspect time to think or become wary that information is being put down in writing.

The Interview

Interview Procedures

The greatest part of any investigation is usually devoted to interviews. The better investigators must have the qualities of a salesman, actor, and psychologist. He or she must establish a rapport with the interviewee. The investigator's presence should induce confidence without an air of superiority. Demeanor should be sympathetic and understanding with an avoidance of any racial or prejudicial traits between both the investigator and the subject interviewed.

The investigator must suit his or her techniques of interviewing to the varied personalities or class of people—children, boys, girls, young persons, middle-aged persons, and older persons. Once the investigator determines the group or class of the subject to be interviewed, he or she must then adjust the method of interviewing to the type of personality and attitude of that subject.

The following procedures elaborated in this section regarding the interviewing of witnesses may be applied to any interview involving a civil or criminal case that the private investigator may be assigned.

Interview of Witnesses

According to psychological practitioners, people forget 50 to 80% of the details of what they have seen or heard within 24 hours of the event. Therefore, witnesses should be interviewed as soon as possible following that event for a more tangible rendering of what was seen or heard at the time.

There are several factors that have a tendency to effect one's testimony as time passes. These are areas in which we all are at fault because we are human, and as humans, we tend to have failings.

The investigator must make a conscious effort to recognize when testimony may be altered for one or more of the following reasons:

1. *Forgetfulness*—It is not uncommon for a person to forget or not recall something that may not have been noteworthy or important at the time.

2. *Rationalization*—People tend to adjust or rationalize their memory of what they have seen with what other people say about the event or their own prejudices, opinions, or convictions.
3. *Memory Substitution*—People substitute what they think they remember, rather than what they actually remember.
4. *Biases and Self-Protection*—People have a tendency to consciously or unconsciously distort testimony the longer they have to think about an event. This may include a personal bias or may be to protect a friend or themselves.
5. *Vanity and Egotism*—The witness pretends to know more than what is actually known and embellishes or cultivates information or facts that only impair an investigation. This person may be a "cop buff" or has the intention of impressing the investigator with his or her knowledge and bearing.

The Interview Process

Segregate the Witnesses

Even prior to any responder or investigator at a scene, people tend to talk and compare information about an event. The tendency to rationalize accident facts or criminal actions is common in that people will adapt their memory to be consistent with what other witnesses say. This is particularly so if one witness is more dominant or outspoken than another. In order to control this, witnesses should be segregated as soon as possible so that their testimony may not be corrupted in any way.

Interview Privately

Witnesses must be interviewed privately, away from other witnesses or bystanders. Choose a location where interruptions and excessive noise will not interfere during the process. Access the witness's condition—is he or she in shock, agitated, or nervous? Try to attend to his or her physical comfort before the interview. Offer a cup of coffee, tea, or a soda, if possible. While the witness is seated, do not stand or sit in a "commanding" position. Do not sit behind a desk; rather sit across or next to the witness while making eye contact that is not harsh but that communicates genuine concern. The interviewer must maintain a calm and caring attitude. Avoid the use of abusive, foul, or threatening language, as it will only create negative reactions. Also, the interviewer must not accuse or place responsibility on anyone and must never express any opinion, particularly regarding the event. Try not to focus on fault or guilt as it may create conflicting feelings within the witness and may offer incomplete or inaccurate testimony. If necessary and if possible, shift the focus from people to things, such as procedures, response, training, and communications.

In this way, the interviewer may be able to underscore the amount of useful or substantial information that can be obtained. Moreover, privacy allows the witness to relay information without the pressure of other people hearing what is said, allowing trust and confidence to be established between the investigator and the witness.

Documentation

Ask first, but if the witness is hesitant, do not take notes or make a recording during the interview process. After talking and making sure the witness is comfortable, advise him or her that you would need to reduce what was said to writing as it is necessary to record facts and information for a report. Indicate that the report will be more complete with written and signed statements regarding the incident. If the witness is willing to give a written statement, the investigator should write down in his or her own hand, single spaced, exactly or as close as possible the words given by the witness. It should be dated and signed by the witness and witnessed by the investigator. See a sample copy of a statement taken from a witness in the Appendix C.

If the witness refuses to give a written statement, as soon as the interview is over, commit your recollection of the interview, relating all facts and information remembered, to writing (or a recording). Note the time, date, place, and person interviewed, and this writing will be attached to and made part of the report, as would an original written statement if taken.

Obtaining Basic Facts for the Statement

Start by asking the witness to tell all that he or she knows about the events that occurred before, during, and immediately after the incident. Do not interrupt, no matter what is said, unless the testimony goes far off track and must be gently guided back to the subject at hand. If conflicting information is offered, make a note of it to be used later for a contradiction if necessary. Interruptions or questioning at this time may cause a witness to hesitate and reflect on what is said and what he or she should have said.

Summarize the testimony given by slowly going over each key point and the essential elements bearing on the incident. Verify that the witness agrees with the investigator's understanding with the facts and information as related.

Once it is clear that the witness has related as much as is expected, and the investigator is satisfied that no more can be added at this time, the questioning of certain portions of the testimony can begin. Witnesses tend to skip from one point to another, skipping areas that may be of great interest to the investigator and failing to fill in gaps in recalling the event which may be of some importance. Follow-up questions will explain, clarify, or detail certain acts or actions by others, along with the consistency of the testimony as given by the witness. If the witness becomes vague or reluctant in answering some questions, rephrase the questions to obtain a specific or factual answer. Try not to ask questions that will provide the witness an opportunity to give a "yes" or "no" answer. Rather, use a question that must be answered with facts. An example might be "Did you hear what John said to Bill before he struck him with the hammer? What exactly did he say?" Be assertive on these points; do not let inconsistency, reluctance, or evasiveness slip by without pursuing a definite answer.

Reluctant or Unwilling Witnesses

Sometimes a witness does not have the communication skills, has a language barrier, or does not have the mental ability to understand the function or purpose of a witness and how it might affect him or others.

There will be times when a witness is reluctant or refuses to give any type of statement for whatever reason. Reasons may vary from fear of being socially ostracized, physical retribution, to wishing "not to get involved."

In any event, because PIs are not police officers with the clout of charging a person with withholding information or not cooperating (Obstruction of Governmental Administration), they have little authority in converting a witness to their way of thinking. Any thought of monetary gain for the witness should be discouraged, because any information of this type would certainly come to light if the witness has to appear in court. Whether the value of the information received is truthful or not, testimony obtained for money will certainly be considered as tainted.

The Interrogation

> The basic principle behind interrogation is that no one can successfully lie consistently to a good interrogator.

It must be taken into account that police officers and police detectives have much more clout during an interrogation than does a private investigator. The threat of criminal charges such as withholding information, lying, or giving false information to the police in an official investigation is usually enough to force the subject to give up and tell all that the police wish for. However, the PI does not have that ability and authority to "force" the truth from someone. Unless the interrogator is involved in an authorized criminal investigation prior to the police becoming involved and can become more aggressive, the investigator may have to rely on the "good faith" or the truthfulness of the subject in offering information rather than "forcing" information from them by coercion of law.

There are many personal aspects in the making of a good interviewer and interrogator. Most investigators will agree that the most important part of an investigation is their skills in the course of the interview, where most of the information they will gather will be obtained. In this regard, the art of interviewing is learned through experience rather than through formal training. To be successful, the interviewer must rely on the cooperation and, in many instances, the collaboration of the person interviewed.

Because private investigators do not have the ability to compel information or testimony from the person as a police officer might, they must stress those techniques and methods they learned in an effort to elicit as much information as possible.

If following an interview an interrogation of a suspect takes place, there are many techniques that will induce positive results. These will include close observation of the subject's behavior, attitude, physical changes, body postures, facial expressions, gestures, tics, and eye movements. Unless the private investigator has previous experience in law enforcement and has had some training in this area, it is suggested that participation in some type of formal instruction be had from a reputable firm that conducts specialized training and seminars in this field.

Bear in Mind the Following Points on Interrogation

- Eliciting worthy information from a subject during an interrogation takes skill and time.
- The interrogator must be cognizant of his or her prejudice, biases, or prejudged adverse opinions that may distort or corrupt the information received.
- If possible, the interrogator should establish a baseline of normal behavior prior to interrogation.
- The interrogation technique practiced can be very good, but body language plays an important augmentation to the process.
- Watch the responses of the subject carefully where he or she tries to convince rather than convey.
- Have the subject of the interrogation sit in front of you with no encumbrances in between. An interrogator loses half of the body language when the subject sits behind a table.
- It is more difficult to analyze older subjects regarding body language. As we age, we become better at lying and hiding our emotions.
- Spiritual or religious values of the subject can cause torment and anxiety if approached correctly.

And concerning mechanical or electronic results, remember the following:

- The polygraph is basically a medical machine involving the measurement of blood pressure, breathing, and perspiration.
- Voice-print analyzation measures one's emotional response.
- When offered as evidence in court, both are subject to vehement confrontation by a defense attorney.

Because of the importance of the interrogation process, the following nine steps of interrogation are offered as a method of an acceptable and proficient procedure.

The Reid Nine Steps of Interrogation[7]

1. *Having Direct Positive Confrontation*—Advise the subject that based on the facts and evidence, he or she is in fact considered the guilty party.
2. *Developing a Theme*—Consider this to be the most important of the nine steps. Once the interrogator identifies the theme, the blame for the offense will be placed elsewhere. It will be an attempt to give social and moral justification to the subject that gave cause or led to the offense.
3. *Handling Denials*—The interrogator should limit the amount of interruptions by the subject during the session, so as to cut down on denials.
4. *Overcoming Objections*—Attempt to develop a theme out of the subject's excuses or objections. Turn and use this behavior against the subject.
5. *Procuring and Retaining the Subject's Attention*—Direct the subject's attention toward you, the interrogator. Move closer to the subject. Touch the subject lightly, physically, on the arm or the hand. Show sincerity, compassion, and some agreement or understanding of how the "act" could or did occur.
6. *Handling the Subject's Passive Mood*—The interrogator should recognize that the subject has reached a point of resignation and is ready to "give up"—ready to confess.
7. *Presenting an Alternative Question*—Attempt to obtain an admission. Offer a "face-saving" solution, an alternative that is not as self-incriminating in the subject's eyes.
8. *Having the Subject Relate Various Details of the Offense*—The interrogator should now gather all the specifics of the offense, including associates, if any, and anyone else who may be involved. Use care at this point. The subject may not wish to involve anyone else.
9. *Converting an Oral Confession into a Written Confession*—The reduction of all oral admissions to a written statement, signed by the subject and witnessed.

We must remember that the process of interviewing and interrogating by an investigator is an art, but it can be learned.

The Miranda Warnings and Other Issues

The Miranda warnings are basically warnings given to a suspect of a crime in which he or she is advised that the suspect has certain constitutional rights, in that the suspect has the right not to incriminate him- or herself as provided in the Fifth Amendment of the U.S. Constitution. The U.S. Supreme Court decreed this requirement for the legal admission of oral and written statements.[8]

A police officer has some restrictions regarding interviewing and interrogation that the private investigator—a private person—does not have to abide with. After interviewing or gathering the facts, once a police officer determines or zeros in on a suspect, the Miranda warnings must be issued, and the interview now becomes an interrogation.

> The requirement that Miranda warnings be given to a suspect of a crime or offense is binding only on police officers or other law enforcement personnel who have custody of a suspect they wish to question. This rule does not apply to private investigators, security officers, security guards, store detectives, loss prevention officers, or any private person, even if the subject to be questioned is in custody and under arrest.9
>
> However, if a private investigator, or any private person noted above, is requested by a police officer to conduct an "interview" or any type of interrogation, or a police officer is present during any interview or questioning by an investigator at any time, the private investigator has now become an agent of the police, and the Miranda warnings must be issued. Otherwise, any admissions or statements made by the defendant under these conditions will not be admissible in court because the warning was not given.[10]

The Warnings

As defined by the Supreme Court, the warnings are *obligatory for a law enforcement officer* once the suspect is now considered the perpetrator or possible perpetrator, and must be given to the suspect *before any questioning*:

1. You have the right to remain silent.
2. Anything you say can be used against you in a court of law.
3. You have the right to the presence of an attorney.
4. If you cannot afford an attorney, one will be appointed for you free of charge prior to any questioning if you so desire.

In addition, almost all police departments and law enforcement agencies have added a fifth element of the warning that was not required by the court, but by giving this extra admonition, it can forestall any subsequent objections by an attorney concerning a client's admissions: "If you wish to answer any questions without an attorney present, you have the right to stop at any time and request an attorney before continuing this questioning. Do you understand what I just said (or read)?"

It must be understood that the suspect must completely understand what he is being told, and if the suspect indicates at any time after the warning or during questioning that he or she does not wish to continue answering any questions, or that he or she wants a lawyer, the questioning must stop. If the suspect states that he or she is willing to answer any question and does not want an attorney, an oral waiver is sufficient. Caution must be used in the case of a mentally challenged person or a person of low intelligence. It will be assumed by the court that the suspect who falls into this category will not have the wherewithal to relinquish his or her right to self-incrimination.

Other Fields of Cautionary Inquiry

Union Employees

If a private investigator is employed by a business client to investigate some criminal act or company offense where the result of such investigation will bring about the arrest or termination of an employee, certain procedures must be acted upon besides the Miranda warnings (if required in a criminal case).

If the employee to be questioned belongs to a union, that employee has the right to request union representation or another member of the union to be present during any questioning.[11] The investigator is not required or obligated to advise the union employee of this right. It is up to that employee or his or her union to make the request.[12] The union representative or another union member may be present during the investigation or interrogation of the suspect employee. However, he or she may not act on behalf of or in an adversary manner as an attorney would if the employee were a client, nor can they interrupt the process other than to make suggestions, clarify facts, or offer other information on other employees.[13]

Juveniles

In some states, the police cannot interview or interrogate a juvenile under any circumstances without a parent, guardian, or court-authorized person present.

As a general rule, however, the interrogation of juveniles is best left to the police and at their discretion. Defenses such as the parent not being present when the child is questioned or that the child is too young to understand the nature of surrendering his or her rights, would most assuredly come up when the client's attorney enters the case.

Juvenile Apprehension Procedures

Without a doubt, many larceny offenses and other crimes against property will come to the attention of the security officer which will involve the juvenile as the perpetrator. The security officer must be aware that there are different laws and procedures concerning the handling, apprehension, and custody of a juvenile. Various states detail specific actions that must be carried out by police or peace officers regarding children. Additionally, these statutes may note the requirements that must be undertaken by a private citizen (security officer) prior to and after a juvenile is taken into custody.

Juvenile Defined

For the purposes of identifying when a child becomes classified as a juvenile and as a delinquent, the following narration is offered:

- "Juvenile delinquency is anti-social behavior by a minor, especially behavior that would be criminally punishable if the actor were an adult" (*Black's Law Dictionary*).
- A juvenile is a minor; a person who has not reached legal age; a child. A minor or juvenile may also be considered one who has not reached the age of legal competence, which may be designated as the age of 18 in most states. Moreover, in some states, a minor may be classified as an infant in civil law.
- A juvenile delinquent is a classification given to a minor who has committed a criminal wrong, and the offender is usually punished by special laws pertaining to children. Recent definitions of juvenile delinquency note that a delinquent is an infant of not more than a specified age who has violated criminal laws or has engaged in disobedient, indecent, or immoral conduct, and is in need of treatment, rehabilitation, or supervision.[14] Infancy is defined as the state of a person who is *under the age of legal majority*.[15]

The Age of Legal Majority Legislated in the United States[16]

21 years of age—2 states	19 years of age—2 states
20 years of age—None	18 years of age—46 states

Generally accepted is that the designation of *juvenile delinquent* is given to a child who engaged in an act that would be a crime if such crime was committed by an adult. Depending on a state's criminal code, juveniles may be classified as such depending on their age at the time of the offense. Some states require a minimum age of 10 or 12 years, and a maximum of 15, 16, or 17 years for a juvenile delinquency specification.[17] However confusing we may view the definition given to a juvenile offender by the various states, we must consider that each year, court decisions reevaluate the status of a juvenile. Moreover, a juvenile court is created by statutory law. Therefore, the boundaries of jurisdiction between the juvenile and criminal courts are subject to review and modification.[18]

The Courts

Depending on the individual state, the court that has jurisdiction over children may be called a Youth Court, Juvenile Court, or Family Court. These courts have been legislated by the state in favor of a specific jurisdiction of a parental nature, over delinquent, dependent, and neglected children.

The first juvenile court was established in Chicago in 1899 by educators and reformers seeking the causes of juvenile delinquency, and what role society, poverty, social status, and the family had in the performance of mischievous behavior. By 1945, every state had a court established with its own set of laws specifically for juvenile offenders. Most experts in the field of juvenile behavior believe that laws pertaining to children were originally conceived in an effort to place the youth, not the offense, at the forefront. Moreover, critics have noted that there is no uniform juvenile justice system in the United States. Unfortunately, the system today leaves much to be desired. Juvenile courts appear to be incapable of addressing the complex needs of children and families, often causing more harm than good to the child.

Some states make no legal definition or distinction between juveniles and adults when it comes to a crime committed or charged. Other states designate children of a certain age as "delinquent offenders" if they commit an act that would be a crime if committed by an adult. For those minor acts not reaching the status of a crime, such as truancy, runaways, or incorrigible conduct, a child could be classified as a "status offender" that might be described as a *person in need of supervision* (PINS). Each state may differ in the classification and treatment regarding children. Depending on the seriousness of the crime committed by the juvenile, the local prosecutor or district attorney along with the judge sitting in the appropriate court may adjudicate that the juvenile should face the charge in a criminal court and suffer the consequences as an adult.

> However, the U.S. Supreme Court set certain criteria for states in deciding whether a juvenile should be transferred or waived to a criminal court for trial.[19] The case before the court that brought about this decision concerned 14-year-old Morris Kent of Washington, D.C., who was arrested for the crimes of rape and robbery. Although admitting to the crimes, the boy was found by the court to have been tried in violation of due process, and the court dismissed the case.
>
> It was found that the parents of Morris Kent were not notified of his arrest, he was interrogated without being informed of his rights to remain silent or have representation by an attorney, he was detained without a probable cause hearing, and the police had matched his fingerprints from previous records on file.[20]

In addition, the U.S. Supreme Court set standards for transferring or waiving a juvenile to a criminal court.[21] These precepts include the following:

- The seriousness of the alleged offense.
- The aggressive, violent, and premeditative nature of the act, whether against a person or property.
- The death or serious nature of personal injury to another.
- Whether the juvenile's associates acting in concert during the crime are adults who will face the charges in criminal court.
- The juvenile's maturity, emotional and social attitude, and the effect of the home environment.
- The juvenile's previous criminal or juvenile record, if any.

In some states, for the purpose of not designating or "branding" a child a "criminal," the child adjudged a juvenile may be considered a *respondent* and not a *defendant* as an adult would be, and when that juvenile is apprehended, he or she is *custodialized,* not *arrested.*

Exceptions to this rule are some of the very serious felonies in which a child who initially falls under the designation of a juvenile delinquent may be charged as an adult in a criminal court. The age categories may differ in some states, but the seriousness of the crime would be the determining factor.

The court and the prosecutor acting in the interest of justice will make the determination as to whether the juvenile is to be charged as a juvenile delinquent in a juvenile court or a defendant in a criminal court. Undoubtedly, the public's view of a horrendous or egregious act by the juvenile, particularly upon another child or person, would have some input in that decision. Depending on the state, extremely grievous crimes would include offenses such as murder, rape, sodomy, arson, or kidnapping.

Other than that proscribed in a particular criminal code in the state of your employment, bear in mind that generally, you cannot take a juvenile into custody (custodial—which is in fact an arrest) for a noncriminal act. The private investigator or security officer can only take a juvenile into custody if the act committed by the juvenile would be a *crime* if committed by an adult.

It is important to reiterate this principle—a juvenile can only be *arrested/custodialized* and detained if the crime committed was one that an adult could be arrested for.

Check with your own state's codes in regard to juveniles.

Juvenile "Custodial" and Detention Procedures

A private citizen (PI or security guard) must advise the juvenile of the cause and purpose of the apprehension and the taking into custody, and require that he or she submit. Thereafter, most states require that *without unnecessary delay,* the juvenile must be turned over to a parent or guardian, taken to his or her home, brought before a family or juvenile court judge, or delivered to a police or peace officer.

In an event where a security officer or an investigator has control or authority over a particular location such as a retail establishment, shopping mall, or other public venue, there may occur an incident where a juvenile conducts himself in such a manner to be a nuisance, become disruptive, or cause a disturbance, but his behavior is not considered serious enough to charge the child with a "crime." However, a business establishment has the right to maintain a secure and protected environment safe from any disorder for their visitors, clients, or customers. It is suggested that a business enterprise establish written policy (guidelines and procedures) to cover this type of juvenile occurrence.

The taking of a child into custody under these conditions is technically an arrest, and business administrators will require that the child who is taken into custody be immediately turned over to a parent or the police for whatever juvenile procedures they follow.

Consequently, it is suggested that for a circumstance where a juvenile is taken into custody but will not be charged and no police action will be requested, that the loss prevention manager or security officer be guided by the merchant or owner's legal counsel concerning action to be taken. Counsel may feel that under some minor noncriminal circumstances that the parent, parents, or guardian of the juvenile be advised immediately by telephone of the particulars surrounding the incident, and that they respond to the caller's location as soon as practical so as to take the juvenile into their care. If the response of the parents or guardian will be delayed or will take an inordinate period of time, the security officer would do well to request police assistance and turn over custody to the police, even though there will be no court action. Generally, they are required to accept custody if a parent is not responding within a reasonable time (check with local police authorities). In this situation, the most that will happen will be that a "Juvenile" or "Juvenile Incident" card will be compiled by the police detailing the incident and noting parental notification following.

Apprehension, Custodial, and Questioning Procedures

If the juvenile is taken into custody and is to be charged, the police should be notified without delay. It then becomes their duty to advise the parents or custodian that the juvenile has been taken into custody, the circumstances surrounding the incident, and that the minor will be charged as a juvenile delinquent.

The private investigator and security officer should also be aware that once detained, there are different procedures for juveniles than those that may apply to adults. The juvenile should be taken from public view as soon as practical and should not be contained in the same room as adult defendants if at all possible. Because a juvenile may become frightened or disorientated, the security officer should attempt to act in a calm manner and not aggravate the situation. Restraints, such as handcuffs, should not be used on a juvenile unless the juvenile is being charged as a juvenile delinquent and becomes unruly, attempts to escape or fight his or her way clear, or acts in such a way where he or she may harm themselves or others. If restraints are used in these situations, and if called upon, the security officer may have to show to the court why it was necessary to do so. In these instances, the security officer should note witnesses to the actions of the juvenile and the necessity of restraints, and make the appropriate notations on the arrest or apprehension report for future reference.

Cautionary Note

Caution must be considered in the questioning of a juvenile. Other than that mandated in some state statutes, detaining a person for a period of time for questioning because of some suspicion and without probable cause, particularly if the subject believes such detaining is by force or threat, should be considered an unlawful arrest or unlawful imprisonment. However, in the case of a juvenile offender, in reality he cannot be considered able to relinquish his civil rights because of age. The juvenile may become intimidated by a security officer and place himself in jeopardy by making admissions that may later be excluded in court. Nevertheless, a private investigator or security officer could question and investigate a juvenile's actions if he receives *voluntary compliance.*

Voluntary compliance may be defined as consent by a person to communicate and respond to questions put to him by another. A juvenile in reality cannot give voluntary compliance if he does not understand what right he is giving up, and the court will definitely rule to that effect. But if a parent or a guardian is requested to accompany or meet the security officer in a security office or a private office along with the juvenile and the child is questioned in that parent's presence without any hindrance from that parent, voluntary compliance may be presumed. This presumption is generally accepted in most states, but some restrictions may apply to the questioning of juveniles in the state in which the security officer is employed.

Many young adults and teenagers carry false or altered identification in an effort to prove an older age. When the age of the person detained is doubtful or cannot be verified, it is recommended that regardless of the person's appearance, size, and maturity, that person should be treated as a juvenile. To reiterate, be cautious—if it is questionable as to the age of the person, treat that person as a juvenile rather than as an adult. There may be sanctions for treating a juvenile as an adult, but none for an adult who is treated as a juvenile prior to police custody.

Remember, be guided by the procedures concerning juvenile apprehension and detention in your state.

Conclusion

At this point in our narrative, it is important to reiterate the apprehension and custodial procedures of a juvenile. Generally stated, a security officer may take a child under the age of legal majority into custody as a juvenile delinquent for a crime that if committed by an adult would in fact be a crime for which he may arrest that adult. The same admonitions apply as to any arrest—informing the child of the cause thereof and requiring him to submit unless custody is made immediately after a pursuit. After taking that child into custody, state statutes require that the child be turned over to a parent, magistrate, or police officer without delay. Most importantly, the security officer is responsible for the complete well-being of the juvenile while in his or her care, and the security officer's actions are ultimately guided by federal and state law.

The investigator or officer should be cognizant of the laws and procedures governing the custody and terminology of a child in his or her particular state of employment.

> Remember and be extremely aware that as legislated in most state statutes, the private investigator or security officer (a private person) may take a juvenile into custody only if he or she committed an act that would be a crime if such an act (the crime) was committed by an adult.

Communication and Observation Techniques

The Communication Process

The communication process includes the following:

- *The Sender*—The person who is sending, offering, or giving the message.
- *The Receiver*—The person or persons to whom the message is directed and received.

> *The Written Word*—This form of communication is used to accentuate a directive, policy, or procedure. In its written form, the message cannot be misunderstood. Policy is not policy unless it is written.

Communication is received by a person's five senses:

1. Sight
2. Touch
3. Hearing
4. Smell
5. Taste

There are three methods of communication—*verbal, nonverbal,* and *written:*

1. *Verbal*—The spoken word to another and that other person hearing those words. This type of communication is used in all conversations where the spoken word is used—announcements, emergency notifications, public and personal relations, among others. Varieties of oral communication include language that is loud, abusive, or offensive, language that is friendly or neutral, and at times the manner of speech can be condescending. The tone or pitch of the articulation, the attitude of the sender, and the clarity of the message can all have some effect on how it is received.
2. *Nonverbal*—A message with meaning that is sent to another by gestures, movements, signs, signals, and body reflexes. It can take many forms that may give a signal that the sender is angry, argumentative, or submissive. At times, gestures may be used to add to or emphasize the spoken word. Depending on one's culture or ethnic background, this type of communication may be practiced more so than other groups within our society. Moreover, consider that any time the PI is in oral communication with another person, for whatever reason, body language can accentuate the message given.

   The first impression given by private investigators to another will be positive and long lasting for those who present themselves in a professional, competent manner.
3. *Written*—The use of words or the message put down on paper or in another form. This form of communication is used to document an incident or activities. It may be used to form directives, policy, and procedure. Rather than complicate a written message in whatever form that it may be presented, it should be short, to the point, and in simple language so that there would be no misinterpretation. It can aid memory at a later time.

Regarding these methods of communication, how that message is received can be greatly affected by the lack of speaking skills, mental competency, prejudice, or bias. The PI must be perceptive to those barriers that are discussed below.

Listening Guidelines

In the communication process for the private investigator, the most important of the five senses noted above is the sense of hearing (listening). People often assume that communicating with and influencing the other person's viewpoint and attitude are dependent upon one's ability to speak clearly and fluently, and to impress them with articulate verbal skills. Human communication is not always accomplished by talking, for it is equally important to be able to listen, and regarding the private investigator, to listen well.

The points described below identify the investigator as the *listener* (receiver), and the subject being questioned as the *speaker* or *talker* (sender).

- *Good communication is a two-way street.* Most of us like to speak more than listen. If we do not allow the other person the opportunity to speak, we are saying that we do not care about them or what they have to say. If we want to be heard, we must be willing to listen.
- *Good listening increases the dialogue.* If you are a good listener, you are usually well received at the start. When you let people know that you are listening and want to hear more, it could be a great compliment to the person who is speaking.
- *Good communication needs information.* If we listen and are listened to, the flow of information will produce good communication and understanding.
- *Good listening demands your attention.* Often we are preoccupied and distracted and we do not listen as we should. Give the talker your entire attention or you will miss the entire meaning.
- *Good listening enables you to understand and respect the other person's intent or point of view.* If we do not listen, particularly attentively, comprehension and *important facts given unwittingly may be lost.*
- *Good listening demands patience.* If we act as if we are impatient or too eager, we create in the other person a need for them to close down or express themselves inappropriately and often incorrectly.
- *Good communication demands sincerity.* If we are inattentive to the other person, or if we show that we are distracted or preoccupied, the talker will become aware of it and a wall will be built between the two.
- *Good listening takes a "third ear."* If we are interested in what the speaker is trying to convey to us, we can hear the emotion and meaning a lot better than merely allowing the words to fall on our ears. We must hear through our ears to our hearts. Basically this would include personal insight and commiseration, knowledge of the talker's background, the expertise and experience of the investigator, and the complete understanding of the case at hand.

Barriers to Effective Communication

The private investigator must be aware of his or her demeanor concerning the following obstacles that may be obvious or present in any contact with the subject. The following deterrents will or may alter the outcome of the dialogue:

- Uses ambiguous words and phrases.
- Has adverse personality or physical traits.
- Has strong biases or prejudices.
- Has an incomplete understanding of the subject matter.
- Lacks or does not have confidence.
- Lacks interest.
- Has poor communication techniques.
- Makes incorrect or incomplete statements.
- Talks too long or says too much.
- Fails to get and hold the listener's attention.
- Does not organize material.
- Sets up one-way communications.
- Tries to confuse intentionally.
- Talks over the head or above the comprehension of the listener.
- Is subject by superiors to excessive pressure for results.
- Has a physical separation or obstacle between the investigator and the subject (wall, glass, desk, fencing).
- Is disrupted by noise or discord that affects the communication.

Remember that in addition to that noted above, we must be conscious that aggressiveness, arrogance, belligerence, and a tough-guy image will produce a negative portrayal of the investigator in any contact with the public or the person interviewed or interrogated. Consequently, this behavior will have an effect on his or her work product.

As to the person being questioned, certain barriers will or may affect how well information is given or received. Examples are as follows:

- Poor timing
- Situation is or becomes too emotional
- Participants have strong feelings about the matter of the subject
- Fatigue
- Personality conflicts
- Distractions (various disruptions in the flow of the conversation between the private investigator and the subject, such as noise, family members, pedestrian traffic, etc.)

Sensitivity Issues

During any interaction with another person, particularly during an interview or an interrogation, the PI should be sensitive to such characteristics noted below and avoid any direct, indirect, or casual reference to them:

- Age
- Sex
- Race
- Ethnic background
- Religion
- Traditions/customs
- Values/beliefs
- Family structure
- Mental disability
- Physical disability
- Physical appearance (height, weight, hair, baldness, physical deformity, etc.)
- Lifestyle
- Homelessness
- Clothing, manner of dress
- Jewelry (type and how worn)

Some Suggestions in the Communication Process

During the communication process, behave in the following manners, by being:

- Polite, calm, and attentive
- Civil and courteous
- Open minded when evaluating the facts
- Business like
- Self-assured
- Respectful
- Helpful
- Responsive

Do not do the following:

- Argue, or be defensive
- Show anger, impatience, contempt, dislike, or sarcasm
- Take reactions to your bearing personally
- Appear to expect trouble
- Give the impression that you are a threat
- Be self-centered
- Let personal biases or prejudices affect your actions

When Communicating

- Be aware that a communication problem may have more to do with style than with the content.
- Learn to understand different styles.

- Concentrate and focus on the subject matter.
- Be constantly aware of what you want to say and how you will proceed in the questioning process.
- Talk about the process of communicating; ask the individual if he or she is comfortable that a clear understanding is taking place.
- Avoid jokes or comments, particularly of sexual, racial, or ethnic content, that may offend.
- Use language that fosters trust and alliance.
- Do not judge a person because of the way an individual articulates, his or her manner of dress, or his or her demeanor.

The Observation Process

Body Language

Obvious Nonverbal Behavior and Mannerisms

Facial Expressions—A person's "smiles and frowns" can signal much more than one's "ups and downs." Approval, disapproval, disgust, revulsion, fear, anger, happiness, sadness, surprise, love, and hate are only a few of the emotions we convey in our facial expressions.

Eyes—The direct unwavering stare is perceived by most people as a threat. Eye contact is what makes us aware of another person as a human being, and most encounters begin with eye contact. When we look away while listening to someone, we show dissatisfaction with what is being said. Looking away also indicates boredom, annoyance, or rejection. When someone is interested, eye contact is obvious. When we divert our eyes, look away or noticeably fail to make eye contact on a face-to-face confrontation during an interview, interrogation, or while being questioned, the indication is that the subject has something to hide or does not wish to face the question or accusation.

Hands—Often illustrate speech, by pointing or outlining shapes or punctuating speech. Signs substitute for language when two people are unfamiliar with the other's native tongue. The extent of the use of hands is partially cultural, as noted in Italian, Jewish, and Middle East cultures. Clenched hands or fists or the wringing of hands indicates the subject is under stress or is very tense.

Posture—Some postures indicate rapport, while others may indicate psychological distance. One set of postures may be evidenced when speaking and another when listening. Speaking postures are often differentiated by the kind of activities with different sets for explaining, asking questions, and giving orders. Crossed arms or legs, body leaning back into the chair, body turned away while being questioned, and body far from a relaxed state indicate that the subject is holding back, is uninformative as possible, or is hiding the truth.

Touching—Is an immediate mutual experience and is the most primitive of the senses. Power relationships are revealed by who touches who—the *toucher* is invariably more powerful than the *touchee.* An investigator can use this method to gain confidence and show empathy, compassion, agreement, or sorrow. This procedure or process of "touching" is considered one of the most effective methods of persuasion or winning one over to accept the reasoning or inception of a confession.

Subject Leaning Forward—Generally are displaying interest in what is being said, while those who lean back are showing their desire to get away from what is going on. A relaxed, open-body, sitting position shows that the individual is accepting what is being said and is not tense or nervous. A crossed-legged, arms-folded position indicates rejection or tension, if it is accompanied by the appropriate facial expressions of annoyance.

Tics—These are actions committed by the subject, sometimes subtle, sometimes not, that the subject being interviewed or interrogated is not aware of. This could include an eye twitch, involuntary facial tics, involuntary head jerks or movements, coughing, clearing of the throat, and finger movements, among others.

If one is observant, certain body movements, gestures, or tics may be considered as indicators or barriers to the communication process between the PI and the subject being questioned during an interview or an interrogation.

These observations may include one or more of the following within a particular characteristic or personal mannerism:

Openness

Unbuttoned coat
Uncrossed legs
Uncrossed arms
Moving closer

Defensiveness

Arms crossed on chest
Fists clenched
Hands or arms tightly gripped
Leg over arm of chair
Sitting with chair reverted
Crossed legs
Downcast eyes
Does not make eye contact
Oblong or constant smile
Turns body slightly away

Tension

Short breaths
Tightly clenched hands
Palm to back of neck
Wringing hands
Clearing throat
Fidgeting in chair
Locking ankles
Scratching or rubbing back of hand
Gripping wrist or arm
Perspiring

Boredom

Doodling
Head in hand
Face turned away
Drooping eyes
Drumming on table

Evaluation	***Readiness to Accept***	***Doubt***
Sitting on edge of chair	Sitting on edge of chair	Pacing
Body leaning forward	Feet on tiptoes	Pinching bridge of nose
Slightly tilted head	Standing, hand on hips (coat open)	Lowered head
Hand on cheek	Unbuttoned coat	Hand over mouth
Stroking chin	Tilting head	Rubbing eyes
Slightly squinting	Moving closer	Sideways glance
Slow and careful cleaning of eyeglasses	Touching	Feet or body facing exit
Relaxed mouth	Rubbing palms together	Rubbing nose
Chin forward	Head at same level	Rubbing behind or pulling ear
Extended eye contact	Relaxed smile	
Slight one-sided smile	Tugging at trousers	

Conclusion

The major divisions of nonverbal or nonoral body language communication are easily identifiable once the interviewer or interrogator is familiar and alert to the clues that the other person may unknowingly project. Facial and body nuances can be recognized over a period of time and experience. Disgust, annoyance, acceptance, and approval can all be read in the expressions of the eyes and mouth and motion of the head and body. Because most human communication is nonverbal, much of what we see can be very informative if we are interested enough to study individuals and recognize the interaction between people. Once a PI becomes adept at viewing the "body language" of a subject being questioned, the communication process will be enhanced and controlled to a greater degree.

Statements and Confessions

The art of interviewing and interrogation will do the investigator little good unless he or she can capitalize on the information by putting it down in written form as long as the subject is willing to cooperate to that extent. It requires little persuasion to sign a written confession of his statement once he has been induced to confess and made convincing admissions. If a suspect admits to certain allegations but refuses to sign any statement or confession, he may renounce any admissions at a later time, even though the investigator may have put down on paper the exact wording of the admission soon thereafter. Therefore, it becomes a matter of who believes whom. At this point in the investigation, the investigator has reached the most important point in the investigation. A confession must not only convince the investigator that the suspect is guilty, but it must satisfy the prosecutor that the accused admitted and acknowledged his guilt. A written and signed confession, correctly accomplished to reveal all the elements of the crime and indicate that it was a voluntary act is much more compelling than an oral confession put down in writing. The investigator must assume that no matter the manner of the confession, the suspect's defense counsel will subject any confession to close scrutiny and attack the truthfulness of the investigator, accuse the investigator of causing duress to the suspect, and claim his client was coerced into "voluntary admissions."

Purpose of Statements and Confessions

1. To discourage a witness from changing his or her testimony at a later time or at trial.
2. To be used by the prosecution at a trial to refresh one's memory and recollection, to impeach a witness, or to show or place guilt on the defendant in the case at hand.
3. To enable the prosecution to plan its presentation by reducing the element of surprise that unseen or unknown testimony may present.
4. To provide a written record for the investigative report.

The reasons described above are more or less directed toward a criminal case, but statements or admissions, written or oral, may also be equally important in a civil case.

- *Admissions*—An admission is a self-incriminatory statement. However, it may fall short of an acknowledgement of guilt. Coupled with circumstances such as motive, the admission made by a suspect may provide an inference of guilt.

- *Confessions*—A confession is a direct acknowledgement of truth by the guilty person who has or had been part of the criminal act or an essential part of the criminal act. To be admissible, it must be voluntary, without coercion, unlawful influence, or inducement, and without any threats or promises.

Statements

If at all possible, statements from witnesses should be reduced to writing, particularly those statements considered important. Written statements considered important will include the following:

- Subject is or may be considered a suspect
- Key witnesses

- Recalcitrant or reluctant witnesses
- Witness who gives an indication or a tendency to change his or her mind
- Witness who will or may not be available for a legal hearing

A statement is a narrated account of an event or occurrence reduced to writing and taken from a witness to that incident, or some part of it. The statement may be written or recorded. In reality, it is what the witness saw or heard in his or her view or presence. It could also include personal knowledge relating to what that particular witness felt, physically and emotionally. What is related by the witness to the investigator must be relevant and material, personal, truthful, and without opinion. Only the facts pertinent to the incident in question should be made part of the statement. If a witness contradicts his or her remarks in later testimony, a written statement may be used to impeach that witness.

Experts, who may be used or thought of as witnesses, may testify to certain facts based on their field of expertise. Once accepted by the court as an expert, they may offer their opinion formulated or based upon the facts as presented to them.

> If nothing else, a witness must have credibility, competency, and believability.

Statements or Confessions May Be Taken in Different Forms

Written Statements

Written statements are articulation put down in writing on paper, usually by the investigator, signed by the person giving the statement, and witnessed by the writer by his or her signature.

> In order to produce a valid written statement that could later be used in a court or hearing, the witness must be credible and mentally competent. Additionally, the witness must be believable and have personal knowledge of the incident or occurrence. If the witness has the motivation to "do right" and to help enforce the law as a good citizen, later court testimony would only reinforce that affirmation of the written word.
>
> A confession is a completely different type of statement. Confessions may be oral, recorded, or in written form.

Recorded Statements

Recorded statements are taken when a statement or questioning by the investigator is recorded in some manner, personally or by telephone. Because a recorded statement will include no signature, the investigator should advise the witness that all remarks will be recorded and should request acknowledgement and consent to such a recording. However, the act of recording may be known to the person being queried or it may be surreptitious. If the recording is being accomplished without the permission or knowledge of the person being aware of the act, certain privacy issues may arise where the investigator may place him- or herself in criminal or civil jeopardy. (See the "Wiretaps" section and the sections on eavesdropping in Chapter 4.)

Court Reporter Statements

In court reporter statements, all statements, remarks, comments, and testimony by anyone are taken down in court or at a hearing and made part of the transcript of the court action. Another type of questioning in this area might be recorded by a court reporter hired by an attorney for the purpose of having the witness appear for a Q & A (question and answer) session. This usually occurs in an attorney's office or a chamber in a courthouse and is most often part of the discovery process. The reporter, as a notary public, will swear in the witness and then record all questions and answers given by both parties. Subsequently, the reporter will reduce the questions and answers to transcript form, which the witness at a later time may view and acknowledge as correct by his or her signature.

Interrogatory Statements

These statements are in a question-and-answer format in writing and are usually submitted to a witness by an attorney, requesting that the specific questions offered be answered in writing, signed, and returned to the attorney. Usually termed a *deposition,* the testimony of a witness is reduced to writing under oath or affirmation before a person empowered to administer oaths in answer to interrogatories (questions) and cross-interrogatories. This type of statement is usually taken by an attorney and not an investigator, although depending on the case, the deposition may be requested at the direction of an attorney not present.

Written Confessions

The purpose of a confession is to have the suspect admit to the crime or the offense. Basically, to put down in writing what he did, why he did it, where he did it, how he did it, when he or she did it, and if applicable, what happened to the proceeds of the crime and did he have any accomplices? The written confession, if completed correctly, can be the best evidence that will convict a perpetrator.

The methods of taking a written confession will vary according to the circumstances, intelligence, and temperament of the suspect. The order of importance in taking a confession is as follows:

1. The suspect may write his own confession in his or her own hand as long as it is sufficiently comprehensive and contains all of the elements of the crime.

2. The suspect may deliver his confession in the form of a Q & A (question and answer) to a stenographer in answer to questioning. The questions and responses are recorded verbatim and are usually conducted by an assistant district attorney in serious or major crimes, but not necessarily so, as an investigator can also conduct a Q & A.
3. The investigator will prepare the statement by writing his version of the information given to him by the suspect, attempting to use the verbalization and expressions employed by the suspect. The investigator then submits the statement to the suspect for corrections or any changes that will be executed in the suspect's own hand.
4. The suspect may give his statement orally to the investigator who will write the statement, again with all the elements covered (see oral confessions below).

A confession given by a person admitting to a crime must be corroborated with additional proof that a crime has in fact been committed, and that the crime in question is the crime that the confession alludes to, otherwise it cannot be admitted in court. Also a confession, if involuntarily made because of promises, threats, or physical force, cannot be admitted as evidence because the act constitutes coercion.

In any written confession, caution must be taken by the investigator not to provide any chance of an allegation of influencing the suspect's admissions.

See the Appendix C for an example of a written confession that may be used against a defendant in an arrest for a larceny.

Oral Confessions

Oral admissions may be used against the defendant in a court of law. There may be times when a subject will confess or give some information to a crime orally that will implicate him (or another), but the subject will refuse to sign anything regardless and for whatever reason.

In the case where a suspect refuses to give or sign a written confession, the investigator should reduce to writing any remarks, admissions, utterances, declarations, or facts made by the suspect concerning the case in question in written form at the first opportunity, which should then be attached to and made part of the final report.

Depending on any oral statements or written confessions under the circumstances given or received, the court will determine if such information can be submitted and used against the defendant.

Oral admissions also include overhearing a suspect admit to the crime, and telephone conversations between the suspect and the investigator. When a telephone conversation takes place in which the suspect admits to a crime, certain conditions must be met for an admission of this type to be accepted as evidence. Such revelations must be reduced to writing and it must be noted where and when the conversation took place, what the conversation was about, and if the investigator can swear to the fact that he or she identifies the suspect on the other end by voice or by other means.

Remember, a confession that includes details and data that could not or are not known publicly or by an innocent party can be described as the most convincing form of proof. Realize also that in the absence of eyewitnesses and admissions by the accused, it is rare that circumstantial evidence will support a conviction, unless such circumstantial evidence is so overwhelming that it would convince the court.

Unless the subject is a career criminal or one who has had previous experience with police questioning in a police-dominated atmosphere and therefore will remain silent, we can presume the average person will be easily swayed to reveal the desired information if questioned with sufficient skill and patience.

Subsequent Investigation after the Confession

At the conclusion of any confession, written or oral, the investigator should attempt to critically review and corroborate all information contained in the statement.

The following three points must be considered:

1. Regarding the information given, are all of the elements of the crime or offense established?
2. What substantiating evidence will be needed to sustain the facts noted in the written statement?
3. Is there, or does the investigator possess sufficient evidence, independent of the confession that can be presented in court that a crime has in fact been committed? As noted previously, the court may not consider the confession as evidence unless it can be proven either by direct or circumstantial evidence that a crime was committed.

Spontaneous Exclamations

Moreover, be aware that an utterance or declaration made without any thought or during the fervor of the moment is admissible as evidence. Admissions such as these are called *spontaneous admissions* or *spontaneous exclamations*. Examples are "I didn't mean to do it . . . give me a break," "Look, this is BS . . . what do you say we take care of this between ourselves," "Can I pay it back?" "I didn't mean it to happen."

Even though the person who made the spontaneous exclamation may not be available (such as he or she is dead or missing), a person who heard the exclamation may testify about it as an exception to the rule against "hearsay" evidence. The court will accept this testimony because such an exclamation lacks "planning" and is assumed to have a ring of truth to it.[22]

The "Hearsay" Rule

This is the basic rule that testimony one divulges or documents which quotes a person or persons who are not in court is not admissible because the person who supposedly knew or told of that information or fact is not present to state his or her exact words. Therefore, the court cannot judge the demeanor and credibility of the witness not present in court, and more importantly, the witness cannot be cross-examined by the other party's attorney if the testimony were to be challenged.

There are several exceptions to this rule, but the most important would be the *dying declaration* by a person mortally wounded, or who believes he or she is dying or about to die, and does in fact die, telling who caused the injury and possibly the circumstances. Any utterance or confession made at this time can be introduced in court.

Examples could be "Frank shot me," "John pushed me," "I did it," "I killed him and no one else helped me," or "It was my fault." Although the subject who uttered these declarations cannot testify in person, it is admissible on the theory that a dying person knowing that he is about to die has no reason not to tell the truth.[23]

Bear in mind also, that if a subject makes a dying declaration with the knowledge that he is about to die and implicates himself or others in a crime but in fact does not die and recovers, and if the subject recants at a later time, such utterance could still be introduced as evidence. Upon examination, the court may accept and admit the declaration as evidence.

Eliciting a confession from a suspect requires training and experience. For further information on taking oral or written statements and confessions, see "Interviews and Interrogations" section in this chapter.

Techniques and Credibility Regarding the Taking of Written Statements and Confessions

> It should be noted that if the private investigator has the ability and is required to take a written confession from a defendant or written statements from witnesses, the investigator should have some training in this regard. The format and what is required to be included in the confession or statement is most important so that the writing will be able to be admitted and stand up in court under scrutiny.

All statements taken in writing must be *single spaced,* particularly so for handwritten confessions. In any statement taken from a pertinent witness, that witness should be identified at least his name, address, and telephone number prior to the body of the statement.

Moreover, all statements and written confessions should begin with the date and page number at the top of the first page in which the statement is being given, with each page following subsequently numbered. Before the body of the narrative, the statement should bear the title, "Statement of John Doe," and following that in the case of a confession, the pedigree of that subject.

Confessions

For a criminal suspect in particular, a confession should contain the pedigree of that person—basically as much identification as possible that will identify the person on paper who is giving the written statement.

The pedigree should include the following:

- Full name
- Age and date of birth
- Whether married or single
- Social security number
- Home address and telephone number
- Business occupation and address

And may include the following:

- Any aliases used
- Wife's name
- Children, if any

As noted above, *the narrative should be written single spaced,* and the person taking down a written confession would do well to make at least one typographical or spelling error on each page of the confession. By crossing out the mistake, and having the perpetrator place his initials above these "errors" at the time he reads and signs the confession will indicate (in all probability) to the court, if necessary, that the defendant did in fact read the statement he gave before signing and was conscious of its contents.

Some local district attorneys or states attorneys require and authorize a defendant to place on paper a confession written in his own hand with as much information contained therein as noted above, particularly in a police-dominated atmosphere. However, in order to determine that all facts and circumstances are covered and put down on paper in a timely manner (before the subject changes his or her mindset), it may be judicious for the private investigator to question and write out the confession for the subject.

Following the pedigree, the body of the written confession taken from a perpetrator should note certain elements of the crime that was committed. As much as possible of the following particulars should be included:

- Date of the crime.
- Approximate time of the crime.
- Place or location of the crime.
- Intent of the perpetrator.
- What the perpetrator was going to do.

- How the perpetrator was going to do it.
- How the perpetrator did it.
- Did the perpetrator act alone in committing the crime, or did someone help him or her before, during, or after the crime.
- What was taken (the stolen proceeds) and its value.
- How the perpetrator left the scene or what he or she did after the crime.
- What the perpetrator did with the proceeds of the crime (if applicable and possibly recoverable).

Particularly in the case of a written confession taken and put down on paper by a PI, the writing should be single spaced, and a paragraph should be contained at the end of the statement indicating the following:

1. That the statement is being written for John Doe (the subject) by "James Roe," private investigator for ABC Detective Agency and contractually employed by XYZ Company (unless the statement by the suspect is given in his own hand)
2. That the subject has read the statement and all that is contained in the statement is the truth
3. That the statement was freely given, without promises, physical abuse, or threats of any kind

Following that, the subject should initial any corrections, sign his name at the bottom of each page, and on the last page at the end of the statement again sign his full name and add his or her address, telephone number, and the date in his own hand.

Moreover, witnesses to the criminal defendant reading and signing the confession should indicate so by their signatures. These signatures must include the person taking (or witnessing) the confession and at least one other, if possible.

All written declarations should contain certain elements so they will stand up against any argument by opposing counsel in court. Confessions other than statements require that certain factors be included that may not be essential otherwise.

Most importantly, the investigator must remember that any statement or confession must be freely given. The subject may not be threatened, cajoled, or promised anything in return for the statement.

The following is offered to reiterate the above procedures concerning written confessions.

The Specific Parts of a Written Confession

Because the investigator is a private person and not a law enforcement officer, no *Miranda warnings* need be included in any statement or confession. However, *all written confessions must include the following:*

1. The date, time, and location that the statement is being taken should be noted at the top of the first page.
2. Following that, the person giving the statement should be identified: "Statement of John Doe."
3. Subsequent to that a full pedigree or as much of a pedigree as possible to identify the subject should be provided. The first paragraph should identify the subject by name, age, date of birth, social security number, home address, home telephone number, marital status, wife's and children's names (if any), occupation, employer, and business address.

   Regarding this point, consider that in a written confession, the more descriptive the suspect's pedigree is as given by the suspect, the more confidence will be placed in the truthfulness of the confession as it will appear that the suspect gave the information willingly.
4. The next paragraph should describe when and where the subject was, what the subject was doing, and if material, what he saw or heard.
5. If the statement is to include the description of a crime or offense, the subject should describe what he was going to do, what he did, how he left or attempted to leave the scene, and how, when, and where he was apprehended.
6. Number each page consecutively (page 1 of 4, page 2 of 4, etc.).
7. Make at least one mistake on each page. This could include a spelling error, time error, or some other inaccuracy that should be corrected *at the completion of taking the statement,* and *should be crossed out and corrected by the subject* with his or her initials next to the deleted or corrected data as the statement is finally read by the subject.
8. In addition, the subject should sign the bottom of each page (an acknowledgement of reading that page).
9. If necessary, in an effort to gain an admission through commiseration, the writer may include remarks that the subject is sorry that he committed the crime, did not mean to hurt anyone by his actions, or would never do anything like this again. This does not change the fact or the intent of the confession in that the subject has admitted to committing the crime, but it may ease or soften the guilt in the subjects' mind.
10. The last part of the statement should include the caveat that the subject gave the statement willingly, with no coercion or threats, and without any promises of any kind. Also that the statement is being written for the subject by

"Michael Smith, private investigator, of Acme Security Services," unless the statement is written in his or her own hand.

11. Regarding the signing of a confession, the subject should place his or her signature at the end of the statement and then print his or her name under the signature, and also include the subjects' home address, telephone number and date of the signing, all in his own hand.
12. The investigator (as the writer or at least present at all times during the statement process) must sign his name and position as witnessing the subject reading the statement and the placing of the subject's signature on the statement. If possible, and recommended, a second person should also sign as witnessing the reading and the signature made by the subject.

To reiterate: A confession or statement should not be taken or received under threat or duress. If found to be received under these conditions, the court will not allow any statement, oral or written, to be accepted and entered as evidence. The court may also disallow any written instrument received because of a promise made to the giver, whether the promise was granted or not. In court, evidence is excluded under the *exclusionary rule* if supported by these circumstances, and the investigator will have placed himself in an unfavorable and unethical perspective in the eyes of the judge and jury.

Statements from Witnesses (Other Than Confessions)

All other statements not considered a confession or a disclosure of a crime by the subject being interviewed should include the following:

- Those points discussed in numbers 1, 2, 4, 6, and 8 above should be part of any statement taken from a person who may be acknowledged as a witness to an event at a later time.
- In number 2 above, the investigator may wish to use the terminology "Interview of John Doe," rather than "Statement of John Doe" if that is more agreeable to the witness.
- The subject need not be as descriptive as noted in number 3 above for a confession. The name, address, and phone number would suffice, and in number 11 a signature and date would be sufficient.
- As described in number 12 above, one witness to the subject's signature would be adequate in an ordinary witness statement. This could be the person taking the written statement.

It must be emphasized at this point for private investigators to be cognizant that any statement, writing, or report compiled and submitted by them must be as truthful to the facts as possible. The investigator must remember that he or she may have to swear under oath before a court, a hearing, or a legitimate deposition that all contained in the writing, confession, statement, or report offered to the court is the truth. To do otherwise constitutes perjury.

Consider also that any formal written report compiled by a private investigator as part of his or her own business practice, or as required by his or her employer is a "business record," and to intentionally falsify a business record may constitute a crime.

Remember that no Miranda warnings need be included in the written confession *unless* the PI or security officer is operating under the *color of state law.*

If the police are going to become involved because the incident is criminal and serious in nature, it is best to let the police investigate in their capacity and not take confessions or witness statements. On the other hand, if a written confession is taken in which the defendant admits to the crime, it will be gladly accepted by the police because they may not have the opportunity to gain such an admission while the subject is in their custody. This is because Miranda warnings given to a suspect by the police might suppress any admissions that might be received in the interrogation process. Therefore, it should be noted that most police agencies look favorably on confessions taken by security officers prior to their involvement, as long as the security officer has the ability and expertise to do so. But any statement, whoever takes it, becomes part of the case file and is subject to scrutiny by the defense attorney or the prosecutor at discovery or trial. Because of this, some police agencies have procedures that vary with jurisdiction. Regarding criminal prosecution, it would be wise for the private investigator to determine what situations should only be handled by the police, and what incidents can and could be handled by private investigators and security officers.

Chapter 6

Commercial and Industrial Threats and Vulnerability

Awareness

Because the private investigator (PI) may become involved in a case that includes the following act or acts, he or she should be aware of what each offense entails. The following pages will cover these business threats in some detail.

> ***Espionage***
>
> The act of surveillance, infiltration, and spying on the activities of a business enterprise or a government agency in order to steal information or something of value for oneself or another entity, such as a competitor or foreign government. Basically, the theft of information by various means.
>
> ***Sabotage***
>
> Other than military action, the intentional destruction of property or a product for the purpose of slowing or destroying a business enterprise, thereby obstructing or hindering productivity of the normal function. Can be caused by employee or customer discontent, or persons with

psychological or emotional distress. Also, the use of treachery and subversive tactics to cause damage or to disable equipment or property of a business or government agency.

Terrorism

An overt act by a person or a group which is committed for religious, political, ethnic, or cultural reasons. An act to cause fear, panic, and apprehension among the populace, and to bring about damage and harm that, as a consequence, will affect the public's psyche and slow the commerce of the country. At this time, the favorite tool of the terrorist is the bomb, with death and destruction by-products that only magnify the act.

Industrial Espionage

The most significant factor of industrial espionage is that the enemy is within. The greatest percentage of espionage occurs or is penetrated by employees of the business in question. Many employees, some who have risen to the status of trusted personnel, have access to a repository of information, much of which may be sensitive and proprietary to that business, of interest to its competitors, and convenient to unlawful penetration.

Today computer espionage has become readily achieved because of our change over the years from paper copy to computers, where information can more easily be discovered and accessed. Personnel who have password access to computers, computer programs, and computer file storage can easily copy all data from the hard drive or record files and leave without a clue of any criminal trespass. Moreover, a miscreant who wishes to sabotage the company's computers and computer programs in an effort to hurt the business may facilitate this crime with the knowledge he or she has gained along with password access.

The private investigator must recognize the most important assets a private business may possess, which may include its research and development reports, business records, business plans, and customer and supplier databases. This is all basically proprietary information that is the essence of that particular business, and if some or all of this information is compromised, that business will suffer a loss.

Espionage in the private sector is basically the illegal accumulation of business information belonging to a business or an enterprise without the permission of the owners of that data by someone for the use of or benefit by another business or person. It was estimated recently that the average cost of a single incident of economic espionage to a nonmanufacturing company is half a million dollars ($500,000), with a total annual loss of $300 billion nationwide. The average loss to manufacturing companies is $50 million.

Espionage in the public sector would, in effect, be treason. It occurs when a subject has the opportunity to steal state secrets, formulas, or prototypes, and offers them to another country with or without compensation. The purpose of this act is that the country accepting this data would greatly aid its nation militarily and economically over the other. The loss of this information by the country harmed could inflict a detriment or great harm in the prestige or protection of that country.

We are concerned with the private sector and the probability that a PI may become involved in the investigation of a company loss due to internal or external espionage by a rival company, and therefore, we should be aware of the types of activity that may be detrimental to the private company. More importantly, PIs should be aware of the various laws, particularly federal law that protects against any type of espionage, and conduct themselves accordingly.

See "The Economic Espionage Act, Title 18 USC §1831" and within the same title, "Protection of Trade Secrets, §1832" in Appendix A.

There are many ways and methods of espionage that a competitive business may employ. The techniques will vary according to the nefarious operator and the information that is to be stolen. The more professional the thief is, the harder it will be to initially discover the loss or the perpetrator. Such an intrusion into a company's secrets can occur as follows:

- *Computer Espionage*—The use of tapping (hacking) into a business computer or communications network to gain useful data. Unless the target company employs the latest countermeasures, the more sophisticated the "hacker," the less of a chance that the theft will be discovered. See also "Computer Crime" later in this chapter.
- *Seduction*—Where a male or female administrator is seduced by one of the opposite or same sex and is successfully pressured by love or threat of exposure to betray his or her employer by handing over sensitive information.
- *Long-Term Employee*—An employee who has been compromised in some manner, is disgruntled in some way, or is in need of money may approach or be approached by a competitor by which method files, records, and other business information are passed on.
- *Undercover Operator*—Where a person seeks employment in a company for the purpose of strategically placing him- or herself in areas that are prone to contain data he or she desires, or of gaining the trust and confidence of top managers and executives. Some of these undercover agents may be considered "sleepers," who may be employed for a long period of time in the target company and surreptitiously pass on data to his or her contact without anyone's knowledge.
- *Burglary*—A burglary may take place for the purpose of gaining the desired information. Once aboard, this may be done by using photographs, copy machines, or computer disk copies with no apparent disturbance to the

sensitive data. If the entry is made surreptitiously without a "break in" or if conducted and set up in a manner to direct a police investigation toward an "ordinary" burglary, the crime may never be discovered, and the loss of data may never be known.

- *Electronic Eavesdropping*—The use of "bugs," wiretaps, and other eavesdropping devices may also be employed in an attempt to glean as much information as possible without the knowledge of the company in question. The interception or tampering with any telecommunication or electronic equipment is covered in detail elsewhere in this book.
- *Exterior Searches*—The routine search by agents of rubbish bins, dumpsters, and garbage cans put out by the target company for any information that may lead them to other sources or any sensitive papers that may have been discarded.

Espionage may occur in all types of businesses, no matter what size that company may be. Research and development (R&D) may be considered the principal core of confidential information. There are always other larger companies willing to enter into espionage or a similar type of activity in order to expand into another geographic region by taking the smaller company that produces similar products or product categories they wish to gain a foothold in. By knowing the company's worth, identifying its weaknesses, winning the confidence of senior employees, and compromising their R&D efforts, the larger company has an advantage in acquiring the smaller company in a buyout or forcing that company to sell. It is not uncommon for a competitor to gain customer lists in any manner so as to sell competing services or products.

Any type of information can be of value to competitors, political antagonists, criminals, or the media, and there is a high probability that the average business does not employ anyone whose function is to prevent and deal with espionage.

Mobile Camera Phones

Today, approximately half of all Americans possess a cell phone, and mobile phones that are able to take pictures are becoming more popular by the day. Many areas such as schools, health clubs, and the courts have banned possession on their premises in an effort to protect the privacy of their inhabitants. Many corporations and businesses that have sensitive areas where the taking of photographs are prohibited already have procedures in place that will cover this type of cell phone use.

However, because mobile camera phones are becoming more popular, diminutive, and compact in size, a person bent on espionage can easily carry one on premises and photograph sensitive information and then send that information off the premises without anyone's knowledge. The possession of a camera phone on a business premises with no expectation of confiscation or being secured in some manner is unrealistic in our present corporate world. Rather than suffer an information loss, a mobile device that allows incoming calls only might be the best solution with a ban on camera phones with strict compliance rules.

Countering Espionage

Remember that all information may have some meaning to a corporate spy. Whether that information is found on a draft or final copy in a dumpster, by computer penetration, or by loosely secured papers found lying on a desk, such information is valuable no matter in what form it may be found. Many employees do not realize that carelessly handled and unsecured information and data can ruin a company if their trade secrets or proprietary data are compromised.

To confront or discover the espionage aggressor, the private investigator must entail the same skills that the perpetrator employs. For the experienced investigator regarding this type of undertaking, it could be advantageous for the investigator to have the knowledge of a company's efforts at protecting their confidential information. Protection may be as simple as the following:

- Lock all doors. Computer passwords alone will not keep an undercover spy from gathering the information he or she seeks.
- All computer files should be encrypted. If not all files, at least the most sensitive must be encrypted.
- All sensitive or apparently sensitive paper documents must be shredded or burned prior to trashing them.
- Protect all laptop computers, particularly off premises, from theft or any transgression by encryption. Traveling executives and salespeople are particularly susceptible to theft of information from their laptops left in their hotel rooms while they are elsewhere.
- Prohibit mobile camera phones on the business premises. Provide a strict no-nonsense policy with confiscation, security in some manner, or termination if a transgression occurs.
- Be constantly aware of company personnel, contractual employees, and consultants who have access to sensitive company information.
- Do not discuss company business, particularly secrets or sensitive information in areas that are not secured.
- A good hiring process and an in-depth background check of all new hires, particularly those who will be employed in sensitive areas of the company, should be considered essential.

Bugs

In the detection and discovery of eavesdropping equipment, the investigator must employ many of the skills and tricks used by the espionage operator. The foremost apparatus to be used in this effort would be electronic surveillance equipment. Initially, the detection should begin with an electronic debugging sweep of a company's key communication system, sensitive research or development sectors, and boardroom areas. Also included would be telephone and fax equipment located in the offices of high-ranking administrators or managers. So as not to arouse suspicion, this search should be carried out after business or working hours and with as little amount of people knowing of the operation. If a bug or series of bugs are discovered, the question will arise as to either remove them or leave them and devise a way to feed false information to the eavesdropper.

Private investigators employed in this type of enterprise can find it very profitable, but an inclination for electronic proficiency and ingenuity along with proficient training in this field is essential.

See also "Eavesdropping Defined" in the "Wiretaps and Bugs" section in Chapter 4.

> Remember that much of the equipment used today in investigations may have originated from governmental spying endeavors and requires a considerable amount of training and constant usage before it can be operated in a thoroughly professional manner. This will include computers, electronics, radios (microtransmitters, bugs), tracking devices, recorders (video or audio), or cameras (fixed, digital, or handheld video), to name a few.

Computer Crime

Computer Usage

The use of the computer in all business applications has become one of necessity. As their use and access to the Internet grows, personal information stored in computer databases has become much more available to anyone who has the wherewithal to access this information. Data such as credit reports, drivers license and auto registration information, work history, tax records, medical records, and marriage records among others can be used for purposes as random as marketing, background checks for various reasons, bill collection, legal proceedings, stalking instances, and missing persons.

Concerns over unauthorized access and misuse of information, and collecting information under false pretenses have caused some apprehension in the public and private sectors. Because the Internet allows almost instantaneous access to numerous databases, consumer awareness of the problem has increased to where pressure has grown in many circles to have governmental controls instituted. The Federal Trade Commission held a public workshop in June 1997 for which comments concerning problems growing within this service industry from database industry members were solicited. To offset thoughts on this political proposal, several database companies that deal in public records access have formed a lobbying group attempting to ward off governmental controls by introducing self-regulation—in effect a code of conduct and ethics. This association is called the *Individual Reference Services Group* (IRSG) and has set up rules that they expected to be in force by the end of 2004. A full *Report to Congress—An Executive Summary* by the Federal Trade Commission (FTC) (December 1997) concerning this workshop, their positive comments on the regulations to be set up by IRSG, and their concerns regarding this group and their expectations can be found on the FTC Web site.[1]

Misuse and misappropriation of information procured from the use of the computer is not the only way that such information can be detrimental to an individual or a business enterprise. How the information is gained and used can become a fine line between what may be a crime and inferior ethics.

No computer is completely secure. Given time and expertise, any computer can be penetrated. Although economic prosperity is a matter of national security, the Federal Bureau of Investigation (FBI) and the Central Intelligence Agency (CIA) advised U.S. businesses that the federal government can do nothing to protect them from insiders or foreign agents committing computer espionage or sabotage. Computer security will depend on the amount of money and factors that a company wishes to assign to this area. This will include security engineers, intrusion experts, and computer or technical response teams.

It has been said that any information contained on a computer's hard drive has left a footprint, and even when thought to have been deleted, the information is still recorded there. The use of a forensic computer investigator who specializes in the rescue of deleted or partially destroyed information stored within the depths of all computers can be a key to uncovering an undercover or unknown espionage operator.

Internet firewalls and extensive virus and privacy protection may keep outsiders from entering a company's computer, but even these measures cannot deter nefarious company employees from accessing valuable information and secrets for personal profit or committing an internal sabotage. As noted previously, the enemy most often lies within the company that suffers a penetration.

Moreover, any computer that has Internet access, particularly one that is left online for periods of time, is subject to intrusion and is accessible to crackers, hackers (particularly professional hackers), espionage, or just someone bent on causing sabotage. Many companies have their computer systems online (group use) for extensive periods of time out of necessity. An example might include financial databases or retail enterprises that maintain stock control between several geographic locations. Firewalls and software that allow access to the system to two or three attempts before closing them out can be effective barriers.

Outside programmers and computer technicians hired to work on company computers should be compelled to undergo extensive background checks. If a company extensively uses computer equipment and peripherals, it might be a good idea to have technicians and programmers in-house who are familiar with the equipage and programs. Of course, prior to employment, the company must also employ extensive background checks of these employees.

Passwords must be secure with no clues of that password left on a desk or in an office. A sports banner attached to an office wall or picture of a husband, or a wife, or children on a desk may offer a hacker a clue for the password. A family name, names of loved ones, dates of birth, nicknames, or pet names should never be used. A combination of letters and numbers in the password along with frequent changes of that password can reduce access by the culprit. A click of the "on" switch without further safeguards offers no protection whatsoever. Additionally, monitor screens should be placed so that they face into an office rather than outward where they can be read easily by others or from a distant remote location.

Computer Espionage

The business world has become more vulnerable than ever to espionage since we moved from paper transfer of communication and storage to computers. Today, computers are a reservoir of company information, which can include concealed and private data, research and development, business plans and strategy, customer databases, and many other secrets specific to that business venture.

Depending on the company's status, the value of the information, and the level of the employee who has access to that information, will determine the worth of that information to a competitor or adversary. It is not unheard of for a miscreant to plant a *Trojan horse* within a computer system in order to cause someone repeated access to company information. Routine intrusion inspections should be carried out as a matter of course.

Personnel traveling with laptop computers that contain valuable company information on disks or the hard drive are highly vulnerable to theft or inadvertent loss. They should not be left in hotel rooms where information can be taken surreptitiously. Laptops that are information sensitive should contain exceptionally high encryption software in order to deter any entry into the hard drive.

Computer Sabotage

The use of viruses or worms that will infect a computer's hard drive, or hackers who invade for the purpose of destroying files or programs for whatever purpose, are of great concern to highly sensitive businesses that wish to protect their secrets. The reasons people do this type of damage include the following:

- Incorrigible malcontents who wish to cause damage for no reason other than it can be done.
- Disturbed individuals who perceive an injustice has been done to them or their cause.
- Company employees who are dissatisfied for various reasons.
- Company employees who are about to strike the company and wish to do harm.
- A prior dissatisfied customer, client, or patient who wishes to get even.

Computer Attacks and Cyberterrorism

It is well known that many international terrorist groups actively use computers and the Internet to communicate. Accordingly, many have developed or acquired the necessary technical skills to direct a coordinated attack against computers in the United States or any locations outside of the United States under our control. A cyberattack intended to harm the U.S. economy would likely be directed toward the financial markets, critical civilian infrastructures, and government agencies.

At this time, there is no publicized evidence that any terrorist organization has or is currently planning an attack against computers or computer systems. However, there have been some random cyberattacks that have harried computers on the Internet, but the quantity and content are really unknown because many organizations and enterprises fail to report these attacks. Security organizations report that these random attacks are increasing and are implemented through the use of automated tools, called *bots,* that direct large numbers of compromised computers to launch attacks through the Internet as *swarms.*[2]

There are some private investigators who are schooled and specialize in this and other types of computer sabotage. Nevertheless, the average investigator should be aware that this type of crime exists and should be attentive to any investigation involving computer espionage or sabotage.

Computer Forensics

Today, because the courts, juries, and defense attorneys frequently question or challenge an expert's science and technological testimony, it behooves the private investigator to correctly process computer evidence and documentation. Moreover, the importance of evidence preservation cannot be overstated. If upon discovery, it is determined that the computer evidence is accurate and complete, and the research documentation is factually correct, criminal or civil trials will rarely proceed to litigation and are usually negotiated or plea bargained.

Therefore, only those investigators schooled and certified in computer forensics, and in court testimony showing consistent reliable processing methodologies that can be understood and accepted as evidence in court should become involved in computer evidence processing.

Fraud

White-Collar Crime

Defined

We can define white-collar crime as "nonviolent crime for financial gain committed by means of deception by persons whose occupational status is entrepreneurial, professional or semi-professional, and utilizing their special occupational skills and opportunities. Also nonviolent crime for financial gain utilizing deception and committed by anyone having a special technical and professional knowledge of business and government, irrespective of the person's occupation."[3] However, this definition fails to account for other types of criminal fraud, such as the "criminal" business or corporation.

In regard to the term of *culpability* (as described earlier), we can assume that *opportunity* would be the most distinctive indication of a white-collar crime. An out-of-work person without funds to feed himself and his family may turn to armed robbery. A bank teller, also short of cash, might embezzle because a different opportunity presented itself. Because criminals will commit crimes with which they are most familiar, and which are most easily accomplished and have a fair chance of succeeding, will do so because the chance of jail time, if any, will be minimal. One could say that the economic and social status of the criminal, the crime against a business entity rather than an individual, and the chance of restitution would fare well in the public's mind because they view white-collar crime as less serious than the more traditional or violent offenses.

Economic conditions such as depressions, recessions, and company "downsizing" will affirm to a degree the level and type of fraud that will occur in our society.

However, the term *white-collar crime* can cover a multitude of criminal behaviors—financial crime, economic crime, business crime, and of course, fraud. These terms are used interchangeably as the common terminology used by experts in the field to describe white-collar crime.

Although white-collar crimes are not highlighted by the media as sensationally as street crimes, violence, and major assaults, the effect on our institutions is far greater. Fraud in any form reaches into all elements of our society and affects our lives far more than most people realize. All parts of our infrastructure such as health care, government operations, military operations, insurance, banking, financial markets, big business, small business, and communications, to name a few, are affected to some degree by white-collar crime.

Types of White-Collar Crime[4]

White-collar crimes are characterized in four distinct areas:

1. *Personal Crimes*—Committed for personal profit on an episodic basis, for example, welfare fraud and tax cheats.

2. *Violation of Trust*—Committed by persons in organizations against organizations, for example, a person with some authority and held in some trust committing embezzlement, bribery, and kickbacks.
3. *Business Crimes*—Committed by organizations in furtherance of their business interests, for example, false weights and measures, antitrust violations, and environmental crimes.
4. *Con Games*—Committed for the sole purpose of cheating people or clients, for example, fraudulent land sales, bogus securities and rare memorabilia and artifacts.

More simply put, white-collar crime can be broken down into two categories—*occupational crime* and *organizational crime*[5]:

- *Occupational crime* is largely committed by individuals or small groups of individuals working in connection with their occupation. This will include the lower levels of offenses such as embezzlements, skimming, asset misappropriation, check forgery and check schemes, credit card fraud, insurance fraud, bribery, shrinkage and inventory shortages, larceny cons, and flim-flams.
- *Organizational crime* is that committed by business and government. It is committed by corporations and business enterprises in an effort to, for example, show an increase in corporate earnings or cut corners on environmental issues for profit gain. It also includes accounting, bank and bankruptcy fraud, insider trading, investment and securities fraud, Medicare and Medicaid fraud, telemarketing and mail fraud, procurement fraud, and Racketeer Influenced and Corrupt Organizations Act (RICO) crimes, to name a few.

Computer Fraud

According to the U.S. Secret Service, computers are being used extensively in financial crimes, not only as an instrument of the crime, but to hack into databases to retrieve account information, store account information, clone microchips for cellular telephones, and corporate checks, bonds, and negotiable instruments that are later counterfeited using desktop publishing methods. Because computers are a tremendous source of both investigative leads and evidentiary material, the Secret Service has established the Electronics Crimes Special Agent Program (ECSAP) that trains agents to conduct forensic examinations of computers that were used in criminal endeavors.[6]

Moreover, computer technology has been used in counterfeiting U.S. currency and creating false identification documents. Under *Title 18, U.S.C., §1030, 1986 (revised),* the Secret Service was given authority in the investigation and prosecution of these crimes.

If during the course of an investigation a private investigator comes across an instance or circumstance of computer fraud, the Secret Service should be notified so that their forensic expertise can be utilized.

Illicit Behavior Identified

In regard to an internal investigation that a PI might become involved in, there are certain attributes or profiles that will indicate the perpetrator of a fraud:

- *Low-Level or Nonmanagement*—Might include a middle-aged male or female, has a stable position within the business which has been long-term, granted a low level of supervision and has been given a position of trust, has the knowledge of company controls and the authority to access corporate assets. This person may feel passed over, neglected or dissatisfied, abused or exploited, or may perceive that a wrong has been committed against him for various reasons and wishes to "get even." Also, the company's internal audits, policy, and procedures are so lax that the crime can easily be accomplished. Add to this perception that this person may be suffering a financial problem, or other various reasons (family sickness, high living or gambling habits), and the fraud committed is for what is "due" him.
- *Administration and Upper-Level Management*—People in these positions are considered fairly intelligent, highly motivated, and thoroughly trusted with little or no supervision. They may act in concert with others of equal or greater status, or with others that they may have control over, and also have the ability and authority over the direction that the company is directed toward. If the business enterprise is a publicly traded company, annual audits must be performed by a reputable certified public accountant. Depending on the size of the company, there may be a chief financial officer (CFO), a treasurer, or an internal audit department. Generally, any wrongdoing will surface during a legitimate audit, but if there is collusion between the CPA or the auditor and the executives in charge of the "books," the chance that fraud will be discovered can be minimal.

Insurance Fraud

Fraud in any form is a crime. It can occur in the form of embezzlement by a respected employee, or it can occur by distortion and deceit in order to lay claim to a false or minute occurrence. The greatest manner and type of fraud occur in the field of insurance claims. This includes claims filed for personal, property, auto, home, or worker's compensation.

According to a survey taken in November 2002,[7] nearly one of every four Americans (25%) say that it is OK to defraud insurers. Statistics from this survey are somewhat bewildering but indicative of society's attitude toward insurance fraud. The results of the survey follow.

The Survey Also Found

- To overstate the value of their claims to an insurance company:
  - 8% find it quite acceptable.
  - 16% find it somewhat acceptable.
- To submit a claim for items not actually lost or damaged or for injuries or treatments not actually received:
  - 4% find it quite acceptable.
  - 7% find it somewhat acceptable.
- What are the main reasons leading people to commit insurance fraud? (Some respondents offered more than one answer.)
  - 49% believed that they could get away with insurance fraud.
  - 30% said they need the money.
  - 24% believe that they pay too much for insurance.
  - 20% said that they would want to make up for the deductible they would pay.
  - 11% stated that their family, lawyer, doctor, friends or insurance agent influenced them.
- If you knew someone who committed an insurance fraud, how likely would you be to report it?
  - 19% stated not at all likely.
  - 20% stated not very likely.
  - 24% stated somewhat likely.
  - 19% stated very likely.
  - 13% stated extremely likely.

Consider also that more than one in three Americans say it is OK to exaggerate insurance claims to make up for the deductible, and one in three say it is OK to pad a claim to make up for the premiums they already paid according to another survey conducted in 2000.[8]

And in a survey conducted earlier, in 1999, one in three Americans say it is OK for employees to stay off work and receive worker's compensation benefits because they "feel pain," even though their doctor says it is all right to return to work. Moreover, seven of ten Americans say worker's compensation fraud is a widespread problem that they are aware of, and 45% say that worker's compensation fraud is increasing.[9]

According to the latest figures, it is estimated that the recent yearly cost of fraud in the U.S. property and casualty industry is approximately $24 billion, which represents

10% of the total claims payments, and as our weakened economy continues, it is expected that fraud by consumers exaggerating claims payouts will continue to grow.[10]

From these figures, we can presume that insurance fraud has inveigled itself into our personal psyche, and it appears that it will continue to grow to even larger proportions if our veracity, integrity, and morality continue to decline. Consequently, we can consider this an unlimited field for the PI.

Internal Fraud

Worker's Compensation

One area of dishonesty committed by an employee is insurance fraud concerning injuries on the job. A common occurrence would be to fake an injury or exaggerate the pain of a minor injury into a major or permanent impairment.

Based on current statistics, we must consider that worker's compensation case fraud is one of the most insidious insurance deceptions that a dishonest employee can engage in. By engaging in a fake injury or a minor injury heightened to appear as a more serious and debilitating impairment is not uncommon, particularly in companies that have a large number of employees.

The PI must be aware during employee injury investigations that pains, aches, and agony can be feigned or imagined, and that he or she must be constantly observant in this area.

The newly hired employee must be made aware at orientation that falsifying an injury and accepting the benefits of worker's compensation commits the crime of insurance fraud. Additionally, all employees must be informed of the required and thorough investigation into all injuries, the safeguards in place, and the companies zero tolerance toward a crime of this type.

The loss of workdays, payment of lost wages, and costs of medical and rehabilitation among other services are substantial losses to the company. Moreover, consider the cost of litigation for a final award to terminate an insurance claim. Insurance premiums are paid to cover these losses, but insurance companies are not in business to lose money. If losses are high, premiums will increase or insurance coverage will cease.

Insurance Fraud by an Employee

As we have seen, internal fraud within a business enterprise may occur in many forms. It could involve various forms of insurance fraud, kickback schemes, bookkeeping deception (commonly called "cooking the books"), having nonexistent "employees" on the payroll, issuing company checks on bogus accounts, or being in collusion with venders with intent to defraud. Moreover, embezzlement, which is covered in some detail in Chapter 7, is a common crime, and the perpetrators may be found in business or government administrations.

See also the section in Chapter 5, "Credit Card Fraud."

Cons, Scams, and Flim-Flams

Because many of the small claims filed against any business may only be a few thousand dollars individually, in total they add up considerably. Though the business owner will have to absorb these petty losses because of the deductible on his or her insurance coverage, insurance rates will typically rise as the claims against the business mount. Close attention and intervention of loss prevention and insurance investigators can identify fraudulent claims in many instances.

Slip and falls are usually staged at major retail and restaurant chains, with these "con artists" most often preying upon supermarket/grocery and department stores, and spacious public areas of large office complexes and malls. These claims of injury appear to be the most common type of insurance fraud as it requires little time or effort to set the stage. The injured party does not have to provide premium money for an insurance policy, as he or she might need in other frauds, and the alleged fall is most often without witnesses and difficult to disprove. Additionally, there is often a delay in reporting the injury and claim. The reasoning for this delay is that the investigation is hindered by no witnesses or witnesses' memories, the alleged accident scene has changed or has been renovated, and the subject has had time to set up doctor examinations, hospital stays, and bills. The dollar amount of the claim is usually under $5,000, and most of these incidents are set up by a group of people known as *gypsies*.[11] Because of the overwhelming volume of these types of claims by this group, the insurance industry finds that they are a tremendous problem to deal with. These gypsies are a mobile group and change names and addresses frequently as they move from town to town. The changing of names and other identification makes matching of these claims difficult for the insurance industry's Property Insurance Loss Register (PILR). The existence and furtherance of the gypsy lifestyle and identification of their scams depends on secrecy. The gypsy claimant does not wish the scrutiny or publicity that a courtroom will bring. The other scam artist also does not wish publicity and usually will not involve an attorney. Therefore, both will want to settle rather than go to court. These types of cases are referred to in the insurance industry as *nuisance cases.*

Note also, that gypsies are also involved in stolen or bogus credit card and bad check scams and flim-flams at cash registers and returns counters. Bear in mind that a larceny committed by trick or false pretenses is still a crime.

The other scam artist is the "upstanding citizen" who finds that by staging a phony slip and fall, or by building a minor fall into a major injury, he or she can wait out the insurance company all the way to a civil trial. This person's claim is usually exorbitant and he or she feels that even if the claim is settled just before trial, he or she will come out ahead. This subject most often has representation by an attorney and the services of a doctor, both of whom may be as shady as is the subject. Again, many times, the report of the alleged injury is made at a later time after the alleged date of occurrence.

Caution should be taken, however, concerning the honest customer or visitor who has in fact sustained an injury through no fault or little fault of his or her own. In any event, in aiding an injured person and the subsequent accident investigation, all cases should be handled with equal consideration and appropriate professional conduct. Whatever you may believe concerning the facts, respond as though the incident is a bona fide accident. Make no personal comments that might be litigious at a later time. Also, this admonition is to be applied to any coworker present or assisting at the scene, because one never knows who may be listening.

Early detection and thorough investigation of claims having involvement by certain groups such as gypsies have proven to be the best defenses in defeating fraudulent and nonmeritorious claims. Once an accident and injury have been reported, security and loss prevention should examine the scene immediately for witnesses, inconsistencies between the "injured person's" statements, and physical evidence observed at the scene. Photographs and measurements should be taken of the accident scene. Comments by the subject, however minimal, vague, or inconsistent, should be noted and written down as soon as practical. Complete identification should be gathered from the subject, particularly from photo ID of an official nature such as an operator's license. Include the social security number, business address, and if possible, the previous home address. Note if any of the corroborating and "overly cooperating" witnesses present are friends or relatives of the subject, and properly identify them and all witnesses for future reference. If the security officer has any suspicions of a possible fraud, he or she should advise his or her insurance representative or assigned investigator upon submission of the accident report.

Make sure that all required information is taken so that an accident report may be completed soon after the incident. Many times the injured party or a relative at the scene of the accident, or a legal representative at a later time, will request a copy of your "official" accident report. Respectfully deny that request. You could offer them any pertinent information, including names of witnesses and the name of the company's insurance carrier, but no company, in-house, or insurance company accident form should ever be supplied to anyone. Advise them that only the company's insurance company representative or attorney representing the company will have that right of disclosure. The business owner and his or her agent have the legal right to deny a request or demand of any written formal report. In fact, the only time a copy of an accident report or any other writing relevant to the case will be offered is on demand by the plaintiff's attorney at a discovery hearing or at trial.

See Chapter 5, "The Interview Process," for further details concerning interviewing a witness.

Warranty Fraud

Any manufacturer that warrantees their product is subject to some type of fraud. A consumer may wish to return a manufactured product, falsely claiming that the product was discovered defective or damaged upon opening the box or upon receipt, when in fact it was the consumer who damaged or destroyed the item. In other instances, frivolous or deceitful litigation may occur when a consumer sues for damages because of some injury or action caused by the product under warranty. Manufacturers accept a portion of these returns or claims as part of doing business, and of course, the costs of settling these claims are placed on other consumers.

Nonetheless, there will be times when a claim, however outrageous, will be brought before the court and found to be legitimate.

Major fraud may be found in other instances. A manufacturer may find that there was an excessive failure of one particular product and was about to discontinue that item. However, in examining the records of this product, it was found that in excess of 50% of all declarations were due to fraudulent claims submitted by a very small group of dealers. In particular, it was found that one of these dealers had submitted claims on a product in excess of the amount received from the manufacturer. Internal inspection and audit procedures should disclose crimes of this type, with company loss prevention following up the allegation. But for intensive outside investigation of the company or persons involved, hiring a PI may be the only way to achieve a satisfactory solution, arrest, prosecution, and restitution.

Fraud by any other name is still fraud, and fraud in any form is a crime.

Accident Investigation

Consider the following procedures as basic in any investigation of an accident or disaster where injury or property damage occurs. The severity of the incident will guide the subsequent investigation required.

Response Procedures

Assess the Scene for Danger—If an accident or an incident happens where the PI or security officer may be the initial responder, becomes aware of, or is assigned to assist immediately thereafter, it may be necessary to assess the situation to determine if there is any danger of further injuries or damages. Basically, it is important to be aware of potential hazards at the location of the accident or in the workplace and be familiar with the company's accident and emergency plan response procedures.

Determine the Correct Response—The natural tendency is to immediately aid the injured person or persons. However, depending on the situation, an immediate response might be to leave and seek help or turn in an alarm.

Prevent Further Injuries or Damages—The responder must take reasonable steps to prevent or minimize further injuries or damage. This will include shutting down equipment or power sources, ventilating the location, and attempting to confine the leak, spill, or dangerous material.

Perform Emergency First Aid—The type of injury will determine the appropriate medical response. Whether the injury is a burn, an electrical shock, broken bones, minor or severe lacerations, or cardiac arrest, the person who will attempt first aid on the victim should have some first aid accreditation or at least be knowledgeable about first aid procedures and the company's established emergency process.

Upon completion of the response procedures, and before initiation of cleanup and restoration of the scene to its original state, take into account the following activity.

Assess the Scene, Identify Witnesses, and Collect Evidence

At this point after the initial response procedures have been completed, the investigation into the accident will begin.

The basic procedures would be as follows:

- Upon arrival, attempt to preserve the scene as much as possible as it was during the occurrence.
- Control the scene; which may include other or extra security officers. If not available, make use of managers or responsible coworkers to secure the scene.
- Identify the complainant if any and any witnesses to the occurrence.
- Attempt to separate the witnesses from each other so that their recollection will be pristine and not be tainted or distorted by talking to others.
- If unable to take witness statements, attempt to gain as much personal information on the subject as possible so that a follow-up can be made at a later time. Make a short notation in your notebook as to what this witness saw or will be able to swear to.
- The collection and preservation of evidence is paramount. This will include photos, hand-drawn diagrams, and any physical evidence such as tools, fingerprints, and so forth.
- All physical evidence should be identified as to where it was found, by whom, under what conditions, and initialed for future identification; but in any event, the security officer or private investigator must be guided by local police procedures on the handling of evidence.

Surveying the Scene

Initially, the following questions should be answered:

- Who is injured? Describe the person and the injury.
- When and where did the accident occur?

- How did the accident happen? What caused the accident, and how was the injury sustained?
- What property, if any, was damaged, and what actions contributed to the damage?
- Were any precautions in place, and if not, why not?

Witness Identification and Interview Procedures

After surveying the scene in order to develop a clear understanding of the accident, identify all witnesses who witnessed the event before, during, and immediately after. Advise the witnesses that an investigation is necessary to determine the cause of the accident. Witnesses should be separated so as not to discuss the event with others, in particular, other witnesses who may sway or muddle another's recollection of the accident. Individual interviews should be conducted as soon as possible after the fact. Procedures regarding the interview of witnesses may be applied to any interview that a PI might conduct during the course of an investigation.

However, it may not be possible to complete some or all interviews. In that regard, see the section in Chapter 5, "Interview of Witnesses."

Secure the Accident Site

Most accident sites may not require the preservation of evidence, but the PI must be familiar with the basic steps in cases where it is required. The protection of the scene is most important if the accident caused a death, major or numerous injuries, or extensive property damage; if there is a continued risk of more injuries or damage; or if circumstances show that the death or injury was not accidental in nature.

Protect anything within the accident scene that will or may be considered to be evidence then or at a later time. This will include parts, tools, weapons, spill samples, and any material physical or otherwise that was or may have contributed to the accident or that could be disturbed if too many unauthorized people contaminate the scene, or if normal activities are about to be resumed. Evidence can be disturbed or destroyed by curious workers and by-standers, inattentive or untrained security personnel, or when rescue and emergency medical activities are performed. Use other security officers (trained) or employees to assist in protecting the scene. The scene should be isolated as long as is necessary to collect evidence and photograph the accident scene.

Collect and Preserve Evidence

If the investigator is an in-house (proprietary) employee of a corporation or a contracted private investigator, he or she should pay attention and be mindful of company policies in this matter. But, remember that the more severe or serious the accident, the greater the need to collect and record physical evidence. And in that regard, the more serious accident would entail photographs or scaled drawings or sketches of the scene. If possible, determine where witnesses were located and the relationships of objects to each other. Use indicators such as arrows or notations to highlight important objects in the picture or drawing. If possible, use rulers to indicate sizes of important objects in the photo. The reasoning is to show machines, office equipment, and so forth, in their relative positions at the time the photo was taken. The rationale that the collection and recordation of evidence is important is as follows:

- To document the facts for an employee's worker's compensation actions
- To record accident facts in compliance with government regulatory reporting requirements (Occupational Safety and Health Administration, OSHA)
- To protect the company (or the client) in potential legal proceedings (criminal or civil)
- To fulfill insurance/underwriting or regulation reporting requirements
- To collect, preserve, and tag anything that may pertain to, be part of, or be the cause of the accident

The investigator assigned to or in charge of the incident must make sure that all evidence is preserved in a controlled area and that any evidence requested by any outside agency or authorized organization be documented and recorded when offered and returned.

Survey the Scene

As part of the evidence collection process, the investigator should take a step-by-step walk, mentally and/or physically, through the accident scene. Review what has happened. Look closely for clues, evidence, or traces of the cause of the accident. Test and record any physical condition such as noise, lighting, air quality, visibility, temperatures, or anything else that may have contributed to the accident. Make extensive notes of anything that may be odd, different, or out of place, or note possible analysis that may require further inquiry.

Other Possible Evidence

Depending on the case or the circumstances, paper evidence may play a part in the investigation of the case at hand. Orders, written instructions, job safety analyses, container labels, operation logs, charts, records, and maintenance records involved in or pertaining to the accident may be helpful or of use. Moreover, review of personnel files of all or anyone involved in the occurrence may divulge information helpful to the case.

Resolving Legal Liability

Legal liability for most accidental claims will occur because of a condition of *carelessness* or *negligence.* In other words, if one person involved in an accident was less careful or more negligent than the other person, the less careful person will be liable for all if not the greatest portion of damages suffered by the other.

The following scenarios also describe how liability may customarily be applied:

- If the injured person was where he or she was not authorized or supposed to be, or was in an area where the kind of expected activity that caused the accident typically occurs, the person who caused the accident may not be liable, because that person has no duty to be careful toward the injured person.
- If the injured person was careless in his or her actions, compensation may be reduced by the extent such carelessness was responsible for the accident. *(Comparative negligence)*
- If a negligent person causes an accident while working for someone else, the employer may also be legally responsible for the accident. *(Vicarious liability)*
- If an accident is caused on property that is dangerous because of poor building methods or conditions, poor maintenance, or unsafe environmental circumstances, the person in charge or managing the property, and vicariously, the owner of the property is liable, whether or not he or she actually created the dangerous condition. *(Premises liability)*
- If an accident is caused by a defective product, the manufacturer, seller, and distributor may be equally responsible for liability, even though the injured person cannot determine how or who created the condition or was responsible for the defect. *(Product liability)*

Arson Investigation

According to a national survey in 1998 by the National Fire Protective Association, one in every four fires in the United States are arson or suspected arson cases, and they account for nearly 500,000 fires yearly.

This particular area of criminal investigation requires specific training and exposure to the various forms and complexity of fires, how they start, how a fire feeds upon itself, the why and wherefore of arson, and its effect on business and people. Most PIs employed in the field of arson investigation have had prior professional experience in a police or fire department, or as a fire marshal. Therefore, the personal expertise required for arson investigation, the collection of evidence, the arrest of the perpetrator, case preparation, and appearance in court as an expert witness require a background in credentials that can only be obtained in a former professional position. Rarely do we find experienced arson investigators who do not have these qualifications.

Fire Emergency

Many business establishments may be unique in the type of materials contained on premises that could cause or fuel a serious fire. Some may have more flammable and combustible materials aboard than a dissimilar type of enterprise and must incorporate special firefighting, apparatus, hardware, and training than another might require.

As an example, retail department stores contain warehouses, storerooms, and closets that house far more combustibles and are more exposed to fire than supermarket or grocery stores. Plastics, wood, wood composition, and plastic foam contained in furniture and bedding ignite and melt easily, generate high heat, and produce toxic fumes and heavy smoke. High piled palletized stock in racking causes the probability of being heavily fireloaded. Sprinklers in the warehouse racking are considered a necessity. Fire-resistant buildings, completely sprinklered and constructed in sections with fire containment walls and doors between major portions of the building, are a major deterrent to the containment or spread of fire until the arrival of the fire department.

The local fire department should have the availability to have routine walk-through inspections, particularly during business hours. This is most important when the building engages in routine construction and renovation. Local fire or building codes will dictate the amount, type, and placement of fire extinguishers and hardware. Such codes will also note the amount and type of fire exits that will be required, how and when they are or are not to be secured, and how all perimeter doors will operate. Housekeeping is one of the most important fire prevention methods that can be had. Clean and orderly areas throughout the store or building can only reduce the probability of fire. But fires do happen, and the initial investigation of a fire scene as to whether the fire was set or accidental will be conducted by fire department personnel, the fire marshal, or the police arson squad.

The Effect of Fire upon People

No matter how much training, fire protection, and fire equipment may be brought to or contained in a facility, we cannot control people once a fire has been discovered. People are harder to predict, protect, and control. And whatever the facility, the consequences of a fire are most serious because people can resist fire and its by-products only for a very short period of time.

Depending on the type of fuel involved in the fire and how fast the fire is spreading, the first indication of effects upon the person will be lack of oxygen, superheated air, and the consequence of smoke, toxic gases, and chemical compounds. Fire uses up oxygen faster than the victim, and suffocation becomes one of the factors for death. Dense smoke becomes an irritant to the eyes, lungs, and air passages. It causes the eyes to water, the nose to run, and irritation to the throat and lungs, causing coughing and vomiting. The most common toxic gas is carbon monoxide, and when absorbed into the body, it causes brain dysfunction. The person becomes confused and disoriented and succumbs to carbon monoxide poisoning without ever seeing or coming in contact with the fire. The final factor is heat, where the body will blister and destroy tissue. When air temperatures reach 200°F, the chances for human survival are minimal to none. The effects on a burn victim cannot be measured in money.

Consider also the factor of panic. Unable to see or exit freely and safely causes people to become frantic in an effort to save themselves. It is common for people to jump from high-rise windows to their deaths. Many die by piling up against exit doors or are trampled by the rushing mass of people in their frenzied attempt to escape. So then, generally speaking, because of panic, superheated air, or smoke, people can die even before flames will reach their bodies.

The toll of human tragedy in deaths and injuries, property damage, and public concern many times cannot be overcome by the extent of the disaster. Therefore, the importance of fire protection cannot be overstated. Protection of the facility with fire-resistive materials, fire hardware, training, inspection, and enforcement are key to life safety initially, and property protection following.

Remember that fire prevention is proactive, and fire suppression is reactive.

Fire Training

Whether the PI has an inclination toward arson investigation or not, he or she should have some instruction in fire science and become aware of the following procedures:

- The science of the chain reaction of heat, fuel, and oxygen
- The four stages of fire development
- The classification of fires—Class A, B, C, and D
- Fire-extinguishing systems, and the type or agent to use on each class of fire
- The procedures in fighting a fire
- Reporting and evacuation procedures
- How to prevent a fire; housekeeping procedures and routine inspection
- The consequences of a fire on a business, people, and property
- The proper response of employees and emergency responders to a report of a fire and evacuation procedures of a facility that the PI or the private investigative agency might become involved with in a fire investigation

Embezzlement

Defined

For our purposes, embezzlement may be defined as the fraudulent appropriation of property in which someone has been entrusted with its care or possession. Basically, it is the taking of property from another, where the offender took or acquired possession of that property legally (had come lawfully into one's hands) by way of employment or trust.

This method of fraud may happen in three ways and usually occurs over a long period of time:

1. Theft of money
2. Theft of inventory
3. Manipulation of accounts

Understanding the Crime

Embezzlement is a rather tough case to investigate. The investigator must have some knowledge of the company's procedures, practices, rules and regulations, and possibly bookkeeping processes in order to pursue basically what is to be considered a paper trail. It can take many man-hours and be time consuming. If the establishment has sloppy business practices or nonexistent records, and little supervisory oversights, the investigation becomes much more difficult.

Embezzlement is considered a white-collar crime. The offender does not look or act "like a crook." He or she could be your friendly next-door neighbor or a well-trusted long-term employee. When an embezzler is caught, juries in this type of case tend to be much more tolerant than if a crime is committed directly against a person. Based upon the defense's argument, they may view the defendant as a working slob taking something due him or her from the "large tyrannical and filthy rich corporation," or that the company had poor bookkeeping practices or oversights to begin with. So then, it is understandable that in crimes against the person (robbery, assault, etc.) convictions usually result in incarceration, whereas crimes against property usually result in restitution with little or no jail time.

Most cases of embezzlement are never discovered or linked to a particular employee. Many are never reported to the police, mostly for fear of publicity. Although a business wishes to find the culprit and terminate the loss, the company may be quick to fire but slow to prosecute. Long-term employment might offer an excuse for the employee's act in stealing. They may have needed the money to cover some financial hardship, and although they hoped to pay it back, never did so. The thief may fall on the excuse that family hardship or sickness caused him or her to steal. The company may feel sorry for the employee and attempt to recover as much of their loss as possible, let the employee go, and forget the incident.

Although a felony is a crime against the State (the people), and in theory cannot be compromised, anyone can do so for a misdemeanor. However, unless it is a very serious case, felony or not, loss prevention and security managers would rather not spend the manpower and time involved in a complicated and long and drawn-out case, along with the possibility of having to proceed with further court action for recovery after conviction. Thus, the recovery of as much money or value of the property stolen as possible, and the termination of the employee will usually be the conclusion of a case of this type.

Indicators

In the crime of embezzlement, we must consider the role of the model executive, because this employee is usually involved in a long-term and excessive amount of money loss. The crime is easily hidden because of his or her position and apparent forthright and honest demeanor. He or she may gamble to some excess at places like Las Vegas or Atlantic City, but only for a couple of days at a time. He or she never takes a regular vacation, taking only a day here and a day there. This person may drink excessively, frequenting bars and nightclubs. He or she may have an association with undesirable characters. Usually this person is critical of others, and visibly displays a dislike of thieves. He or she may be a religious fanatic, or appear to be. This person may give the impression that he or she has many "contacts" or friends who give him or her great deals on cars, jewelry, and gifts. He or she borrows money from other coworkers and pays back late. He or she borrows from the company's petty cash box, and the IOUs are rarely paid off in a timely manner. This employee asks that his or her personal checks be cashed postdated or "held" for a time before cashing. He or she often works overtime regularly, needs coaxing to give up records, and is usually fastidious and excessively neat in the maintenance of records. When questioned about his or her record keeping or on a particular point about a record, he or she may become argumentative, arrogant, and abusive.

Although the executive may exhibit some or most of the above traits, that does not prove that he or she is a thief; this person may possess only personality or character flaws. However, if the PI is involved in this type of internal investigation, he or she should consider all of the above as indicators of possible wrongful conduct. Moreover, other than the executive position, we must bear in mind that the long-term, well-respected, and responsible employee with similar access to money and other accounts may also commit this type of crime.

Chapter 7

Distinctive Situations

Undercover Operations

Objectives

The undercover agent places him-or herself in a position for obtaining evidence, either direct or physical. He or she can observe criminal or offensive activities, identify perpetrators and associates, listen and record conversations in his or her presence, and obtain copies of or photograph documents. By gainfully obtaining the confidence of the perpetrator or the illicit group, he or she may be able to obtain information as to the complete criminal procedure—how and when the crimes are committed, the people involved, and where the proceeds of the crime are located or disposed of. The undercover agent (UC) may be placed in a location to confirm or contradict information given by an informant. The closer the UC gets to the perpetrator or the group as a friend and confidant, the more information he or she will gain. The discovery of loyalty in a person's makeup may be hard to come by based on coworkers or associates. Undercover work can determine the true feelings or moral sense of the subject in question. Moreover, undercover work may be the only way to discover subversive groups or organizations, or illegal union activities. Some benefits gained by the UC could be the identification of poor supervisors and supervision, the malcontents, and the basis or cause of security or safety problems.

Concerning the services of a private investigator (PI), most undercover operations will be directed toward the dishonest employee. Once the client identifies the particular loss to the agency or the possible target of the investigation, the selection for the undercover operative or agent will be directed by the expertise required to facilitate the investigation.

The objective of an undercover operation is twofold:

1. To obtain information
2. To determine if in fact a crime is the primary element of the investigation, and once established, the identification of the perpetrator(s), and the preparation of evidence for court presentation.

Undercover operations could include investigation into the following:

- Inventory or paper loss, loss surveys
- Larceny of merchandise, equipment, and supplies
- Cashier theft, credit and debit card misuse
- Theft of services, schemes, and scams
- Sabotage
- Espionage
- Gambling or drug use on premises
- Sexual harassment
- Gender, racial, and ethnic discrimination, and other civil rights violations
- Assaults on company property

We must also remember that during a criminal investigation, certain misdeeds may be identified, and that the client may wish to ascertain information for reasons other than crimes within the facility.

Therefore, other than criminal behavior, an investigation could uncover consequential enlightenment that may be beneficial to the business in question.

- Offenses against company policy (rules, regulations, and procedure)
- Employee misconduct
- Work performance
- Morale
- Poor supervision
- Labor or union issues

Selecting the Right Agent for the Job

The undercover operative must be carefully considered by the agency for the particular position he or she will be placed in. Whatever the assignment, the agent must fit in with the profile of the subject or subjects, the neighborhood and social environment, and the work assignment he or she is to infiltrate and investigate. The agent should have the same compatible background in age, ethnicity, culture, social situation, demeanor, and dress of the employees or subjects under suspicion. In reality, his or her physical and racial characteristics should not stand out but should fit in with the persons or group he or she will be assigned to infiltrate. The agent's temperament and intellect will be assets. Self-confidence along with a calm and affable personality, and the ability and the resources to change or adjust plans and situations as may be required on short notice may be considered a skillful trait.

An ideal UC is a combination of an actor and a good investigator. The best placement of a UC would be in an assignment to which he or she could easily adapt or acclimate. Work experience in a job or position that the UC will occupy would be a positive factor.

The Cover Story

A most important factor to be considered is the investigator's cover story. Preparations should be made prior to placing any agent in an undercover operation. A fictitious personal background and history of the "new" character should be processed to include a new name, addresses, assumed education, employment, associates, neighborhoods, trades, and travels, among other details that may be required for the assignment. Additionally, provisions must be made for the agent's freedom of movement and justification of actions, along with the background that will permit the investigator to maintain a financial and social status equivalent to that of the subject. Personal possessions should be acquired for the UC that would be appropriate to the character he or she will assume. This includes clothing, jewelry, vehicles, photographs, letters, certificates, and of course, money.

In some quarters, there is a sense that the cover story should not be completely fictional. But it is usually advisable that the UC maintain that he or she is from a city or location that he or she has lived in and is quite familiar with. However, such a location should not be one that the subject or subjects lived in or are from and would have more knowledge of than the agent. In case the subjects under investigation question the agent's history or claims, arrangement must be made for principals in the fictitious history to be able to corroborate any background account.

Depending on the assignment, the agency may opt for a more seasoned agent rather than a novice or someone less experienced. Proven ability and performance will be controlling factors, along with this agent being less likely to become involved in any unlawful or unsavory actions. However, the novice agent may be more effective in certain situations, because that agent may not have developed prejudices, opinions, or habits that may compromise the investigation.

Rules for the Undercover Investigator

The following rules must be absolutely adhered to for the protection of the investigator while operating as an undercover operator and for a successful investigation. Remember that when employed by a private investigative agency or any security company in any manner, you are considered an agent of that agency or company.

Any action by you, lawful or not, will have an effect upon your employer, possibly the client, and upon the results of the investigation:

1. Agents are prohibited from violating any laws.
2. Agents must never reveal their true cover or identity to anyone. They must never carry or bring anything or any item that would identify them as other than the individuals they portray. Identification and company forms and reports must never be left in the agent's automobile, handbag, or locker.
3. Agents must be careful not to entrap a suspect employee into committing an unlawful act, or to trick anyone into disobeying or contravene company regulations. By suggesting, tempting, or acting on a person's weaknesses so that an offense is committed, the agent could be placed in an unlawful and litigious situation. Moreover, such behavior will compromise an investigation and is unprofessional to say the least.
4. Agents must be careful not to draw attention to themselves. This would include quizzing other people or acting overly intrusive or suspiciously, thereby becoming subjects of public scrutiny, particularly by the individuals under investigation.
5. Agents should not borrow money for any reason from any employee on the job or from the client company, and they should not compromise themselves by lending money to anyone on the target job site.
6. Agents should never bring any employee to his or her home. Instead, they should attempt to meet at the employee's home so that the agent may view the contents of the home and the lifestyle of that employee.
7. Agents must never contact the client for any purpose unless given specific reason to do so under certain circumstances by his or her supervisor.
8. Once hired as an undercover investigator, agents should attempt to fit in with the group of employees that he or she will be around or working with.
9. Unless it is part of the scenario that the agent wishes to portray, for whatever reason, agents should not become a discipline or behavior problem for client company supervisors. This will include lateness, absenteeism, insubordination, or idle behavior.
10. If an arrest takes place by law enforcement authorities where the subject or subjects are taken into custody, the agent should act in accordance with his orders. If the agent has no previous direction, he or she should act according to his or her judgment as to whether disclosure of his or her true identity should be made at the time of arrest or at a later time.

Written reports by the UC must be definitive in nature, indicating any incident or occurrence by date, time, location, person or persons involved, along with a complete description of the occurrence. If possible, any evidence collected must be gathered surreptitiously and cautiously.

Accountability

Agents must be in contact with their supervisors on a daily basis, and depending on the activity of the UC or the investigation, written reports will be compiled on a routine basis or as safety permits. Accountability of the agent must be considered a high priority, including account supervisors and agency administrators. In order to warrant the value and virtue of the information reported by the agent to his or her superiors, and then to the client, various provisions by the agency must be proscribed and controlled in order to achieve a favorable outcome.

Precautions

All undercover operatives must always be aware of their actions and personal behavior. They must learn to relax and relieve any tension that will become obvious to others. They must thoroughly live their cover and know their cover story meticulously. During the "break-in" period, the agent should ease him- or herself slowly into the group and must not appear to be anxious by asking a lot of questions. They should observe individuals within the group they will be working with, listen to their conversations, and watch these employees perform their jobs. As time passes, the agent will become acclimated and accepted by the group, with the duration of this period depending on the unity or secretiveness of the clique.

Regarding the process of placing an undercover operative within the client's facility, care must be taken in the hiring procedure. There are two courses of action that can be taken in placing the agent. The first is known as the *cold placement,* when the agent applies for a position with a bogus background and a plausible story. Because no one at the company is aware of this attempt to gain entry, there is no guarantee that the agent will end up in the area of investigation. The second is known as *controlled placement*. In this way, someone within the company is aware of the agent and his or her purpose for applying for a position. Along with the human resources or personnel manager, the agent can be placed where the investigation is to take place. The problem in this case is that the agent and the agency will have to depend on the confidence of at least two people in the company. In any event, the undercover operative should never use his or her own personal identity or background when working in this type of environment.

The client must be completely involved in the operation, whether undercover or not. To hire an investigative agency, and after initial input, sit back and leave everything up to the agency can often lead to partial or inaccurate information, along with the investigation gearing toward other tangents. The client and the agency must work together in order to motivate agents and receive valid positive feedback.

There will be times when a client will become overanxious or meddle in some form or another into an investigation. Any contact with the agent most probably will compromise the operation, particularly so if employees become aware that the agent is personally involved with the company administration in some way. Whether employees feel they are being watched or not, they will certainly shy away from the agent because of what they presume to be some type of special relationship with the boss. Any type of approach by the client should be rejected, and the agent should contact his or her superiors as soon as practical so that conduct of this type by the client can be terminated.

If some type of emergency exists to the extent that the client or the agency must contact the agent quickly, a code or signal should be incorporated into all investigations so that the agent may break off all contact with the participants and operation instantly or contact the agency or his or her supervisor immediately.

Sting Operations

Many undercover operations may take several weeks and up to a year before coming to a productive or fruitless conclusion. A sting operation usually occurs and is completed within days or at most a couple of weeks. It may be a secondary investigation conducted to protect and substantiate the cover of an agent on the premises, a reaction to information regarding a serious theft or a safety issue that must be acted upon in a timely manner, or to correct problems on an immediate basis. It may be initiated to protect an undercover agent, or to protect and enforce the agent's cover. By acting quickly and including the apprehension of the undercover operative along with the group of suspects, the UC will solidify his or her position as part of the "gang." Moreover, the conclusion of a sting operation where criminal or civil litigation is the result will definitely add to the credibility of an undercover agent's testimony in court.

Government entities are usually the most creative and productive in sting operations, particularly because of the money, time, and manpower that can be put to use in addition to the privileged use of the law and the courts.

Most types of stings include the offering of money for merchandise, expensive or priceless objects, or other items of value. Setting up a scenario where the suspect is photographed, taped, or recorded in some manner during the transaction would place that suspect in possession of stolen goods, to say the least. Care must be taken by the agency not to become involved in any type of entrapment where the agent and agency can be placed in criminal and civil jeopardy. In addition to apprehending the perpetrators, the recovery of property is to be considered a fundamental objective for the operation.

Executive and Celebrity Protection

The U.S. Secret Service makes use of a process based on government research called "threat assessment approach" in an attempt to evaluate potential threats to an individual or a group. This process identifies three fundamental factors in possible violent acts targeting these subjects.[1]

The Secret Service is the only known operational research unit concerning assassinations and personal attacks on prominent public officials or figures. This unit, known as the U.S. Secret Service Exceptional Case Study Project (ECSP), has been in effect publicly since 1949, focusing on effective assessments, behavioral information, identifying patterns of thinking, and prevention of targeted attacks prior to the attack or near attack[2]:

1. Acts of targeted violence are neither impulsive nor spontaneous. They are the result of patterns of thoughts and behavior, which can be a source for identifying and understanding the threat. Some sources could be informants or social actions, or diaries and letters that may describe the intent of the attacker.
2. Violence can originate from a connection between the potential attacker, the subject target, and a current situation. A situation could be because of political or religious reasons, or the stalking of the target for a period of time and committing the act for a fervent desire to become famous.
3. Those persons who are likely to commit targeted acts of violence often engage in telltale behaviors that are preceded and linked to their attack. This will include concentrated planning and logistical preparations. An example would be of a potential attacker hanging around locations frequented by the target subject or closely researching schedules of the target subject.

The investigation and procedures initiated by the Secret Service can be well applied to any PI assigned to executive or celebrity protection. For more detailed information regarding this subject, visit: www.secretservice.gov, and click on "Executive Protection."

Private Protective Services

Considering that any political figure will likely have federal or local police protection permanently, at public or media events, or during the possibility of an attack, we in the private sector can learn from the professionals and apply their expertise to our vocation.

The threat of any physical action against a figure of celebrity status, political personage, or an important business individual is greater today than ever before in our history, particularly because of increasing terrorist activity. But it is not necessarily so that terrorist actions are the predominant factor in the motives that can occur against a personage who is considered a celebrity. Where terrorist activity will most likely be directed toward a political figure, it is not uncommon for business executives to be targeted, particularly so if their company is well known internationally or is involved in foreign holdings.

The term used today for this service is *executive protection.* Forget the terms "bouncer" or "bodyguard" as there is a difference between them and the executive protection professional. One specializes in muscles and most often has a gun, and along with the celebrity lifestyle with all its problems and uncertainties can be very useful if the protected subject wishes to enter a dance club of some renown or an area of concern.

However, they are not effective for business executives or public figures, because although executive protection professionals may be less physically imposing, they are better prepared to identify threats against the protected subject before they materialize. Recognizing and analyzing the threat level, and preparing for and against probabilities require training and constant awareness. Blending into the executive's business and lifestyle with one's bearing and attitude befitting the person under protection is important for the public and corporate image, ensuring the subject's safety, and minimizing the impact of the security presence on his or her daily life—in essence, knowing how to walk, talk, and dress like the executive under protection.

Today, executive protection can apply to any executive who has control or propriety information in financial services, pharmaceutical or energy industries, government contractors, or any large company having international endeavors. Threats can include assassination or the threat of assassination of the person or his or her family, kidnapping, carjacking, explosives (fixed, delivered, or mailed), or biological or chemical agents, to name a few—all for the purpose of political or financial gain, or personal notoriety.

Actions such as these can include foreign as well as nationalistic criminals, extremists, or fanatical zealots. Other than the protection and securing of a facility from any harm, the security and personal protection that surrounds an executive of great interest can be costly and many times intrusive to the subject and his or her family.

In any event, there are certain procedures that must be taken into account in setting up any type of an individual's protection, or for that matter, a group of individuals.

These procedures will include the following:

- Identify those individuals who are critical to the organization.
- Assess the impact of any act against these individuals, to the country, corporation, or the business sector.
- Examine the risks that may befall these individuals. What are the public and private profiles of this individual? Does the individual court public or media attention attracting undesirables, fans, or extremists? What are his personal and family habits? Does he or she travel frequently, in and out of the country, or have business groups or private clubs he or she periodically attends? How private or extensive are announcements concerning this individual (public, corporate, industry wide, Internet, media)?
- Consider that the family members are also subject to the same attacks as the individual and may require equal protection.

Of course, all of the above depend on the constant analysis of the threat level that may affect the individual, and the cooperation permitted by that individual and the corporation. The difference between a bodyguard and a protection professional can be notable. One proclaims muscle and strength; the other, although less physically imposing, creates a cool, calm, and level-headed approach to any situation.

The designation of *protection professional* requires that certain abilities be attributed to him or her and are noted as follows:

- The ability to identify threats before they materialize and to employ appropriate countermeasures
- Training and experience in defensive driving
- Emergency medical training and certification
- The ability to enforce security recommendations with the subject, immediate or not, whether or not agreeable or acceptable to the subject
- The physical ability to defend the subject against a physical attack
- If required, the ability to be licensed to carry a concealed sidearm, and to be firearms proficient in pistols, rifles, and automatic small arms
- The ability to blend into the subject's environment and surroundings in dress, demeanor, and speech
- The ability to keep a low profile in the subject's personal and family life
- The ability to communicate and establish a rapport with the subject while maintaining a professional attitude
- The ability to work with law enforcement agencies, public authorities, fellow security professionals, hotel personnel, and event organizers

In regard to the hiring of a protection professional, many companies hire protection agencies that employ ex-Secret Service agents, former police officers, or military personnel. However, we cannot overlook the possible employ of in-house corporate security personnel who have the right character, dedication, discretion, and integrity, and are trainable in the art of protection. Prior knowledge of company management and operation can only add to their value.

For the novice who wishes to enter into this field of security without prior training, it would be beneficial that entry be made into a protective agency that employs adjutant or subordinate personnel, along with adequate training, until the opportunity arises for an entry-level position as a protection professional.

See also the sections, "Types of Terrorist Incidents" and "Targets of the Terrorist," later in this chapter.

Intellectual Property Protection

Intellectual Property Defined

Intellectual property can include a particular manufacturing process, an invention, a chemical or engineering formula for a new prototype or product, patent information, literary and artistic works, symbols, trademarks, brand names, and images, among others. Proprietary information may be more of a loss to certain companies than others. As an example, pharmaceutical enterprises regard their research, development, and sales information as the most important physical asset, which must be considered the major element to be protected.

In regard to the various threats and vulnerabilities discussed earlier, there are four types of intellectual property that can be attributed to a company reversal if an infringement occurs. Any transgression will constitute a crime, and the individuals or companies committing such an act can be prosecuted:

Patents—The registration of an invention or other tangible items, giving complete right to the patent holder concerning manufacturing and marketing rights. Both U.S. and international patents are issued. Patents last for 20 years and can be renewed. If not renewed, the patent is considered to be expired, and the company loses the right to keep others from manufacturing and marketing the product.

Trademarks—Considered a name, phrase, sound, symbol, color, or corporate logo that is associated with a company or product, where once marketed and widely accepted connects that trademark with the product without doubt. This trademark may also be called a "service mark," and the legal protection is equal. Once registered with the Patent and Trademark Office, protection from competitors will last for 10 years and can be renewed. The designations ®, ™, or "Reg.U.S.Pat.Off." must be placed next to the trademark.

Copyright—Copyright protection for artistic expressions such as novels, textbooks, manuals, movies, poems, songs, and music that are "fixed in a tangible medium of expression." Essentially copyright protects newly creative work placed in written form. Although it is not necessary to solicit a copyright, to do so gives protection to the author or developer if any infringement occurs. If the copyright is sought and granted, the symbol © along with the date of publication should be noted on the publication. A copyright lasts for the life of the author plus 50 years.

Trade Secrets—Any formula, recipe, pattern, device, or collection of data that gives an advantage of one company over another company or competitor may be considered a trade secret. To prove that the item or information is proprietary, appropriate measures must be shown to protect the secret, such as restricting knowledge of the secret to a select few. Moreover, it adds to the value of the business and should be kept a secret. Loss would do great harm to the company. Any infringement could cause the owner to seek damages.

Vulnerabilities

Be aware that the enemy may lie within.

Obstacles to maintaining a protected environment for intellectual property include:

- Sensitive computer files not encrypted.
- Failure to shred or burn *all* sensitive papers and documents.
- Failure to conduct in-depth background checks when hiring personnel for sensitive positions, and constant supervision and quality facilitation thereafter.
- The company executive on the road with a laptop computer containing highly classified or secret company information, including his or her company's latest and most vital activities, many times will leave the laptop unprotected in the hotel room while socializing or dining elsewhere. Entry or access into this room will allow a spy to easily copy data from the hard drive. CDs or floppy disks usually located nearby in the room may be available, and given enough time, all data can be compromised. Available encryption technology can protect laptop data.
- The company manager, administrator, or executives who have access to company reports, statistics, or important data that can be sold to the highest bidder, could be compromised by blackmail and coerced into providing company information.
- Personnel who are in-house or contracted programmers could be unscrupulous, larcenous, or disgruntled employees having a tendency for nefarious schemes. These employees could plant a "back door" into the company computer system so that repeated access can be made, conduct money transfers to their benefit, or completely sabotage the whole system which can seriously affect the company's operations and cause financial calamity.
- Foreign governments have been known to "bug" first-class seats on aircraft and hotel rooms frequented by executives.
- Computer data are much more easily obtained than data from the older method of paper reports.

Counterfeiting/Fraudulent Merchandise

Today, one of the more insidious exploits of deceit are those criminals who commit copyright and trademark fraud by copying music or movies onto CDs or producing look-a-likes ("knockoffs") such as luggage, clothing, handbags, and jewelry. We can assume that the more expensive the item or merchandise, the more someone will attempt to copy it and offer it for sale to the unknowing customer at "discounted prices." There is a loss of earnings and goodwill (eventual discovery of poor workmanship and material) for the manufacturer and also for the deceived customer who believed the item, although "discounted," was in fact genuine. Generally, though, the purchase is made because of price and brand name status.

Whether it is a movie on a CD, a reproduction of a sought-after publication, unlawful manufacturing of drugs, or the manufacture of high-end big name jewelry and soft goods, there will always be a customer willing to seek out these items. A buyer is willing to purchase counterfeit merchandise because of the lower cost, and in many cases, the perception that the fake goods convey a degree of status similar to that of the authentic items. However, the intellectual property owner suffers a devalued product, particularly if the counterfeited item becomes widespread.

Although street venders in large cities, house parties, and flea markets have long held the designation of the place to obtain fraudulent wares, along with small privately owned retail operations, the Internet has proliferated the sale and marketing of fraudulent merchandise. This includes auction venues such as e-Bay, Internet e-commerce Web sites, and message boards.

Protection from Loss

Investigation of this type of crime would include the PI and a knowledgeable company employee who can positively identify recovered "faux" merchandise as bogus. Further, the use of a sting operation would be the most incontestable method for conviction and closing down the operation.

Generally, once a counterfeiting operation has been determined and identified, a cease and desist letter to specific individuals will usually result in a cessation of operations and a voluntary surrender of merchandise for destruction. If not, then criminal action must take place against the offender.

Nevertheless, customarily, the protection of intellectual property must fall on the legal department of the business in question, where not only prosecution is difficult, but recovering stolen information is even harder. The education of employees, particularly those select employees who have access to intellectual property, tools; programs that track sensitive documents as to use, users, and location; good communication between the company's security and management groups regarding intelligence and perception of employees; and secure areas where such information is retained, are a few methods of protecting this type of company asset.

Industrial Espionage

Industrial espionage could be considered a form of intellectual property theft or theft of proprietary information.

Realize also that foreign businesses and governments are notorious for being implicated in industrial espionage. European and Asian countries in particular have had reputations of this sort for years. Corporate and industrial espionage have become so extensive that the Federal Bureau of Investigation (FBI) and the Central Intelligence Agency (CIA) advised U.S. businesses in 2001 that these agencies were unable to protect American businesses, and in reality, "they were on their own."

Moreover, be aware that most espionage committed within American companies is perpetrated by employees of the affected companies. Computer firewalls and assorted programs may prevent or alleviate the problem of outsiders gaining information, but the insider may have full access to intellectual property.

In addition to applying certain procedures for the management and protection of operations and devices of all intellectual property possessed by a business, the proprietary investigator or the PI must be aware of how an interloper—a professional industrial spy or a competitive intelligence expert (commonly called a *Snoop*)—accomplishes his or her task.

Other than "dumpster diving," intelligence is collected in bits and pieces, with the spy putting it all together for a positive result. Remember that this type of intelligence gathering is used not only by business competitors but also by foreign governments.

Some examples of how information may be gathered follows:

- Obtaining private and personal information, particularly salacious details concerning an employee which if made public would place that person in some jeopardy if the desired information is not forthcoming
- Pretending to be a "student" working on a research project, requesting meetings and information from personnel in a company's R&D department
- Being present or presenting oneself as a potential customer at trade, industrial, or electronic shows where new or upcoming products are shown
- Monitoring company employees who unknowingly or consciously post comments on Internet chat rooms and Web sites
- Observing lax security by company employees, particularly those in research and development (R&D) departments
- Burning sensitive papers, manuals, and so forth, in a secure facility by security personnel rather than shredding
- Following companies that employ or have publicity departments issuing press releases regarding new products or new patents
- Studying complete listings of sensitive personnel, including biographical, professional, and academic information in company annual reports, brochures, and other company publications
- Noting the company's failure to have confidentiality or nondisclosure agreements for sensitive personnel while in service and upon separation from the company
- Noting suppliers boasting about sales Web sites

- Looking through job listings that describe research and development positions for certain companies, including job interviews where a competitor's employee or a hired investigator pretends to be a job seeker
- Realizing employees have a propensity to talk, especially when a new product or idea is developed, and in their excitement and titillation, fail to realize that they might be overheard
- Hanging out in public areas such as restaurants, bars, and airports located near the place of business where employees must know not to talk about sensitive business subjects
- Seeking public records at agencies such as the Environmental Protection Agency or the Occupational Safety and Health Administration (OSHA), where regulations require certain information be forthcoming on new or upcoming procedures or programs that are within the privy of that regulating agency

Once an investigator has some knowledge of how intellectual property can be stolen and the safeguards that should be in place to prevent such thievery, the easier an inquiry on a theft can occur with a positive conclusion. However, as stated earlier, realize that the prosecution of a competitor who has possession of the stolen information is difficult, and rarely is a recovery made that benefits the original owner.

Terrorism

In the event a PI is assigned to a business that may encompass or be subject to some or all of the offenses or incidents noted below, he or she should be cognizant of the following information and guidance regarding acts or actions committed by internal (national) or external (international) individuals or groups.

Terrorism Defined

Terrorism may be defined as any overt act by a person or a group that causes death, bodily injury, and destruction. Moreover, the act instills fear, panic, and apprehension to the public at large, which ultimately disrupts the normal working environment of a business, a government agency, or the community in general.

The favorite device used by the terrorist is the bomb, because the bomb is easy to make, can be easily transported and concealed in various shapes and sizes, and many times is easily placed within or near a building, structure, or populated area. It is loud, and it is very destructive, therefore serving the purpose intended. The use of a nuclear or incendiary device must also be considered because the terrorists will regard the performance and the outcome equivalent to meeting their goals, no matter how much loss of life or devastation will result.

The placing of a bomb within a building or in a crowded locale so as to cause physical damage, personal injury or death, panic, and fear, has become the norm in many third-world countries, particularly in Europe and the Middle East. Recently, our country has become the target of national and international radicals, and business and government have suffered damage to life and property. Consider also the public apprehension and fear that follows such an incident. The disruption of a business is a natural development following a bomb explosion, where people fear using public transportation or entering into public areas where they may expose themselves to possible harm.

Terrorist activity has increased dramatically in recent years, and our country has not been immune to such attacks, whether the terrorist was national or international. The intent of the criminal act, along with the suicidal nature of the terrorist in giving up his or her life for the chosen cause can only give rise to our need for awareness and security protection. Given the nature and reasoning for such an act, we can be sure that other attacks will continue to occur in the United States.

Intention and Design of the Terrorist

As noted, the favorite tool of the terrorist is the bomb, and the justification given for such an act is usually a religious, social, cultural, or political agenda. Criminal extortion cannot be ruled out as a factor, but the criminal activity in these instances is for some gain, monetary or otherwise, rather than to punish or validate a point of view.

During this period of our country's history, it must be understood that there are many terrorist organizations, both domestic and international, that are dedicated to disrupting the American way of life. By causing death, serious injury, and property damage where the destruction causes an economic loss to the business under attack, they in essence cause fear and apprehension among the innocent public at large as we go about our daily routines. They do this with the terrorist's primary weapon of choice—*the bomb*.

Terrorist activity has greatly increased in recent years, particularly in Europe and the Middle East. The favorite tool of the terrorist is a bomb device, and the basis for such an act is usually for a political, religious, cultural, ethnic, or social agenda. In essence, the act may be for retribution or for creating a political statement. Criminal extortion may also be used as part of the terrorist act, but this is rarely the case. In recent years, our country has also become the target of radicals who have caused business and government to suffer damage to life and property, including the public apprehension, panic, and fear that follow such an incident.

International terrorists have attacked us not only on American soil, but also overseas in actions against American political and business interests. It is not unusual for American corporations to be targeted or American businessmen to be kidnapped or killed in other countries. The national terrorist, who may or may not belong to the various fringes or hate groups in our country, also has no apparent reluctance to follow through with actions that may cause death, injury, and destruction.

As we have seen in recent years, the car or truck bomb is becoming more useful to the terrorist. Consider that the larger the bomb, the larger the destructive power. The Oklahoma City tragedy and the 1993 World Trade Center bombing caused severe destruction, death, and injury. In both cases, trucks laden with explosive material entered in close proximity or within the structure itself to perpetrate the act. We are beginning to learn that some buildings must be protected by barriers, so as to keep vehicles at some distance from these structures. The farther a vehicle is kept from a building, the less damage and injury will be received from an explosive device.

Because the terrorist has no compulsion regarding who and how many people will be killed or injured or how much property will be devastated, and the purpose of the terrorist act is to cause fear and apprehension, *there will be no warning.* In some instances, communication to the media or law enforcement authorities will be made after the occurrence, detailing the purpose of the act, but not necessarily so. Such disclosure is becoming rare. It is becoming more prevalent that the perpetrators are identified only after investigation by law enforcement authorities.

As terrorism becomes more common throughout the world and in our own country, we should consider that the bomb is not the only device that can be used to cause death and destruction, fear, and apprehension. We saw such an occurrence on September 11, 2001, when two aircraft were flown into the towers of the World Trade Center, a third aircraft flew into the Pentagon in Washington, DC, and a fourth plane crashed in Pennsylvania after a struggle onboard with the terrorists. Other than the severe death and destruction caused by these terrorist acts, it had a profound effect on the American psyche, and for more than a few days, American commerce and travel came to a standstill.

The bomb can be disguised in many ways, and it can be designed to cause specific damage and injuries that the terrorist may wish. They can be planted indiscriminately or in specific places depending on the access that the perpetrator may have or the purpose of his or her intent. The terrorist will usually make his or her attempt at buildings or facilities that contain or will contain large numbers of people. As we have seen in Europe in the recent past, business and transportation sectors are viable and accommodating targets because of the likelihood that large groups of people will be present. In our country, it is a matter of time when the terrorist will turn his or her energies away from notable and extraordinary structures that contain very large groups of people and include government facilities and business establishments.

In spite of these facts, terrorists as a group are not the only people who may make use of a bomb for a particular purpose. The criminal may make actual use of a bomb or the threat for extortion purposes, revenge, a perceived wrong, or simply because he or she wishes to disrupt normal activities. Unless mentally unstable, his or her reasoning is not to injure or cause damage, but to elicit money or something of value or cause a business interruption.

Types of Terrorist Incidents

Today the threat of terrorism is becoming more and more prevalent. According to federal and national police agencies, the following occurrences can be expected in any terrorist activity:

Bombings—To bring about as much destruction and injury as possible, and to increase attention to the terrorist's cause. The bomb is presently the most used weapon against large groups of people without any regard to humanity, infrastructure, transit, the government, or business establishment. This is a serious threat to public safety. It could include an occurrence of some magnitude such as an attack against areas of large gatherings, a national landmark, or an historical structure. The ultimate would be a nuclear threat.

Hijackings and Kidnappings—Usually directed toward high-ranking politicians and business executives, for the purpose of assassination or negotiation in freeing fellow terrorists.

Murder and Assassination—Toward a targeted politician or business executive at any location convenient for the act.

Atomic, Radiological, Chemical, or Biological Attacks—A serious threat to public safety concerning an attack upon a large group of people causing extreme injuries and death among the populace, and a complete stoppage or slowdown of the social order and structure.

Targets of the Terrorist

In addition to the type of attack, we must be cognizant of the threat of seizure of public transportation, buildings, property, territory, and objectives, for the purpose of promoting the terrorist's cause.

The following locations or significant factors have been terrorist targets in the past and are expected to be so in the future:

- Tourist regions or other areas where large crowds will be found
- Major governmental or historical monuments or landmarks
- Buildings housing federal or state agencies
- Large buildings with a large capacity of tenants and visitors, and those that are of national or international significance
- Major utilities, including electric, gas, and water

- Airlines, aircraft, airports, rail, bridges, subways, and other significant transportation facilities
- International business establishments, or businesses that have large holdings in another country
- Universities, colleges, and research laboratories
- Abortion clinics
- Courthouses, town halls, schools, churches, police stations, post offices, and tourist and foreign trade offices
- Persons such as political leaders and principal business executives

Bomb Threats

Consider it obligatory that the PI should become apprised of the fundamental characteristics of bombs and bomb threats at this time of our history. Historical reality has indicated that bombs are becoming more and more prevalent at all levels of our society, here and abroad. Therefore, the PI should have some knowledge as to what a bomb is and how a threat may be received by a business facility.

Other than the terrorist's use of a car or truck bomb, or the nefarious use of a smaller bomb device against a particular group or location, we must envision other acts that threaten our way of life. In essence, the following should be of great concern because of their effect on life and death, and may be considered as weapons of mass destruction, not only within the business facility, but also within the community and some distance from that facility.

Types of Bombs

The basic types of bombs are as follows:

1. *Mechanical*—Where there is an intense buildup of heat, gas, and pressure inside a container until it explodes or shatters. This type of bomb includes the following:
    - *Small Bombs*—A small bomb can be very powerful in nature and can easily be concealed in a backpack, handbag, briefcase, or shopping bag. It may be disguised as a pack of cigarettes or a hand-carried radio, and although small, the consequences of detonation can be severe.
    - *Car Bombs*—A large bomb can be concealed in any type of vehicle, and when detonated, it can cause complete devastation to anything in the vicinity. Any vehicle operated by a person determined to achieve this type of destruction would be difficult to deter unless known beforehand. One way to reduce the damage and injury is to install barriers around a building so that a vehicle would not have the opportunity to park too close.

These bombs are difficult to deter or reduce injury and damage other than through the use of barriers or the strict control of vehicle access, particularly to underground or outside tier parking.

- *Incendiary Devices*—Although not perceived as a mechanism in which a buildup of heat or gas will initiate the mechanical action, these devices are normally designed to ignite after a business has closed for the night, so that once the fire has started, discovery is not immediate. The usual scenario is where the perpetrator slips or places the device down the sides of upholstered chairs and sofas. Retail stores that carry furniture of this type are at great risk, but it should be remembered that such a device could be placed anywhere, so all businesses are susceptible. Loss prevention must consider that it is almost impossible to prevent a device of this type from being brought onto the retail premises or any premises open to the general public. If an incident such as this happens once, it can be expected that it will happen again. At times where a high risk is anticipated, security officers may be required to conduct as complete a search as possible after the store or building has closed for the evening.

2. *Chemical*—Where the explosion is caused by an immediate rapid conversion of a solid or liquid substance into a gas which has much greater volume. Bomb contents using common substances such as fertilizer and other ordinary products are easily purchased and easily transported in bulk.

3. *Nuclear (Atomic)*—The most extreme device and the ultimate weapon causing severe and extensive damage to people, businesses, institutions, and property over a very large area. The results can include complete devastation, the mass slaughter and injury to humanity, and finally, immediate and chronic radiation sickness and fallout unto other areas.

   The nuclear weapon must achieve a chain reaction with material that is very hard to acquire or accumulate. The making of a nuclear device requires a sizable infrastructure and scientific know-how. Moreover, it requires fissionable material that is under close scrutiny by the international community.

Other Implements Considered as Weapons of Mass Destruction

There are other types of weapons that can cause cataclysmic effects on the general public and their way of life in a given area. These may be described as follows:

1. *Chemical Agents*—Poison gases or other toxic agents can be used that can cause harm by inhalation, ingestion, or topically on the skin, particularly in closed areas such as buildings, theaters, subways, and aircraft.

2. *Biological Agents*—Bacteria and viruses can be introduced into the air, water, or food supply, or into other manufactured products consumed and that come in contact with the public.
3. *Dirty Bomb (Radiological Dispersion Bomb)*—Although a dirty bomb makes use of radiological material, it is not a nuclear device. It is a device where contamination by radiation is activated by the use of a mechanical device that sets off a high explosive (basically a mechanical bomb described above) in order to disperse the radioactive material. A device of this type will not be as destructive as an atomic bomb because it will be only as destructive as the size or amount of the explosive. However, the aim is for the conventional mechanical/chemical explosive to disperse the radiological material contained in the bomb container. Depending on the wind and other environmental factors, the dispersal of radioactive material would cause the land to be contaminated and unusable for many years and adversely affect a large portion of the populace with immediate and long-term radiation sickness.

All three weapons described above will cause acute and chronic ailments.

4. *Electromagnetic Pulse (EMP) Bomb*—The effects of this type of weapon are not widely known. Although new to the terrorist, this implement has long been known to the military. There are basically two types of design and initiation for this device:

   Electromagnetic Radiation from a Nuclear Explosion—The resulting electric and magnetic fields may couple with electrical or electronic systems to produce damaging current and voltage surges.

   - *This Phenomenon May Also Be Caused by Nonnuclear Means*—A device specifically produced and designed to cause havoc by shutting down or destroying all electronic, electrical, and computer systems and components, which will include, among others, financial, transportation, and telecommunications. This weapon can be considered primitive in nature as it can be simply fabricated into a bomb. The device consists of an explosive filled copper tube, surrounded by coiled copper wire and batteries to trigger the explosion in which the electric current racing down the tube creates a magnetic field in the coil, compressing the magnetic field as the coil bursts. The result is a powerful wave of magnetic energy that can penetrate walls, concrete, and most metal shielding.

The Manufacture and Handling of These Weapons

We must consider that a terrorist may have possession of and use any one of these implements to further the chosen cause. Whatever the design, the achievement of the device is to cause death, great harm, a destroyed or weakened infrastructure, fear, panic, and apprehension. The making of an atomic device requires a sizable infrastructure and scientific know-how. Moreover, it requires fissionable material that is under close scrutiny by the international community. Unless the terrorist is involved with a country or political organization that has the ability to manufacture a nuclear device, chemical and biological methods are most likely to be used. The Defense Department has stated that regarding biological and chemical employment, "the low technology required lends itself to prolific and even potential terrorist use."

Concerning the implements described above, the most difficult to manufacture would be the nuclear weapon; and it would be, of course, the most lethal. Following that, of the two other agents, biological weapons are more lethal than chemical weapons.

Biological agents are more difficult to manufacture into weapons, or to enter into the air, water, or food supply to any great degree. Chemical agents, however, are more easily produced and dispersed and are, therefore, probably the terrorist's first choice. Based on present technologies, the employment of chemical weapons can cause the death of tens of thousands of people, and the use of biological weapons could kill hundreds of thousands of people. Readily available commercial materials and technologies found at pharmaceutical and chemical plants, or fly-by-night laboratories, can produce these agents with ease. The more sophisticated devices for biological or chemical dispersal would require the use of scientists and engineers, but the greater the cause, the greater the chance of recruiting confederates with that expertise. Small quantities can cause extreme devastation and can be transported and smuggled easily. Depending on the nature of the implement needed to spread the particular agent, we must consider that both contaminates can be entered into the air we breathe, the food we eat, or the municipal water supply that services what we drink.

Awareness

An attack that includes the devices or schemes described above would be sudden and without warning; therefore, the only action to take would be to recognize the type of threat and react accordingly. In an atomic blast, regular bomb procedures would take effect. Once the loss prevention professional recognizes that a person or persons are becoming ill or are reacting to an unknown agent, medical attention must be forthcoming. Regarding a biological or chemical exposure, medical and public safety authorities must determine the cause and the method of treatment, and it is at this point, that proper caution, procedure, and care will be disseminated.

The above types of occurrences will most probably occur surreptitiously by an international or a national terrorist acting on behalf of a cause. We must also bear in mind the deranged person, whom for whatever reason may wish to do cause serious harm or death to a large segment of the general public. In any event, the public emergency services, local, state, and national, will become involved and control the incident depending on the extent of the threat.

The Warning

Noted below are the various ways in which the business establishment can become aware that there is a threat of or the presence of a bomb on premises.

Bomb Threats without Demands

The language of this kind of threat is concise and deliberate, short and to the point. The caller gives little warning before the bomb will explode, or may not say when the bomb is to explode. The threat may have been made to a third party—the police, the newspapers, or a telephone operator. As soon as the statement about the bomb is made, the perpetrator hangs up and answers no questions.

Under these circumstances, the threat must be considered genuine. Call for police assistance immediately. Depending on company policy and procedures for evacuations, if there is time before the bomb is to go off, wait for the police to arrive. If not, the decision to evacuate or not must be made.

Some of the reasons that the threat may be considered a hoax are that the caller gives more than 1 hour warning, the caller uses slurred speech and may be intoxicated, the threat is made in a joking manner, or the threat is made in a fit of temper where loud, abusive, or foul language is used.

Bomb Threats with Demands

This is the bomb threat of extortion, and most often for money. A manager or someone such as an administrator will usually receive the call so that the caller will be able to speak to someone in authority and can expect directions to be carried out. The person receiving this type of call should attempt to delay the delivery for more than an hour, advising that only certain people are able to conduct a transaction of this type, and it will take that long to set up the procedure for such a sum of money. Advise the police immediately after the caller hangs up.

Remember that the extortionist will try and put pressure on the manager in regard to time, but that if his or her threat is carried out and a bomb explodes, the extortionist has failed to achieve his or her goal. So then, if anything, we have somewhat of an advantage. Any information concerning an extortion of this type should be strictly confidential and information held to only those people who must be involved.

Threats Received by Telephone

Generally, the bomb threat will be received by telephone. Any store telephone at which the outside public can have access to the retailer, switchboard operator, or customer service representative for a large business, should be manned by personnel who have been trained to remain as calm as possible and to obtain as much information as possible from the caller. Every telephone that can receive incoming calls must have a copy of a "Bomb Report Checklist" (see Appendix D) handy so that by following directions on this form, the person receiving the call can easily attempt to gain as much information from the caller as possible. The employee receiving the threat most probably will be the store receptionist, security guard/receptionist, or a customer service representative. They must be trained and directed to write down on the checklist all information that can be elicited from the caller, and whatever can be remembered after the caller hangs up. The assessment of what the caller said, the time the device will go off, the possible location of the device, how the caller acted, his or her attitude, his or her speech, and various other indications may well determine how loss prevention, store administration, and the police will react to the threat.

If nothing else, the employee receiving the bomb threat must attempt to determine the following from the caller:

- When will the bomb explode (exact time if possible)?
- Where will the bomb explode (exact location if possible)?
- What type of bomb is it (if given, responding police may find it useful)?
- How or why will it explode (same as above)?
- Who is the caller and whom does he or she represent? If given spontaneously and inadvertently, the answer may be noteworthy.

Upon completion of the call, the employee should follow the company instructions—notification of the police, appropriate management, and supervisory personnel; and compilation of a Bomb Report Checklist regarding the report and notifications.

Threats Received by Mail or Messenger

Letter or package bombs are made to kill and maim when opened. Such devices can be received from terrorists, extortionists, deranged persons, or disgruntled customers. It is not uncommon for this type of hazard to occur, and therefore, it should not be taken lightly. The employee who receives or handles incoming mail or packages by messenger should be aware of the following information.

If a letter or package is received and the mail handler or the recipient has the slightest suspicion that it may contain a bomb, loss prevention or security should be immediately notified. Once the suspicions have been confirmed, the police should be called. *If there is any doubt, do not open it.* The envelope or package should be isolated in a locked room away from windows and thin partitioned walls to await the arrival of the police.

Listed below are a number of indications that should alert the mail handler or receiver that the letter or package *might* be considered suspicious:

- Greasy areas or grease marks may be found on the envelope or wrappings.
- The envelope or package may feel overly heavy for its size.
- Uneven weight distribution may be felt within the package or the contents appear to be rigid within a flexible envelope.

- A package has excessive wrapping or is very poorly wrapped.
- There may be some type of resistance upon opening.
- Foreign mail, or the amount or type of postage may not agree with the type or class of package mail.
- An odor of almonds or marzipan emanates from the envelope or package.
- There appear to be too many stamps for the weight of the envelope or package.
- The letter or package may appear to have been delivered by hand from an unknown source, and if so, it may be a timed device.
- The letter or package contains special markings, unusual endorsements, or restrictions such as *Fragile, Handle with Care, Private, Confidential, Personal, Addressee's Eyes Only, Please Deliver Directly To,* or *Rush.*
- As to the address,
  - The handwriting, typing, or spelling may be very poor.
  - It may be wrongly addressed or have an incomplete correct address.
  - No return address is noted, or the return address is from an unknown or suspicious source.

Written bomb threats received by messenger or by mail often provide excellent evidence for the police. Threats of this type are usually made for the purposes of extortion and imply that if the demand is not complied with, an act of terror, most likely a bomb, will befall the company in question. Once a written threat is recognized as such, avoid any further or needless handling so as to preserve fingerprints, handwriting, postmarks, and any other markings on the letter or envelope for forensic examination. Loss prevention should notify the police immediately upon discovery.

Finding a Suspicious Object without Warning

The PI should realize that not all bomb devices placed in a business facility would come with a warning, particularly if the work of a terrorist. It is essential, therefore, that during the security officers' ongoing routine inspection or walk-through of the facility, that he or she be constantly vigilant of any suspicious object or package. Moreover, all employees should be trained to be vigilant regarding suspicious objects and situations.

Basically, they should be concerned about anything

1. That should not be where it is found
2. That cannot be accounted for
3. That appears to be out of place

If something suspicious is found under these circumstances, it should not be handled, and the police should be notified immediately.

For pertinent information regarding the merits of a veritable bomb risk, see Appendix C, "Guidelines for Evaluating Threat Credibility on a Bomb Threat."

Workplace Violence

Workplace Violence Defined

The most common understanding of workplace violence by the general public are those disputes or confrontations between employee and employer that escalate into serious altercations, and where serious injury or death may be a consequence. These actions can occur in and around the place of employment or business premises. But as we have seen in recent years, violence can be precipitated by other factors that do not include the employee/employer relationship.

Because violence is becoming more prevalent in today's society, particularly in the workplace, it is important that we cover the problem in some detail.

As described by Occupational Safety and Health Administration (OSHA), violence in the workplace may be considered to fall into three categories[3]:

Type I: Stranger Violence—This type of violence occurs when a stranger, unknown to the occupants of the premises, be it a business, school, or place of worship, enters with the intent to commit a crime. It could include an armed robbery or a sexual assault upon an employee, customer, or visitor. Moreover, it might include a deranged or hate-filled individual who believes that his or her actions will bring him or her some type of recognition, whether reasonable or not. It is estimated that this type of violence accounts for 60% of all workplace homicides.

Type II: Customer/Client Violence—Occurrences such as these may take place when a client attacks an employee during the course of a business transaction. This could include a welfare recipient attacking a social worker, a patient striking a heath care worker, or a disgruntled customer attacking a sales person. It is estimated that 30% of all homicides fall into this category.

Type III: Employee Violence—Although this area accounts for only 10% of workplace homicides, it appears to be the most prevailing aggression as perceived by the general public. This area is all encompassing, as it will include employee versus employee; employee attacks upon supervisors, managers, and bosses; and domestic violence. The subjects of the conflict can also include former employees, temporary or contractual employees, or subcontractors who may spend a significant amount of their workday on your premises.

Workplace Violence—A Perspective

The available percentage figures noted above have been the well-accepted statistics at this time, but recent criminal activity is rewriting the percentages and the types of violence within each category.

Workplace violence can strike anywhere, in supermarkets, shopping malls, retail department stores, offices, government buildings, schools, banks, libraries, and even restaurants. The escalation of violence in these accessible, open public locales places not only the employee at danger but also the visitor. The assault may be random in nature, or it may include targeted individuals.

The occurrence of violence that can occur in Type I and Type II as described above is exceptionally hard to identify, because these assailants will be strangers where no prior knowledge of them is known. Once that person enters your premises, it will usually be the first time you will have any interaction with him or her. Other than employing certain safeguards that will reduce crimes such as robbery, and specific actions by an employee to reduce or curtail an attack, the threat will never be completely eliminated.

However, there is one area in which we can apply some effort to address the problem of violence. That area is *Type III: Employee Violence*. Because there can be no inquiry into a person's private life during the hiring process, the employer must depend completely on prior employment and hope that the information received is complete and forthcoming. Other than that, the employer has no further recourse than to observe the demeanor and performance of the newly hired employee during his or her probationary period. If not observed during this period, sooner or later there will be obvious and clear warning signs that can alert an observant supervisor or boss to possible serious occurrences. Although the employer may view workplace violence as minor and an additional problem that he or she must face, there is also the problem of compliance under federal law that states the employer must provide a safe and healthful work environment for all employees.[4]

Other than the social or physical disorders that could identify a violent person, we should be more concerned with Type III as identified above, which we may be able to recognize to some degree. That individual may be a disgruntled or former employee, or a person who is or becomes uncontrollable or erratic because of alcohol or drugs. In addition, it is not uncommon for an angry or irate spouse or lover of an employee to cause an altercation in and around the business premises.

Employee Violence

Although workplace violence between coworkers would not normally be considered an emergency where security officers must become physically involved to control the situation, it does happen. There is little doubt that violence in the workplace is on the increase, and it can occur under various conditions. Anger, frustrations, competitiveness, theft between coworkers, and stress, for example, can make emotions and tempers escalate into physical confrontations. Moreover, minor or negligible problems can also simmer and increase to where harm or destruction most likely can occur. In that respect, this is why the security officer must have his or her eyes and ears tuned to the employee community, where fellowship and silence are most often the norm.

The first and most important step in anticipating workplace violence is to know your employees. Hopefully, human resources/personnel has gone beyond a cursory check of prospective employees during the hiring process so that those persons who have a troubled or violent background can be identified and refused employment.

Petty instances can lead to serious overt actions; therefore, the security officer must be aware of everything around him or her. Unless the occurrence has already become critical, it is in the company's best interest for the security officer to bring these minor instances to the attention of the human resources or personnel manager as soon as he or she is made aware. Theft of personal property by one coworker from another is not only a cause for concern by loss prevention, but also whether the culprit is truly identified or not can lead to serious physical violence. Moreover, there will be times when tempers flare and fists fly for no other reason than jealousy, work habits, or girlfriend/boyfriend situations.

In addition, certain business situations or events may trigger a violent incident among workers. These could include negative performance ratings, disciplinary actions, terminations, strikes, downsizing, love triangles, and just plain personality dislikes. Depending on the seriousness of the situation, some immediate action must be taken. This could include some type of consultation by managers on up to immediate dismissal. In most occurrences, a warning and subsequent close attention of the combatants will suffice.

But in the more critical events, the security officer must remember that even the most docile employee will react to mob behavior during labor actions or strife, simply because a person's livelihood may be at stake. During these serious situations, the security/loss prevention department must protect those employees and management personnel still on the job and the facility itself from any risk or harm. When an employee is threatened with bodily harm on premises, or threatened off premises and an assault takes place within the facility, loss prevention should attempt to have the threatened employee make a police report of the incident.

> During all terminations for cause, a security officer should be present or in close proximity in case the situation becomes loud, abusive, or physical. The terminated employee should be escorted to his or her locker for confiscation of company property or to gather his or her own private property, if necessary, and should then be immediately escorted off premises. He or she should be given a trespass warning if the company feels that it is a necessity, written if possible, noting that he or she is not to enter into any area of the business establishment other than that which is open to the public. Further, he or she is not to contact former fellow coworkers while they are working and disrupt them while at work. He should be advised that any violation of this trespass notice could result in an arrest.

Caution should also be used in how and when reason or evidence is presented to the employee. Do not give the impression, if possible, that another employee assisted, gave help, or in any way caused the termination of the fired employee. If he or she believes that another coworker is involved in his or her dismissal, attempt to dissuade or deny such belief. If the security officer feels that the fired employee may take some retribution against another, advise him or her that if such action is taken, he or she will be arrested and charged with the appropriate crime.

Additionally, we must consider the possibility of an incident that could occur because of some event that may provoke an employee so intensely as to seriously injure or kill people that the subject believed were or could have been the cause of his predicament. A random act of this type and the possibility of a hostage situation on premises call for the immediate assistance of the police and emergency medical assistance, if required. The security officer should not become involved directly with the person committing the assault or the hostage taking. The security officer's only duty is to protect as many employees, customers, and visitors as possible from harm by removing them from the crime scene. Whether the subject remains on premises or is involved with a hostage, the police will be the controlling factor once they arrive, and the security officer will stand by to give whatever assistance or information the police may require during the incident.

Identifying the Potential Perpetrator

There are several early warning signs that may be considered in attempting to identify the employee who may have a propensity toward violence. Some of these traits can be identified during the hiring process, and others may not be observable until the subject has been employed for a period of time.

This could include the following traits and personal history of an individual:

- A migratory work history, which might describe an involvement in serious disagreements or violence in prior employment; a criminal history of violence, or any history of violence outside of the workplace; a substance abuser, alcohol or drugs
- A history of domestic or child abuse, or as a victim of abuse; a history of psychological problems or personality disorders, resolved or not, which would include obsessive compulsive behavior, abnormal, inappropriate, or odd and erratic behavior; romantic or sexual obsessions, particularly if observable
- A loner or a socially isolated individual with no or very few friends. Paranoid, has an unwarranted sense of entitlement; views change, coworker promotion, or little or no wage increases as a personal indignity; chronically disgruntled, always complaining; does not accept criticism, has contempt and disdain for authority; holds grudges against anyone who has "offended" him or her; externalizes blame, will never accept or own up to his or her own shortcomings
- Easily justifies other acts of violence or violence elsewhere as permissible. Views intimidation, force, fury, or violence as legitimate and acceptable; a bigot or a devotee to racial, political, religious, ethnic, or cultural biases; an

obsession with, access to, or possession of weapons, including attraction to or participation in paramilitary groups or training

Results of Violence in the Workplace

Any serious incident of violence that may occur on a business property can cause the following aftereffects:

- Business disruption
- Civil lawsuits and legal expenses
- Need for increased security
- Property damage
- Employee trauma
- An effect on productivity, a reduction in the business enterprise
- An effect on the company's image

Strikes

There are many instances where corporations procure the services of a private investigative agency when they are subjected to a strike or picket situation. One of the more difficult situations that company security officers will face will be fellow coworkers who decide to conduct a strike against their employer, more so if the security officer is a member of the striking union, or a member of a union that sympathizes with the goals of the striking members. In order to be effective and ethical, security officers must remain neutral. They may sympathize with the strikers, but outwardly their attitude and emotions must be kept to themselves. Unfortunately, this is not always the case.

For this reason, company management may wish to use outside professionals for the purpose of photographing, videotaping, and identifying the antagonists and malcontents for any subsequent action.

Depending on the severity of the strike and its effect on the safety and security of people and property, it will be up to the company administration to reduce its operation, close down, or to continue with business as usual. Remember that any enterprise has the legal right to remain open for business with as little disruption as possible, and the police will enforce that right. Corporate security's key function during a strike is to control violence, and to protect people and property from harm. However, in the event that the strike may have escalated to some serious extent, the police may request that the company curtail certain business operations or services for reasons of safety.

Union Representation

Employees who belong to a union or wish to gain entry to a union have certain rights regarding union activities and are protected under certain circumstances.

In that regard, under the *National Labor Relations Act* (enforced by the National Labor Relations Board, a federal agency), it is illegal for an employer, his or her subordinate, or an agent acting on behalf of the employer to commit or enter into any of the following:

1. Employees may not be threatened or coerced.
2. The employer may not threaten to close or shut down the facility if a union comes in to represent the employees.
3. The employer cannot deny an employee the right to vote for union representation.
4. The employer cannot spy on union activities or positions before the vote for representation or after representation has been acted on and the union comes aboard.
5. The employer cannot inquire of employees about union activities and positions.
6. The employer cannot fire, transfer, or demote an employee in retaliation for union activities.

> The striking union is protected by public law but is also required to act within that law. Accordingly, the company and its employees (including managers, security personnel, and contractual agents) cannot commit strikebreaking tactics.

There are two types of strikes:

1. *Economic*—The union must give the company 60 days notice of its intent to strike. This period will provide the company time to negotiate a settlement or make plans for the strike.

2. *Unfair Labor Practice*—This type of strike can take place suddenly and without notice. This would include a "wildcat strike" where there is a walkout or work stoppage in violation of a valid union contract. The company must react quickly, usually by requesting a court order to return to work.

Loyal security officers, whether proprietary or contractual, must remember that their primary responsibilities are the protection of employees, visitors, and customers from harm, and the protection of property. Depending on the business enterprise, some businesses are susceptible to great loss and damage during a riot or a civil unrest, which may have started as simply a strike or a demonstration that got out of control.

A private investigative agency contractually hired for the duration of the strike will be guided and their actions will be restricted by the law. An agent may be used to photograph or record the leading agitators or instigators of the strike for future court presentation, executive protection, or for the investigation (in addition to the police) of apparent sabotage to personal or company property. They are in no way to become involved in strikebreaking activities, coercion, threats, or constraints on the strikers or their leaders. Federal law enforced by the NLRB provides severe sanctions for those people, groups, or businesses that interfere with a labor union's right to strike.

As soon as an employee or manager learns that a strike will occur or has begun, the company administration and the security manager should be advised as soon as practical. Subsequent to that, the company should notify the local police department, particularly if the strike has occurred or is imminent. Strikes and picket behavior are covered under various laws, and such laws determine how and what parameters the strikers will operate under. Generally, strikers and pickets may only *congregate and picket off the property of the business in question,* and under certain lawful conditions may picket only on the public highway (sidewalk, curb, and street). The police will become involved, if for no other reason than to keep an eye out for any violations of law and keep the peace.

If the strikers and their supporters become unruly or get out of hand in any way which would cause a disturbance or a business interruption, or there is an attempt to stop or impede the flow of traffic or people onto the business property, the police will be the group to handle the situation and not company security. Security officers must not become involved in physical confrontations with strikers unless an assault takes place on their person or on the property they are protecting.

The security officer or private investigator will be guided by the laws of arrest and the use of force as noted elsewhere in this book.

Security and the company administration will be guided by police actions in any situation and any request by them during an emergency. This might include the closing down of the premises in order to protect individuals and groups from harm, prevent property damage, or to quiet or disperse an unruly assemblage.

One must remember that protection and access to the facility for customers, visitors, and other employees who wish to continue to work are major concerns. Sabotage may also be a problem because there will be some strikers who become frustrated as time passes and attempt to disrupt business in various ways, some of which may be considered very serious. This could include bomb threats, the obstruction or interference of public utility services (electric, gas, and telecommunications), or outright physical damage to property. The police should be advised of any sabotage or threat of sabotage.

The Right to Picket

1. Pickets have the right to picket, demonstrate, and hold meetings as long as such activity does not violate local, state, or federal law.
2. Pickets have the right to picket as long as it does not cause a disruption of any of the functions or objectives of the business; they may not interfere with business operations.

3. Picketing is legal as long as it does not limit or deny access of employees, customers, visitors, vehicles, deliveries, and so forth, to the business and any of its components. Blocking anyone or any vehicle from entering or leaving the business property, physically or by threatening behavior, is illegal.
4. Pickets may act as individuals but not in the name of the employer or any of its component parts.
5. Handout literature may be given out by pickets to passersby but cannot be forced upon them.
6. Any picketing activity must be peaceful. Pickets may not cause a reduction of any element of safety or the preservation of order.
7. Pickets cannot apply secondary pressure or boycotts against neutral or secondary employers or businesses.
8. Depending on the circumstances, the police have the authority and power to impose conditions and number of pickets where they believe large groups of people might engage in or are likely to cause disruptive or criminal acts.

Other Picketing Issues

Other than a strike and picket action by a group of employees, unionized or not, against an employer for the purpose of economic pressure to gain some wage increase or to gain or retain some benefit, we must consider that other demonstrations may take place that might affect a business enterprise.

Under various federal laws and sanctions, a business may seek injunctive relief, monetary damages, criminal sanctions, unfair labor practices, and disciplinary actions against individuals and the union as a group.

However, concerning a demonstration other than a labor issue, a citizen has the right to *peaceful assembly* under the First Amendment of the U.S. Constitution. This peaceful assembly protects the right to picket whether the purpose is a labor dispute, civil rights, or *other demonstrations*. Generally, picketing is protected when it is for a lawful purpose, is conducted in an orderly manner, and publicizes a grievance of some kind.

Groups or crowds that may form or picket a company because of some business practice or circumstance that they feel affects or offends them or others as a group, should be handled as that of a strike incident. An example of such activity could include issues such as offensive hiring practices, discrimination or harassment practices, animal rights (retail stores that sell furs or animal products), and conduct considered abhorrent to certain religious groups (abortion clinics). If management cannot resolve the situation, the police should be requested. If the occurrence causes a business disruption or their presence is illegal, they can be removed. Caution and discretion in tactics must be considered for fear of bad press and publicity.

Business Practices

What a Business Should Do

The administrators and management of a business enterprise may wish to engage in all or some of the following actions depending on circumstances and developments as they occur:

1. Upon determining that there will be some type of picketing movement laid against the company for any reason, company management should notify the local police precinct. The police will determine if any permits are required for assembly and picketing, control the size of the picket action, and monitor their conduct according to law.
2. Where picketing may be spontaneous or with the appearance of no direction or organization, management may wish to inquire of the demonstrators or pickets the reason or issue for such activity against the company. If the activity cannot be resolved, the police should be advised so as to examine, control, *or* disperse the group.
3. Depending on the number of pickets and their demeanor, police officers may or may not be permanently assigned to the demonstration. If the picketing is of a minor nature, the regular radio motor patrol car on post will give intensive patrol to the scene. Under these circumstances, company security personnel should monitor the demonstration closely and request police assistance as may be required. If the picket line is large or must be closely supervised, police officers will be assigned to fixed posts at the picketing location.
4. Corporate management or their agents (this would include PIs and security officers) may videotape any picketing action for the purpose of recording and identifying any violent or unlawful act by individuals or groups (strike leaders, organizers, or strikers). Videotaping for any other reason cannot be justified and may be illegal.
5. Corporate management or their agents may make use of undercover operatives or employee loyalists for the purpose of advising the business owner of any criminal acts that occurred, acts that may occur, or any actions that might affect the operation of the business enterprise.
6. Corporate management may wish to proclaim a trespass advisement. Once the pickets or the organizer of the picketing action are advised and notified by business management that the picketing group, acting individually or in concert, is not to enter upon the property of the business for any reason, such an intruder *may* be arrested for trespassing by company security personnel and turned over to the police for adjudication. Be aware that proper notification and documentation of the trespassing warning should be compiled for future reference and court action.

7. Management should advise company personnel not involved in the protest not to openly commiserate, interfere, agitate, or in any way become involved with demonstrators or pickets.
8. Company security personnel must be made aware of the precautions and actions noted herein, which must be avoided, and those they may react to within the law *and* the parameters the company may authorize.
9. Consider that whatever the size and reason for the picketing action, the media will surely be advised. Company management should be in readiness to respond to any questioning by the media. This will include a prepared statement ready for distribution.

What a Business Can Do

Regarding any violation concerning any activity by the pickets or the organizers of the picketing action that affects the business operation, that causes adverse publicity, or that has affects the goodwill of the corporation, business management may seek an injunction in court to cease and desist. Videotapes and personal observations reduced to sworn statements may be required to bolster the initiation of any criminal or civil litigation:

1. Picketing may be limited to one site (e.g., the main entrance to the business).
2. Pickets do not have the right to picket on the business property. They should be removed to public property or public right-of-way (sidewalk, curb, street).
3. Physical obstructions or creating a blockade are unlawful and may not interfere with another person's rights, whatever the protest.
4. Pickets may not block access to the business facility, its parking fields, or its property. They may not obstruct a sidewalk, driveway, parking field, or any right-of-way from use by anyone who desires to drive, walk, or in any way enter upon or leave the business being picketed.
5. If the amount of people on the picket line appears to be excessive (*mass picketing*), and where it appears that such a large group makes that picket line intimidating to people attempting to cross the line to work, deliver goods, or conduct business in any way, such action *may not* be considered as an attempt at *peaceful persuasion,* but may be considered a breach of the peace.
6. Pickets parking their autos in the company parking lot or field may be towed off premises. The business may reserve the right to park vehicles to employees, customers, visitors, and other persons who wish to conduct legitimate routine business activity.
7. Pickets may not demonstrate within a private business facility. This will include parking fields and areas owned or leased by the company.
8. Pickets may not picket on an adjacent business property without the permission of that business or landowner.
9. Pickets may not cause a disturbance or commit a disorderly act, individually or in concert. This will include loud and abusive language, obscene or foul

language, offensive gestures, threats, shoving, pushing, or fighting among themselves or others.

10. Any malicious damage to vehicles or any other personal or corporate property, entering, leaving, in, or on the business property must be addressed immediately with corporate and police response against the violators.
11. Trash bins or baskets may be located at staff entrances or public entrances for the purpose of discarding or disposing of handbills or handout material from the demonstrators to employees, passersby, or visitors. Disposal must be voluntary by the individual.
12. Company personnel may remove any unauthorized postings or signage concerning the demonstration in question *in* or *on* the business property.

What a Business Cannot Do

1. An owner, administrator, or manager of a business, their agents, and their employees, contractual or not, are restrained in certain conduct that may arise or take place regarding union activities and strikes.
2. An employer cannot threaten or coerce an employee from engaging in union activities, or threaten to close the facility if a union comes in.
3. An employer cannot deny an employee the right to vote for union representation.
4. An employer cannot spy on union activities. This includes company informants paid for such actions or outside contractual agents (PIs).
5. An employer cannot ask an employee about his or her union activities or attitudes.
6. An employer cannot fire, transfer, or demote in retaliation for union activities.
7. If for no other reason than committing a bad business practice, the corporate management and their agents may not interfere in any way with the picketing action, other than by lawful means (seeking a court order) or by entering into some communication, interaction, and agreement between the parties in an effort to end the demonstration.

In Conclusion

People have a right to protest, but such protest is not unlimited. If union members wish to picket, the picketing must be lawful. In an effort to control any action that may get out of hand, the police or local governing authority may set a reasonable time, place, and manner of restrictions.

Although many of the tasks and functions are attributed to loss prevention or security officer personnel employed or contracted to a business enterprise; the information, procedures, or processes in this section and in many other parts of this textbook are insights that a private investigator must or should be aware of and should be a part of his or her body of knowledge.

Appendix A

Cautionary Statutes for Licensed Private Investigators

Introduction

The private investigator must consider that whether he or she accepts a fee or not, contracts for a service to be performed or not, and inquires or investigates into an action that gathers information that is, will, or can be used in any manner, the investigator could be held liable for his or her actions under various federal and state laws, and can be subject to arrest, imprisonment, fines, or forfeiture of his license.

Therefore, before the private investigator becomes involved in certain types of inquiry, he or she would do well to examine in some detail the pertinent laws, both federal and state, that control his or her actions or could place them in jeopardy in the performance of his or her duties. Some of the more important laws that can have a cause and effect on the private investigator in the course of business are noted below. If private investigators believe that they may become involved in a case that could encompass some law or regulation, they should research those codes or the legal processes in detail.

In addition, the private investigator must be aware of the local and state regulations and laws that cover his or her actions and licensing requirements.

Other than those state and local laws that govern our conduct, the following synopsis of laws will have a dominant effect on the private investigator or security

> During the course of a private investigator's career, he or she will most likely become involved in a case that may encompass one or more of the following federal laws, statutes, or regulations. This will be in addition to any local and state laws that also have the power and authority over the professional performance of a private investigator.

If the investigator believes that some adjudication will occur and a particular law or laws will control the consequence of that investigation, he or she should become mindful of any law that could govern his or her actions. Although not complete, set forth below are the more common federal laws and regulations that a private investigator may regard.

officer during the practice of his or her vocation. And because of their importance, particularly in the area of civil litigation, it would be incumbent on the private investigator or security officer to have a relevant knowledge of these laws in directing their behavior.

Federal Civil Rights Law

A civil right is an enforceable right or privilege, which if interfered with by another gives rise to an action for injury. Examples of civil rights are freedom of speech, press, and assembly, the right to vote, freedom from involuntary servitude, and the right to equality in public places.

Discrimination occurs when the civil rights of an individual are denied or interfered with because of their membership in a particular group or class. Statutes have been enacted to prevent discrimination based on a person's race, sex, religion, age, previous condition of servitude, physical limitation, national origin, and in some instances, sexual preference.*

The Civil Rights Act of 1964

The Civil Rights Act of 1964 protects constitutional rights in public facilities and public accommodations such as hotels, restaurants, and places of entertainment, public education, health care, public assistance, and various social services, and prohibits discrimination in any other federal financially assisted program. It also prohibits unlawful employment practices for employers, labor organizations, and so forth because of race, color, or national origin. It also creates the Equal Employment Opportunity Commission (EEOC) and its powers of enforcement.

Sexual Harassment

Also included in this act is sexual harassment, which is a form of sex discrimination and is considered a violation of the Civil Rights Act of 1964. Sexual harassment includes unwelcome sexual advances, requests for sexual favors, and other verbal or physical conduct of a sexual nature. It also includes any writings or pictures of

* Legal Information Institute, Cornell Law School; www.law.cornell.edu/topics/civil_rights.html. The information contained herein has been garnered and extracted from the above Web site in particular, along with other law resources.

a sexual nature, or the posting of those writings or pictures. Sexual harassment occurs when submission to or rejection of this conduct explicitly or implicitly affects an individual's employment, unreasonably interferes with an individual's work performance, or creates an intimidating hostile or offensive work environment. Sexual harassment of an individual may take several forms. The victim as well as the harasser may be a man or a woman. The victim does not have to be of the opposite sex. The person committing the offense may be the victim's supervisor, a coworker, an agent of the employer, an employee or supervisor in another area, or a nonemployee. The victim need not be the person harassed but could be anyone affected by the offensive action or conduct. Unlawful sexual harassment may occur without economic injury to or discharge of the victim, and the harasser's conduct must be unwelcome.

The Civil Rights Act of 1991 modifies and makes additions to the Civil Rights Act of 1964, Age Discrimination in Employment Act of 1967, and the Americans with Disabilities Act of 1990.

Title 42, Chapter 21, USC

The following sections of this title pertain to civil rights in particular, but also are a concern for security officers and private investigators—those who act on behalf of, perform as, or pretend to be a public officer.

§1981—Equal Rights under the Law

All persons within the jurisdiction of the United States shall have the same rights in every state and territory to enter into contractual agreements, etc., . . . and to the full and equal benefit of all laws and proceedings for the security of persons and property as is enjoyed by white citizens, and shall be subject to like punishment, pains, penalties, taxes, licenses and exaction's of every kind, and to no other. The rights protected by this section are protected against impairment by non-governmental discrimination and *impairment under color of state law.*

§1983—Civil Action for Deprivation of Rights

Any person who, under color of any statute, ordinance, regulation, custom or usage, of any State or territory, or causes said person, a citizen of the United States *or any other person* within the jurisdiction thereof to be subjected to the deprivation of any right, privilege or immunities secured by the Constitution of the United States, shall be liable to the party injured in any action at law, suit in equity, or other proper proceeding for redress.

Any public servant or private person acting on behalf of or at the request of a police officer (under the *color of State law*) must offer and declare to the person in custody or under arrest the Miranda Warning regarding self incrimination. Any admission or evidence gained without this warning cannot be used against that person.

> Consider this law, *Title 42, Chapter 21 USC, §1983,* as one of the more important federal civil rights statutes that can affect the private investigator in his or her actions.

Basic Provisions of the Act—Section 1983 of Title 42 provides a right to sue state officials *and others* acting under the *"Color of State Law"* to deprive "any rights, privileges or immunities secured by the Constitution and Laws." Further, it provides that any person who, under the color of state law, subjects another to a deprivation of rights secured by the United States Constitution shall be liable to the injured party. In other words, the offender can be charged in federal court for the crime and also be liable in civil court for damages. The right to be free from false imprisonment is among the rights protected by the Act.

Note that the defendant (violator) may also be subject to this federal law over and above any state actions. *Double jeopardy does not apply.*

The "Color of State Law"

To be in violation of this Act, the violator must have acted under the color of state law. This federal statute prohibits those who act under the color of law from violating a person's rights and privileges. It is intended to protect a citizen from illegal actions by a law enforcement officer or agency—the misuse of lawful authority.

Therefore, the Federal Civil Rights Act can rarely be satisfied in the case of anyone except a state or government official. But, if a private investigator or security officer acts on behalf of, in cooperation with, or at the request of a law enforcement officer, his or her actions are subject to the same restrictions as the law assigns to that law enforcement officer.

A §1983 action could lie against the defendants alleged to be police officers who used excessive force, or a citizen who collaborated with a police officer in making an unlawful arrest.

Consequently, we can say that the following occurrences in which a private person (a private investigator or security officer) can be held accountable under this Act are circumstances that they must be aware and cautious of in their actions:

1. Where a person's conduct (the private investigator/security officer) is the direct result of a state agent's encouragement or command. The "state agent" can be a police officer, sheriff, district attorney, or any law enforcement officer in which the security officer acts on that person's behalf.
2. Where a private person (a private investigator/security officer) undertakes the performance and activities that are ordinarily exclusive to or only within the purview of a governmental entity. This would include *any private citizen* who professes and acts as if he or she were a police officer.
3. Where the private person has been granted certain benefits by the state (or any municipal authority) of such a nature that the individual and the state are inseparably linked. Note that this may include private security guards or private investigators employed by a municipality or a school district.

§1985—Conspiracy to Interfere with Civil Rights

1. Preventing Officer from Performing Duties:

   If two or more persons in any State or territory conspire to prevent by force, intimidation, or threat, any person from accepting or holding any office, trust, etc., or from discharging any duties thereof, or to induce any officer to leave any State, district or place where his duties as an officer are required to be performed, or to injure his person or his property on account of his lawful discharge of the duties of his office, or while engaged in the lawful discharge thereof, etc., so as to molest, interrupt, hinder or impede that officer in the discharge of his official duties . . . is guilty of this section, and may have an action for the recovery of damages against any one or more of the conspirators.

2. Obstructing Justice—Intimidating a Party, Witness, or Juror:

   If two or more persons in any State or territory conspire to deter, by force, intimidation, or threat any party or witness in any court of the United States from attending such court, or from testifying in or to any matter pending therein, freely, fully and truthfully, . . . etc., or to influence the verdict, presentment or indictment of any grand or petit juror in any such court, or to injure such juror in his person of property on account of any verdict, etc., or to conspire for the purpose of impeding, hindering, obstructing or defeating in any manner the due course of justice in any State or territory with the intent to deny any citizen the equal protection of the law, . . . is guilty of violating this section, and may have an action for the recovery of damages against any one or more of the conspirators.

§1986—Action for Neglect to Prevent

Every person who, having knowledge that any of the wrongs conspired to be done and mentioned in §1985 of this Title . . . are about to be committed, and having the power to prevent or aid in preventing the commission of the same, neglects or refuses to do so, and if such wrongful act is committed, shall be liable to the party injured, or his legal representatives, for all damages for such wrongful act, which such person by reasonable diligence could have prevented.

Title 18, Chapter 13, USC

§242—Deprivation of Rights under Color of Law

Any person who under the color of any law, statute, ordinance, regulation or custom subjects another person in any state, territory, etc., to the deprivation of any rights, privileges, or immunities secured or protected by the U.S. Constitution or any law of the United States, or subjects that other person to different punishments, pains, or penalties because of that person being an alien or by reason of his color or race, than that prescribed for the punishment of all citizens, shall be in violation of this law and may be subject to a fine and/or imprisonment. More severe punishment is noted for any act in violation of this law in which a dangerous weapon or device is threatened or used, or if bodily injury or death occurs because of such use, or if the act includes kidnapping or attempt to kidnap, sexual abuse, or attempt to kill.

> Note that bona fide visitors to the United States, permanent resident aliens, and aliens, documented or undocumented, are covered under these sections of federal law (§1981, §1983, §1985, §1986, and §242).

The Racketeering Influenced and Corrupt Operations Act (RICO)

Title 18 USC, §1961 et seq.

This covers fraud and related activity regarding identification documents, activity regarding access devices, gambling information, mail fraud, wire fraud, financial institution fraud, obstruction of a criminal investigation or law enforcement activity, and tampering with a witness, victim, or informant to name a few. The law is very broad and all encompassing. Penalties include up to 20 years of imprisonment (or life imprisonment if the violation is based or tied to racketeering), including seizure, detention, forfeiture, and disposal of property. (See Criminal Penalties §1963 of this Act.)

The Economic Espionage Act of 1996

Title 18 USC, §1831, et seq., (1996) (Uniform Trade Secret Protection Act—Federal Economic, Espionage and Protection of Trade Secrets Law)

This is model legislation prepared for the ultimate purpose of creating the same trade secret laws in all 50 states. It makes the theft or misappropriation of trade secrets a criminal offense, punishable with fines up to $10 million and prison terms up to 15 years.

A trade secret is defined as "any formula, pattern device, or compilation of information, which is used in one's business to obtain an advantage over competitors who do not know or use it." (See §1832—Theft of Trade Secrets.) Trade secrets are generally protected by state law following the guidelines of this federal law, but not all states have elected to create state trade secret laws. At present, 40 states have done so; New York State is not one of them, and New York has not adopted the Uniform Trade Secrets Act. In New York, trade secrets are protected under common law.

Interception and Disclosure of Wire, Oral, or Electronic Communications Prohibited

Title 18 USC, §2511 (Wiretaps, Eavesdropping)

Prohibits the interception or endeavoring to intercept any wire, oral or electronic communication, or procures another to do so, and prohibits any electrical, mechanical or other device, when affixed, used to intercept or to interfere with any wire or radio communication.

See also New York State Penal Law, Section 250.00 (definitions of terms); §250.05—Eavesdropping (wiretapping), a class E felony; §250.10—Possession of eavesdropping devices; §250.25—Tampering with private communications; and §250.30—Unlawfully obtaining communications information.

Check with your local and state laws or statutes regarding wiretaps and eavesdropping in which a private investigator will be employed in concerning the subject of wiretaps, illegal recordings or facsimiles, and bugging devices.

The Electronic Communications Privacy Act of 2000

Title 18 USC, §2701 (Unlawful Access to Stored Communication)

Prohibits intentional access without authorization a facility where electronic communication service is provided, or obtains, alters or prevents authorized access to wire or electronic communication while it is in electronic storage, and depending on first or subsequent offenses, sets punishment of not more than $250,000.00 and/or 2 years imprisonment. The law also makes it illegal for a private citizen to own, manufacture, import, sell, or advertise any eavesdropping device having reason to know that such devices will be primarily used for surreptitious interception of wire, oral, or electronic communications.

The Computer Fraud and Abuse Act

Title 18 USC, §1030 (Fraud and Related Activity in Connection with Computers)

Prohibits entry or access to a computer without authorization, which is determined as protected from disclosure by the U.S. government, and obtains information or causes transmission of information or code to a computer or computer system and causes damage to equipment or a person.

The Freedom of Information Act (FOIA)

Title 5 USC, §552 (1966) (as amended by Public Law No. 104-231, 110 Stat. 3048)

The Privacy Act

Title 5 USCA, §552a (1974)

The Freedom of Information Act (FOIA) is a federal statute that allows any person the right to obtain federal agency information and records unless the records, or part of the records, are protected from disclosure by any of the nine exemptions contained in the law (see below).

The access provisions of the FOIA and The Privacy Act overlap in part with the two laws having different procedures and different exemptions. Therefore, it might be possible to access the requested information in one law that may be denied in the other.

Nevertheless, there are several important distinctions between the FOIA and the Privacy Act. For this reason, you might wish to request access to a record under both statutes.

About the Freedom of Information Act

The FOIA gives the private investigator access to many different types of records in various agencies and departments of the federal government.

There is protection of disclosure where access may be denied by the nine exemptions contained in the FOIA.

These exemptions are as follows:

1. Classified documents
2. Internal personnel rules and practices
3. Information exempt under other laws

4. Confidential business information
5. Internal government communications
6. Personal privacy
7. Law enforcement
8. Financial institutions
9. Geological information

Additionally, 1986 amendments to the FOIA added certain exclusions to the law including the right of an agency not to respond to a request of information or confirm that such a record or information does in fact exist.

The exclusions are as follows:

1. Information that is exempt because disclosure could reasonably interfere with a current law enforcement investigation
2. Information concerning all records of informants maintained by a law enforcement agency
3. Records maintained by the Federal Bureau of Investigation pertaining to foreign intelligence, counterintelligence, and international terrorism

About the Privacy Act

The Privacy Act may be used only by U.S. citizens or permanent resident aliens, and only to obtain access to records that can be retrieved from a system of records—by your name, or by a number, symbol, or other identifying particular that is assigned to you.

The FOIA, on the other hand, allows any person to obtain access to any records, as stated above.

The Privacy Act carries broader exemptions than does the FOIA, particularly where law enforcement records are concerned. Some agencies may routinely refuse your FOIA request for that reason. The Privacy Act permits an agency to charge requesters for copying, but not for search costs. The statute of limitations for filing a lawsuit is only 2 years under the Privacy Act, but under the FOIA, it is 6 years.

The Privacy Act basically gives the right to an individual to access his or her own records, and to correct, amend, or delete information that is incorrect, inaccurate, irrelevant, or outdated. The act also notes that the misuse of information can threaten employment, insurance, and credit opportunities, and the increased use of computers and other sophisticated technology enhances the possibility of harm to the privacy of the individual. The Privacy Act not only allows you to obtain your own records, it also gives you the right to correct, amend, or delete information about you that is inaccurate, irrelevant, outdated, or incomplete. In fact, the Privacy Act gives you the right to sue the agency if it refuses to correct or amend your record, or if it refuses to give you access to it.

Requests for agency records about yourself can also be made under the Privacy Act of 1974. You should make requests for personal records under both the FOIA and the Privacy Act.

Moreover there are two other federal "Open Government Laws." These laws are commonly called the *"sunshine laws"*:

Federal Advisory Committee Act of 1972 allows individuals to attend federal advisory committee meetings.

Sunshine Act of 1976 gives us the right to attend meetings of the governing boards of 50 federal agencies and to obtain the records of these meetings.

The Bank Secrecy Act of 1970

Title 31 USC §5311

Covers money laundering, regulation of check cashing and other similar instruments, currency exchange, and money transmitting businesses.

The Right to Financial Privacy Act (RFPA)

Title 12 USCA §3401 et seq. (1978)

Protects the rights of consumers in financial institutions in keeping financial records private and free from unjustified government investigation. The act appears to have no direct impact on private individuals. Intrusive or unlawful access by a private investigator may place him or her in jeopardy under this law.

The Consumer Credit Reporting Reform Act (CCRRA)

Title 15 USC §1681 (1996) (Formerly the Fair Credit Reporting Act)

Regulates the manner in which consumer information is obtained and used. It affects anyone who conducts preemployment background investigations, credit reports, or credit inquiry. For detailed information, see the following sections:

- §1681b—Intent to use the report of employment purposes.
- §1681d—Disclosure of investigative consumer reports.
- §1681e—Complaint procedures.
- §1681m—Requirements on users . . . regarding adverse action taken by an employer based on information in the report, incl. information obtained from third parties, other than consumer reporting agencies.
- §1681o—Civil liability for negligent compliance.

Fair and Accurate Credit Transactions Act of 2003 (FACT)

Title 15 USC §1601 PL 108-159 (12/4/03) (Amends the Fair Credit Reporting Act)

Enacted to prevent identity theft and allow victims of identity theft to place fraud alerts in their credit files, and the prevention of retention of fraudulent information on these files. In particular, this act concerns anyone who possesses consumer information for business purposes, keeps or maintains records containing personal information, including social security numbers, accepts credit cards for payment, or performs credit checks.

It also grants the consumer the right to a free credit report once a year in order to determine accuracy and fraudulent actions.

The Fair Debt Collection Practices Act

Title 15 USC §1692

Prohibits persons from engaging in unfair, deceptive, abusive, and unfair debt collection practices, including overcharging, harassment, and disclosing the consumer's debt to a third party.

Public Company Accounting Reform and Investor Protection Act

Title 15 USC §7201, 101-1107 et seq. (Sarbanes-Oxley Act of 2002) [Short Title] (Public Company Accounting Reform and Corporate Responsibility)

This Act, passed in January 2002 by the 107th Congress, was brought about by the reckless actions of corporations such as Enron, which caused devastation among investors and employees and was instituted in the public interest and for the protection of investors.

The Act authorizes commission rules and enforcement by the installation of the *Public Company Accounting Oversight Board.* Sets auditing and accounting standards, and the oversight, notifications, and penalties by the Security and Exchange Commision (SEC) and General Accounting Office (GAO), and duties directed to state regulators. In essence, it lists corporate responsibility for the following:

1. Internal controls or rules
2. Corporate information
3. Financial reports, financial statements
4. New standards for corporate accountability and penalties for corporate wrongdoing

5. Improper influence on the conduct of audits
6. Forfeiture of bonuses and profits, and other penalties
7. Insider trading
8. Prohibition of personal loans to executives
9. Disclosure of all transactions involving management and principal stockholders

The Polygraph Protection Act of 1988

Title 29 USC Chapter 22 (Employee Polygraph Protection)

There is no doubt that at some time in the career of a private investigator, a "lie detector" could be utilized in the investigation of a crime. Many times when the polygraph exam results in deception and the suspect is confronted with the details, it has produced a confession. Varied results can at least reduce the number of suspects or zero-in on the apparent suspect.

Considering the sensitivity of one's personal and civil rights, the following condensed version of this Act is presented as an introduction and a cautionary tool for the private investigator who may wish to make use of a polygrapher and in following the lawful procedure so noted in the law.

Consider that this law may become an important part of an investigation, and the private investigator should have at least a fundamental knowledge of the legal process.

Basically, the following narrative is an abridgement or summarization of the Polygraph Protection Act to a more readable rendition and noting the more important provisions for the private investigator. For full details and enumeration of this law, refer to the actual statute.

§2001 Definitions

As used in this section:

1. *Employer*—The term *employer* includes any person acting directly or indirectly in the interest of an employer in relation to an employee or prospective employee.
2. *Lie Detector*—The term *lie detector* includes a polygraph, deceptograph, voice stress analyzer, psychological stress evaluator, or any other similar device (whether mechanical or electrical) that is used, or the results of which are used, for the purpose of rendering a diagnostic opinion regarding the honesty or dishonesty of an individual.

3. *Polygraph*—The term *polygraph* means an instrument that records continuously, visually, permanently, and simultaneously changes in cardiovascular, respiratory, and electrodermal patterns as minimum instrumentation standards and is used, or the results of which are used, for the purpose of rendering a diagnostic opinion regarding the honesty or dishonesty of an individual.

§2002 Prohibitions on Lie Detector Use

Except as provided in Sections 2006 and 2007 of this title, it shall be unlawful for any employer engaged in or affecting commerce or in the production of goods for commerce

1. directly or indirectly, to require, request, suggest, or cause any employee or prospective employee to take or submit to any lie detector test;
2. to use, accept, refer to, or inquire concerning the results of any lie detector test of any employee or prospective employee;
3. to discharge, discipline, discriminate against in any manner, or deny employment or promotion to, or threaten to take any such action against
   A. any employee or prospective employee who refuses, declines, or fails to take or submit to any lie detector test, or
   B. any employee or prospective employee on the basis of the results of any lie detector test; *or*
4. to discharge, discipline, discriminate against in any manner, or deny employment or promotion to, or threaten to take any such action against, any employee or prospective employee because
   A. such employee or prospective employee has filed any complaint or instituted or caused to be instituted any proceeding under or related to this chapter,
   B. such employee or prospective employee has testified or is about to testify in any such proceeding, or
   C. of the exercise by such employee or prospective employee, on behalf of such employee or another person, of any right afforded by this chapter.

§2003 Notice of Protection

The Secretary (Secretary of Labor) shall prepare, have printed, and distribute a notice setting forth excerpts from, or the summaries of, the pertinent provisions of this chapter. Each employer shall post and maintain such notice in conspicuous places on its premises where notices to employees and applicants to employment are customarily posted.

§2005 Enforcement Provisions

a. Civil penalties

1. In general
   Subject to paragraph (2), any employer who violates any provision of this chapter may be assessed a civil penalty of not more than $10,000.00.

2. Determination of amount
   In determining the amount of any penalty under paragraph (1), the Secretary shall take into account the previous record of the person in terms of compliance with this chapter and the gravity of the violation.

3. Collection
   Any civil penalty assessed under this subsection shall be collected in the same manner as is required by subsections (b) through (e) of Section 1853 of this title with respect to civil penalties assessed under subsection (a) of such section.

b. Injunctive actions by the Secretary

The Secretary may bring an action under this section to restrain violations of this chapter. The Solicitor of Labor may appear for and represent the Secretary in any litigation brought under this chapter. In any action brought under this section, the District Courts of the United States shall have jurisdiction, for cause shown, to issue temporary or permanent restraining orders and injunctions to require compliance with this chapter, including such legal or equitable relief incident thereto as may be appropriate, including, but not limited to, employment, reinstatement, promotion, and the payment of lost wages and benefits.

c. Private civil actions

1. Liability
   An employer who violates this chapter shall be liable to the employee or prospective employee affected by such violation. Such employer shall be liable for such legal or equitable relief as may be appropriate, including, but not limited to, employment, reinstatement, promotion, and the payment of lost wages and benefits.

2. Court
   An action to recover the liability prescribed in paragraph (1) may be maintained against the employer in any Federal or State court of competent jurisdiction by an employee or prospective employee for or on behalf of such

employee, prospective employee, and other employees or prospective employees similarly situated. No such action may be commenced more than three (3) years after the date of the alleged violation.

3. Costs
   The court, in its discretion, may allow the prevailing party (other than the United States) reasonable costs, including attorney's fees.

d. Waiver of rights prohibited . . .

The rights and procedures provided by this chapter may not be waived by contract or otherwise, unless such waiver is part of a written settlement agreed to and signed by the parties to the pending action or complaint under this chapter.

§2006 Exemptions

a. No application to government employers

This chapter shall not apply with respect to the United States Government, and State or local government, or any political subdivision of a State or local government.

b. National defense and security exemption

National defense—Nothing in this chapter shall be construed to prohibit the administration, by the Federal Government, in the performance of any counterintelligence function, of any lie detector test . . .

Security—Nothing in this chapter shall be construed to prohibit the administration, by the Federal Government, in the performance of any intelligence or counterintelligence function, of any lie detector test to

A. (i)–(v) . . . any individual employed by, assigned to, or detailed to, the National Security Agency, the Defense Intelligence Agency, or the Central Intelligence Agency, any expert or consultant under contract or employee of such contractor to such agency, an individual applying for a position in any such agency or any individual assigned to a space where sensitive cryptologic information is produced, processed, or stored for any such agency; or

B. . . . any expert, or consultant (or employee of such expert or consultant) under contract with any Federal Government department, agency, or program whose duties involve access to information that has been classified at the level of top secret or designated as being within a special access program under Section 4.2(a) of Executive Order 12356 (or a successor Executive Order).

§2007 and §2009 Private Employers

Subject to Sections 2007 and 2009 of this Title, this chapter shall not prohibit an employer from requesting an employee to submit to a polygraph test if:

1. The test is administered in connection with an ongoing investigation involving economic loss or injury *to the employer's business,* such as theft, embezzlement, misappropriation, or an act of unlawful industrial espionage or sabotage;
2. The employee had access to the property that is the subject to the investigation;
3. The employer has a reasonable suspicion that the employee was involved in the incident or activity under investigation; and
4. The employer executes a statement, provided to the examinee before the test, that
   - A. sets forth with particularity the specific incident or activity being investigated and the basis for testing particular employees,
   - B. is signed by a person (other than a polygraph examiner) authorized to legally bind the employer, is retained by the employer for at least three (3) years, and . . .
   - D. contains a minimum—an identification of the specific economic loss or injury to the business of the employer,
     - ii. a statement indicating that the employee had access to the property that is the subject of the investigation, and
     - iii. a statement describing the basis of the employer's reasonable suspicion that the employee was involved in the incident or activity under investigation.
   - E. Exemptions for security services
     1. In general

        Subject to paragraph (2) and Sections 2007 and 2009 of this Title, this chapter shall not prohibit the use of polygraph tests on prospective employees by any private employer whose primary business purpose consists of providing armored car personnel, personnel engaged in the design, installation, and maintenance of security alarm systems, or other uniformed or plainclothes security personnel and whose function includes protection of
        - a. facilities, materials, or operations having a significant impact on the health or safety of any State or political subdivision thereof, or the national security of the United States, as determined under rules and regulations issued by the Secretary within 90 days after June 27, 1988, including:
        - i. facilities engaged in the production, transmission, or distribution of electric or nuclear power,

ii. public water supply facilities,
iii. shipments or storage of radioactive or other toxic waste materials, and public transportation, or . . .

b. currency, negotiable securities, precious commodities or instruments, or proprietary information.

2. Access
The exemption provided under this subsection shall not apply if the test is administered to a prospective employee who would not be employed to protect facilities, materials, operations, or assets referred to in paragraph (1).

F. Exemption for drug security, drug theft, or drug diversion investigations.

1. In general
Subject to paragraph (2) and Sections 2007 and 2009 of this Title, this chapter shall not prohibit the use of a polygraph test by any employer authorized to manufacture, distribute, or dispense a controlled substance listed in schedule I, II, III, or IV of Section 812 of Title 21.

The exemption provided under this subsection shall apply if the test is administered to a prospective employee who would have direct access to the manufacture, storage, distribution, or sale of any such controlled substance; or . . .

b. in the case of a test administered to a current employee, if
i. the test is administered in connection with an ongoing investigation of criminal or other misconduct involving, or potentially involving, loss or injury to the manufacture, distribution, or dispensing of any such controlled substance by such employer, and
ii. the employee had access to the person or property that is the subject of the investigation.

§2007 Restrictions on Use of Exemptions

a. Test as a basis for adverse employment action

1. Under ongoing investigations exemption . . .

Except as provided in paragraph (2), the exemption under subsection (d) of Section 2006 of this Title shall not apply if an employee is discharged, disciplined, denied employment or promotion, or otherwise discriminated against in any manner on the basis of the analysis of a polygraph test chart or the refusal to take a polygraph test, without additional supporting evidence. The evidence required by such subsection may serve as additional supporting evidence.

2. Under other exemptions
   In the case of an exemption described in subsection (e) or (f) of such section, the exemption shall not apply if the results of the analysis of a polygraph test chart are used, or the refusal to take a polygraph test is used, as the sole basis upon which an adverse employment action described in paragraph (1) is taken against an employee or prospective employee.

b. Rights of examinee

The exemptions provided under subsections (d), (e), and (f) of Section 2006 of this Title shall not apply unless the requirements described in the following paragraphs are met:

1. All phases
   Throughout all phases of the test
   A. the examinee shall be permitted to terminate the test at any time;
   B. the examinee is not asked questions in a manner designed to degrade, or needlessly intrude on, such examinee.
   C. The examinee is not asked any question concerning
      i. religious beliefs or affiliations,
      ii. beliefs or opinions regarding racial matters,
      iii. political beliefs or affiliations,
      iv. any matter relating to sexual behavior,
      v. beliefs, affiliations, opinions, or lawful activities regarding unions or labor organizations; and . . .
   D. The examiner does not conduct the test if there is sufficient written evidence by a physician that the examinee is suffering from a medical or psychological condition or undergoing treatment that might cause abnormal responses during the actual testing phase.

2. Pretest phase
   During the pretest phase, the prospective examinee is provided with reasonable written notice of the date, time, and location of the test, and of . . .
   B. such examinee's right to obtain and consult with legal counsel or an employee representative before each phase of the test;
   C. is informed in writing of the nature and characteristics of the tests and of the instruments involved;
   D. is informed, in writing—whether the testing area contains a two-way mirror, a camera, or any other device through which the test can be observed,
      ii. whether any other device, including any device for recording or monitoring the test, will be used, or

iii. that the employer or the examinee may (with mutual knowledge) make a recording of the test;

E. is read and signs a written notice informing such examinee
   i. that the examinee cannot be required to take the test as a condition of employment, that any statement made during the test may constitute additional supporting evidence for the purpose of an adverse employment action described in subsection (a) of this section,
   iii. of the limitations imposed under this section,
   iv. of the legal rights and remedies available to the examinee if the polygraph test is not conducted in accordance with this chapter, and
   v. of the legal rights and remedies of the employer under this chapter (including the rights of the employer under Section 2008(c)(2) of this Title); and . . .

F. is provided an opportunity to review all questions to be asked during the test and is informed of the right to terminate the test at any time.

3. Actual testing phase
   During the actual testing phase, the examiner does not ask such examinee any question relevant during the test that was not presented in writing for review to such examinee before the test.

4. Posttest phase
   Before any adverse employment action, the employer shall
   A. further interview the examinee on the basis of the results of the test; and
   B. provide the examinee with
      i. a written copy of any opinion or conclusion rendered as a result of the test, and
      ii. a copy of the questions asked during the test along with the corresponding charted responses.

5. Maximum number and minimum duration of the tests
   The examiner shall not conduct and complete more than five (5) polygraph tests on a calendar day on which the test is given, and shall not conduct any such test for less than a 90-minute duration.

c. *Qualification and requirements of examiners*

The exemptions provided under subsections (d), (e), and (f) of Section 2006 of this Title shall not apply unless the individual who conducts the polygraph test satisfies the requirements under the following paragraphs:

1. Qualifications
   The examiner
   A. has a valid and current license granted by licensing and regulatory authorities in the State in which the test is to be conducted, if so required by the State; and
   B. maintains a minimum of a $50,000.00 bond or an equivalent amount of professional liability coverage.

2. Requirements
   The examiner
   A. renders any opinion or conclusion regarding the test
      i. in writing and solely on the basis of an analysis of polygraph test charts,
      ii. that does not contain information other than admissions, information, case facts, and interpretation of the charts relevant to the purpose and stated objectives of the test, and
      iii. that does not include any recommendation concerning the employment of the examinee; and . . .
   B. maintains all opinions, reports, charts, written questions, lists, and other records relating to the test for a minimum period of three (3) years after administration of the test.

§2008 Disclosure of Information

A. In General

A person other than the examinee, may not disclose information obtained during a polygraph test, except as provided in this section.

B. Permitted Disclosures

A polygraph examiner may disclose information acquired from a polygraph test only to

1. the examinee or any other person specifically designated in writing by the examinee;
2. the employer that requested the test; or
3. any court, government agency, arbitrator, or mediator, in accordance with due process of law, pursuant to an order from a court of competent jurisdiction.

C. Disclosure by employer

An employer (other than an employer described in subsection (a), (b), or (c) of Section 2006 of this Title) for whom a polygraph test is conducted may disclose information from the test only to

1. a person in accordance with subsection (b) of this section; or
2. a governmental agency, but only insofar as the disclosed information is an admission of criminal conduct.

§2009 Effect on Other Law and Agreements

Except as provided in subsections (a), (b), and (c) of Section 2006 of this Title, this chapter shall not preempt any provision of any State or local law or of any negotiated collective bargaining agreement that prohibits lie detector tests or is more restrictive with respect to lie detector tests than any provision of this chapter.

Cautionary Note

Be aware that the most important sections for the private investigator which will decide who, when, and how a polygraph test will take place are controlled under §2007 and §2009 of this law. Because this Employee Polygraph Protection Act is rather explicit and thorough, some of the narrative has been removed or abridged by the author so that it can be easily read. Nevertheless, the general fundamental facts remain as described herein.

For full details and complete content of this law, see the actual statute: Title 29 USC Chapter 22.

The National Labor Relations Act (NLRA) (The Wagner Act of 1935)

Gives the worker the right to form a union, join a union, and the right of collective bargaining concerning work hours, working conditions, and wages.

Among other restrictions, it prohibits employers and employees from interfering in the formation of a labor union, the right of legal union actions, discrimination of union workers, and any illegal intrusion of a lawful strike.

Health Insurance Portability and Accountability Act (HIPAA)

Public Law 104-191, August 21, 1996

A set of regulations designed during the Clinton Administration to protect the privacy rights of patients.

The purpose of this law is to improve the efficiency and effectiveness of Medicare and Social Security, and to combat waste and fraud within the health care system. It affects the use, release, and transmission of private medical data and mandates a set of rules, which include regulation, security, privacy, and compliance, in addition to guidelines, violations, and penalties.

The restrictions obligate doctors, hospitals, pharmacies, health providers, insurance companies, benefit managers, claims processors, and payers in the use of data and disclosing medical information to anyone for any reason.

Threats to information security and privacy include the following:

1. Intentional misuse from internal personnel
2. Malicious or criminal misuse from internal personnel
3. Unauthorized physical intrusion of the data system via information networks
4. Unauthorized physical intrusion of the data system by an external person

Americans with Disabilities Act (ADA) of 1990, Eff.7/26/92

Title 42 USCA 12291, §501 (1990); Title 29, 47 USCA

This law prohibits private employers, state and local governments, employment agencies, and labor unions from discriminating against qualified individuals with disabilities in job application procedures, hiring, firing, advancement, compensation, job training, and other terms, conditions, and privileges of employment.

Prohibits preemployment inquiries concerning whether an applicant has a disability, or inquiry into workman's compensation history prior to hiring.

Applicable to employers with 25 or more employees (added 1992).

An individual with a disability is a person who

1. Has a physical or mental impairment that substantially limits one or more major life activities
2. Has a record of such an impairment
3. Is regarded as having such an impairment

A qualified employee or applicant with a disability is an individual who, with or without reasonable accommodation can perform the essential functions of the job in question.

Reasonable accommodation may include, but is not limited to

1. Making existing facilities used by employees readily accessible to and usable by persons with disabilities
2. Job restructuring, modifying work schedules, reassignment to a vacant position
3. Acquiring or modifying equipment or devices, adjusting modifying examinations, training materials, and policies, and providing qualified readers or interpreters

An employer is required to make an accommodation to the known disability of a qualified applicant or employee as long as such accommodation would not impose and "undue hardship" on the operation of the employer's business. Undue hardship is defined as action requiring significant difficulty or expense when considered in light of factors such as the employer's size and financial resources and the nature and structure of its operation. An employer is not required to lower quality or production standards to make an accommodation, nor is an employer obligated to provide personal use items such as glasses or hearing aids.

Medical examinations and inquiries:

Employers may not ask job applicants about the existence, nature, or severity of a disability. Applicants may be asked about their ability to perform specific job functions. A job offer may not be conditioned on a medical examination, unless the examination is required of all applicants for similar jobs. Medical examinations must be job related and consistent with the employer's needs.

Employees and applicants currently engaging in the illegal use of drugs are not covered by the Americans with Disabilities Act (ADA), when the employer acts on the basis of such use. Tests for illegal drugs are not subject to the ADA's restrictions on medical examinations. Employers may hold illegal drug users and alcoholics to the same performance standards as other employees.

The provisions of this law are enforced by the Equal Employment Opportunity Commission. It covers all employers with 15 or more employees.

Refusal to hire: There are only three valid reasons to rescind a job offer to a person with a disability:

1. The applicant lied on his or her application or résumé.
2. The applicant is a threat to him- or herself and to others.
3. The applicant is unable to perform essential job functions for the position offered.

Driver's Privacy Protection Act (DPPA)

Title 18 USC, Chapter 123 (eff. Sept. 13, 1997)

Prohibition on release and use of certain personal information from state motor vehicle records. In New York State, regulated by the Department of Motor Vehicles as required by the federal law. This law has affected many employers who may rely on certain information for hiring, promotion, and retention decisions. The intent of this federal law was to protect the personal privacy of certain information maintained by some or all of the states on persons licensed to drive. Under the federal law, states have the ability to enact a much stricter law concerning the issuance of personal information that may be contained in their motor vehicle records. Some states have gone as far as to deny access to any information unless dictated under other federal laws.

Personal information is defined as name, address, telephone number, individual's photograph, social security number, driver identification number, and medical or disability information. However, the law does allow the release of certain information for clearly defined purposes [DPAA §2725 (3)].

Following is a list of permissible uses (by a private investigator) for personal information under the federal DPAA:

1. Personal information may be disclosed for use in the normal course of business by a legitimate business or its agents, employees, or contractors in the normal course of business only:
   a. To verify the accuracy of personal information submitted by the individual to the business; and . . .
   b. if such information as so submitted is not correct or is no longer correct,
   c. to obtain the correct information, but
   d. only for the purposes of preventing fraud by pursuing legal remedies or recovering on a debt or security interest against the individual.
2. Personal information may be disclosed for use in connection with any civil, criminal, administrative, or arbitral proceeding in any Federal, State or local court or agency, or before any self-regulating body, including:
   a. The service of process,
   b. An investigation in anticipation of litigation,
   c. The execution or enforcement of judgements and orders, or
   d. Pursuant to an order of a Federal, State or local court.
3. Personal information may be disclosed for use . . .
   a. In research activities,
   b. For use in producing statistical reports, so long as the personal information is not published, redisclosed or used to contact the individual.
4. Personal information may be disclosed for use by any insurer or insurance support organization, or by a self-insured entity, or its agents, employees or contractors in connection with:
   a. Claims investigation activities,
   b. Antifraud activities,
   c. Rating, or
   d. Underwriting.
5. Personal information may be disclosed for use by a licensed private investigative agency or licensed security service for any purpose permitted under this law . . . may be disclosed for use by an employer or its agent or insurer to obtain or verify information relating to a holder of a commercial driver's license that is required under the Commercial Motor Vehicle Safety Act of 1986 . . . may be disclosed for use by any requester if the requester demonstrates that it has obtained written consent of the individual to whom the information pertains.

In addition, restrictions note that a private investigator may share personal information with others only if they have a permissible use. If shared, a record shall be compiled of the transaction noting the individual inquired of, the nature of the information, the identity of the recipient to whom shared, and their purpose for this information. The record must be maintained for five years. There are criminal and civil penalties and liabilities for any violation (see DPAA, §2722, 2723, and 2724).

Appendix B

The Elements and Clarifications of Specific Major Crimes

The novice private investigator should have a fundamental understanding of the elements of the various crimes that are committed on a daily basis, and those he or she may have to investigate. The following major crimes are delineated to their basics in an effort to at least acquaint the novice to what constitutes a particular crime.

Arson

Arson may be described as the malicious burning of a house, building, or any property of value. There must be malicious intent, but the building or property in question need not be completely burned. The ignition of the fire satisfies the requirement of burning and any appreciable burning is sufficient. The gravity of the offense will depend on the dwelling or building being occupied at the time of the fire. The crime may be committed for insurance fraud, revenge, intimidation, concealment of a crime, or economic gain (e.g., business competitors), and it may be committeed by a disgruntled person or a deranged person (pyromania). Fraud or economic gain is the greatest motive for arson.

Natural causes of fire may include a carelessly tossed lit cigarette, combustible materials improperly secured, spontaneous combustion, and lightning or electrical accidents. These causes do not fall under the arson statutes.

The methods and techniques of the arsonist in setting a fire will vary depending on the emotion of the arsonist at the time of ignition, or they may be carefully planned in an effort to employ some ingenuity in its execution. In order to create a fire, there must be a combustible material, and the material or fuel may be already present or brought to the scene. The use of liquids (gasoline, kerosene alcohol), gases (natural gas, propane, butane, acetylene), solids when used finely ground or in powdered form may generate intense heat when mixed with water or other liquids (sodium, sodium peroxide, potassium, and calcium carbide). The devices used to ignite the fire may be a mechanical arrangement or something as simple as a candle.

Attempted arson is a crime with specific intent which would have been completed except for the intervention of some preventing cause. The major element in this circumstance is the overt act in carrying out the intent.

Any injury or death resulting from the crime of arson will cause additional charges to be laid against the perpetrator.

Burglary

The definition of burglary may vary by state. In some state jurisdictions, the degree or seriousness of the crime depends on whether the building is a dwelling, a business facility, or another type of structure, whether the crime is committed at night, or whether there is a person present within at the time of the crime. Basically, to have the crime of burglary, the following elements must be established:

1. *Breaking and Entering* (entering and remaining unlawfully)—Breaking into a premises (building and any real property) will definitely show intent, but the actual breaking need not occur. The perpetrator may simply walk though an unlocked or open doorway or window.
2. *Intent to Commit a Crime Therein*—The crime committed therein may be a larceny (breaks into a safe or cash box to steal the money, takes jewelry from a business or dwelling), a rape, or a murder. The crime may not have been completed, as long as it can be proven that there was an intent to commit a crime satisfies this provision.

   If the perpetrator has the *intent* to commit a crime *within the building he or she has entered*, he or she commits a burglary. If there is *no intent* to commit a crime, but the perpetrator has in fact *entered unlawfully*, he or she commits a trespass.
3. *Dwelling House of Another, or Any Building*—If it is a dwelling house (a building where a person is usually lodged therein at night), whether occupied or not, and whether the crime occurs at night or during the day will determine the seriousness or degree of the burglary. Substantiality, a burglary of a building can be any edifice wherein a business may be conducted, a school, a church, or temple, and depending on the various state statutes, entry into with intent to commit a crime may include a garage (unattached from the dwelling), an enclosed truck, a vehicle, a boat (with or without sleeping/living arrangements therein), or any structure, secured or not.
4. *During the Nighttime or Daytime*—Particularly in the case of a dwelling, the time of day and whether occupied or not during the commission of this offense will determine the degree (serious) of the crime.

See the following regarding the offense caused by trespass.

Trespass

A person is guilty of trespass when he or she enters and remains *unlawfully* in or upon a premises. Again, there are degrees of culpability (the charge as an *offense, violation,* or a *misdemeanor*) depending on the circumstances. A few examples follow:

- A homeless person breaks a store window to enter a grocery store in order to keep warm because of very cold weather. He goes to a quiet corner of the building and falls asleep. He is awakened by the police in response to a silent burglar alarm. This subject committed a trespass, because there was no intent to commit a crime therein. (He may be charged with breaking the window glass to gain entry—that is, criminal or malicious mischief.)
- A homeless man commits the same activity as above with the same thought of keeping warm, but he notices that in passing, a refrigerator is full with bottled beer. He decides to take two six-packs and drink the beer. When the police arrive in response to the silent alarm, they find him somewhat intoxicated having drunk 12 bottles of beer. This subject committed a burglary because he had the intent once within to commit the crime; the larceny of the beer.
- A person enters a theater or a sports ballpark surreptitiously without paying the required fee, thereby committing a criminal trespass.
- A person causes a disturbance in a public place or in a business establishment and is asked to leave by a security guard or a manager of the establishment with the admonition that if he returns at any time thereafter, he is subject to arrest for trespass. If the subject disregards the warning and does in fact return, he may be arrested and charged for the trespass.

Embezzlement

As noted and covered earlier in this book, the offense of embezzlement is usually known as a white-collar crime. The methods employed by the perpetrator will depend on the nature of the transactions in which he or she has the ability to defraud and the position that gives him or her that opportunity. In the banking industry, the employee in the performance of his of her duties may have the competency to manipulate transactions and accounts so that the loss may not be found except by a complete audit.

Moreover, an accountant or bookkeeper may be the only person in an organization familiar with the comprehensive knowledge of the financial operations, and who may have the ability to cut checks or manipulate accounts or funds to his or her own use. These criminal activities may take place over a period of years, and he or she may be considered above reproach in his behavior, personal habits, and financial status. Unless there is an outside audit by professionals, the theft or loss may never be found. This is particularly so if the perpetrator has the authority and confidence of the company's administrators, and the know-how and ability in hiding the losses.

Forgery

Negotiable instruments, stock and bond certificates, business and personal checks, or bills of laden and similar documents are the tools of commerce. Destroy the confidence or trustworthiness of these transactions and the financial establishments will suffer notably.

A person who with intent to defraud, deceive, or injure another, falsely makes, completes, or alters a written instrument, is guilty of the crime of forgery. The seriousness or degree of the crime will depend on the instrument designed and intended to be a true representation. It may be a deed, a will, codicil, contract, any commercial instrument, or the unlawful use of a credit card, which does make evident, create, transfer, terminate, or otherwise affect the legal right, interest, or status. It may also include a public record, an instrument required and filed by law, a prescription of a duly licensed physician or other authorized person, tokens, transportation transfer certificates, money, stamps, securities, or any valuable instrument issued by a governmental authority, and any stock, bonds, or other instruments with an interest in a claim against a corporation or other organization. As we can see, there is a vast area where forgeries may be committed.

Today, most forgeries are committed by uttering business and personal checks. In fact, about 80% of fraudulent checks are lost or stolen and then uttered with a forged endorsement. Some check forgeries may be "raised checks" (i.e., checks with the amount altered to a higher sum).

If a previously forged instrument as described above is found in the *possession* of a person who has the *knowledge* that it is forged and *with intent to defraud or deceive* another, *he or she utters or possesses* a forged instrument, he or she may be guilty of criminal possession of a forged instrument.

The private investigator assigned to a case that may involve a forgery of a business certificate or instrument may solicit the services of a document examiner for expert analysis and documentation.

Kidnapping

Kidnapping is the act of abducting or stealing away a man, woman, or child through force or fraud and detaining that person against his will. The perpetrator's purpose may be one of holding the subject for revenge, ransom, some compensation, or to fulfill a sexual desire. Any abduction of a person is a kidnapping, even though no ransom is demanded. It is a capital crime (death penalty) in many states whether the victim is killed or not. It is also a federal crime, and the Federal Bureau of Investigation (FBI) will enter the case officially after 7 days have passed, even after it cannot be proved that a state line has been crossed.

Larceny

If one was to check state penal codes, he or she would find that the larceny and fraud statutes contain much more narrative and pages that the more serious crimes of murder, assault, and robbery. The reasoning behind this is that in the general heading of "larceny," the criminal has the ingenuity, time, and ability to devise many methods of taking and disposing money or property against the will of the owner.

Larceny may be described as the wrongful taking, obtaining, or withholding from the possession of the true owner any property such as money, personal property, or any article of value of any kind in any manner, and the perpetrator has the intent to deprive or defraud the true owner of that property and appropriate it to his own use. The elements of the crime are that there was *intent* to deprive, *stole* (took, obtained, or withheld), *property* (no matter what value), *owned by another* (person or specific possessor). Basically, the perpetrator did take, steal, and carry away property belonging to another.

The taking or withholding may take various forms such as fraud, false pretense, unauthorized use or possession of articles (credit and debit cards, counterfeit money, etc.), swindles, cons and flim-flams, or the theft of services (telephone, electric, gas). The most common cause of larceny is greed or economic gain. The seriousness or degree of the charge of larceny depends on the value of the property taken. As an example, the theft of $10 from a cash register would fall into the category of *petit (petty) larceny,* and the theft of property in the value of $10,000 would elevate the crime to a *grand larceny.* Once the larceny is committed, the return of said property or payment is no defense. The degree of larceny attributed to the value of the loss will depend on the State statute in which the crime occurred.

Additionally, the taking of property *without force from the person* is always *grand larceny* no matter the property value. Take, for example, a woman on a bus who has her wallet surreptitiously taken from her pocketbook suspended from her shoulder by a strap. The subjects who commit this type of theft generally fall into a category known as "pickpockets."

In another example, a woman walking down a street is approached by a thief who grabs the woman's pocketbook, which slips from her shoulder, and runs away. The thief committed a *grand larceny* (the theft of property from the person—no force was used).

However, in another scenario, the woman holds on to the pocketbook and resists. The perpetrator strikes the woman with his fists until she falls to the ground and the pocketbook is finally ripped from her grasp. Although the pocketbook may have only contained personal papers and change but no paper currency, there still was a larceny of property. And since *force* was used, a *robbery* was committed; the value of the property taken is not a requirement—the thief committed a *grand larceny* and a *robbery.* An additional charge of *assault* could be made because of the force used, whether a serious injury occurred or not.

There are many ways and ruses in which a larceny may be committed, which are too numerous to list here. Check with your local state laws for the legal definitions of what constitutes a larceny and its degrees or levels.

Homicide

> Homicide is defined as the death of a human being; it need not be caused by a criminal act.

Homicide may be classified in various forms depending on the type of death and the circumstances or facts surrounding one's demise:

A. *Criminal Homicide*—Any homicide that is not excusable, justifiable, or natural is a criminal homicide. It includes the following:

Murder

1. The killing *with* malice aforethought (premeditation).
2. It may also include the killing of a person, while committing a crime, or during the commission of any crime someone, anyone, is killed intentionally or not. Any accomplice to the crime, whether that person had any intent or action in the killing, is a principal and is equally guilty of murder during the commission of the crime.

Manslaughter—The unlawful killing of a person *without* any *malice aforethought* (no premeditation), where there is no malice but recklessly causes the death or another and in which the death might have been avoided. Or with intent to cause serious physical injury to another person, causes death to that person, or under mitigating circumstances which a death does not constitute murder acts under the influence of extreme emotional disturbance, where because of some provocation there was no intent to kill just before the act, or where the killer lost control of him- or herself and thereafter did in fact kill.

This may also be termed *voluntary manslaughter,* which could be defined as the killing committed during the "heat of passion."

Examples:

1. Ralph comes home and finds his wife in bed with his brother. In the heat of passion, he obtains a gun from the bedroom closet and kills both.

2. Bob hits Joe over the head with a beer bottle during an argument in a bar. Subsequently, Joe dies a day later in the hospital.
3. John, during the commission of a burglary, is surprised by a security guard and while fleeing the scene the guard falls down a flight of stairs causing the death of the guard.

   In number 1 above, the charge most probably will be voluntary manslaughter as long as the district attorney accepts the heat of passion or emotional disturbance theory.

   In the number 2 and number 3 cases cited above, the charge most probably would be manslaughter. However, in case number 3, if the perpetrator while during flight in his attempt to escape, pushed the guard who lost his balance and fell down the stairs causing his death, the charge most probably would be murder. Case number 1 might rise to the state of a murder if the facts so warrant.

Involuntary Manslaughter occurs when a death is caused by a violation of a "non-felony," where there is no malice but which might have been avoided. For example, Jack is driving at a high rate of speed (75+ MPH) on a twisted mountain road. His car crosses over to the guardrail and the vehicle flies over the cliff. Wilber, the passenger who was with Jack, is killed in the crash. Jack survives and is charged with involuntary manslaughter. A death as a result of reckless driving may be also called vehicular manslaughter.

Today, there is increased enforcement against a perpetrator, who in driving while intoxicated (DWI) is involved in an accident that caused the death of one or more individuals. The state could charge the perpetrator with murder if the state (under their criminal code) can prove that the commission of reckless endangerment was exceptionally severe, or that the circumstances warrant such a complaint.

Additionally:

1. Where some task or responsibility by a person which was supposed to be accomplished and was not executed.
2. A person who does not have authority or purpose to do something, but in fact through laxity, carelessness, intoxication, negligence, or without reason, the act was completed.

   Someone dies as a result of these actions, such person can be charged in the classification of manslaughter (also called *negligent homicide*).

   There are several degrees of murder and manslaughter depending on the seriousness and the performance or accomplishment of the killing or the death. Check with the criminal statutes in your state for the degrees and reasoning in each classification.

Abortion—Considered a crime (criminal homicide of a fetus) where a pregnant female commits a self-abortion upon herself causing a miscarriage, or the abortion is committed by another person depending on the term of the fetus. Most states consider the abortion of a fetus justifiable in order to save the mother's life or within 24 weeks from the commencement of her pregnancy. Check with your state law.

B. *Innocent Homicide*—This type of homicide includes two classes of death:

Excusable Homicide—Where the outcome is death caused by an accident or misadventure while committing a lawful act in a lawful manner and without negligence. It may include the killing of a person when the subject believes that he or she is in danger of death or serious physical injury to him- or herself or another, kills that person but later finds that the gun being held by the perpetrator was a toy gun. If the subject believes that the imitation pistol was real and lethal at the time of the offense, it is an excusable homicide.

Justifiable Homicide—A killing is justifiable if it is authorized by law. Examples might be killing in battle within the rules of war, executing a death sentence authorized by a competent tribunal, or the act of a subordinate performed in good faith in compliance of orders, within the scope of his or her authority, and without negligence. It may also include killing in self-defense, where the subject was reasonably in fear of his or her life, someone else's life, or of serious physical injury. Moreover, a killing to prevent the commission of a violent crime such as a rape or murder is authorized by law.

C. *Natural Homicide*—A natural homicide is a death that comes naturally to a person without assistance of another person; essentially the will of God. Death may be caused naturally by old age, heart attack, an acute illness, or a long-term chronic illness such as cancer.

D. *Accidental Homicide*—Death that is caused by an accidental injury such as a vehicle or a transportation accident, a lightning strike, electrical shock, fire, drowning, falls, structure collapse, or poisoning by gases or noxious fumes.

E. *Suicide*—The killing of one's self; it is a voluntary and intentional destruction of the body. At one time under common law, it was considered a felony crime (and therefore under religious impediments burial restrictions were severe), and an attempted suicide was considered a misdemeanor crime. Many state laws carry suicide and attempted suicide as crimes but no specific provisions for punishment are provided, but the *attempt* is considered as punishable.

F. *Homicide Undetermined*—When the cause of death cannot be determined by the medical examiner or the coroner, the Certificate of Death will state "Undetermined" and will remain as stated until or when new evidence is brought to light. A situation of this type is very rare, but there are deaths that do occur that cannot be explained by present-day science.

Physical evidence is considered very important, particularly in a criminal homicide, and significant in any homicide investigation in order to determine if the death was criminal in nature. It is for this reason that a crime scene search by the police must be crucial and substantial.

Robbery

Robbery is the forceful taking of property from another person or in the presence of another person against that person's will. Force need not be used with a weapon, such as a gun or a knife. It may be the threat or fear of harm (a robber holding a bat threatens to hit the victim with the bat unless the victim gives over all his or her money, or threatens immediate physical harm unless the victim complies). By placing the victim in fear of immediate or subsequent violence (to the victim or another) where he or she can make no resistance is sufficient justification to sustain a charge of robbery.

Robberies can take place anywhere and in varied conditions. They could take place in a bank, a retail store, liquor store, gas station, and upon an armored car, a payroll messenger, a person on the street, a cab driver, or the forceful taking of a vehicle from the person (carjack).

Another aspect of robbery is the truck highjack (formerly known as highway robbery). Today tractor-trailers may carry a quarter of a million dollars in electronic equipment, or other products and merchandise of similar value. This crime is conducted usually by a competent group of suspects who are well connected to a fencing operation or with a nefarious and lawless merchant willing to accept delivery for his or her own use at a discount. If the modus operandi (MO) of the hijack crew is consistent (electronics, cigarettes, or liquor only), they may be highly organized. Other than the possibility of a conspiracy between the driver (or freight terminal loaders or dispatchers) and the hijackers, the actual robbery can take place anywhere and at any time convenient along the truck route. If the driver is an occupant of the truck at the time of the crime, it is a robbery. If the truck is stolen from a rest stop while the driver is not present, it is a larceny.

For example, a subject enters a bank during banking hours, walks up to the bank managers' desk and states that his partner has his family, his wife and two daughters, bound and in custody at the manager's home, and that if he, the manager, did not allow him to enter the bank vault and take whatever money he wanted, the manager's family will be killed. He is requested to call home to verify the truth of what the subject said. He calls and a man answers and confirms that his family is being held hostage. The manager under fear that his family will be killed or physically harmed then escorts the subject into the vault where the subject fills a large bag with currency. The subject then tells the manager to return to his desk, wait 10 minutes before calling his home first to verify that his family is safe and then the police.

A robbery was committed, and although no force was used, fear was the major factor in this crime.

Sex Offenses

A sex offense may be described as rape, sodomy, perverted sexual practices, and the mere touching of another person's private parts. In sexual harassment cases, any overt action such as language or pictures with sexual overtones, touching, or stalking can be construed as a crime. Because a sex crime can be especially traumatizing for the victim, discretion, tact, and special care in the investigation and interview must be considered.

Rape—Unlawful carnal knowledge—sexual intercourse with actual penetration (however, slight) of a female's vagina with the male's penis. Essentially, *rape is the sexual intercourse of a female regardless of her age without her consent* (against her will—without conscious or voluntary permission) or intercourse of a female child not old enough to understand the nature of the act. Moreover, if the female is under a certain age and the male is over a certain age when the act is committed, with or without the permission or consent of the female, it is considered a *rape* or *statutory rape* depending on the ages or age difference between the participants (check your state law).

If the woman is of unsound mind, unconscious, or intoxicated, and the accused is aware of this condition, and has sexual intercourse with her, that is also *considered a rape.* Penetration, however slight, is sufficient to complete the offense. The force required may simply be the penetration as described, however, if the woman is in a normal mental condition and not intoxicated, unconscious, or otherwise incapable of rejecting the advance, the sexual act must be committed against the reluctance, resistance, and will she is capable of at the time of the attack.

Remember that the accusation of a sexual crime by a female adult, although easily made, may at times be difficult to substantiate or disprove. Evidence to corroborate the victims' complaint would include significant signs of physical resistance made by the victim on the perpetrator or signs of the assault on the victim by the perpetrator, medical examination of the victim and the suspect, examination of the clothing of each, and examination of the crime scene.

Any person present during the commission of the rape and who did not participate, but in fact by his presence aided, incited, encouraged, and shared in the criminal intent and purpose of the perpetrator, is considered a principal in the crime and may also be charged with rape.

Sodomy—Depicted as a "crime against nature" and is considered the carnal copulation of humans in other than the "natural manner." In addition, sodomy can be described as bestiality or carnal copulation by a human with an animal. Although sodomy is usually practiced by homosexuals, it may also take place between a male and a female, male and male, or female and female.

Generally, the definition of sodomy is "deviate sexual intercourse" where sexual conduct between persons not married to each other consists of contact between the penis and the anus, the mouth and penis, or the mouth and the vulva. In the recent past, both parties were guilty of sodomy even though they were willing partners. Many, if not all, states have either done away with some aspects of the sodomy laws or completely disregard any thought of prosecution unless the crime consists of the use of force against an unwilling partner and penetration, however slight, constitutes the crime of sodomy.

See the Glossary for further clarification of *rape* and *sodomy.*

Other sexual offenses or forms of sexual perversion include the following:

Incest—Sexual intercourse between persons closely related to each other—generally persons "of the same blood"—parent and child, brother and sister, and in some states, uncle and niece, aunt and nephew. Whether willingly or unwillingly by each partner, it is considered a felony *(mala in se).* Marriage between persons of such close relationship is not permitted because there is medical and legal logic in punishing the sexual acts between them.

Pederasty—Sexual intercourse (anal) with a boy.

Pedophilia—An obsession with children (male or female) as sex objects. Includes taking sexually explicit photographs, molestation, exposing one's genitalia, sodomy, and rape.

Indecent Exposure—The exposure of genitalia to one of the opposite sex, usually conducted by a male in the presence of one or more females. It is considered compulsive neurosis labeled *exhibitionism.* The individual who commits this act is usually timid and has a lack of aggressiveness in his or her character and is often incapable of the normal sex act. The exposures may take place in private and public areas.

Voyeurism—The "peeping tom" and is a derivation of the sexual excitement by one viewing the genitalia or nude body of another, usually a female. He prefers to remain hidden and his activities frequently include or are followed by masturbation.

Sadism and Masochism—The sadist achieves sexual excitement by inflicting physical punishment or pain on another. The masochist, however, achieves pleasure by submitting to physical ill treatment or pain by the sadist or another person. A sadist and a masochist may have the same deviations and submit to either practice. Whips, chains, bindings, and other forms of "punishment" are used by either party male on male, female on female, or male and female.

Fetishism—The use of some type of clothing, such as shoes or intimate wearing apparel of the opposite sex in order to excite sexual satisfaction. This is mostly committed by men, rarely by women.

Transvestitism—The practice of wearing clothes of the opposite sex in order to simulate erotically the attributes thereof. Many homosexuals are involved in this type of activity, but it is not uncommon for other males to act in a similar manner. The same offense among females is more common, but it is socially accepted more openly since the implication is not perverted as that possessed by the male.

Frottage—The sexual perversion in which excitement is aroused and satisfaction achieved by rubbing against the clothing or the body, usually the buttocks, of a person of the opposite sex. Almost invariably committed by males. *Toucherism* is closely connected to *frottage,* in that the subject has an irresistible desire to touch the body or body part of another person. Occurs mostly in crowded areas (such as on a bus or subway), and acts such as pinching and caressing are made to appear like a casual contact.

Appendix C

Statement Taken from a Witness

Sample Confession Taken from a Perpetrator in a Larceny

Sample Initial Lead Form

A Case Report on a Larceny Investigation

Guidelines for Evaluating Threat Credibility on a Bomb Threat

Statement Taken from a Witness

The following is an example of a statement taken from a witness.

January 6, 2004

Statement of Jane Roe

My name is Jane Roe, I am 32 years old and I am married and have one daughter. I live at 334 Rockaway Avenue, Brooklyn, New York.

A few of days ago, on January 2, I was standing outside my apartment house where I live with my daughter who was in her carriage. It was about 3:30 in the afternoon when it happened. I know what time it was because I had just come downstairs from my apartment after dropping off some groceries, looked at my clock in the kitchen which said 3:15, and I figured I could give my daughter some fresh air. So I went down.

I was only there a few minutes when I heard some "bangs" . . . it sounded like firecrackers going off. I heard three "bangs," so I looked at the direction of the noise and saw a man on the ground and another man running towards me. The man on the ground was about one hundred feet from where I was standing. The man running towards me had a gun in his hand and I grabbed my daughter out of the carriage and fell on the ground covering her. The man ran passed me towards Beckmann Street.

I found out later that the man on the ground was shot and died there. I also was told that the police had arrested a man for the killing but the next day when I saw the picture in the paper of the guy that the police had caught, I knew that this wasn't the man who I saw.

The man I saw who did the killing and who ran past me was white, with a medium complexion, I think Hispanic. He was about 6 feet tall, and very thin with long black hair and he had a black gun in his left hand. He was wearing a light green jacket. That's all I remember about him, but I'll never forget his face and this was not the man that the police arrested.

I am giving this statement to John Adams who is writing it for me and who identified himself as a private investigator. What I said here is the truth, and I have not been threatened or received any promises or reward for this statement. I just feel that they got the wrong guy.

Witnessed:

John Adams *Jane Roe*
Private Investigator
NYS License 137939
Telephone (718) 456-1234

Sample Confession Taken from a Perpetrator in a Larceny

The following example of a written confession may be used in court as evidence against a defendant caught shoplifting and charged with the crime of larceny.

June 26, 2001

Statement of John Doe

My name is John Doe, am 35 years of age being born on December 16, 1966. I live at 421 Halestone Street, Morristown, NH 12345 with my wife, Jane, and my two children, John Jr., age 6, and Jennifer, age 8. I am employed by RDD Contractors in Morristown as a carpenter. My social security number is 111-22-3456.

Today, Monday, June 26th, 2001, at about 1:30 PM I was in Henshaw's Department Store, Maple Street Mall, Anytown, NH with my wife. My kids were home being cared for by my mother-in-law, Martha Jones. While in the store on the first floor, I decided to take a man's ring that I saw laying on the counter in the jewelry department. I describe this ring as yellow gold with a large white stone on the face. I believed this ring to be expensive. I always wanted one like it, but I could never afford it. I put the ring in my jacket pocket and continued to shop with my wife in the store. After she made several purchases, we were about to leave the store when someone stopped me. This person said he was a security officer and he wanted me to go with him to the security office. When I asked why, he said I was under arrest for stealing some jewelry. In the office, the security officer found the ring that I took in my jacket pocket where I had put it. I have been told that this ring is valued at $1249.00, and that the white stone on the ring is actually a diamond.

I realize now that what I did was wrong, and I'm sorry that I took this ring. I want to say that my wife, Jean, was unaware that I did it. She had nothing to do with it. I did it on my own.

I give this statement to George Smith who is writing it for me and it is the truth. I have not been threatened or harmed in any way, or given any promises for giving this statement.

Witnessed:	*X John Doe*
George Smith	421 Halestone St.
Security Officer	Morristown, NH 12345
Ted Blackstone	(123) 456-7890
Loss Prevention Manager	June 26, 2001

Comments: Notice that the first paragraph completely describes and identifies who the subject is, his domicile, and his employment.

The second paragraph notes the date, time, and the place of occurrence, why he was present, and who was present with him. Included also are the opportunity, his intent and desire to commit the larceny, describing from where and what he stole, and where he placed the stolen object on his person. He describes the arrest and where the security officer found and recovered the stolen property. Notice that the value of the ring is noted (which constitutes grand larceny, a felony), but he is not advised at any time that he will be charged with the felony, only that he is to be arrested.

The third paragraph shows that he is sorry (shows remorse) for committing the crime, and lays blame on himself.

In the final paragraph, the subject states that he was not threatened, harmed, or given a promise for this statement, that it was given voluntarily, and that all the above is the truth. Note that if a police officer were taking this confession, Miranda warnings and a caveat would be included; that making or giving a false statement is a crime and the subject could be charged as such. As civilians, private investigators and security officers need not include these admonitions.

If possible, the private investigator or officer writing the statement should make one or two spelling or grammatical mistakes in the text. When the subject reads the finished statement before signing, the mistakes should be brought to the subject's attention and requested that he or she cross out, correct, and initial those corrections. This is an indication he or she has read the statement and acknowledged or made the corrections him- or herself. The statement must be signed by the subject along with him or her noting address, telephone number, and date. When the statement is signed by the subject, it should be witnessed by at least two persons and so noted by their signatures.

Sample Initial Lead Form

CASE REPORT

Initial Lead/Request for Service

ABC Investigative Agency
Johnstown, New York, 12345
(T) 819-132-5634 (F) 819-132-5639

Case Report - Assigned?	Case - Number	Date/Time of Initial Report	Date of Occurrence
Yes ☐ No ☑		Feb. 13, 2005 1425 hrs	Unknown

Contact Person/Client -	Telephone Number -	Address of Contact
Mr. John Simmons	(612) 826-2233 X213	Simmons Electronics, Ltd. 3264 Ames Ave. Benning, Vermont 11339

Investigator Assigned -	Type of Incident/ Investigation	Supervisor Assigned
J. Rolling	(To be assigned)	Abe Congolewski

At above date and time, Mr. John Simmons contacted this office via land-line from his office requesting the possibility of hiring a private investigator. He stated that he believes that his company, which is privately owned by his family has been systematically drained of money that had been allocated toward pay raises for his employees. It is his belief that the company comptroller, a Ted Brookings, is the culprit and can show the writer evidence found by him exposing Brookings as the guilty party, his method and apparent total loss to date.

A personal meeting has been set up with the writer to meet Mr. Simmons off-site at the MaryBill Diner, 212 Main St., Benning, Vt. at 1015 hours, Feb. 14, 2005, in order to discuss the matter.

Note: The form represented here may be titled an Initial Lead Form, which would establish a request for investigative services.

Note that all names of the principals mentioned in a case report are in bold letters so that they are easily identified in the narrative. Some police departments and a few private investigative agencies make use of this procedure but it does not effect the narrative in any way if bold letters are not used in this manner. The sample case reports following will utilize this model.

A Case Report on a Larceny Investigation

<table>
<tr><td colspan="3" align="center">CASE REPORT
ABC Investigative Agency
Johnstown, New York, 12345
(T) 819-132-5634 (F) 819-132-5639</td></tr>
<tr><td>CR Number
38-2005</td><td>Investigator Assigned
Robert Alexander</td><td>Date of This Report
May 9, 2005</td></tr>
<tr><td colspan="3">Lead Investigator/Supervisor
William Jones   Page 1 of</td></tr>
<tr><td>1308 hours
May 5, 2005</td><td colspan="2">The writer was contacted via land line by a Mr. John Jensen who stated that he was interested in hiring a private investigator. Upon questioning, it was determined that Mr. Jensen is the CEO of Jensen Computer Associates. He stated that on information and belief his in-house accountant is stealing from the company. He further bases this assumption on the fact that he has been contacted by one outside vender claiming some type of fraud regarding their accounts payable and other financial business exchange with his company.

Arrangements were made for an appointment at Mr. Jensen's office located at Jensen Computer Associates, 1609 Jefferson Way, Johnstown, New York, 12345 on May 6, 2005 at 1000 hours.</td></tr>
<tr><td>1000 hours
May 6, 2005</td><td colspan="2">The writer was present at Mr. Jensen's office in which he stated that his company's accountant is Edward Jensen, his nephew, who resides with his wife and children at 32 Walnut Lane, Johnstown, NY, 12346. Edward Jensen has been employed as an accountant for eight (8) years, and John Jensen has never had a problem prior where he questioned his nephew's fiduciary procedures. The writer was given certain documents and billing statements (copies of which are attached to and made part of this report) from two venders that he has done business with for several years and which he believes are above reproach.

Discussion took place between the writer and Mr. J. Jensen regarding the law concerning this particular crime in question, the action to be taken if E. Jensen is found to be a thief, the initial investigation and the continuation required for a possible closure of the case. Remuneration was fully discussed</td></tr>
</table>

	regarding payment for services rendered to ABC Investigative Agency.
	A contract between Jensen Computer Associates, the client, and ABC Investigative Agency, with the writer and investigator assigned Robert Alexander, acting as agent for the Agency, was signed and is attached to and made part of this report. A copy of the contract along with appropriate business documents and certificates was given to Mr. J. Jensen, and copies of which are attached to this report.
	The writer advised that the investigation would begin at 0900 hours, May 7, 2005.
May 7, 2005	While in the office of ABC Investigative Agency this date, the writer investigated the background of Edward Jensen. A check of criminal history locally or statewide was negative with no outstanding warrants. Financial check found that the subject of this investigation had declared personal bankruptcy in 2002 and presently had hit his limit on Citibank Visa credit card, account number 1243-26-5004 and Bank of America Mastercharge credit card, account number 1336-36-00012. Accounts have been frozen for lack of payment and outstanding finance charges. Subsequent inquiries by Mr. Jensen to open other credit card accounts and loan applications from various institutions have been denied. Mr. Jensen's home mortgage is in jeopardy as foreclosure proceedings have begun by the holder, American Savings Bank of New York. Based on the investigation to date, Mr. Jensen is in financial failure and about to lose his home. Credit card and mortgage holders documents regarding the aforementioned information are forthcoming and will be attached to and made part of this report when received.
	In addition, the writer was in telephone contact with Mr. Arthur Bernstein, part owner of Bernstein Electronics, Ltd., advising him of the investigation of Edward Jensen requested by his Uncle, John Jensen concerning the possibility of some type of embezzlement. Mr. Bernstein stated that after a conversation with Mr. J. Jensen, he was aware that an investigation would take place. An appointment was made to meet with him at 1000 hours, May 8, 2005.
	Case Active

CASE REPORT
(Supplemental)

CR Number 38-2005	Jensen Investigation	Page 2 of **Date of This Report:** May 9, 2005

(Continued)
1000 hours
May 8, 2005

The writer was present at Mr. Bernstein's office at 203 Piper Street, Johnstown, New York, 12345.

Present with Mr. Bernstein was his attorney, Mr. Barry Finkelstein, whose office is located at 1900 Piper Street, Johnstown, NY. Mr. Finkelstein's business card is attached to and made part of this report. Mr. Bernstein states that his company has received eight bills that he is aware of from Jensen Computer Associates totaling Twelve Thousand Four Hundred and Sixteen Dollars ($12,416.00) that he believes to be bogus as communicated to him by his company's accountant. Based on his company's accountant, Black and Black C.P.A. Associates, these bills were received over a period of five (5) months, intermingled among veritable bills that could be accounted for. According to Mr. Bernstein, these bogus billings were received by Miss Abigail Wentworth, his accounts receivable and accounts payable bookkeeping clerk. These bills were paid to Jensen Computer Associates routinely as far as Mr. Bernstein is aware of and states that Miss Wentworth has been employed by his company for eight years, and on a question by the writer of possible collusion, he states that she appears to be competent and has had no indication that she is dishonest.

Since Mr. Jensen refused to turn over the original bills and checks in question on the advice of his attorney, Mr. Finkelstein, copies of the bills along with copies of the cancelled checks for these bills were given to the writer. All are attached to and made part of this report. The writer cautioned Mr. Bernstein and Mr. Finkelstein that these original documents are to be saved and kept safe for the

	possibility that they may be introduced as evidence in court. Both agreed to do so.
May 8, 2005	The writer was advised by his office manager, Jay Sweet, that an anonymous message was received at about 1400 hours and directed to me in which an unknown party, a female, stated that I should look into the background of Miss Abigail Wentworth because I would find a personal connection between her and Edward Jensen if I dug deep enough. The party refused to identify herself and hung up without any further comment. Upon returning to the office, the writer began an investigation of Miss. Wentworth. Determining a list of friends of Miss Wentworth from Mr. Bernstein and his secretary, Amelia Underwood via telephone, the writer attempted to gather as much information as possible about Miss Wentworth's personal and business habits.
May 9, 2005	After contacting three female friends of Miss Wentworth by telephone and personally off the business site, the following information is noted: 1. All three friends of Miss Wentworth are coworkers, working in the same office of on the same floor as the subject in question. 2. All three wish to remain anonymous and will deny any information attributed to them. 3. All three agree that the subject in question knows Mr. Edward Jensen personally. 4. Two agree that they have overheard personal telephone conversations between Wentworth and Jensen. 5. Two agree that Wentworth has been flaunting what appears to be expensive jewelry and clothing in recent months, whereas she was usually a very plain dresser. 6. One of the informants had observed both Wentworth and Jensen on two occasions together in a local restaurant in a social setting within the last three months.

Case Active

<table>
<tr><td colspan="3">CASE REPORT
(Supplemental)</td></tr>
<tr><td>CR Number
38-2005</td><td>Jensen Investigation</td><td>Page 3 of
Date of This Report:
May 11, 2005</td></tr>
</table>

After interviews with her coworkers on May 9th, and believing that the demeanor, background and beliefs of Miss Wentworth were worth inquiring into with possible positive responses, it was felt that a personal interview was favorable.

1900 hours
May 10, 2005 Determining that Miss Wentworth was at her home, 1630 Sunset Ave., Johnstown, NY, at this time, the writer was present at that location to interview her. Miss Wentworth acknowledged that she had heard there was an investigation into Jensen Computer Associates. She does not remember who told her or how she became aware of this information. Further interview with Wentworth elicited the following admissions:

1. That she has known Edward Jensen for approximately ten (10) months having met by chance at the Boxtail Restaurant on Ames Avenue in Johnstown.
2. Based on information from Jensen, she believed him to be single without any children.
3. That after about two (2) months, they became lovers. Neither her friends or family knew that she had a boy friend or that they were intimate.
4. Approximately three (3) months into their relationship, Edward proposed the possibility of his company offering bogus bills to her company, where she would pay them as accounts payable.
5. Because of his attitude and insistence, and afraid that he would break off the relationship, she agreed to do as he wished.
6. About three (3) months ago, Edward Jensen sent her a bill, which she paid. She believes that this first bill was for Three Thousand Dollars ($3000.00) and some change.
7. She was unable to recollect the total amount of money she paid out of her accounts payable to Jensen Computers Associates, but she believed it was more than Ten Thousand Dollars ($10,000.00).

8. Jensen *kept most of the money. The money that* Jensen *kept was for their honeymoon and new* lifestyle in Hawaii. Jensen gave her some money that she spent on some jewelry and new clothes.

A written confession was taken from Abigail Wentworth, in which she details the larcenous activity between her and Edward Jensen, particularly her involvement in the scheme. She further stated that she knew she would be caught sooner or later, and was sorry that she stole the money, particularly from Mr. Bernstein who was good to her. Wentworth's confession is attached to and made part of this report.

Comment: As a single and apparently a lonely woman, the writer wishes to note that Miss Wentworth appears to be somewhat naive and easily led. It is evident that Edward Jensen relied on these characteristics to induce her into his larcenous scheme.

Case Active

CASE REPORT
(Supplemental)

CR Number 38-2005	Jensen Investigation	Page 4 of **Date of This Report:** May 11,2005

1015 Hours May 11, 2005	The writer was in telephone contact with Mr. Bernstein at May his office and advised him of the case so far, in that Miss Wentworth had confessed to her part in the bogus billing scheme, and that her co-conspirator was Edward Jensen. The writer advised him that if Mr. John Jensen was to demand an arrest in this case, both his nephew and Wentworth would be prosecuted. Mr. Bernstein stated that as long as he received complete restitution for his losses, and the termination of Wentworth, he was not inclined to pursue a prosecution in this case.
1100 hours May 11, 2005	The writer was in telephone contact with Edward Jensen at his office and requested that he come to the offices of ABC Investigative Agency for a further interview regarding the case in question. Since he acknowledged that he was aware from his uncle that there were some inconsistencies in his bookkeeping methods, he agreed to respond.

Case Active

<table>
<tr><td colspan="3">CASE REPORT
(Supplemental)</td></tr>
<tr><td>CR Number
38-2005</td><td>Jensen Investigation</td><td>Page 4 of
Date of This Report:
May 11,2005</td></tr>
<tr><td>1220 hours
May 11, 2005</td><td colspan="2">Mr. Edward Jensen was present at the writer's office and was interviewed as to the variance in funds billed to and funds received by his company concerning Bernstein Electronics, Ltd.

During the interview, it was apparent that his answers were inconsistent and incompatible with the facts in this case. He became very agitated and uneasy as the questioning continued, and when confronted with the signed confession of Abigail Wentworth, he broke down, tearfully explaining that he was in an extreme financial state, owing money on his mortgage and that his credit cards were maxed out. The reason why he did it was to pay off his debts and stop the foreclosure on his home before his wife found out. He had no excuse regarding his conduct with Wentworth, stating that he was sorry for her and did not think of the consequences. He stated that he spent some of the money he stole on necessary items, and gave some to Wentworth. Most of the money he had placed in a savings account under his name at Sunrise Savings and Loan, 2212 Central Avenue, Johnstown, NY, in account number 8913612. He stated the reason he placed the money in a bank was because if he started to pay off the credit card bills in large sums, someone might get suspicious. Once he made some sort of arrangement with the credit card companies, he would begin a small but constant flow of payment until he was free and clear. He wished to note that his wife is unaware of the stolen money or of his affair with Wentworth.

Telephone contact was made with a Mr. James Teller of Sunrise Savings and Loan. It was determined that savings account 8913612 in the name of Edward Jensen had a total of Eight Thousand Forty Dollars and 37 cents ($8040.37).</td></tr>
<tr><td>1335 hours
May 11, 2005</td><td colspan="2">A written and signed confession was taken from Edward Jensen, describing his involvement and actions in the larceny of money from his company, how he manipulated company's books, how and why he got Wentworth involved into the scheme, and what he did with the money he stole.</td></tr>
</table>

1530 hours	While Edward Jensen was still in the writer's office, the May 11, 2005 writer was in telephone contact with Mr. John Jensen and advised him that his nephew, Edward had confessed to the crime of grand larceny, given a signed confession and that most of the money he stole was in a bank account at Sunrise Savings and Loan. Mr. John Jensen stated that he now wished that the police become involved and that an arrest in this case be made, including the arrest of Miss Wentworth, noting that he didn't care if the crime was perpetrated by his nephew or anyone else. Based on the advice of his immediate family and his attorney, Mr. Jensen felt that he should go forward and prosecute.
1555 hours May 11, 2005	The writer was in contact with Detective William Maguire at the 7th Pct., Johnstown P.D., advising him of the circumstances in this case and that a full confession was received and a partial recovery was to be made. Mr. John Jensen was to be the complainant and would swear to the information requesting the arrest of his nephew, Edward Jensen and Abigail Wentworth. Arrangement were made with him for Edward Jensen to surrender himself accompanied by his attorney at 1000 hours, May 12, 2005 at the 7th Pct. Stationhouse.

Case Active

CASE REPORT

(Supplemental)

Page 5 of

CR Number 38-2005	Jensen Investigation	**Date of This Report:** May 11,2005

(Continued)

1615 hours May 11, 2005	Edward Jensen was then in contact with his attorney, Jason Gottleib, 360 Central Avenue, Johnstown, NY, via telephone, and advised him of the events to this date. The writer was then advised by Mr. Gottleib on the same telephone contact that he would be present at the stationhouse and meet Jensen at 1000 hours the next day. At the conclusion of the telephone call, Edward Jensen left the office for home.

1625 hours May 11, 2005	The writer advised Mr. John Jensen of the arrangements for surrender to the police the next day. He stated that he would be present at 1000 hours as a complainant to swear to the information as required.

An ABC Private Investigative and Security Services arrest report has been compiled and is attached to and made part of this report.

Case Active

CASE REPORT
(Supplemental)

CR Number 38-2005	Jensen Investigation	Page 6 of **Date of This Report:** May 12,2005

1000 hours May 12, 2005	The complainant, **John Jensen, Edward Jensen** and attorneys **Barry Finkelstein** and **Jason Gottleib,** along with the writer were present at the 7th precinct stationhouse. At that time, the original copy of **Edward Jensen's** confession was given to **Detective Maguire** by the writer. A copy of this confession is attached to and made part of this report.

Police Case Report # 7-154-05 A formal complaint was taken by Maguire from the complainant, **John Jensen** and a Case Number was assigned. **Edward Jensen** was placed under arrest and processed by **Det. Maguire.**

He was charged with the crime of Grand Larceny, Penal Law Section 302.10.

The defendant **Edward Jensen** promised to **Mr. John Jensen** that on the advice of his attorney, he expected to plead guilty to the crime because of the embarrassment he has caused to the his family, the family name and to the company, and that he would pay back any and all monies stolen by him prior to him being sentenced.

A copy of the police case report and an ABC Arrest Report is attached to and made part of this report.

Personal contact was made by the writer with **Mr. John Jensen** on this date. **Mr. Jensen** stated that he was satisfied with the results of this investigation and felt that our services were no longer required after court proceedings are concluded.

A copy of this investigative report and a bill for services rendered will be sent to **Mr. John Jensen,** CEO of **Jensen Computer Associates** following the arraignment of **Edward Jensen** for the crime of grand larceny.

Case Closed

Comment

A supplementary page/s could be compiled in the completion of the case. This will include the court proceedings (arraignment of Edward Jensen, his plea, return date, and the setting of bail or release conditions).

Following that, the case would be marked as *Case Closed,* with a complete copy of the case report along with a closing letter and final billing statement to Mr. John Jensen.

Even though it would be not necessary to note if the complainant received any restitution since that would fall under the purview of the court, such addition would definitely complete the case.

Guidelines for Evaluating Threat Credibility on a Bomb Threat

The determination of the credibility of a particular threat frequently involves a decision made by a number of persons. This could include security, building ownership or management, and law enforcement personnel who will base that decision upon the consideration of many factors.

The following guidelines cover some of the more common factors that should be considered when evaluating the believability of a threat. There may be others directly related to a particular situation. However, each is worthy of consideration, and as a general rule, the more indicators present, the more credible the threat.

Credibility Guidelines for the Evaluation of a Bomb Threat

Indicator

Regard the quality of the facility's access control systems.

Consideration

If a bomb threat is received at a facility that has good perimeter protection, the chances that an outside group or individual placed a bomb in a work area are limited. Conversely, if a limited, or *no* access control system exists or the building is open to the public, the placing of a bomb could occur more easily.

Indicators

- Did the caller of the bomb threat display specific and definite knowledge of the facility?
- Did the caller provide details as to the time of the explosion, location, and reason the bomb was placed?
- Did the caller sound intoxicated? Was there laughter in the background, or other signs that the call is a prank or hoax?

Consideration

The more specific the threat, the higher the level of credibility. More credence should be given to the caller who displays first-hand knowledge of the physical layout of the building or the operating function of the facility, and who is willing to provide greater details as to when the bomb will go off.

Indicators

- Has there been unfavorable publicity? Is the company presently/about to be involved in a strike situation?
- Is the company involved in an incident or publicity that is highly controversial?

Consideration

Unfavorable publicity to a company may focus unwarranted attention on its operations and may make the facility vulnerable to bomb threats that prove to be false. On the other hand, involvement in highly controversial issues, or emotional and volatile situations may require the threat to be taken more seriously.

Indicator

Was the time limit given realistic?

Consideration

Since the threat of *most* serious bomber who call in a threat is to avoid hurting people who may be sympathetic to their cause, a serious threat usually timed to enable innocent people to leave the area without injury. However, if the threat has political, cultural or religious overtones, the probability of a bomb causing catastrophic destruction, serious injury and death will usually take place immediately or very soon after the call.

Indicator

Was there a threat of multiple bombings or the placing of multiple bombs?

Consideration

Experience has shown that threats of multiple bombings within a single facility will more likely be false because of the difficulty in coordinating such an undertaking, although multiple bombings are possible and must be considered.

Indicator

Have there been previous bomb threats or terrorist threats?

Consideration

If a terrorist group has recently made declarations or threats against an institution or a company, particularly if that company has international holdings, any subsequent bomb threat should be seriously considered in conjunction with other indicators. Similarly, if the details of the threat fit other actual incidents, the threat has more credibility.

Indicator

Have previous bomb threats resulted in evacuation?

Consideration

Media and in-house publicity of a bomb threat incident where an evacuation occurred often fosters more bomb threats. Threats may be made to try and halt company operations again and again. If there is no history of an evacuation and if the bomb threats are isolated incidents, the threats' credibility increases.

Appendix D: Forms

(The following form may be used as a sample disclosure release to be completed upon application for employment.)

(COMPANY LETTERHEAD)

Information Disclosure Release Form

This is to inform you that as part of our procedure for processing your employment application, and/or your evolving progression of employment or advancement at XYZ Company, XYZ Company will examine and inquire into your background and the information provided and noted on your application and/or resume. In addition, we may use an independent agent or agency to conduct a complete inquiry and/or investigative report on your background.

This inquiry and/or investigative report may include information obtained through personal or telephonic interviews, and/or by written communication to family members, business associates, financial sources, public records, friends, neighbors or other third parties with whom you are acquainted or so noted on your application and/or resume. The information may include inquiries as to your character, general reputation, personal characteristics, or mode of living. Further, inquiry may include credit history, workers compensation records as may be lawfully obtained, previous employment histories, education and credentials verification, motor vehicle records, and/or criminal history if any.

Please Read This Document Carefully before Signing

By signing this document below, you are releasing XYZ Company, any and all persons employed by XYZ Company, and any person, agent or agency contracted by XYZ Company from any and all liability whatsoever for this purpose.

You have the right to make a written request for additional disclosure concerning the complete nature and scope of the investigation conducted, and we will provide that information to you as required by law.

____

Print Your Name

____

Signature

____

Home Address

____

Telephone No. (_____)________________ Today's Date ________________

ABC Private Investigative and Security Services, Ltd.

Arrest/Apprehension Report

Refer to Case Report Number ____________Date of Original Occurrence/ Report ______________________

Date of Arrest ____________________ Time of Arrest__________ Date of this Report __________
Month Day Year

Location of Arrest____

Original Report by ______________________________Dep't _________

Classification of Crime _______________ No. of Subjects _____This Subject No.________

Name of Subject _________________________________

Aliases/AKA______________________

Age______ Date of Birth ___________ Social Security # ______________ Home Tel. # _______________

Home Address ____

Business Name/Address ____________________________________

Tel.#________________________

Height_______Weight______Build______Race_____Complexion_______ Eye color _____ Hair color ______

Hairlength/type____________Mustache/type/color__________________ Beard/type/color __________________

Tattoos/Scars (describe in detail) __________________________________

Idiosyncrasies with jewelry/dress/appearance ________________________

Witnesses to the Crime/Arrest ____________________________________

____

Police Officer/Detective Assigned ____________________________ Shield # __________________

Police Report # __________________ Subject released: To Police ________ To Parent____________________________

Other type of release ___________________ Time/date _______________

Comments/details____

Security Officer/Private Investigator Assigned	Approved By	Date

Attach to Case Report with any other originals. Use Continuation/Supplemental Report for additional details, witnesses, etc.

ABC Private Investigative and Security Services, Ltd.

123 Main Street, Suite 202
Anytown, Illinois 11334
Tel. (808) 678-1324

CONSENT TO SEARCH

I, ______________________________ having been informed that I have a
(PRINT NAME)
constitutional right not to give permission for a search of my personal property or any property owned by me, possessed by me, or under my control, including any motor vehicle in my possession, and that I have the right to refuse consent for any type of search by any security officer of the Loss Prevention Department of A.B. Henshaw and Company, or any search by a manager employed by that company or any Private Investigator employed by ABC Private Investigative and Security Services acting as an agent of A.B. Henshaw & Company.

Having been so advised, I hereby authorize ______________________ a Security Officer/Private Investigator to conduct a complete search of__________ ____________________ located at ______________________________.

I understand that any property found and seized as a result of this search may be used against me in any legal hearing or court of law.

This written permission is being given by me freely and voluntarily, and without threats or any promises made to me of any kind.

Today's Date ______________________

______________________________ ______________________
Print Name Sign Name

____________ ______________________________
Date of Birth Home Address

______________________________ Telephone # ____________________

Witness ______________________ Witness ____________________
(Signature) (Signature)

____________ ____________ ____________ ____________
Title Date Title Date

File original with Case Report. If an arrest is made, attach original to police report and file copy with Case Report.

BOMB REPORT CHECKLIST

GENERAL TELEPHONE INSTRUCTIONS UPON RECEIVING A BOMB THREAT

ATTEMPT TO WRITE OUT THE COMPLETE MESSAGE GIVEN BY THE CALLER. PROLONG THE CONVERSATION. DETERMINE AND NOTE AS MUCH OF THE FOLLOWING INFORMATION AS POSSIBLE.

EXACT WORDS OF CALLER ____
____
____
____

TODAY'S DATE:________ORIGIN OF CALL: Local___Long Distance___Booth ___Within Bldg.___ Unknown___

TIME OF CALL: ________CALLER'S IDENTITY: Male_____Female____ Juvenile____ Approx. Age:___

PRETEND DIFFICULTY HEARING THE CONVERSATION. KEEP CALLER TALKING.
BUT DO NOT ANGER THE CALLER.
IF CALLER SEEMS AGREEABLE TO FURTHER CONVERSATION, ASK QUESTIONS SUCH AS THE FOLLOWING

BOMB FACTS

When will the bomb go off?______________ Hour?_________ How much time remaining?__________

Where is it located?________________________________What area of the bldg.? __________________

How do you know so much about the bomb? ____

Why are you doing this? ____

Where are you now? ____

What is your name/address? ____

IF THE BUILDING IS OCCUPIED, INFORM THE CALLER THAT DETONATION COULD CAUSE INJURY OR DEATH.

CHARACTERISTICS OF CALLER

Check off all that apply.

VOICE	SPEECH	ACCENT	LANGUAGE	MANNER
___Familiar	___Fast	___Local	___Excellent	___Calm
___High pitched	___Slow	___Not local	___Good	___Rational
___Deep	___Distinct	___Foreign	___Fair	___Coherent
___Raspy	___Stutter	________Type?	___Poor	___Angry
___Loud	___Deliberate	___Race?	___Foul	___Laughing
___Soft	___Slurred	_______Region?	___Righteous	___Irrational
___Pleasant	___Nasal		___Other	___Emotional
___Incoherent	___Distorted			___Intoxicated?
___Other?	___Lisp			
Explain ____	___Other?			

Apparent familiarity with this facility? _____
Yes _____No ____
Much: ____Some: ________________________
Explain:________________________________

BACKGROUND NOISE

___Factory machines
___Bedlam
___Music
___Trains
___Voices
___Party atmosphere

___Office machines
___Mixed/noisy
___Street traffic
___Animals
___Airplanes
___Quiet

Police Notified? Yes__ No __Time Ntfd.______

Time of Arrival______Police Report No.____

PERSON REPORTING ________________

Use other side of this form for further information if needed. Attach copy to Case Report; original to Police.
NOTIFY YOUR SUPERVISOR IMMEDIATELY OR FOLLOW THE EMERGENCY PROCEDURE PLAN.

Appendix E

National and International Organizations and Associations for the Private Investigator

State Associations for Private Investigators

State Licensing of Private Investigators

Professional Certifications and Standards

National and International Organizations and Associations for the Private Investigator

The following organizations or associations offer national or international membership for licensed investigators and detectives, in addition to extending affiliation and certification for the private investigator.

In addition, these organizations may provide regular meetings for interacting and reciprocation among members and seminars and training within a particular field of endeavor.

The following are but a few that can be explored on the Internet.

1. ASIS International (formerly The American Society for Industrial Security [ASIS]), Arlington, VA 22209, (703) 522-5800. The world's largest security and investigation association of professionals, including private investigators and corporate loss prevention and security officers at all levels. Offers a complex application and examination for the sought-after titles of Certified Protection Professional (CPP), Professional Security Investigator (PCI), and Physical Security Professional (PSP). In addition to certifications, holds an annual national seminar and monthly meetings in local chapters in most U.S. cities. www.asisonline.com
2. American Academy for Professional Law Enforcement (AAPLE), New York. Law enforcement personnel, active and retired, who possess college degrees, including college professors and institutions.
3. American College of Forensic Examiners (ACFE), Austin, TX 78701, (800) 245-3321.
4. Association of Certified Fraud Examiners (CFE), Austin, TX (CFE certification). Accounting, auditing, and fraud investigation; certification/training/education. www.acfe.com
5. American Academy of Forensic Sciences, Los Angeles, CA.
6. American Institute of Executive Protection, Bridgewater, NJ.
7. American Polygraph Association (APA), Chattanooga, TN.
8. The Academy of Security Educators and Trainers, Berryville, VA.
9. Center for Interviewer Standards and Assessments, Downers Grove, IL (CFI certification).
10. Council of International Investigators, Inc., Seattle, WA.
11. Defense Investigators Association (DIA), Stuart, FL (CCDI certification).
12. Information Systems Security Association (ISSA), Oak Creek, WI (CISSP, SSCP, GIAC, CIA, and CISA certifications), international organization of information security professionals and practitioners.
13. International Association of Personal Protection Agents, Arlington Heights, IL.
14. International Narcotic Enforcement Officers Association, Albany, NY.
15. International Association of Personal Protection Agents.

16. International Narcotic Enforcement Officers Association.
17. International Association of Professional Security Consultants.
18. International Association of Professional Security Consultants, Des Moines, IA.
19. International Association of Credit Card Investigators, Novato, CA 94945, (415) 897-8800. Investigators of credit card fraud; sponsors national and regional seminars.
20. International Association of Arson Investigators, St. Louis, MO 63102, (314) 621-1966. Includes government, insurance, and private arson investigators; sponsors national and regional seminars and meetings through state chapters throughout the United States.
21. International Association of Special Investigative Units, New York, NY 10038, (212) 669-9274. Insurance industry investigators; offers seminars and training.
22. International Foundation for Protection Officers (IFPO), Naples, FL (CPO certification). Develops and certifies training of security officers.
23. Loss Prevention and Security Association (LPSA), Tempe, AZ.
24. National Association of Legal Investigators, Alton, IL 62002, (618) 465-4400. (www.nalionline.org) Specializes in personal injury and criminal defense investigation for trial attorneys; holds national and regional seminars.
25. National Association of Investigative Specialists (NAIS). General investigative work; holds annual seminars.
26. National Association of Professional Process Servers (NAPPS). (www.napps.org) State laws regarding licensing, with directory of chartered state associations.
27. National Association of Investigative Specialists (NAIS), Austin, TX.
28. National Association of Fire Investigators (NAFI), Sarasota, FL (CFEI certification).
29. National Association of Legal Investigators, Sacramento, CA (CLI certification).
30. National Association of Professional Accident Reconstructionists (NAPARS), Brandywine, MD.
31. National Association of Professional Insurance Investigators (NSPII), Delaware, OH; includes arson, accident, bomb, theft, and fraud investigators.
32. National Council of Investigation and Security Services, Baltimore, MD.
33. National Retail Association. Specializes in retail loss prevention, security, and safety.
34. The National Council of Investigation and Security Services, Severna Park, MD 21146, (800) 445-8408. (www.nciss.com) General investigative services.
35. World Association of Detectives, Severna Park, MD 21146, (800) 962-0516. General investigative services with international contacts.
36. Women Investigator's Association, Encino, CA.

State Associations for Private Investigators

Most states have their own investigative associations or organizations that provide networking, business contacts, camaraderie, fellowship, and training. Some associations hold annual seminars or affairs, and many include local chapters that meet monthly. In addition, some state associations may not have Web sites, but do have e-mail.

For a full listing by state, see PI Resources and Locator (www.piresourcesand-locator.com/invesassoc.html).

Nevertheless, the reader may wish to explore the various states licensing divisions such as the Department of State, Secretary of State, the State Police, State Department of Public Safety, Office of the Attorney General, or the Department of Commerce regarding the following inquiries:

1. To determine the private investigator or private detective association or organization that caters to investigators in the private sector in your state
2. To determine whether certain licenses or permits are required by the state or local municipal authorities, such as investigator's license or pistol carry permit, and the necessary requirements or provisions for possession
3. To determine if there are reciprocity agreements between states regarding being licensed in one state and functioning as an investigator in another

The following are a *sample* of professional associations that can be found in various states:

- California Association of Licensed Investigators (CALI), www.cali-pi.org
- Massachusetts Licensed Private Detectives Association of Massachusetts, Inc., www.lpdam.com
- Associated Licensed Detectives of New York State (ALDONYS), www.aldonys.org
- Private Detectives Association of New Jersey. www.pdanj.com
- Texas Association of Licensed Investigators. www.tali.org
- The Pacific Northwest Association of Investigators (PNAI), www.pnai.com
- Pennsylvania Association of Licensed Investigators, www.pali.org
- Washington Association of Legal Investigators, www.wali.org

State Licensing of Private Investigators

There are only a few states that do not require licensing:

Alabama
Alaska
Colorado
Idaho
Mississippi
South Dakota

Pennsylvania has no licensing at the state level, but there is licensing county by county.

Missouri also has no licensing at the state level. However, some cities within the state require licensing.

All other states, including Puerto Rico and Washington, D.C., have licensing requirements and standards for private investigators.

Professional Certifications and Standards

Those noted in the following short list offer professional certification to private investigators and loss prevention and security personnel within their particular field of expertise:

- Certified Public Accountant (CPA)
- Certified Fraud Examiner (CFE)
- Certified Protection Professional (CPP)
- Certified Internal Auditor (CIA)
- Certified Forensic Interviewer (CFI)
- Certified Information Systems Auditor (CISA)
- Certified Protection Officer (CPO)
- Certified Information Systems Security Professional (CISSP)
- Certified Information Systems Auditor (CISA)
- Global Information Assurance Certification (GIAC)
- Professional Certified Investigator (PCI)
- Physical Security Professional (PSP)
- Systems Security Certified Practitioner (SSCP)
- Certified Fire and Explosive Investigator (CFEI)
- Certified Legal Investigator (CLI)
- Certified Criminal Defense Investigator (CCDI)

Glossary

Abbreviations

As Found in Law Citations

A.D.	Appellate Division Reports
A.D.2d	Appellate Division Reports, Second Series
Aff'd.	Affirmed
Cal.Rptr.	California Reporter
Cir.	Federal Circuit Court of Appeals
C.F.R.	Code of Federal Regulations (rules made by federal agencies and executive departments)
E.D.	Eastern District (Federal)
EDNY	Eastern District New York (Federal)
F.Supp.	Federal Supplement
F. 2nd	Second Circuit (Federal)
NDNY	Northern District New York (Federal)
N.Y.	New York Court of Appeals Reports
N.Y.2d	New York Court of Appeals Reports, Second Series
N.Y.S.	New York Supplement Reporter
N.Y.S.2d	New York Supplement Reporter, Second Series
SC	U.S. Supreme Court
S.Ct.	U.S. Supreme Court Reporter
SDNY	Southern District New York (Federal)
Sup.	Supplement
Sup.Ct.	U.S. Supreme Court
U.S.	United States Supreme Court
USC	U.S. Code (Federal Law; laws made by the U.S. Congress)
U.S.C.A.	U.S. Code Annotated (Federal Law)
Federal Register	Official daily publication for Rules, Proposed Rules, and Notices of Federal agencies and organizations, as well as Executive Orders and other Presidential Documents

Terms

Abduction: (1) The carrying away by force or fraudulent persuasion, a wife, child, or ward. (2) The unlawful taking away or detention of a male, female, or child for illicit purposes. (See also *Kidnapping*.)

Abscond: To secretly leave the court's jurisdiction, or to hide within the jurisdiction in order to avoid legal proceedings.

Access Control: Terminology that covers the management, mechanism, and capability of people who wish to enter a building or an enclosure, or entry into an information system. In access to a structure, a hard key, a magnetic or electronic card key, personal identification number (PIN), eye (iris), handprint, fingerprint, or voiceprint may be utilized. In giving access to information and data via computers may include *authentication* and *encryption*.

Authentication—A method that confirms the user's identity. Generally the techniques used are something only the user knows, such as a password or PIN, the use of a smart card or ATM-type card, or something that is part of the user, such as a fingerprint, iris, etc. The use of two or all three of these methods in combination would provide the strongest authentication.

Encryption—A process where a coding and decoding is used in an effort to secure communications (computer, telephonic) between the receiver and the sender.

Accessory: Although not the principal actor in the commission of an offense, a person who solicits, requests, commands, or intentionally aids the principal actor to engage in the commission of such offense. Accessories are divided into two classes—one who *before the fact* aids, abets, or procures another to commit the crime, and one who *after the fact,* knowing the crime has been committed, receives or assists the criminal.

Accomplice: A person who is liable to prosecution for the identical offense charged against the defendant on trial. One who is so connected with a crime that he or she might be convicted as a principal to the crime (for example, acting in concert).

Accusatory Instrument: Can be described as an indictment, an information, a simplified traffic information, prosecutors information, a misdemeanor complaint, or a felony complaint. Every accusatory instrument, regardless of the person designated therein as the accuser, constitutes an accusation on behalf of the State as the plaintiff and must be entitled "The People of the State of New York" (or the particular state in which the instrument is sworn to) against the designated person known as the defendant. (Also known as and interchangeable with the *complaint, information, affidavit,* or *bill of particulars.*)

Accused: The person charged with a crime, felony, or misdemeanor; also the defendant in a criminal case.

Acquittal: A deliverance from an accusation of guilt; the setting free from a criminal charge by process of law, a court, or a jury.

Actus Reus: *Latin.* To commit the criminal act; the mental component of criminal liability. In order to find the defendant guilty of most crimes, he or she must have committed the criminal act (the *actus reus*) in a mental state of being conducive to a culpable mental state (the *mens rea*). (See *Mens Rea* and *Culpability.*)

Adjudication: The giving or pronouncement of a judgement or degree in a cause; also the judgement given or passed down. The equivalent of *determination.*

Adult: In common law, a person who has attained his or her age of *majority,* usually 21 years, although in some states a woman attains her majority at 18. In most states one must be an adult to enter into a contract or to start or defend a legal action. Also depending on the state in criminal law, a juvenile becomes an adult generally at the attainment of age 16.

Age of Majority—Generally, the legal age when a person achieves the capacity for independent action and responsibility in personal affairs.

Age of Consent—When a person may legally enter into a marriage contract without the consent of a parent or guardian, or when a woman may consent to sexual intercourse before such intercourse constitutes the crime of statutory rape. The age in both instances noted herein vary in different states.

AIA: The American Insurance Association—includes property, casualty, and surety companies. Also includes the *Fire and Theft Index Bureau,* a department of AIA, which compiles and shares fire and theft claims information in an effort to prevent fraudulent claims. (See also *PILR.*)

ALR: The Art Loss Register—A private international database of lost and stolen art, antiques, and collectibles.

Amicus Curiae: *Latin.* A friend of the court. Also a lawyer who volunteers information or a person who has no right to appear in a suit but is allowed to introduce an argument, authority, or evidence to protect his or her interests.

Arraignment: Calling or bringing a defendant before the court to answer an accusation or complaint.

Arrest: To take a person into custody for the purpose of holding that person so as to answer to a criminal charge or civil demand. The term is synonymous with *apprehension.* A private person may arrest anyone for a felony anywhere in the state in which it was committed, and who has in fact committed that felony. The arrest must be under the conditions that a felony has in fact been committed and that the person arrested is in fact the perpetrator.

A private person may also arrest a person who has committed an offense in his or her presence (actually witnessed the act), and the arrest can only be made in the county where the offense took place.

Such arrests can be made without a warrant at any time of the day or night, and depending on the circumstances, physical force is justified. Check with your local and state laws to resolve any question of interpretation.

Arrest Warrant: Issued by a judge and directed to a law enforcement officer (police officer, sheriff, or a uniformed court officer) calling for the arrest of a defendant after an information (bill of particulars) attesting to a crime committed by the subject has been sworn before the court, or has been convicted of a crime but failed to appear for sentencing, owes a fine or is in contempt of court. Sometimes called a *bench warrant.* (See also *search warrants* issued by the court.)

Arson: The willful or malicious burning of or causing to be burned a dwelling house, building, a structure, vehicle, ship, or boat. Some states may include the criminal burning of any property. The act may be one of revenge, insurance recovery, a depraved mind, or to cover up some other crime.

Assault: Any intentional, unlawful offer, attempt, or threat of corporal injury to another by force, or force unlawfully directed to the person of another, under such circumstances as to create a well-founded fear of imminent peril, coupled with the apparent present ability to effectuate the attempt if not prevented. An attempt to offer or beat another, without touching him or her, as if one lifts up his fist in a threatening manner at another. The least touching of another's person, if done willfully or in anger, constitutes battery.

Also, intentionally, recklessly, or with criminal negligence causing physical injury to another person.

Assault and Battery: Always includes an assault; therefore, the two terms are used together and combined as assault and battery. An unlawful touching of the person of another by the aggressor, or by some substance put in motion by him or her (the swinging of a bat or pipe, a knife or bullet causing injury).

Bail: To set free, liberate, or deliver from arrest, or free of custody to the keeping of other persons, on their undertaking the responsibility for the appearance as directed by the court of the person bailed. If a defendant "jumps bail" (fails to appear on the date required and directed by the court), bail is forfeited and a bench warrant is issued for his or her arrest.

Bail-Bond: A bond or obligation given by a defendant and his surety under the condition to be void upon the performance by the accused of such acts as he or she may legally be required to perform. The bondsperson will provide the bail (money) required in return for some collateral equal or greater than the bail in the form of some property, holdings, or other asset. If the defendant fails to appear in court as required, the defendant forfeits his or her collateral. Upon application, the collateral offered is now owned by the bondsman.

A *surety* is one who undertakes to become responsible for the debt of another; one who binds him- or herself for the performance of some act of another. A surety need not be a bail-bondsman.

Battery: Intentional and wrongful physical contact with a person without his or her consent which entails some injury or offensive touching. The unlawful beating or unlawful touching of the person.

Bench Warrant: A court order, in which a criminal action is pending, directing a law enforcement officer to take custody of the defendant and bring him or her before the court. May sometimes be called an *arrest warrant*. It can also be an order to appear issued by the court, when a person does not appear for a hearing which can be resolved by posting bail or appearing before the court.

Blackmail: The extortion of money or something else of value by means of intimidation, which may include a threat of prosecution, a civil action, or injury to a person's reputation.

Breaking and Entering: An unlawful entry even though no force was used to gain entry. It is not necessary to prove an actual forceful entry, although an entry of this type would be a proving factor. Entry may be made through an unlocked door or window, an open unsecured door or window, or any opening giving access to the interior of a building, dwelling, or structure.

Bribe/Bribery: A price, reward, gift, or a favor bestowed or promised with a view to pervert the judgement or corrupt the conduct of a judge, public officer, witness, or other person.

Burglary: To knowingly enter or remain unlawfully in a building with the intent to commit a crime therein. The degrees of the crime will depend on the building type, time of day, and the presence or not of a person.

Case Law: The application of a particular case opinion with those facts as close to the facts as possible in the current case before the court. To be of use, the former opinion must have relevancy, value, precedent, or persuasive authority to the present case. The closer the facts are to each case, the more authority the former case will provide for that case now before the court. (See also *Holding, Precedent,* and *Persuasive Authority.*)

CERT: (1) *Computer Emergency Response Team*—Coordination center operated by Carnegie Mellon University; federally funded by the Department of Homeland Security and the Department of Defense as a research center providing computer forensics and security, incident execution, training, research and development, and public advisories. Excellent information source available to the private investigator.

(2) *Computer Emergency Readiness Team*—Analyzing and reducing cyber threats and vulnerabilities. The dissemination of cyber threat information. Part of the Department of Homeland Security.

Chain of Evidence: The number of persons who have handled the evidence between the time it was collected and the ultimate disposition, and each transfer of custody should be logged and receipted. It must be properly secured and protected from any corruption, destruction, or decay and accounted with time, date, and the person or department of custody.

Child: A descendant of the first degree. Generally, a child under the age of 7 years old is considered not capable of committing a crime. A child of the age of 7 years and under the age of 12 years is presumed to be incapable of crime unless it can be proved the child has sufficient mental capacity to know the wrongfulness of the act charged. A child 12 years of age and before the 16th birthday who is incorrigible or has committed an offense that would be a crime if committed by an adult may be charged as a juvenile delinquent. However, if the crime committed by the juvenile is so egregious, offensive, or hideous, the juvenile may be charged as an adult at the discretion of the prosecutor and the presiding judge.

Check with your state laws regarding any change in age requirements noted above.

Civil Action: Action brought to enforce, redress, or protect private rights. In general, all types of actions other than criminal proceedings.

Civil Law: A body of statutory and common law with private rights and remedies available to a citizen; regulates arrangements, contracts, and claims between individuals and corporations.

Collusion: A secret agreement or action between two or more persons (whether their interests conflict or not) made or performed for a fraudulent, unlawful, or deceitful purpose, or committing some act forbidden by law.

Color of State Law: Actions by a private investigator or a security officer (private persons) acting on behalf of or at the direction of a law enforcement officer acts under the federal law (the Color of State Law—§1983) and, in so doing, must be guided by the procedures that control a law enforcement officer, such as giving the Miranda warnings prior to an interrogation.

Common Law: Introduced and carried over into the United States from England by early settlers. Law that originated from usage and custom prior to statutory (written) law. Judicial decisions were based on or incorporated into the customs of society at the time. Today, common law includes those nonstatutory precedents, customs, and traditions that may be used as a guide in the judicial process.

Community Property Law: There are eight states that observe community property laws: Arizona, California, Idaho, Nevada, New Mexico, Texas, Louisiana, and Washington. Community property is everything that a husband and wife own together. This will include all money earned, debts incurred, and any property acquired during the marriage. Both own and owe equally, regardless of who earns the income. Held separately from this law are all debts or property owned by a spouse prior to marriage, property received as a gift or inheritance during the marriage from a third party, among others. Assets, debts, business interests, pensions, and retirement programs (for example, Roth, 401K plans) are split 50/50 between each spouse.

Compensatory Damages: Those damages directly referable to a breach or tortious act, and which can be readily proven to have been sustained, and for which the injured party should be compensated as a matter of right.

Complainant: A person who files a bill of complaint; the party who starts a legal action in Criminal Court. When the action is in Civil Court, the complainant is called the *plaintiff*.

Confidential Informant: Designation used by law enforcement authorities for informants who must or wish to remain unknown to everyone except his or her *handler*.

Consent Search: A search carried out with the voluntary authorization of the subject of the search; permission is granted by the subject. It can be given orally or in writing.

Conspiracy: In criminal law, a combination or agreement between two or more persons to commit an act punishable by law, or to effect a legal purpose by criminal or unlawful means.

Contraband: Originally defined as goods prohibited to be imported or exported. Presently defined as something held or possessed unlawfully, particularly that which is controlled or licensed in some manner. Any material object or substance that is unlawful for a private person to possess.

Contract: A legally enforceable agreement between two or more parties to do or not to do a particular thing upon sufficient consideration. A legally binding contract may be oral or in writing.

Coop: Any location where a private investigator or security officer can be hidden from view, and where he or she can observe the conduct and behavior of customers, visitors, and company personnel. The location may be within an interior wall, closet, or other contrivance, and where a two-way mirror may be put to use for the purpose of covert observation.

Copyright: (1) An author's right of literary property, recognized by common law, in unpublished literary and artistic productions.

(2) The statutory protection of the author's exclusive privilege of multiplying, publishing and selling copies of his production for a specified period of time (U.S. Copyright Statute).

The statute includes any original writing, dramatic or music composition, artistic productions, works of art, lectures, sermons, maps, scientific or technical matter, motion pictures, photographs and prints, among others.

Corporation: An entity or artificial person created by law, consisting of one or more natural persons united in a body bearing a distinctive name. A corporation is endowed by law with the capacity of perpetual succession—remains the same though its members may die or change—and is empowered to act as a unit or as a single individual.

Corpus Delicti: *Latin.* The body, substance, or foundation of a crime. In homicide, the dead body. In larceny, the stolen property. In an arson, the burnt building. (See also *Corpus Delicti Evidence.*)

Crime: A crime is an *act* or *omission* forbidden by law, and punishable upon conviction by some penalty, such as a fine, imprisonment, or death; it is an offense against the state.

Stated otherwise, a crime is an act or omission forbidden by society—*the people*—through their representatives. As an example, consider that possession of marijuana is a crime today, but it may not be a crime tomorrow. A crime proscribed is whatever society says it is—what is a crime today may not be so in the future.

Criminal: A popular term for one who has committed a crime and has been convicted of that crime. Repeat offenders are sometimes called *habitual criminals.*

Criminal Justice: A generic term for the procedure by which criminal conduct is investigated, evidence gathered, arrests made, charges brought, defenses raised, trials conducted, sentences rendered, and punishment carried out.

Criminal Law: The body of statutory (written) law that proscribes those acts or omissions as crimes committed by or against the individual or the state, and the punishment to be dispensed after conviction for those offenses or actions detrimental to the state (the people). A distinct body of rules governing the definition, trial, and punishment of crimes.

The criminal laws of the United States are found in the Constitution of the United States, the constitutions of the respective states, the common law offenses, the statutes enacted by the congress or the legislatures of the respective states, and in municipal or local laws enacted by counties, cities, towns, and villages.

Criminal Mischief: The unlawful and willful destruction or injuring of any property belonging to another. Also known in some states as *malicious mischief.*

Criminal Possession of Stolen Property: A person is guilty of criminal possession when he or she knowingly possesses stolen property with the intent to benefit him- or herself or a person other than the owner of the property thereof, or to impede the recovery of said property to the rightful owner. The value of the property will decide whether the crime is a felony or a misdemeanor; and may be added as a second charge if the perpetrator also committed larceny of said property.

Criminal Trespass: To knowingly enter or remain unlawfully in or upon premises. A person commits a trespass when he or she does not have license and privilege to enter therein.

Criminalist: A crime scene search technician/investigator; a specialist or expert in the collection of evidence. May also be called a forensic examiner or technician. Some law enforcement agencies use the terminology *criminalist* and make use of these technicians outside of the direct control of the police department (directed by another department such as a Medical Examiner).

Culpability: In order for a suspect to be charged with committing a crime, he or she must have a *culpable mental state*—where the suspect *intentionally* (willfully, by design, had the intention to commit or attempt to commit the crime), *knowingly* (knew what they were doing and that the act about to be committed was wrong), *recklessly* (recklessly and without concern or due regard of the consequences of the act, did commit the act), or by *criminal negligence* (an act committed with negligence; doing or omitting to do something required of them, or what people of ordinary prudence would not have done or omitted to do). Proof of any one of these mental states of being at the time of the criminal act is sufficient. (See also *Actus Reus* and *Mens Rea*.)

Damages: An award sought after by the plaintiff for some "wrong" (an injury to his or her person, property, or rights) that has been committed against him or her by some unlawful act, default, or negligence by another. The award is usually in the form of money (monetary damages), but not necessarily so. The action may be to right a wrong or change a procedure.

Deadly Physical Force: Defined as physical force that, under the circumstances in which it is used, is readily capable of causing death or a serious physical injury. To commit deadly physical force upon another, a person may use such force when he or she reasonably believes it to be necessary to defend him- or herself, or a third person in imminent fear of death or serious physical injury. Also, such force may be used against a perpetrator to prevent or terminate the commission or attempted commission of murder, kidnapping, forcible rape, forcible sodomy, robbery, arson, and certain burglaries.

Some states may have more severe restrictions on a private person using deadly physical force. Check your state criminal codes in which you are employed for further clarification. (See also *Physical Force*.)

Decision: A determination arrived at after consideration of facts, and, in legal context, law (the court's judgement). (See also *Holding*.)

Defamation: The spoken *word* or *written material* that was said or made known with malice and caused special damages. (See also *Libel* and *Slander*.)

Defendant: The adverse party to an action:

(1) *In a criminal case,* one who has committed the crime, has been arrested, and is to face the charges in court.

(2) *In a civil action,* one who has committed the wrong against another, and the plaintiff who has suffered that wrong, seeks damages from the defendant.

Discovery: In legal or court practice, the disclosure of facts, documents, depositions, statements, evidence in any form, etc., by one party at the request of the other for use by the latter as material evidence in a case that is being prepared for trial or expected to be tried. Essentially, the purpose is to determine what the other side possesses and expects to produce in their claim or defense. The process may be used in criminal and civil cases.

Due Process: The fundamental rights of the accused to a fair trial; the prescribed forms for conducting a criminal proceeding; the safeguards and protection of the law given to one accused of a crime. In criminal law, the right to have crimes and punishments clearly defined in the law.

Duress: Any illegal imprisonment, or legal imprisonment, used for an illegal purpose, or threats of bodily or other harm, or other means amounting to or tending to coerce the will of another, and actually inducing him or her to do an act contrary to his or her free will.

Eavesdropping Terminology:

PBX Cable—Private Branch Exchange; located at the telephone company exchange and use is only given by their permission or court order.
REMOBS—A system called remote observation.
ESS—Electronic switching system.
VLF Bugs—Very low frequency bugs.

EEOC: The Equal Employment Opportunity Commission; a federal agency overseeing employment practices.

Embezzlement: Misappropriation or misapplication of money or property entrusted to one's care, custody, or control. It is a crime.

Encryption: See *Access Control.*

Entrapment: Setting a trap to catch criminals in the act; legitimate and proper. Wrong, however, to induce a person to commit a criminal act.

Ethics: A Code of Ethics that has been established for any group, organization, or business enterprise is conducive to a more cohesive workforce, a positive attitude among workers, the integrity of the unit, an increase in effectiveness, and a fostering of better relationships between the public and other agencies. It also provides, measures, or prescribes the standard required and contributes to a low turnover rate and a better caliber of employees and applicants.

Evidence: Generally, it includes all the means by which any alleged matter of fact, the truth of which is submitted to investigation, is established or disproved. See also:

Associative Evidence—Evidence that links the suspect to the crime scene or the offense. For example, physical or trace evidence found on the suspect that can be connected to the crime scene or the offense.

Testimonial Evidence—Oral testimony of a sworn witness; subject to cross-examination. There are two types: direct and circumstantial.

Direct—Actual knowledge of facts using ones senses (i.e., eyeball witness, smell, taste).

Circumstantial—Evidence used to prove a fact (i.e., fingerprints, blood type, DNA).

Best Evidence—Concerns documents or writings. Simply means to produce the original.

Circumstantial Evidence—Evidence of facts and circumstances as distinguished from direct proof, which circumstances, when established, lead the mind to certain conclusions.

Continuity of Evidence—That evidence secured or kept in custody and how it was passed from one to another, an unbroken chain that protects the integrity of the evidence.

Corpus Deliciti Evidence—Consists of objects or substances that are an essential part of the body of the crime.

Corroborating Evidence—Evidence supplementary to that already given and tending to strengthen or confirm it.

Direct Evidence—Evidence, which if believed, proves a fact or matter in issue without the intervention of proof of any other fact, or without any inference or presumption. Testimony by a witness who actually saw, heard, or touched the subject or issue of interrogation.

Documentary Evidence—Evidence supplied by papers, books, writings, etc. (A type of real evidence.)

Hearsay Evidence—Evidence of what some other person has been heard to say. This is usually excluded unless it falls within one of the recognized exceptions (i.e., dying declaration, a spontaneous utterance or admission, etc.).

Indirect Evidence—Evidence that does not actually prove the facts, but from which they may be presumed.

Material Evidence—Sufficiently important; it is not trivial.

Opinion Evidence—Generally, witness testimony based on the expertise of the witness.

Physical Evidence—Evidence that proves that a crime was in fact committed, and can be connected to the perpetrator. Any item or physical thing that may be found that has a connection to the crime. Examples are fingerprints, blood, blood type, DNA, hair, a bullet, a weapon, personal property left at the scene, tools and tool marks, recovered stolen property in possession of the perpetrator, VCR tapes of the act.

Presumptive Evidence—Evidence that is not direct and positive; evidence afforded by circumstances from which a presumption may be drawn.

Real Evidence—Objects or persons; something that can be seen, heard, or observed by the court.

Relevant Evidence—Direct bearing on the *fact in issue,* pertinent and worthy of consideration by the court.

Tracing Evidence—Articles that assist in locating the suspect (e.g., a laundry mark or personal papers found among the suspects' personal effects).

Evidence; To Suppress: In a court of law, an attorney may attempt to suppress evidence on a motion based on several motion factors, which may include unlawful search, illegal eavesdropping, right to privacy offenses, unlawful confessions, illegal identification, and the *poisoned tree concept.*

Ex Parte: *Latin.* On one side only; by or for one party; done for, on behalf of, or on the application of one party only.

Ex Post Facto: *Latin.* After the fact.

Ex Post Facto Law: *Latin.* A law that has been passed after the occurrence of a fact or the commission of an act which retrospectively changes the legal consequences of such fact or deed. Basically, where a law was enacted and signed into law, and thereafter a subject cannot be charged with violating that law if in fact the commission or the occurrence took place before the law took effect.

Forbidden by all the states and the federal government by the U.S. Constitution.

Exclusionary Rule: Evidence illegally seized or obtained; evidence obtained unlawfully and which is excluded from the court proceeding. This rule commands that when evidence has been obtained in violation of the privileges guaranteed by the U.S. Constitution, the evidence must be excluded at trial. This includes that any evidence obtained by unreasonable search and seizure is excluded under the Fourth Amendment of the U.S. Constitution, (applicable to all states—*Mapp v. Ohio,* 367 U.S. 643; 6L.Ed.2d 1081; 81 S.Ct. 1684 [1961]).

Exemplar: A specimen or a standard to be compared against a questioned document, writing, seal, stamp, or impression. The required exemplar will depend on the type of investigation and must be obtained lawfully.

Extradition: Delivery of a fugitive or fugitives of justice by a nation or a state to another. A court proceeding may be required for the transfer if the defendant challenges or contests the deliverance.

False Arrest: An unlawful arrest; an unlawful imprisonment. (See below.)

False Imprisonment: Detention of a subject without justification. The same as false arrest; the terms are synonymous.

Felony: A crime punishable by death or more than 1 year in a state prison or correctional facility. What constitutes a felony is determined by statuary regulation.

Finding: The result of the deliberations of a jury or a court (judge or jury).

FOIA: The Freedom of Information Act; *USC Title 5, §552.*

Forgery: The false making, counterfeiting, and alteration of a genuine instrument in whole or in part; the false making or counterfeiting of the signature of a party or witness with intent to defraud. Includes the fraudulent making or altering of a writing to the prejudice of a man's rights. The term "writing" includes typed, printed, and engraved matter as well.

Fraud: A false representation of a matter of fact, whether by words or conduct, by false or misleading allegations, or by concealment of that which should have been disclosed, which deceives and is intended to deceive another, and thereby causes injury to that person. (See also *Injury.*)

Grand Jury: A body of citizens whose duty is to receive and hear complaints in criminal cases, and if found sustained by evidence will find for a bill of indictment (a *true bill*) against the person or persons complained of. Depending on the state, a grand jury will consist of 21 jurors, with a minimum and necessary number (quorum) legally and duly assembled to transact business. A *true bill* is the endorsement made by a grand jury upon a bill of indictment when the evidence submitted is sustained.

A *petit jury* is an ordinary jury sitting in judgement as distinguished from a grand jury.

Gypsy: Also Gypsies; (Gipsy) (See also *Romany*):

(1) A secret criminal organization in Europe and the United States; in operation since about AD 1000.

(2) A self-perpetuating, structured, and disciplined association of individuals and groups, combined together for the purpose of obtaining monetary gains, wholly, or in part by covert or illegal means, while protecting their criminal activities through silence and kinship, and a pattern of graft and corruption.

Habeas Corpus: *Latin* for "you have the body." It is a writ (court order) directing law enforcement officials who have custody of a prisoner to appear in court with that prisoner to help the judge determine if the prisoner is lawfully incarcerated. It is a protection against illegal confinement when due process has been denied, where a person is held without charges, bail is excessive, or parole has been granted or improperly surrendered by a bail enforcement agent. The writ can also be used in child custody or deportation proceedings in court, or in federal court in challenging the constitutionality of a conviction in state court.

Hearing: In its broadest sense, whatever takes place before a court or a magistrate that has or sits in a judicial function without a jury. A trial is a hearing, but not all hearings require the formalities of a trial.

Hearsay: Evidence not derived from the personal knowledge of the witness, but from the mere repetition of what that witness has heard others say. Evidence of this type cannot be examined by opposing counsel and cannot be admitted as such.

Holding: A decision by the court; a holding is a legal principle to be drawn from the opinion (*decision*) of the court. (See also *Decision*, *Finding*, and *Judgment*.)

Homicide: *Common use of the term*—The death of a human being by the act, procurement, or the omission of another; *the death of a human by criminal means* (intentional, premeditated, manslaughter, or by culpable negligence). The correct term under these circumstances would be *Criminal Homicide*.

However, all deaths are homicides (death of a human); it need not be criminal in nature. There is also *accidental homicide, natural homicide, suicide,* and *innocent homicide* (excusable and justifiable).

To further define:

Murder—The unlawful killing of a human being with malice aforethought. In many states, murder has been made a crime punishable with greater or less severity according to the atrociousness or depravity under which it is committed. The more serious degree would be the willful, deliberate, and premeditated killing.

Manslaughter—The unlawful killing of another without malice either expressed or implied. As an example, committed when one kills another in a fight arising upon a sudden quarrel, in the heat of passion, or upon great provocation. It may also be occasioned by an omission of duty on the part of some person, or negligence on his or her part, whereby death ensues.

Abortion/Self-Abortion—Unless justified by statute (to save the life of the mother or the length of term/gestation of the fetus), the destruction or killing of a human fetus is in violation of the statutes protecting that fetus from harm.

Justifiable Homicide—The killing of another when it is strictly lawful and necessary, as when one shoots and kills an enemy in war, or when a warden of a prison executes a person in pursuance of a mandate of the court. Also, the killing of a perpetrator to prevent escape from certain felonies, a prisoner charged with a felony in order to prevent his or her escape, or in the lawful defense of another.

Excusable Homicide—When committed by misadventure (such as accidental), or in his or her own defense, or in the defense of another, or to prevent the commission or completion of certain felonies.

Although less used, the following terms may also apply to a particular homicide:

Patricide—The killing of one's father.

Matricide—The killing of one's mother.

Fratricide—The killing of one's sibling.

Infanticide—The killing of an infant or very young child.

ICPI: Insurance Crime Prevention Institute—A group of insurance companies that investigate and seek prosecution of fraud involving property and casualty insurance claims.

Illegal: In violation of a statute, regulation, or ordinance that may be criminal or merely not in conformity. For example, an armed robbery is illegal and a crime, and an access road that is narrower than the county allows (in violation of their ordinance) is not criminal, but is illegal and must be corrected.

In Camera: *Latin.* When the doors of the court are closed from the public and only persons connected to the case are admitted. Also a court proceeding held privately and in secrecy.

Incumbrance: With regard to property; a claim, lien or liability attached thereto.

Indictment: An accusation in writing found and presented by a Grand Jury, charging that the person named therein has been guilty of a public offense punishable on indictment.

Informant and Informer: An *informant* is a person who informs or offers an accusation against another person whom he or she believes or suspects has violated some penal statute; any person who reports a crime because of civil responsibility,

An *informer* is a person who reports or offers information on a crime from motives other than his or her responsibilities as a good citizen. Reasons for informing range from jealousy, revenge, malice, monetary reward, or a falling out between accomplices or coconspirators. The informant may also wish to escape responsibility for his or her part in a crime in return for a "free pass" by the police, or in the case of a prosecutor, the dismissal of a charge against him or her, or a reduction of the charge in return for testimony as a witness.

A *confidential informant* is one who has direct contact with a police officer or a law enforcement official and is unknown to anyone else outside or within police control. Information is solicited from this source for various reasons; the officer has information or evidence detrimental to the informant which could be used against him or her (under duress), the officer may offer money, other inducements, or incitements in return for information, or the officer offers protection from any legal entanglements and becomes his "guardian angel." Once determined to be reliable in information received in the past, the informant's intelligence is a great source for further inquiry or legal search warrants by the court. (See also *Snitch.*)

Information: An accusation sworn to and laid against a person for a criminal offense. (See also *Accusatory Instrument.*)

Infraction: A minor offense not considered a crime. Usually attributed to traffic offenses.

Injury: Any damage done to another's person. It includes that person's rights, reputation, property, or physical and mental harm.

Intent: A mental desire and will to act in a particular way. Intent is a crucial factor in determining if a certain act was criminal. At times a judge or jury may find that there was "no criminal intent" by a defendant, and the complaint was dismissed. However, the lack of intent in certain crimes may reduce the charge to a lesser crime.

Intentional Tort: A tort or wrong perpetrated by one who intends to do that which the law has declared wrong; also cited as a *willful tort.* (In contrast with a negligent act in which the tortfeasor fails to exercise that degree of care in doing what is otherwise permissible.)

Interrogatory: A question or a set of questions in writing intended to be proposed to a witness requesting an answer or answers.

IRC: A leading nonprofit, independent research organization supported by leading property and casualty insurance companies and associations.

IRSG: Individual Reference Services Group—A lobbying group consisting of 13 of the largest commercial database companies attempting to fend off a government crackdown by introducing self-regulation into the information brokering business. Their rules are to go into effect by the end of 2004 and will restrict access to certain data types.

Judgment: A decision or sentence of the law handed down (given) by a court, justice, or other tribunal on the claims of parties to a litigation.

Judicial Process: The sequence of steps taken by the court in deciding cases or disposing of legal controversies.

Kidnapping: The unlawful seizure, carrying off, and detention of a person by force, fear, or fraud for illicit purposes, such as revenge, perversion, or sexual desires, but usually for ransom.

Larceny: A person with intent to wrongfully take, obtain, withhold, defraud, deprive, or appropriate property of another for him- or herself or a third person by trick, false pretenses, or embezzlement or has control over property not his or her own without the owner's permission, commits a larceny. A determination of a *grand larceny* or a *petit larceny* will depend on the value of the property stolen, how it was stolen, and the state in which the crime took place.

Law: The formal means of social control that involves the use of rules that are enacted, interpreted, and are enforceable by the courts of a political community. It is an effort of society to protect persons, their property, enforce their contracts, and hold them to liabilities for their torts, and to punish those who commit crimes or offenses by means of remedies administered by government.

Legislature: A representative body that makes the laws of the people. In a state government, it may be the Senate and the Assembly. In the federal government, it is the Senate and the House of Representatives.

Libel: A malicious publication in printing, writing, signs, or pictures tending to blacken the reputation of one who is dead, or the reputation of one who is living. (See also *Slander.*)

Litigant: Any party to a lawsuit. This includes the complainant, plaintiff, defendant, petitioner, respondent, cross-complainant, or cross-defendant. It does not include a witness or an attorney. Usually referred to in a civil court action but it may also include persons in a criminal proceeding.

Litigation: Any lawsuit or other resort to the courts to determine or resolve a legal question or matter.

Litigious: Subject to contention; disputable. Inclined to judicial contest; one who constantly brings or prolongs a legal action or actions, particularly when legal schemes are unnecessary or unfounded, all for various purposes such as using the courts to punish enemies, seek an advantage, or gain a profit.

Mala In Se: *Latin* for "wrong in themselves"; acts or offenses immoral or wrong in themselves. For example, murder, larceny, sex offenses, and crimes against nature, and so forth.

Mala Prohibita: (Also termed *Malum Prohibitum.*) *Latin* for those crimes or offenses that embrace acts prohibited by statute as infringing on another's rights, though no moral turpitude may be attached and constituting crimes and offenses only because they are prohibited. For example, gambling, minor trespass, environmental statutes (dumping toxic materials), health codes (spitting on sidewalk, violation of quarantine, failure to report certain diseases or sicknesses), failing to obey traffic/motor vehicle codes and laws, and so forth.

Malfeasance: Committing an *unlawful act;* often used to describe misconduct by a public official. Also note:
Misfeasance—Lawful act performed in a wrongful manner.
Nonfeasance—Failure to act when duty required.

Malice: A willful intent to do mischief; ill will. A wrongful act done intentionally and without just cause or excuse.

Malicious Prosecution: An intentional tort arising from the institution or instigation of unjustifiable and unreasonable civil or criminal actions. An action instituted with the intention of injuring the defendant without probable cause and which terminates in favor of the person prosecuted. A prosecution that is begun with malice and without probable cause. A person may seek criminal and civil action against the offender. This could include a district attorney, police officer, or any private person as the offender.

Mens Rea: *Latin* for a "guilty mind." The mental state in which the crime is committed (*actus reus*). The defendant must commit the criminal act (the *actus reus*) in a certain mental state. For example, the crime of larceny requires the physical taking (to take, steal, carry away, and deprive the owner of his property)—the mental state or *mens rea*. (See also *Culpability.*)

MIB: Medical Information Bureau—A group of health and life insurers. Maintains a centralized computer database for storing health histories of persons who have applied for insurance and who have omitted or misrepresented facts.

Miranda Warnings: The warnings that must be given to a person who is now considered a suspect in the crime under investigation, advising him or her of their constitutional rights before any questions are put forth. As declared by the U.S. Supreme Court, unless all points of the warning are presented and understood by the suspect, a conviction of the accused may be jeopardized.

Miranda v. Arizona, 384 U.S. 436, 86 S.Ct. 1602, 16 L.Ed.2d 694 (1966).

Misdemeanor: A crime punishable by a fine or no more than a year in jail. Incarceration is usually served in a local or county jail.

Modus Operandi (MO): *Latin.* The manner of operation; the criminal's MO. In reality, based on the criminal's experience, limited or enhanced by his mental and physical capabilities. If his or her activities have shown great or some success in the past, he or she usually will continue the same method of operation in committing following crimes. Depending on the type of crime, the MO may include the motive, time or day of the crime, nature of entry and egress, nature of property stolen, nature of attack on another, the method and use of particular weapons. Consider also personal particulars or idiosyncrasies by the perpetrator before leaving the scene such as partaking of the victim's liquor, eating, and leaving a "calling card" (some marking, object, or feces in plain view). The detection of one's MO at a crime scene is an important factor in identifying the perpetrator.

Negligence: The failure to exercise a degree of care a reasonable person would exercise given the same circumstances, and thereby causing injury or damage. Negligence could be equated to carelessness (negligent tort).

Negligence Per Se: Conduct, whether of action or omission, which may be declared or treated as negligence without any argument or proof as to the particular surrounding circumstances, because it is contrary to the law.

NICB: The National Insurance Claims Bureau—Formerly the *National Automobile Theft Bureau.* Includes property and casualty insurance companies that have joined together to stop crime and vehicle theft. Maintains a computer database.

NIOSH: National Institute for Occupational Safety and Health; a federal subagency of OSHA.

NLRB: The National Labor Relations Board; a federal agency.

Nola Contendere: *Latin* for, literally, "no contest." A plea that has the same effect in a criminal action as a plea of guilty, but does not bind the defendant in a civil suit for the same wrong.

OSHA: Occupational Safety and Health Administration; a federal agency.

Parole: The release of a convicted criminal after he or she has completed part of his or her prison sentence. The concept being that the prisoner has earned his release by good behavior while in prison and the hope that the prisoner can be rehabilitated into society. A specific period and terms are set; routine reporting to a parole officer, obligation to a halfway house assignment, and hours of home (curfew), and constraint on the use of alcohol and drugs. (See also *Probation.*)

Peace Officer: Distinct from a police officer; *powers are not as broad.* Limited to certain lawful acts of authority or jurisdiction. For example, parole or probation officers, court officers, corrections or prison officers, game wardens, bay constables, fire inspectors. Powers may be further defined in the various state laws. Some states may differ in that some police officers are also peace officers.

Pendency: The state or time of something pending, as in a lawsuit awaiting settlement.

Perjury: The act of a person under oath who knowingly and willfully swears falsely after sworn in by a notary public, court clerk, or a public official in a matter material to the issue or point in question, which may include a court proceeding, administrative hearings, depositions and answers to interrogatory questions, or by falsely signing a legal document. Perjury is a crime.

Physical Force: Physical force is justifiable and not considered an offense when used in defense of self or another person, in defense of a premises, in order to prevent a larceny or criminal mischief to property, or in order to effect an arrest, or to prevent an escape from custody. Such force must be reasonable under the circumstances and not excessive. Check with your state criminal codes, which may be more or less restrictive in the interpretation of the use of physical force upon another. (See also *Deadly Physical Force.*)

Physical Injuries: A *physical injury* may be defined as an impairment of a physical condition or substantial pain (bloody lip, black eye, swollen facial injuries, minor lacerations, or loss of teeth that require medical attention, and so forth).

A *serious physical injury* is defined as an injury that creates a substantial risk of death, causes death or serious and protracted disfigurement, impairment of health, or the loss or impairment of the function of any bodily organ or extremity (loss of an eye, arm, leg, bullet wound, knife puncture, broken bones, paralysis, and so forth).

PILR: The Property Insurance Loss Register—A national data registry where insurance underwriters may inquire of subjects under investigation for excessive claims or insurance fraud.

Also includes a list maintained by the American Insurance Association (AIA) of all fire losses over $500,000, and maintains a database to access information of duplicate coverage or loss. (See also *AIA.*)

Plagiarism: The taking of another person's writings or literary concepts (plots, characters, words) and selling or publishing them as one's own product. Quotes or brief excerpts from a literary work which are acknowledged to the original author are not considered to be plagiarized. It is not considered a crime but if found to be true and can be proved, can be the basis of a fraud charge or copyright infringement.

Plaintiff: One who brings suit, bill, or complaint against another; one who seeks damages for some wrong. See also *Defendant* (the opposing party).

Plain-View Doctrine: Other than to comply with search and seizure laws, if a private investigator or security officer has the right to be in a certain place or area and happens to observe evidence or contraband in plain sight, those items can be seized and be admissible in court (*the plain-view doctrine*).

Poisoned Tree Concept: If the rights of a suspect are violated in any way such as an improper arrest, false imprisonment, or unlawful search and seizure, then any evidence arising from that arrest or seizure is inadmissible. This would include any incriminating oral or written statements made by the suspect, recovery of stolen property, and any evidence acquired as a result of that arrest will be inadmissible in court and the subject released under the *fruit of the poisoned tree concept.*

Police Officer: A person employed by the State, municipality, a special district, or public authority; a member of a Force sworn to protect the community and maintain public order, safety, morals, and health. To prevent and detect crime, and to uphold and enforce all laws and regulations, with the power to arrest, control, and direct, all within his or her "geographic area of employment." May also be known as a *sworn police officer.*

Persuasive Authority: Anything that may be cited as an excellent analysis of the legal issues and provide guidance for any court that happens to read it is therefore considered "persuasive authority." It is not binding in another state court, but may be considered.

Possess: As defined, "means to have physical possession or otherwise to exercise dominion or control over tangible property" (has been defined as to whether on the person or not).

Precedent: A decision from an earlier case that has been adjudicated by an Appellate Court and is relevant to the present case being decided in the lower court. Correspondingly, it furnishes a rule or model for deciding a subsequent case—if there is nothing to distinguish the circumstances or facts of the current case from a case already decided, the earlier holding is considered binding on the court. A holding from one state is not binding upon another state but may be considered. (See also *Stare Decisis.*)

***Prima Facie* Case**: *Latin.* A case made out of evidence sufficient to counterbalance the general presumption of innocence. Enough presentable evidence for an arrest or a case to proceed in court.

***Prima Facie* Evidence**: *Latin.* Evidence showing the existence of the facts, and which if uncontradicted is sufficient to maintain the proposition affirmed. Evidence sufficient enough to indict or arrest.

Principal: (1) A chief actor in a crime, or one who is present at its commission; as distinguished from an accessory.

(2) Property or capital, as distinguished from interest or income.

(3) The employer of an agent.

(4) The person primarily liable on a note or a debt, for whom another has become surety.

Probable Cause: Reasonable cause; having more evidence than against. Those facts and circumstances that would lead a reasonably prudent person in like circumstances to believe that a crime has been committed and that the person committing such act is guilty.

Probation: Adjudicated by a judge to a person convicted of a crime that rather than being sent to jail, certain conditions are set such as staying out of trouble and maintaining good behavior, performing a public service, staying away from alcohol and drugs, and reporting routinely to a probation officer. Violation of the terms set will usually cause the judge to enforce the jail time originally acknowledged.

Pro Bono: *Latin.* Short for *pro bono publico*; "for the public good." Usually referred to legal work performed by lawyers without compensation for the indigent, those with limited funds, a charity, or for a social cause.

Product Liability: The legal liability of manufacturers and sellers of a product to compensate buyers and users of a harm caused, which can also include browsers and bystanders, for damages or injuries suffered because of a defect or defects in the goods owned, purchased, or provided for sale.

Provocation: The act of inciting another to commit a particular deed; that which arouses, moves, calls forth, causes, or occasions.

Proximate Cause: That which, in a natural and continuous sequence, unbroken by any efficient intervening cause, produces the injury (or damage), and without which the result would not have occurred.

Punitive Damages: Compensation in excess of *Compensatory Damages,* which serves as a form of punishment to the wrongdoer who has exhibited malicious and willful conduct. Moreover, this form of punishment serves the purpose of making an example of the defendant to deter others from acting in the same way.

Quid Pro Quo: *Latin* for "something for nothing"; used to describe a consideration that passes between parties to a contract, rendering it binding and valid. Can be used as a colloquialism: "You do something for me—I'll do something for you."

Rape: Unlawful carnal knowledge of a woman (sexual intercourse with actual penetration of a woman's vagina with the man's penis) by threat of violence, intimidation, or forcibly without her consent and against her will. In certain states and under certain ages, it is a crime *with* or *without* the consent of the female. Intoxication or unconsciousness of the woman of any age cannot consent to the act, and does not admit or grant to the perpetrator his willfulness or purposeful intent. Entry, however slight, must be made for a charge of rape, otherwise a charge of attempted rape will ensue.

Reasonable Grounds: Knowledge (reasonable belief) that a person has possession of stolen property or merchandise on his or her person that belongs to a business retail establishment or another. Such knowledge may be based on probable cause.

Reasonable Time: The manner in which a suspect is handled based on lawful and reasonable custodial and arrest tactics; a reasonable time and manner for imprisonment with no intentional delaying tactics prior to turning the subject over to the police.

Reciprocity: (1) The quality or state of being reciprocal—mutual dependence, action, influence.

(2) In the lawful sense concerning the private investigator or the public servant: The mutual exchange of privileges, *specifically* a recognition by one of two countries, states, or institutions of the validity of licenses or privileges granted by the other. In essence, once one state recognizes the other state as to mutual compatibility, ability is granted to private investigator to operate in one state as long as he or she performs under the same controls or provisions of the state that licenses him or her.

Respondent: (1) The party called upon to answer an appeal. If the defendant appeals the decision of a lower court, the original *plaintiff* becomes the *respondent* in the Appellate Court.

(2) In some states for the purpose of not designating or "branding" a child a "criminal," the juvenile may be determined a *respondent* in court proceedings and not a *defendant* as an adult would be.

RFID: Radio Frequency Identification Tag; may be used to track the movements of employees, people, things, stock, and commodities.

Robbery: The unlawful taking of personal property from the person against his or her will by means of force or fear of injury to him- or herself or another.

Romany or "Rom": Also *Romanies*; *Roma.* (See also *Gypsy.*)

(1) Of India, its people, or their language.
(2) A native or inhabitant of India, or a person of Indian descent.
(3) The gypsies collectively.
(4) Rom—the language spoken by the gypsies.

Rough Shadowing: Shadowing done in such a manner as to cause the subject under observation to be aware he or she has been discovered, causing discomfort or annoyance, or to interfere with him or her in any way. Generally used to make the subject uncomfortable enough to leave a location.

Search and Seizure: The examination of a person's premises, his or her property, or of his or her person in an effort to find stolen or illicit property or contraband, or to discover evidence of guilt that may be used in the prosecution of his or her crime. Because the Fourth Amendment of the U.S. Constitution gives a citizen the right of security in his or her home, papers, and effects, search and seizures must be under the authority of a search warrant issued by a judge, or when a law enforcement officer has solid facts that give him or her *probable cause* to believe there was evidence of a specific crime on premises or evidence about to be disposed of but there was no time to secure a warrant. Any evidence obtained in violation of the Fourth Amendment is not admissible. (See *Fruit of the Poisoned Tree.*)

Search Warrant: An order by the court permitting a law enforcement officer to search a particular premises or person for certain types of evidence, based on a declaration of a law enforcement official. The warrant may be broad or very restrictive as to limit the search to a particular area.

Secret Rebate: A "kickback" of money by a business to a "preferred customer" not offered to the public or by a subcontractor to a contractor not shown or itemized on a job estimate. Considered as an unfair business practice in most states and could result in criminal penalties. The court may refuse to enforce any contract, written or oral, where there is such a secret rebate.

Secret Service: The U.S. Secret Service, a division of the *Department of Homeland Security* (formerly of the Department of the Treasury) has the statutory obligation to protect the President, Vice President, their families, and other important individuals (executive protection); and to investigate and prosecute the following crimes:

- Financial Institution Fraud and related criminal investigations
- Money laundering
- Counterfeit money and fraudulent identification
- Forgery of government checks and bonds
- Asset seizures and forfeitures
- Access device fraud; credit cards, debit cards, ATM cards, computer passwords, credit and debit card account numbers and personal identification numbers (PINs), long distance access codes, and computer chips in cellular phones that assign billing info
- Computer and Telecommunications fraud
- Food stamp violations, Electronic Benefits Transfer (EBT) cards, and program fraud investigations

Sentence: The judgment formerly pronounced by the court or the judge upon the defendant after his or her conviction in a criminal prosecution awarding the punishment to be inflicted. Sentencing is generally regarded as the province of the judge, but in some states and depending on the severity of the crime, the duty to sentence is placed upon the jury. Statutes may require a minimum or maximum sentence to be imposed, but all sentences must be within the limits set by the legislating authority for the particular offense.

Suspended Sentence—A conviction, but in lieu of incarceration or a fine, the defendant may be assigned to a community service, some correctional supervision (probation) for a set period, or ruled completely free of any encumbrances.

Multiple Sentencing—If convicted of more than one crime, the court may sentence the defendant to a *concurrent term* (the sentence for all crimes will be served together at one time) or to a *consecutive term* (the defendant must serve his or her time for one crime before he or she must serve time for the second or subsequent crimes).

Service of Process: The *personal service* of writs, summonses, subpoenas, rules, and so forth, signifies the delivering or leaving them with the party to whom or with whom they ought to be delivered or left, and when they are so delivered, they are then said to be served. *Constructive service* is made by sending the process through the mails, delivering it to an authorized representative, or by publishing it in a newspaper.

Sexual Harassment: Unwelcome sexual advances, requests for sexual favors, and other verbal or physical conduct of a sexual nature, when submission to or rejection of this conduct explicitly or implicitly affects the individual's employment (as per the EEOC). Victim may be female or male.

Shadowing: An unobserved close watch of a subject; a subject under surveillance.

Shoplifting: A form of larceny; a type of theft. The theft of merchandise or property from a retail merchant. The offender is charged with the crime of larceny, not "shoplifting" (although some states may have enacted specific "shoplifting laws").

Slander: Defamation by words *spoken;* false, malicious, and defamatory words tending to damage another's reputation or means of livelihood. (See also *Libel,* a malicious writing or publication.)

Snitch: Slang expression for an informant (sometimes used by police personnel). The present legal term used today is *confidential informant*. The terms "stool pigeon," "stoolie," and "rat" are usually given to informers by criminals, convicts, or underworld characters.

Sodomy: Carnal copulation in other than a "natural manner" (anal or oral). Also described as *bestiality* by a human with an animal. In the past, willing partners (male and female, male and male, female and female) committing the act was considered a crime. Considered a form of sexual perversion (crime against nature) in many states, but some states have done away with some sodomy laws or completely disregard the thought of prosecution unless the crime consists of the use of force upon an unwilling partner. In any case of this crime, penetration, however slight, constitutes the crime of sodomy.

Sovereign Immunity: The doctrine that the government (state or federal) cannot commit a legal wrong and is immune from civil suit unless it gives its consent.

SPO: Special Police Officer (as in New York State). Additionally, in some states a citizen who is not a police or peace officer may be given police powers under certain circumstances.

Stare Decisis: *Latin* for "to stand by a decision," the doctrine that a trial court is bound by Appellate Court decisions (precedents) on a legal question which is raised in the lower court. Reliance for such a precedent, and which cannot be ignored, is the rule until such time that the Appellate Court changes the ruling. This doctrine also requires that once the highest court of the state has announced a legal principle, all the courts in the state must follow that principle in future cases where the facts are substantially the same and regardless of whether the parties are the same, unless and until it is overruled by the U.S. Supreme Court or is reversed by the highest court of the state in some future decision.

Statutory Law: A law enacted by or with the authority of a legislature; written law authorized by statute.

Subpoena: *Latin.* A writ or order requiring the attendance of a person at a particular time and place to testify or present him- or herself as a witness.

Subpoena Duces Tecum: *Latin* term for a subpoena commanding a person to attend and produce some book, paper, or a document that is pertinent to the issue in question; the court's order to *produce the record,* or other identifiable evidence.

Surveillance: To keep close and constant watch over someone or something. Certain types are not permitted or considered decent and appropriate, such as in some situations with closed-circuit television (CCTV) which may raise the issue of privacy.

Tort: A private or civil wrong or injury, other than a breach of contract, for which the court will provide a remedy in the form of an action for damages. A willful/negligent wrong committed against a person by another. A tort can be willful (intentional), for example an angry punch in the nose, but the tort is far more likely to be a result from negligence (carelessness). While the injury or wrong that forms the basis of the tort may be physical, it is not a requirement; libel, slander, intentional infliction of mental distress, and public humiliation are a few examples not based on physical injury.

A *personal tort* involves or consists of an injury to a person or to the reputation or feelings. It is distinguished from a *property tort*—an injury or damage to real or personal property.

Trade Secret: A trade secret is one that if known could effectively damage a business operation. *The Uniform Trade Secret Act of 1979* classified and extended protection for business continuation for the theft or criminal loss of prototypes, formulas, specifications, patterns, strategies, and techniques, that if produced by another entity, could cause a serious loss of earnings. Secrets would include knowledge or data not yet in the public domain, information disclosed by owner/proprietor to those bound to protect the secret, to those who obtained the information knew that it was a secret, the information is identifiable (specific class or category), and there were indications that the owner tried to prevent or protect unauthorized use.

Trademark: A distinctive name, sign, or mark, officially registered, attached to goods offered for sale to distinguish them from others. An identifying mark or symbol that is different from any other and clearly distinguishes it as one of a kind.

Trial: The judicial examination of the issues, whether of law or of fact, between the parties of a criminal or civil action, such examination being conducted by a competent tribunal (a judge alone or a judge and jury) in accordance with the law of the land.

Usury: Unlawful interest; contracting or charging a premium for the use of money borrowed beyond the legal rate of interest.

Utter, Uttering: Putting into circulation, offering. To deliver, offer, or put into circulation a note (counterfeit currency) or a check known not to be legal and/or genuine.

Venue: The neighborhood, place, or county in which the injury or crime is declared to have been done, or the fact declared to have happened. *Jurisdiction* of the court means the inherent power to decide and/or rule on a case, whereas *venue* designates the particular county or city in which the court with jurisdiction may hear and determine the case.

Verdict: The formal and unanimous decision or finding made by a jury (or one concurred in by the majority of jurors required by law), impaneled and sworn for the trial of a cause and reported to the court upon the matters or questions duly submitted to them during the course of the trial. The court may accept or reject the decision made by the jury for cause.

Vicarious Liability: Where liability is not only attributed to the wrongdoer, but to the wrongdoer's trainer, supervisor, and employer; one who has delegated authority to the wrongdoer, or who has all or some authority over the wrongdoer's actions.

Voir Dire: *Latin* for "speak the truth." The preliminary examination of a witness or a juror as to his or her competency, interest, truthfulness, etc., before acceptance to the panel.

Warrant: A process under seal of a court or justice authorizing the arrest of the person named, or the ability to legally search a dwelling or particular place or locale, or directing the doing or completion of some act.

The Weingarten Rule: The right of employees to the presence of a union representative during any and all investigatory interviews and interrogations was confirmed by the U.S. Supreme Court in 1975 concerning *The National Labor Relations Board v. J. Weingarten, Inc.* The case involved a clerk being investigated by the Weingarten Company and the court ruled in favor of the NLRB for the employee. The Weingarten Rule applies only to interviews and interrogations concerning the investigation of any crime or infraction of company regulations. The rule applies to the following:

(1) The employee must make a clear request for union representation before any questioning.

(2) If the request is made, the employer must choose among three options:
- Grant the request and delay the questioning until a representative arrives and has time to consult with the employee
- Deny the request; end the interview (the employer may pursue other avenues of investigation)
- Give the employee the choice of having the interview without representation or ending the interview

(3) The union representative may not sit silently and only observe the process and cannot be forced to do so; the union representative has the right to assist and counsel workers during the interview regarding the reason that the employee is under investigation.

It must be noted here that the union representative has no right to advise the employee not to answer questions or to provide false answers.

White-Collar Crime: "A planned or organized illegal act of deceit committed by an individual or organization, usually conducted as a deviation from legitimate business or governmental activity, for personal or corporate gain." (Definition by Albanese and Pursley, *Crime in America,* Copyright 1993.)

A violation of criminal law whereby a person or persons of respectability, high position or social status commit the offense in the course of his or her occupation or fiduciary position. Generally the reason given is greed, job dissatisfaction, failure of recognition or promotion, and getting even with the employer. Poverty or psychopathic tendencies appear to be less confirmed for this crime.

Terms that are used interchangeably include *fraud, financial crime, economic crime*, and *business crime.*

Willful Tort: See *Intentional Tort.*

Witness:

(1) A person who sees or has knowledge of something and testifies to it.

(2) A person who gives evidence under oath or affirmation, either orally, by deposition, or by affidavit.

(3) A person who affixes his or her name to an instrument executed by another in order to testify as to the genuineness of the maker's signature.

Endnotes

Chapter 1

1. *Occupational Outlook Handbook,* 2004–2005 Edition, Bulletin 2540, U.S. Department of Labor, Bureau of Labor Statistics, Washington, DC.
2. Professionalization of Private Eyes, *Newsday,* Business and Technology Section, pp. 43–45, December 19, 2005.
3. Ibid.
4. Op cit., *Occupational Outlook.*
5. Ibid.
6. Op. cit. *Newsday.*
7. Ibid.
8. Op. cit., *Occupational Outlook.*

Chapter 2

1. For example. See *New York State Business Law, Article 12-B Mercantile Establishments, §218-Defense of Lawful Detention.* Check your own state of employment; many states have similar laws.
2. *Black's Law Dictionary.*
3. *The People's Law Dictionary*, by Gerald N. and Kathleen Thompson Hill, ©2002, MJF Books/Fine Communications, New York.
4. *State v. Perry,* 140 So. 2d 587 (Florida 1962), reversed on other grounds; 373 U.S. 379 (1963).
5. *Dauphin County Bar Association v. Mazzacaro,* 351 A. 2d 229 (PA 1976).
6. *Green v. UPL Committee,* 883 S.W. 2d 298 (Texas App., Dallas, 1994).
7. *The Evolving Constitution,* by Jethro K. Liebermann, p.124, ©1992, Random House, New York.
8. Ibid.
9. *Newman v. Bloomingdales,* 543 F. Supp. 1029, SDNY (1982).

10. *Alexnian v. New York State Urban Development Corp.*, 5544, F. 2d 15 (2d Cir.) (1977).
11. *Pratt v. Taylor,* 451 U.S. 427, 101 S. Ct.
12. *Rojas v. Alexanders,* 654 F. Supp. 856 (EDNY), (1986).

    Note: Under the Administrative Code of the City of New York, special patrolman may be appointed by the NYC Police Commissioner pursuant to the law, and will possess the same powers and be subject to the same rules and regulations as regular members of the New York City Police Force; *New York City Administrative Code, §14-106.*

    However, as described in the *New York State Criminal Procedure Law, §2.10, Subd. 27,* all special patrolmen appointed by the Police Commissioner are *peace officers* and have only the powers conferred upon peace officers by New York State Law. This appears to be in contrast to the NYC Administrative Code.
13. *Follette V. Vitanza,* 658 F. Supp. 492, modified 658 F. Supp. 514, vacated in part 671 F. Supp. 1362 (NDNY).
14. *Hauptmann v. Wilentz,* 50 F. Supp. 351 (DCNJ), (1983).

Chapter 4

1. Op. cit., *The People's Law Dictionary.*
2. Ibid.
3. Ibid.
4. *Jackson v. Police Department of the City of New York,* 447 N.Y.S. 2d 320, 86 A.D. 2d 860 (1982).
5. *Boughton v. State,* 37 N.Y. 2d 451, 373 N.Y.S. 2d 87 (1975).
6. *Ippisch v. Moricz-Smith,* 1 Misc. 2d 120, 144 N.Y.S. 2d 505.
7. *Jorgensen v. Pennsylvania R.R. Co.,* 118 A.D. 2d 854 N.Y.S. (1956).
8. *Mapp v. Ohio,* 367 U.S. 643; 6L Ed. 2d 1081; S. Ct. 1684 (1961).
9. Op. cit., *The People's Law Dictionary.*
10. Ibid., The "Hearsay Rule"—The testimony (or document/s) that quotes persons or records not in court is not admissible, because the person (or document) who knew or knows the facts is not in court to state his or her exact words or deeds and, therefore, such information cannot be cross-examined by opposing counsel.
11. *Burdeu v. McDowell,* 41 S. Ct., 574 (1921).
12. *Chimel v. California,* 395 U.S. 752 (1969).
13. Reaffirmed position found in *Trupiano v. United States,* 334 U.S. 699 (1948).
14. *Wolf v. Colorado,* 338 U.S. 25 (1949); *Mapp v. Ohio,* 367 U.S. 643 (1961); and *Chimel v. California,* Op. cit.
15. *People v. Santiago,* 43 Misc. 2d 264, 278 N.Y.S. 2d 260 (1967).
16. Op. cit., *The People's Law Dictionary.*
17. *Black's Law Dictionary; The People's Law Dictionary,* Op. cit.; and *Dictionary of Legal Terms,* ©1996, Oceana Publications, Dobbs Ferry, NY.
18. *Employee Polygraph Protection Act of 1998,* Title 29, USC §2001 *et. seq.*
19. Ibid.

Chapter 5

1. Op. cit., *The People's Law Dictionary.*
2. *Police Integrity: Use of Personality Measures to Identify Corruption-Prone Officers.* Summary of a Research Study by Jennifer O'Connor, Callie Chandler, and Howard Timm. Published by Community Policing Exchange, Phase V. #19, March/April 1998; Police Ethics/ Standards, Integrity/Trust. Included as part of various studies and surveys published by the Community Policing Consortium, Office of Community Oriented Policing Services (COPS), National Institute of Justice. See www.communitypolicing.org/publications/ exchange
3. Ibid.
4. Ibid.
5. Fingerprints Aren't Foolproof, *Newsday,* by Kathy Wollard, p. 31, September 19, 2005.
6. *The Reid Technique of Interview and Interrogation,* workbook and course materials. ©1993, by John E. Reid Associates, Inc., 250 South Wacker Drive, Suite 1100, Chicago, IL, 60606.
7. Ibid., *The Reid Nine Steps of Interrogation,* used with permission.
8. *Miranda v. Arizona,* 394 U.S. 436 (1966).
9. *People v. Ray,* 65 N.Y. 2d 282, 480 N.E. 2d 1065 (1985); *People v. Frank,* 52 Misc. 2d 266, 275 N.Y. S. 2d 570 (1966).
10. See "The 'Color of State Law'" in Appendix A.
11. *NLRB v. Weingarten,* 420 U.S. 251 (1975).
12. *Pacific Telephone V. NLRB,* 711 F. 2d 134 (1983).
13. *Southwestern Bell v. NLRB,* 667 F. 2d 470, 5th Circuit (1982); *NLRB v. Southwestern Bell,* 730 F. 2d 166, 5th Circuit (1984).
14. Op. cit., *Dictionary of Legal Terms.*
15. Ibid.
16. *Juvenile Justice and Children's Law,* p. 119, by Margaret C. Jasper, ©2001, Oceana Publications, Dobbs Ferry, NY.
17. Ibid.
18. *American Youth Viol*ence, p. 117, by Franklin E. Zimring, ©1998, Oxford University Press, New York.
19. *Kent v. U.S.,* 383 U.S. 541 (1966).
20. *Delinquency and Criminal Behavior,* pp. 37, 40, by Ellen Heath Grinney, ©1992, Chelsea House, New York.
21. *Kent v. U.S.,* Op. cit.
22. Op. cit., *The People's Law Dictionary.*
23. Ibid., *The Hearsay Rule.*

Chapter 6

1. See http://ftc.gov/; click on Testimony and Reports—105th Congress (December 1999).
2. *Dictionary of Criminal Justice Terminology,* Bureau of Justice Statistics.
3. *The Fraud Examiners Manual,* p. 4305, attributed to Herbert Endelhertz, ©1993, Association of Certified Fraud Examiners, Austin, TX.

4. Ibid., p. 4305.
5. *Financial Crimes,* U.S. Secret Service Web site; www.secretservice.gov.
6. Ibid.
7. A survey conducted between the dates of November 13 and 18, 2002, and released February 2003 by Taylor Nelson Sofres (TNS) Intersearch, commissioned by the consulting firm Accenture, Ltd., to conduct a national survey about insurance fraud. The study included telephone interviews with 1,030 adult respondents. Of these respondents, 298 acknowledged that they had previously filed a property/casualty insurance claim for personal, property, auto, or homeowner insurance or for worker's compensation.

   The survey was publicized by The Coalition Against Insurance Fraud, 1010 Vermont Avenue, Washington, DC 20005.
8. The Insurance Research Council, 718 Providence Road, Malvern, PA, 19355. Statistics are from the year 2000 survey. This is described as a leading nonprofit independent research organization supported by leading property and casualty insurance companies and associations.
9. Ibid., statistics from the year 1999 survey.
10. The Insurance Services Office, Inc. (ISO), 545 Washington Boulevard, Jersey City, NJ, 07310. This is described as the property/casualty insurance industry's leading supplier of statistical, actuarial, underwriting, and claims data.
11. The author wishes to note that the term or word *gypsy,* when used in this book does not refer to a particular ethnic group, but rather it refers to a criminal lifestyle and is not intended to include law-abiding members of the Romani people or their culture. See the Glossary for the definitions of *Gypsy* and *Romani.*

Chapter 7

1. *Threat Assessment: Defining an Approach for Evaluating Risk of Targeted Violence,* by R. Borum, R. Fein, B. Vosselkuil, and J. Berglund, *Behavioral Sciences and the Law,* 17:323–337.
2. *Protective Intelligence and Threat Assessment Investigations: A Guide for State and Local Law Enforcement Officials,* by R.A. Fein and B. Vossekuil, 1998, NIJ/OJP/DOJ publication no. 170612; Assassination in the United States: An Operational Study of Recent Assassins, Attackers, and Near Lethal Approachers, by R.A. Fein and B. Vossekuil, *Journal of Forensic Sciences,* 44:321–333, 1999.
3. *Title 29 USC 1900, §5(a)(1),* OSHA's General Duty Clause.
4. Ibid.

Selected References

Barker, Lucius J. and Barker, Jr., Twiley W., *Civil Liberties and the Constitution,* 6th edition, ©1990, Prentice Hall, Englewood Cliffs, NJ.

Black, Henry and Campbell, M.A., *Black's Law Dictionary,* 7th edition, ©1999, West, St. Paul, MN.

Cushman, Robert F., *Leading Constitutional Decisions,* 18th edition, ©1992, Prentice Hall, Englewood Cliffs, NJ.

Hill, Gerald N. and Thompson Hill, Kathleen, *The People's Law Dictionary,* ©2002, MJF Books/Fine Communications, New York.

Lieberman, Jethro K., *The Evolving Constitution,* ©1992, Random House, New York.

Manley, Anthony D., *The Retail Loss Prevention Officer—The Fundamental Elements of Retail Security and Safety,* ©2004, Prentice Hall, Saddlerock, NJ.

McKinney's Consolidated Laws of New York—Annotated (with supplements), ©1998 with updates, including annotations from state and federal courts and state agencies. West, St. Paul, MN.

New York Consolidated Laws Service—Annotated Statutes (with supplements), ©1998, Lexis Law, Charlottesville, VA.

New York State *Criminal Procedure Law.*

New York State *Family Court Act.*

New York State *General Business Law.*

New York State *Labor Law.*

New York State *Penal Law.*

The Reid Technique of Interviewing and Interrogation, ©1993; Workbook and course materials presented at training seminars conducted by John E. Reid Associates, Inc., 250 South Wacker Drive, Suite 1100, Chicago, IL, 60606.

United States Code Service—Lawyers Edition; ©1998, *Volume 42 USCS—The Public Health and Welfare §1983*—1998 supplement, Lexis Law, Charlottesville, VA.

Webb, Garn H., LL.B., *Plain Language Law—Civil Wrongs (Torts),* ©1981, Professional Impressions, Atlanta, GA.

Web Sites of Interest

Web sites are routinely redesigned and file names may change. Home pages that are popular today may not be found tomorrow. Noted below are the more popular sites that have been active and in service for some time or are national in status. They are continually updated with current information.

www.dni.gov: National Intelligence Council; provides information about trends in foreign and domestic espionage against American businesses.

www.aria.org: The American Risk and Insurance Association; the study and promotion of risk management.

www.artloss.com: The Art Loss Register.

www.asisonline.org: American Society of Industrial Security; security news and legal updates via ASISNET. Some inquiries may require membership in ASIS.

www.cert.org: Computer Emergency Readiness Team; operated by Carnegie Mellon University and funded by the Department of Homeland Security and the Department of Defense.

www.dss.mil: Defense Security Service (DSS); can assist businesses in search of government contracts.

www.fbi.gov: Federal Bureau of Investigation; information about FBI programs, National Infrastructure Protection Center (NIPC). Awareness of National Security Issues and Response (ANSIR), and the Uniform Crime Report (UCR).

www.fedworld.gov: Location and search and clearinghouse for government information.

www.ftc.gov/bcp: Federal Trade Commission, Bureau of Consumer Protection—Fraud Deception, and so forth. Also interesting testimony and reports before U.S. Congress: 105th—(1991 to 1998) through to 111th (2009 to 2010) concerning all subjects of interest to the private investigator.

www.irsg.org: Individual Reference Solutions Group; an association of database providers which includes the 3 major credit bureaus and 11 other companies.

www.iso.com: Insurance Services Office (ISO). Includes the Property Insurance Loss Register (PILR), which includes lists maintained by the American Insurance Association (AIA); both of which merged in 1997 with Index Systems Insurance Services Group, Inc., and operates at ISO. Provides statistical data, claims, actuarial data, risk management, and legal and regulatory services.

www.lib.msu.edu/harris23/crimjust.assn.htm: Assorted list of law enforcement and professional associations and organizations for education, training, and networking purposes. Criminal justice resources.

www.mib.com: The Medical Information Bureau; includes health and life insurers.

www.nicb.org: The National Insurance Claims Bureau; merged with the National Automobile Theft Bureau in 1992 and Insurance Crime Prevention Institute (ICPI)—more than 1,000 insurerers involved in insurance fraud.

www.nsi.org: National Security Institute; security policies and procedures, employee information security awareness service, seminars, special reports, and travel advisories.

www.secretservice.gov: The U.S. Secret Service Web site; may be searched for topics such as fraud, executive protection, computer offenses, and financial crimes.

www.us-cert.gov: Computer Emergency Response Team; part of the Department of Homeland Security.

www.vitalrec.com: Search any state for vital records.

Some of the Following Web Site/Database Providers Charge a Fee for Their Service

www.555-1212.com: A Web-based information services business with monthly renewal rates for access. Data on residential searches, business searches, reverse search of phone numbers and addresses, and toll-free numbers.

www.lexisnexis.org: Searches include 10 unique nationwide databases. Can be viewed by product services, occupation, industry, task, and by search products offered.

http://directory.westlaw.com: Westlaw's commercial database called "People Finder." Searches for witnesses, defendants, heirs, beneficiaries, debtors, missing persons, and so forth. Will include name, address, date of birth, telephone number, and present and previous address (click on *public information, records and filings*).

www.IRBsearch.com: Individual and multiple search reports. Offers a search of company profiles, executive profiles, and board memberships, including international businesses. Fee and membership required along with professional status and license for account activation.

www.TracersInfo.com: For current, accurate business and consumer information gathered from government and proprietary sources. All types of search descriptions offered. Fee required for membership.

www.merlindata.com: Merlin Information Services—for professionals needing to locate people or assets, public records, proprietary databases, and skip tracing. Various fees required for assorted reports.

www.intelius.com: Verification, information, and business services offered. Volume discounts for access.

www.locateplus.com: For searchable and cross-referenced public information. Various price plans for assorted services.

www.choicepoint.com: Provider of decision-making technology and information for the reduction of fraud and the mitigation of risk. Premier source for the insurance industry, businesses, and government. Now part of the LexisNexis® Risk and Information Analytics Group; see www.risk.lexisnexis.com

Index

J

L

M

N

O

9781439815427